Helpmates, Harlots, and Heroes

Helpmates, Harlots, and Heroes
Women's Stories in the Hebrew Bible

SECOND EDITION

Alice Ogden Bellis

WESTMINSTER
JOHN KNOX PRESS
LOUISVILLE • KENTUCKY

Book design by Drew Stevens
Cover design by Lisa Buckley
Cover art: 'And Miriam the prophetesse, sister of Aaron, tooke a timbrell in her hande and all the women came out after her with timbrells and dances', illustration from 'The Story of the Exodus', published 1966 (colour litho) by Chagall, Marc (1887–1985) © Private Collection / The Stapleton Collection / The Bridgeman Art Library Nationality / copyright status: French / in copyright until 2056

Second edition
Published by Westminster John Knox Press
Louisville, Kentucky

This book is printed on acid-free paper that meets the American National Standards Institute Z39.48 standard. ∞

09 10 11 12 13 14 15 16—10 9 8 7 6 5 4 3 2

Library of Congress Cataloging-in-Publication Data

Bellis, Alice Ogden.
    Helpmates, harlots, and heroes : women's stories in the Hebrew Bible /
Alice Ogden Bellis. — 2nd ed.
        p. cm.
    Includes bibliographical references.
    ISBN 978-0-664-23028-9 (alk. paper)
    1. Women in the Bible.   2. Bible. O.T.—Biography.   3. Feminist theology.
    4. Womanist theology.   5. Bible. O.T.—Feminist criticism.   6. Bible. O.T.—Black
interpretations.   I. Title.
BS575.B45 2007
221.9'22082—dc22   2007012353

To my parents,
whose prayers undergird my life
and whose faith,
evident in thoughtful reflection
and compassionate living,
inspires and challenges me

Contents

Contents

Preface

Clarence Newsome, former Dean of the Howard University School of Divinity, asked me to develop a course on the women of the Hebrew Bible. I had taught Hebrew language and other Old Testament courses but had not done any work in the area of feminist interpretations of the Bible. It was not that I lacked interest, since I considered myself a feminist. It was more for lack of opportunity. I was ready for a new area of research, and this one was especially intriguing. Womanism was a new concept to me. I was eager to learn about it from my colleagues Kelly Brown Douglas and Cheryl Sanders, both leaders in the emerging movement of black feminists.

As I began searching for books and articles, I discovered a wealth of material on methodological and philosophical issues as well as on individual biblical women. However, there was very little that surveyed the field in an easily accessible fashion for the general reader and student, and what little existed was not scholarly. Now that I have taught the course many times, I am convinced of the need for a book to bring together the latest contributions that feminist and womanist biblical scholars have made. The difficulties in such a project are daunting. Can so much material and so many points of view be represented adequately in the space of one book? Will such a book become immediately dated, as ever-new studies pour forth from the pens and computers of scholars? The answer to this second question is undoubtedly yes. Nevertheless, my goal is to present the fruits of feminist biblical interpretation in a way that will be accessible to the public as well as to the academic community for such a time as this.

My thanks go to Clarence Newsome, former Dean of Howard School of Divinity, who launched me on this field of study. I owe much to my students at Howard and to members of Providence Presbyterian Church in Fairfax, Virginia, where I was Associate Pastor for nearly fifteen years; to Southminster Presbyterian Church in Oxon Hill, Maryland, where I was a summer pastor; to St. Marks Episcopal Church in Washington, D.C., Fairfax Presbyterian Church, Church of the Covenant, Vienna, and Burke Presbyterian Church in northern Virginia, where I lectured and received helpful feedback; and to the educators of National Capital Presbytery to whom I presented some of this material. They stimulated my thinking and asked important questions of the texts. I am indebted to Howard University, which provided me a research

grant to work on this book. I am grateful to Jeff Hamilton of Westminster
John Knox Press, my first editor, who saw the value in this book when it was
still at an early stage, and to all the staff there who shepherded this book in
its first and revised edition through to the final stage. I especially thank
Stephanie Egnotovich, the executive editor at Westminster John Knox, for
encouraging me to revise and update this book. My thanks also go to my col-
league Dr. Cheryl Sanders, whose thoughtful reading of the first edition
helped me formulate more clearly what I wanted to say and who encouraged
me to ask hard questions about womanist scholarship.

Most especially I must thank my husband Jeff Nicoll, whose thoughtful,
sometimes challenging, but always supportive comments and questions have
contributed immeasurably to this new edition.

Abbreviations

AAR	American Academy of Religion
ABD	*Anchor Bible Dictionary.* New York: Doubleday & Co., 1991.
BA	*Biblical Archaeologist*
BARev	*Biblical Archaeology Review*
BETL	Bibliotheca ephemeridum theologicarum lovaniensium
Bib	*Biblica*
BibInt	*Biblical Interpretation*
BZAW	Beihefte zur Zeitschrift für die alttestamentliche Wissenschaft
CBQ	*Catholic Biblical Quarterly*
FCB	Feminist Companion to the Bible
HTR	*Harvard Theological Review*
JAAR	*Journal of the American Academy of Religion*
JBL	*Journal of Biblical Literature*
JFSR	*Journal of Feminist Studies in Religion*
JRT	*Journal of Religious Thought*
JSOT	*Journal for the Study of the Old Testament*
JSOTSup	Journal for the Study of the Old Testament: Supplement Series
NIB	*The New Interpreter's Bible*
RB	*Revue biblique*
RelSRev	*Religious Studies Review*
SEÅ	*Svensk exegetisk årsbok*
SBL	Society of Biblical Literature
SBLBSNA	Society of Biblical Literature Biblical Scholarship in North America
SBLDS	Society of Biblical Literature Dissertation Series
SJOT	*Scandinavian Journal of the Old Testament*
TS	*Theological Studies*
USQR	*Union Seminary Quarterly Review*
VT	*Vetus Testamentum*
WBC	Newsom, Carol A., and Sharon H. Ringe, eds. *The Women's Bible Commentary: Expanded Edition with Apocrypha.* London: SPCK; Louisville, KY: Westminster/John Knox Press, 1992.

WIS   Meyers, Carol, ed. *Women in Scripture: A Dictionary of Named and Unnamed Women in the Hebrew Bible, the Apocryphal/Deuterocanonical Books, and the New Testament.* Grand Rapids: Wm. B. Eerdmans Publishing Co., 2001.

ZAW   *Zeitschrift für die alttestamentliche Wissenschaft*

Part 1
Background

1

Introduction

This is a story about stories. It is a story about feminist and womanist inter-pretations of sacred stories. Women's stories in what Jews call the Hebrew Bible and Christians term the Old Testament[1] are very powerful. They have profoundly affected women's self-understanding and men's perception of women. In the nineteenth century, women who dared to speak in public (which was considered unseemly) were labeled "disobedient Eves" or "Jezebels."[2] Abby Kelley, a Quaker and radical abolitionist, was especially disturbed when this latter epithet was hurled at her.[3] Black women have dis-proportionately been called Jezebel, suggesting that they are more sexual than other women. Women's stories in the Hebrew Bible have also been used in positive ways. Angelina Grimké, another prominent abolitionist, held up biblical women such as Miriam, Deborah, Jael, Huldah, and Esther as exem-plars for women to emulate.

Even in dawning years of the twenty-first century, biblical stories of women still influence the way women think of themselves and the way the rest of the world thinks about them. Much of this influence is negative. Eve, Jezebel, Delilah, and other female biblical characters represent seduction and evil.

Today both women and men feel liberated when they hear new readings of these stories. Both men and women are disturbed when they hear about some of the more atrocious stories of female victimization. Both are excited when they hear some of the more "feminist" of the stories, especially when they have not been exposed to such readings before. Stories have been used against women, but stories can also provide tools to use in the struggle for wholeness and dignity.

A great deal of work has been done in the last third of a century by feminist biblical scholars on women's stories in the Hebrew Bible. This research has produced new and exciting readings of the stories, whose traditional interpretations have been foundations for Western negative attitudes toward women. Was Eve really the terrible temptress and was Rebekah the demonic deceiver depicted in many a traditional interpretation? Is Ruth the "sweet little thing" we find in children's Bibles, or does her story undercut the narrow religious attitudes of its day and perhaps even of our own? These and many other areas have been explored, debated, and reconceived by feminist and womanist scholars. Before the 1990s very little of these discussions had reached the woman or the man in the pew or even the pastor or seminary student, in part because the sources are scattered among various scholarly journals and in part because, until recently, such work was suspect even in academia.

At the time *Helpmates, Harlots, and Heroes* was first published, I believed the time had come to share with the people in the parish the fruit of the last quarter century of work. Not all questions had been answered, not all problems solved, but enough progress had been made that a vast amount of refreshing, exciting—sometimes disturbing—material needed to be shared broadly, freely discussed, and evaluated by those whose lives are touched by these issues in very practical ways. A dozen years later, the need is still there, and fortunately many voices are now singing in this choir. Before, my voice was soft and in many ways uncertain. Now, I want to sing a little louder and with new conviction.

A BRIEF HISTORY OF FEMINIST STUDIES
OF HEBREW SCRIPTURE

The roots of feminist interpretation of Scripture lie in the nineteenth century in the women's rights movement. Opponents of that movement used the Bible to buttress their opposition to it. They interpreted the story of Eve's secondary creation from Adam's rib to mean that woman is subordinate to man. They understood her leading role in eating and sharing the forbidden fruit with Adam as indicative of the evil and subordinate nature of women.[4]

By the 1830s and 1840s some women's rights activists were becoming articulate about the need for a different approach to biblical interpretation.[5] Not only were white women active, but African American women were also understanding the Bible in new ways. Jarena Lee, a member of the American Methodist Episcopal (AME) Church, felt the call to preach and found biblical support for her position.[6]

In the 1880s, Elizabeth Cady Stanton and a committee of women compiled *The Woman's Bible*[7] in an effort to counteract the oppressive use of the power of the Bible against women. Although it did not use the then-new techniques of higher criticism (based on the assumption of multiple sources of the Bible rather than Mosaic authorship), it was a serious effort at a new understanding of the Scriptures.[8]

In the late nineteenth century many feminist Christian voices dealt with the Scriptures and debated traditionalists. Few of these women were trained biblical scholars, although some of their arguments foreshadow later, more sophisticated versions of their approach.[9] It was not until 1894 that the first woman became a member of the Society of Biblical Literature, the biblical scholarship "establishment."[10]

In the early part of the twentieth century women made significant contributions to biblical scholarship. Nevertheless they were not advocating new approaches that we would today call feminist.[11] Treatments of women in the Bible came from women outside the profession. Dr. Katherine Bushnell, medical missionary to China and Women's Christian Temperance Union leader in the late nineteenth century, wrote[12] God's Word to Women.[13] Reverend Lee Anna Starr, a Methodist minister in the early twentieth century, wrote The Bible Status of Women. Both believed that the Bible, when properly translated and interpreted, presents a vision of the equality of the sexes.[14]

In the 1960s a few more voices were heard. In 1964, Margaret Crook, professor of religion and biblical literature at Smith College and thirty-nine-year member of the Society of Biblical Literature, published Women and Religion. She raised the issue of the male domination of the Judeo-Christian tradition and urged women to take an active role in reshaping the faith.[15]

In 1967 Elsie Culver, a professional lay church worker, wrote Women in the World of Religion. She pointed out the lack of research by modern biblical scholars on women's status and roles in the biblical culture and suggested the importance such research would have for contemporary women.[16]

Feminist hermeneutics did not really develop momentum until the 1970s, often considered the beginning of the second phase. At first, the approach was to restore the proper meaning of biblical texts by exposing the masculine-dominated and often misogynist interpretations of Scripture. In books such as The Liberating Word,[17] by Protestant theologian Letty Russell, interpreters assumed that once the veneer of patriarchal interpretation was removed, the Bible would be liberated from sexism.

Soon it was recognized, however, not only that past interpretations were sexist but that many of the texts themselves also presented serious problems. For example, how do we handle the difference between the way God reacts to Sarah's and to Abraham's incredulity at the news of an impending old-age pregnancy (Gen. 17:17; 18:12)? How do we deal with the fact that for many purposes women were viewed as little more than chattel? These and other questions raised the issue of biblical authority. How could a book that included so much that ran directly counter to feminism be accepted as authoritative, religiously or culturally? In one form or another, this question has dominated much feminist biblical thought in what some view as the third phase of feminist biblical criticism, beginning in the 1990s. Before considering this crucial question, we will first define what is meant by feminism and womanism and related terms.

DEFINITION OF FEMINISM

Feminism has a long history. No one definition would satisfy all feminists; rather, a range of understandings is needed. Nevertheless feminism may be broadly defined as a point of view in which women are understood to be fully human and thus entitled to equal rights and privileges. In no sense can they be considered subordinate or inferior.

Most feminists would agree that differences exist between men and women. Clearly, reproductive and other physical differences exist. Growing scientific evidence also shows that the female brain and the male brain develop differently because of differing hormonal influences.[18] In addition, it is evident that culture has provided different sets of experiences for women and for men. Perhaps differently developed brains, different experiences, or some combination of these has resulted in different perspectives. Although not all women have had precisely the same experiences and women's brains are not all identical, there is some commonality, as well as some important differences, in the experiences that have shaped women of all races, creeds, and social classes.

Many people, both men and women, agree on a theoretical level with the proposition that men and women are morally equal.[19] Being a feminist usually involves something more than assent to this principle. Feminism includes an awareness that society's norms are masculine and that to be a woman in such a society involves marginality. Since humans are adaptable, women are able to identify themselves with the masculine norms, just as members of ethnic minorities often identify with white norms.

As a child growing up in North Carolina, I was not aware that I had an accent. I heard the national commentators on television, and they sounded normal. I thought I sounded normal too. Therefore I reasoned that I sounded just as they did. Only when I went to college in Massachusetts did I become truly aware of my southern accent. Once recognized, it quickly disappeared. I cannot even imitate it anymore!

We might think that people would automatically experience life and literature from their own particular vantage point. In reality, the dominant culture trains everyone to identify with white males. For example, one of the Ten

Commandments prohibits coveting a neighbor's wife. In spite of the fact that the norm is male, the Ten Commandments are accepted by Jewish and Christian women as authoritative. Many women do not even notice that they have to edit this commandment in order to make it fit their situation. The continual process of translating directions to fit their concepts may result in women's alienation from themselves. It is analogous to the experience of ethnic minorities who rarely see positive role models from their ethnic group. Many are trained to think of themselves as unattractive, poor, and criminal. As a result, both ethnic minorities and women often must learn all over again how to be themselves.

A few years ago I read a very good book on the ministry. I assigned it to one of my classes at Howard University School of Divinity. Some of the students also liked it very much, but two women students noticed how sexist it was. Once they pointed it out to me, it was obvious, and I regretted that I had assigned the book. I had simply focused on the main points the author was making and ignored the sexism. I identified with the male norm so easily that I didn't even see the problem.

Feminists want to change the way people experience both life and literature. We want everyone, men and women, to be aware of the sexual codes in life and in books, even in the Bible. We want readers to notice not just the Moseses, the Davids, and the Solomons. We want them to consider also the Miriams, the Bathshebas, and the queens of Sheba. We want to unmask sexism and any other codes that are oppressive.[20]

Some feminists view the goal of the feminist movement as the ascendancy of women. Others take the position that equality and reconciliation are the aims for which we should fight.[21] The former group includes many separatists. Men are excluded, and most Christians in this camp reject existing religious institutions as hopeless. Mary Daly, a former Roman Catholic, is a good example.[22] Very few feminist biblical interpreters today share this perspective, in which both men and traditional organized religion are completely rejected. More now may be termed post-Christian, or culturally rather than religiously Jewish. These feminists are not closely identified with a confessing faith tradition but still view the Bible as their cultural heritage. As Carole Fontaine puts it,

> [W]e must continue to deal with the Bible because it is ours. That may sound too self-evident to be meaningful, but, restated the Bible is part of the religious and literary heritage of Jews and Christians. To jettison it because we see it with all its pits and valleys, all its byways into oppression, is to lessen our understanding of how we got where we are and what we are up against on the paths that we now choose to travel. Give up the loving intimacy and restored paradise of the Song of Songs? Do without the active, compassionate women of the book of Exodus? Throw aside the first

successful slaves' rebellion in recorded history? Live without the creation celebrated in Proverbs 8 or Job 38–42? Give up Jesus, the Jew who envisions a new humanity, demonstrating that there may be another paradigm of maleness, another way to be human, perhaps even another way to understand God than by the traditional means of structures of domination and submission? Never.[23]

These feminists are also open to men with feminist perspectives, who believe in and are also working toward sexual equality and reconciliation. Although most of the commentators whose views are discussed in this book are female feminists, a few male feminists are included because their work, in my view, has contributed substantially to the work of feminist criticism. André LaCocque and David Gunn are examples of male feminists.

A significant portion of the work of all feminists is the analysis of present and past cultures regarding their failure to recognize women's full value and their oppression of women. Only as problems are named and their dynamics understood in detail can we develop strategies for overcoming them. At the same time, some of this analysis has been marred by a tendency to judge ancient cultures by modern standards in a way that does not take into account the economic, social, technological, and other constraints that shaped the peoples of the past (and the present, for that matter).

As early as 1982, but especially in the 1990s, the term "postfeminism" gained prominence. Like feminism, postfeminism is complex and multifaceted, but in general views feminism as no longer relevant. Some postfeminists criticize feminists for forcing women into a victim mentality; others suggest that many women agree with feminist goals but do not identify themselves as feminists, perhaps because of the stridency of some feminist voices; still others believe many women have become disenchanted with feminism and want traditional domestic roles. There is some truth in each of these critiques, even though they may be criticized for being simplistic. At the same time, postfeminism itself has suffered as a result of being viewed as overly right-wing and reactionary. As long as gender-based discrimination continues to exist, feminism will continue to have a reason for being and will continue to evolve, in part in response to critiques such as those leveled by postfeminists.[24]

DEFINITION OF WOMANISM

Since womanism is less well known than feminism, we will consider it at greater length. Cheryl Sanders writes this in an opening essay for a roundtable discussion:

Womanist refers to a particular dimension of the culture of black women that is being brought to bear upon theological, ethical, biblical and other religious studies. These new interpretations of black women's religious experience and ideas have been sparked by the creative genius of Alice Walker. She defines the term womanist in her 1983 collection of prose writings *In Search of Our Mothers' Gardens*. In essence, womanist means black feminist.[25]

Some may ask why a special new name is needed. There are many varieties of feminism. Why can't black feminism be one among many? In responding to Sanders's roundtable essay, Shawn Copeland answers this question:

The adaptation of the term signals the acute and seething dissatisfaction of African American women scholars at the "stepsister" treatment we, and indeed all women of color, have received from white feminists inside and outside the church. The embrace of the term womanist by African American women scholars signifies our demand for serious, sustained, and substantive dialogue with white feminists. Such dialectic is crucial given Walker's *first* definition of womanist: "A black feminist or feminist of color." The very term, then, implies black women's reworking of the notion and term *feminist*. . . . It seems to me that black feminists and/or womanists seek a new and common ground from which all women and men may vigorously oppose racism, sexism, homophobia, ageism, class exploitation, intentional limitation of the disabled, and—I add, as Christians must—anti-Semitism.[26]

Not only have black feminists felt like stepsisters but they also have felt isolated from one another. Michelle Wallace wrote in 1982, before the beginning of womanism:

We exist as women who are Black who are feminists, each stranded for the moment, working independently because there is not yet an environment in this society remotely congenial to our struggle—because, being on the bottom, we would have to do what no one else has done: we would have to fight the world.[27]

Womanism is a banner under which black feminists celebrate their unique identity. Cheryl Gilkes describes her reaction to the new term this way:

When I first read Alice Walker's definition of "womanist," it engendered the same joy and sense of good feeling within me that I felt that day, now twenty years ago, when I acquired my "Afro" (a hairstyle I still wear). It just felt good. It fit. It provided a way of stating who I was and how I felt about a lot of things.[28]

Womanism as defined by Alice Walker, in the preface to *In Search of Our Mothers' Gardens*, has four parts. The term derives from the adjective "womanish," as opposed to "girlish." A mother says to her daughter, "You acting womanish," meaning that she is acting grown up, but in a way that is willful, courageous, audacious, even outrageous.[29] This does not mean that acting womanish is bad; nor is the mother who describes her daughter this way a bad mother. Emilie Townes explains:

> Having been a participant in such dialogue in my youth, I can attest that the mother involved is far from resigned to such independent behavior. As a true mentor, she endeavors to encourage, restrain, and guide assertions of moral autonomy, liberation, and sexuality in a hostile society. She is an active participant in the liberative process, but also a circumspect guide. Both women are in tension, yoking dynamically the quest for personal growth and liberation with collective struggle.[30]

The second part of Walker's definition has to do with the womanist's relationships with other adults. The womanist loves other women, sexually or nonsexually, but is also involved in the struggle to liberate her people from oppression. Womanists are not separatists.[31] The third part of the definition lists the things womanists love: music, dance, the moon, the Spirit, love, food, roundness, struggle, the folk, and themselves. The last part of the definition compares womanism and feminism. Womanism is to feminism as the color purple is to lavender.[32]

Precisely how black feminist Christians should use the womanist label and four-part definition is a subject of much debate in the womanist scholarly community. This much is clear: there is more to womanism than celebration. Sanders writes:

> As early as 1985, black women scholars in religion began publishing works that used the womanist perspective as a point of reference. The major sources for this work are the narratives, novels, prayers and other materials that convey black women's traditions, values and struggles, especially during the slavery period. Methodologically, womanist scholars tend to process and interpret these sources in three ways: (1) the celebration of black women's historical struggles and strengths; (2) the critique of various manifestations of black women's oppression; and (3) the construction of black women's theological and ethical claims.[33]

Womanism is something more than feminism for black women. It is more colorful, exuberant, and audacious than its white counterpart.

Perhaps the most fundamental difference between white feminism and black womanism is in the attitudes toward men. White women feel less solidarity with white men in particular and men in general than black women feel with black men. White women tend to view white men as the problem. Womanists are concerned about sexism within African American men in particular and men in general. Nevertheless, the common history of the suffering of black women and black men because of their ethnicity forms a strong bond between African American women and men. The experience of slavery and the ways in which that institution tore the fabric of black families apart, sexually exploited black women's bodies, and denied the manhood of black men left deep impressions on African American culture. Thus there is a tension within womanism between the desire to fight sexism and the solidarity felt with black men.

This tension is one of the reasons that since the early nineties, black feminism has emerged as an alternative name for womanism. Womanism tends to support bonds between black men and women, minimizing the problems of the oppression of black women by black men, while feminism (at its best) focuses on the connections among women of all backgrounds in their common fight against marginalization.

In addition, according to Patricia Hill Collins, womanism is associated with black nationalism with its claims of racial superiority. Walker's famous "womanist is to feminist as purple to lavender" suggests that black women are womanists, while white women are merely feminist. However, working from a slightly different definition of black nationalism, Pearl Cleage believes that black feminism and black nationalism need not be at odds, because dedication to the freedom of black people includes working for the political, social, and legal equality of women, who constitute the majority of blacks.[34]

Nevertheless, black women are in a bind. Claiming the womanist label tends to distance them from global women's issues, while choosing to be called black feminists may similarly put off some within the African American community. Collins suggests that perhaps the time has come to get beyond naming, by applying the central ideas in womanism and black feminism to analyzing gender issues in a range of relationships within black communities. She also recommends shifting the perspective from women's oppression to the gender-specific ways institutionalized racism works. This also helps reduce defensiveness, as it recognizes that "just as feminism does not automatically reside in female bodies, sexism does not reside in male ones."

Collins concludes with these thoughts:

> Finally, despite the promise of this approach, it is important to consider the limitations of womanism, black feminism, and all other putatively progressive philosophies. Whether labeled "womanism," "black feminism," or something else, African American women could not possibly possess a superior vision of what community would look like, how justice might feel, and the like. This presupposed that such a perspective is arrived at without conflict, intellectual rigor, and political struggle. While black

women's particular location provides a distinctive angle of vision on oppression, this perspective comprises neither a privileged nor a complete standpoint. In this sense, grappling with the ideas of heterogeneity within black women's communities and hammering out a self-defined, black women's standpoint leads the way for other groups wishing to follow a similar path. As for black women, we can lead the way or we can follow behind. Things will continue to move on regardless of our choice.[35]

One additional term needs definition. *Bosadi* (womanhood) is the name of choice of African–South African women. *Bosadi* interpreters are concerned with what ideal womanhood should be for African–South African women. Five elements are involved:

1. A critique of elements that oppress women in African culture and revival of aspects that uplift women
2. A critique of elements in the Bible that oppress women, while high-lighting liberating elements
3. Awareness of the interplay of postapartheid racism, sexism, classism, and African culture that shape the reading of the Bible
4. Awareness of the African concept of *botho/ubuntu,* which stresses the unity and communality of all Africans, which means that the liberation of all African women requires the involvement of all Africans, both men and women
5. Awareness of the significance of the family, which however should not be interpreted to require rigid gender roles[36]

Whenever I have had access to the work of womanist, black feminist, *feminista, mujerista* (Spanish for "feminist" and "womanist," respectively), Asian, and *Bosadi* feminist biblical scholars, I have included it. I celebrate their insights and contributions to our understanding of the Judeo-Christian tradition. Indeed, in the early twenty-first century, postcolonial biblical interpretation by men and women from around the globe has emerged in solidarity with feminist perspectives as a vital new approach that shares much with feminist methodologies and agendas. This can be seen especially clearly in the title of Caroline Vander Stichele and Todd Penner's edited volume *Her Master's Tools? Feminist and Postcolonial Engagements of Historical-Critical Discourse.*

HERMENEUTICS

With working definitions of feminism and womanism in hand, we turn now to hermeneutics, the theory of interpretation. The insight that dominates biblical scholarship today is the recognition that neutral, objective readings of texts, religious or otherwise, are a myth.[37] What have masqueraded as neutral readings were actually biased in the direction of the dominant group, that is, white men of a particular class, nationality, and time. They were no more neutral than feminist readings, and perhaps less so, because they were unaware of the point of view behind the interpretations. At the same time, at least some feminists value the *goal* of objectivity, especially in terms of trying to understand what women's lives were like in the past, even if we must acknowledge that in matters of history complete objectivity is an impossibility.

MY LIFE EXPERIENCES

Because our life experiences affect the way we interpret texts and interpretations of texts, I will describe my background briefly. I grew up in North Carolina and was raised as a Presbyterian in a family where religion was very important. My family is white and middle class, but that does not tell the whole story. From my mother, Helen DaVault Ogden, I received a grounding in Hebrew Bible stories. She read these stories to me nightly from a book that became so tattered that we covered it with pink floral wallpaper to keep it together. I still remember the print vividly. When the book disintegrated further, we finally discarded it. For years I longed to know which children's Bible storybook had such a profound impact on me.

After my mother read these words in the first edition of this book, she found a copy of the book we had used, Jesse Lyman Hurlbut's *Hurlbut's Story of the Bible*, and gave it to me for Christmas. Originally copyrighted in 1904, it was recopyrighted by his son Charles C. Hurlbut in 1932 and 1947. The author told Bible stories to his children and their children and their friends for fifty years before writing the stories down for additional generations to hear. In reading through this book now, I am fascinated to see that though the stories are told from a precritical point of view, women do not fare too badly. Eve eats the fruit first, then gives to her husband who eats, but she is not vilified. Rahab is included, though not her profession. The story of David and Bathsheba's affair is omitted. Ruth and Esther are there with positive roles.

Hearing those stories over and over again, I learned to rejoice when through God's power the weak overcame the strong. I also learned from my mother a profound concern for the dignity of every human being. When I was a teenager, my mother was a leader for a black Girl Scout troop. Today she is deeply concerned about the rights of Palestinians in Israel.

My father, Henry Allen Ogden, gave me a strong sense of control over my destiny. He impressed upon me the conviction that I could do whatever I set my mind to. These seeds later sprouted into a sense of self-worth in spite of what my culture told me. In his retirement my father, who worked as an engineer and manager during his professional years, has found tremendous satisfaction in doing a variety of service projects utilizing his carpentry skills. His concern for helping people has made a deep impression on me.

I am also grateful for the intellectual awakening that my high school English teacher cultivated in me. I can never thank Leslie Pearse enough for what she did for me. She taught me how to think critically and ask the right questions.

Beyond the seeds my mother planted in me as a child, my consciousness began to be raised about racial issues when I went to Howard Divinity School. I chose to go there, not because of any particularly liberal ideas, but because my personal circumstances brought me to Washington. I wanted to go to a university-related nondenominational seminary, and Howard is the only one in Washington.

The consciousness-raising process continued over thirty years of living in Washington, D.C., where my children attended public schools that were more than ninety percent black. My return to Howard as a faculty member fifteen years ago accelerated the recovery from racism. Howard Divinity School is an exciting, cutting-edge seminary with some of the sharpest students and faculty anywhere.

My feminist consciousness also gradually developed as a result of experiences of mostly subtle, but some not so subtle, sexism and sexual harassment in the church, where for almost twenty years I served in various capacities as an ordained Presbyterian minister. The opportunity to teach a course on women in the Hebrew Bible at Howard immeasurably contributed to my acceptance of my own feminism.

Graduate training was a formative time for me intellectually. My PhD is in Semitic languages (Hebrew, Akkadian, Arabic, Ge'ez—the classical language of Ethiopia, etc.) from the Catholic University of America. My dissertation was a rhetorical critical study of Jeremiah 50–51. While at Howard, I learned about African American culture; at Catholic University, I experienced and came to appreciate Catholic culture for the first time.

My experience of Jewish culture has been more limited. I have attended services in Reform, Conservative, and Reconstructionist congregations and have officiated at a number of interfaith weddings with a liberal Reform rabbi. Jews from Austria, Russia, and Georgia (formerly part of the Soviet Union) are friends my family made because of our common involvement in music and art.

The metropolitan Washington area is increasingly multicultural. Among my friends have been women born and raised in the Dominican Republic, Thailand, and Canada. My adult children's friends include Asian Americans, African Americans, and Latinos. Although such friendships do not make us experts on the cultures of our friends, they do change our perspectives in important ways. When I wrote this book I was married, but after over thirty years of marriage my former husband and I divorced. I was single for several years and have recently remarried. My daughters graduated from college and law school and are embarking on work in law firms. I am now much freer than ever before to pursue my intellectual and creative interests.

ASSESSING DIFFERING INTERPRETATIONS

The recognition that interpreters bring different life experiences to the reading and interpreting task does not mean that all interpretations are equally valid. Several criteria may be used to judge the quality of an interpretation: internal consistency, logic, coherence with the text and with the stated interpretive principles of the interpreter.

An example from history may be helpful. In the nineteenth century, it was common for Southern slavery apologists to use the Bible as justification for their position.[38] Today we find it difficult to understand how they found warrant in Scripture for this cruel practice. Certainly slavery exists in the Bible, but slavery in ancient Mediterranean cultures was of a different sort than that practiced in the United States in modern times. In addition, although the biblical authors took slavery for granted, as they did that the earth was flat, this does not mean that the Bible is proslavery any more than that its view of the shape of the earth is normative.[39]

Is the modern consensus that slavery is immoral correct? I believe that it is. The apologists for slavery drew false conclusions from the biblical materials they used. There is a lack of coherence between text and interpretation. Today, most biblical readers recognize that a form of slavery existed in biblical times and was accepted as part of life. However, nothing in the Bible suggests that slavery as it evolved in the modern world is morally acceptable, and much suggests its immorality. Thus we may say that the contemporary understanding of the Bible's position on slavery is more nearly correct than the one espoused by the advocates for slavery. Some interpretations are better than others. Contrary to popular opinion, one cannot prove everything one wants to by the Bible. Such "proofs" are based on proof-texting: taking texts out of their literary and cultural context, as well as ignoring other, equally relevant, biblical texts.

Although some interpretations do not stand up to close scrutiny, there are many gaps in the text that leave room for more than one interpretation. Such texts are said to be polyvalent or multivalent. The author who originally wrote the text or the editor who brought it into its final form presumably had something specific in mind, but the text as it stands is open to more than one interpretation.

Sometimes we are not even aware that we are filling in a gap. A personal example will illustrate. When I was teaching an adult Sunday school class on Esther, I commented to the class that Vashti was expected to present herself to a drunken male audience with nothing on but her crown. My class was surprised. They had not read the story that way at all. When we looked at the text closely, we discovered what it said: "On the seventh day, when the king was merry with wine, he commanded Mehuman, Biztha, Harbona, Bigtha and Abagtha, Zethar and Carkas, the seven eunuchs who attended him, to bring Queen Vashti before the king, wearing the royal crown, in order to show the peoples and the officials her beauty; for she was fair to behold" (Esth. 1:10–11). The text does not explicitly say that Vashti was to appear wearing only her crown, but it is possible to read the text this way.[40] My Sunday school class got a good laugh out of this, because I, the minister, had read the story in a more risqué way than they had and in a way that was not strictly necessary.

Although we may fill in some gaps in a number of ways, the cultural context of the stories provides some constraints. We need to be careful that we do not unconsciously read contemporary values into the ancient stories. We also should not fill in literary gaps in a way that is inconsistent with information in the story. There is not an endless number of acceptable readings, and not all readings are valid.

We may distinguish between emic and etic readings. Emic readings involve looking at the story from an insider's perspective, as much as is possible, given the distance in time and geography from the text. Etic readings, on the other hand, view the narrative from an outsider's perspective. For example, an emic reading of the biblical high valuation of women's roles as mothers understands that in a subsistence farming economy women's birthing and nurturing of children, especially the males, who could devote more manual labor to the farm operation, was of great economic importance and thus practically was highly valuable to the community. In addition, the fact that most women probably did not live much past thirty meant that women did not have a long life span in which to do much other than domestic responsibilities and some physical labor in the fields. An etic reading from a contemporary Western feminist perspective is not as appreciative of this high valuation because of the modern awareness that women have many more gifts and talents to offer than simply giving birth and taking care of children. Both the emic and the etic reading have validity; together they are more balanced than either one alone.

Heather McKay, in reacting to some of the more negative etic readings suggests that

it is time to resile from the recent (and current) practice of blaming and apostrophizing male-authored and androcentric texts. Admittedly this has been a necessary procedure . . . , but the procedure should now be modulated, if not abandoned. That negative and angry stance will no longer serve the purpose of forward-looking feminist scholars who wish to move beyond a rhetoric of blame and who wish to foster the creation of, and be able to work within, a gender-neutral, or, better, a both-gender-friendly, climate of discussion in biblical studies.[41]

In a similar vein, although dealing with a slightly different issue, Alicia Ostriker advises:

Yet if a feminist's stance toward Scripture is inevitably adversarial, it can also be more than that. For to diagnose is not to heal. If our object is to retrieve from the palimpsest of patriarchal narrative what the narrative attempts to bury and deny, we may seek for traces or tracks of the female story. Reading with the eyes of desire, we may peer between the lines for a lost past, and we may discover fresh and transforming meanings within supposedly familiar stories. Further, remembering that the Bible was—whether inspired from above or not—written down here below, by human beings over a period of millennia in acts of composition not so very different from our own, we may want to recognize how filled it is with gaps and fractures, and take advantage of its contradictions. When we do so, we cease to posit a simple polarity or adversarial relationship between male text and female re-writers. Instead, we begin to discover that our revisionist interpretations of the Bible are not simply forbidden by the text and tradition we are challenging. They are also invited and supported.[42]

The pluriform nature of interpretation is sometimes disturbing to modern believers. Even more upsetting is the discovery that biblical texts do not always give a uniform or consistent picture. Kathleen Farmer comments on this situation as it exists in Proverbs, but her words could be extended to the entire Hebrew Bible:

I suggest that the literary conventions of Israel were quite different from our own, that those who collected the "words of the wise" and those who found them worthy of inclusion in our canon of Scripture were not as concerned with unanimity or consistency as we often are. Studying the texts themselves leads to the conclusion that plurality of thought was not merely tolerated but was actually embraced and celebrated by the wise and those who held them in esteem. We modern readers ought not to expect the biblical writings to conform to our own literary notions of propriety.[43]

Between the postmodern awareness that all interpretations are influenced by the context of the interpreter and that the texts themselves are often multivalent and inconsistent, on the one hand, and the human yearning for handles on the truth, on the other, tension exists.[44] What we accept as truth are the readings that resonate with our experiences. These resonances are not just individual. They are to some degree conditioned by the various communities of which we are a part.[45]

Human knowledge is limited. Nevertheless we can be aware of our limitations and simultaneously have firmly rooted convictions. Such convictions empower us to work energetically for the benefit of the larger human community.

FEMINIST HERMENEUTICS

Feminist hermeneutics may be defined as the interpreting of texts with the principles of feminism in mind. To put it another way, feminist hermeneutics is the business of reading texts with sensitivity to issues of gender. That, however, is a rather cold definition of an enterprise that is anything but emotionally cool. Phyllis Trible has a wonderful definition: "a critique of culture in light of misogyny."[46] Renita Weems broadens the focus: "A challenge for marginalized readers in general, and African American women in particular, has been to use whatever means necessary to recover the voice of the oppressed within biblical texts."[47] It should be added, however, that not all feminists are looking at gender issues with the assumption that everything was negative; some are seeking to understand ancient women's experience with less judgmental lenses. Nevertheless, the fact that they are interested in what the world was like for biblical women still sets them apart from traditional mainstream biblical scholars who rarely concern themselves with the clues in texts relating to women.

The energy for feminist hermeneutics comes principally from the experience of women, many of whom are painfully aware of living in a society in which the norm is still largely masculine, in spite of a great deal of progress. For womanists and other nonwhite feminists, the pain is intensified by the awareness of the Eurocentric nature of the norm.

Yet even the interpretation of our experience as oppressive comes in part from the Judeo-Christian tradition with its liberation themes.[48] So we critique the tradition with tools derived from the tradition in the first place. Christians, Jews, and scholars from other faith traditions, as well as those not identified with any religious community, are involved in feminist interpretation of biblical texts. Blacks and whites, as well as people from Asian, Latin, and other ethnic backgrounds, are making important contributions. Each brings a slightly different perspective to the work, but all share in the bond of struggle against sexism.

Renita Weems has addressed the issue of womanist hermeneutics. Her approach, cited above, suggests that womanists may use many different approaches to interpret texts and that the focus may be on any characters, men or women, who are especially marginalized or oppressed.

Mexican biblical scholar Elsa Tamez believes that interpreters need to gain distance from traditional interpretations. This distance will make it possible to come closer to the text. She suggests that Latin American readers will then be able to take into account their own particular experiences as they read the Scriptures. In particular, Latin American women need to distance themselves from what she describes as the "macho culture." Latin American women also read within a framework of poverty, malnutrition, repression, torture, Indian genocide, and war. Finally, Latin American women need to bring their perspective to bear not just on texts about women but on the entire Bible.[49]

Kwok Pui-Lan, a Chinese Christian feminist, reads the Bible in a non-Christian world and questions whether the Bible contains all the truth. She measures the authority and meaningfulness of the Bible within the context of her Christian community. She uses Asian cultural and religious traditions and sacred texts as the context for biblical reflection and sees the social biography of her people as the key for biblical interpretation.[50]

Similarly, Chung Hyun Kyung believes that Asian women's theology must locate God's revelation in the lives of Korean people in order to overrun the legacy of the Bible's colonizing function, which served to make Asian Christians dependent on Western biblical interpretation.[51]

CONTRIBUTIONS OF FEMINIST INTERPRETERS

Some of the areas in which feminist interpreters have made important contributions are:

1. Beginning a systematic investigation into the status and role of women in ancient Israelite culture
2. The rediscovery and assessment of overlooked biblical traditions involving women
3. The reassessment of famous passages and books about women, such as the book of Ruth
4. The discovery of feminine biblical images of God
5. Developments in the area of translation principles relating to women's concerns[52]
6. Consideration of the history of the reception and appropriation of biblical texts about women, in various cultural settings, especially in art, both graphic and cinematographic, literature, and most recently music

Another area that feminists in general and womanists in particular could fruitfully address is biblical women with special ties to Africa. I have tried to do some of this work in this volume, but much more needs to be done.

PATRIARCHY

Patriarchy, a term that feminists frequently use, needs clarification before we move on. Most of the words that feminists employ to describe "the problem," such as androcentrism, misogyny, and sexism, are used with their ordinary dictionary definitions. The word "patriarchy" is different. Technically, it means the rule of the father. In feminist literature, it includes androcentrism, misogyny, and sexism.

Not all feminist interpreters are satisfied with the word patriarchy.[53] They contend that it is emotionally charged and somewhat vague. Because it is used so frequently by feminist interpreters, however, I will use it in its generally accepted meaning of "male dominated" and "oppressive of women."

However, I want to challenge some of the modern blinders that sometimes prevent contemporary readers from a fair assessment of ancient culture. Gut reactions need to give way to knowledgeable, critical reflection on biblical texts and the ancient milieu in comparison with the modern world. For example, as discussed above regarding emic and etic readings, biblical women who produced many children, especially male children, were highly esteemed. In a premodern agricultural setting, sons were valuable economic commodities. Today, in the modern Western economic world, children are economic liabilities, though highly valued for other reasons. Is modern culture's tendency to value women who bring home large paychecks, especially when their work may be drudgery, any more humane than the ancient world's esteem of fertile mothers? In both the ancient and modern context, economics matters. It shapes our values and choices.

FEMINIST APPROACHES TO THE AUTHORITY
OF SCRIPTURE

For post-Christian, culturally Jewish, and separatist feminists, Scripture has no religious authority. For feminists who identify themselves with a faith tradition tied to the Hebrew Bible, however, the issue of the authority of Scripture is very important. This matter has been debated for centuries. The development of higher criticism in the nineteenth century started heated discussions that continue in some religious communities to this day.

Feminist studies of Jewish and Christian Scriptures have provided a new focus for these issues. The problem is: How can a feminist accept a sacred literature that includes so much that suggests or even sanctions the inferiority of women? Either the sanctity of the Scripture or the principles of feminism are called into question. Trible puts it this way: "I face a terrible dilemma: Choose ye this day whom you will serve: the God of the fathers or the God of sisterhood. If the God of the fathers, then the Bible supplies models for your slavery. If the God of sisterhood, then you must reject patriarchal religion and go forth without models to claim your freedom."[54]

For most feminist Jews and Christians, the basic tenets of feminism are nondebatable. How one understands the Scriptures is open to consideration. On one end of the spectrum are those who can find no way of resolving the tension between feminism and the Bible. For them, the Bible is irremediably androcentric, irredeemably sexist. Many feminists in this group do not wish to renounce religion entirely, only the sexist forms of it they find oppressive. Mary Daly is the leading example. Women of this persuasion are finding spiritual nourishment in the worship of goddesses, drawing from ancient sources. Although philosophically their position may appear extreme, the insights of these women are touching the larger American spiritual community.

Those who do not categorically reject the Bible deal with it in a number of ways. One of the most helpful discussions comes from Elisabeth Schüssler Fiorenza.[55] She outlines three basic approaches and a number of categories within the first two. The first one, she says, is used by feminists who belong to conservative churches, although these methods are used by feminists who consider themselves liberal as well. The more conservatively inclined Christians hold to the traditional belief that the canon forms an inerrant unity in which there can be no theological inconsistencies. Schüssler Fiorenza outlines five hermeneutical strategies within this first approach:

1. The *loyalist* approach uses a hierarchy of truth method. For example, many feminists believe that the admonition to submission in Ephesians 5 should be understood as mutual submission and that it must be understood in the light of Galatians 3:28: "There is no longer Jew or Greek, there is no longer slave or free, there is no longer male and female; for all of you are one in Christ Jesus."

2. A *universalist* and *essentialist* approach is used by some feminists, often in conjunction with the loyalist approach. Texts that are timeless, such as Galatians 3:28, take priority over texts that speak to a particular historical situation, such as 1 Corinthians 11:2–16, which enjoins women to wear a head covering or a certain style of hair.

3. The *compensatory* strategy seeks to balance the androcentric nature of Scripture with emphasis on stories of strong women, feminine imagery, and so forth.
4. The *contrast* strategy involves making a contrast between biblical culture and contemporary culture. For example, to compare Abraham's action of passing Sarah off as his sister, with all its attendant sexual danger for Sarah, to the insights of modern feminism on rape, is to compare not just apples with oranges but apples with camels.
5. The *redemptive* strategy seeks to redeem Scripture from patriarchal confines, similar to the third strategy. The redemptive method involves gathering texts that show signs of feminine strength and retelling the stories in memory of the victims. This approach has been used extensively by Phyllis Trible.[56]

Schüssler Fiorenza's second approach describes feminists who recognize the pervasive androcentric character of Scripture and who seek to isolate a central authoritative biblical principle that validates equal rights and liberation struggles, which in effect creates a canon within a canon. Four strategies within this approach can be discerned:

1. Some feminists seek a liberating theme, tradition, text, or principle from the Bible as *the* hermeneutical key to interpreting the Bible. For example, Letty Russell suggests "God's promises for the mending of creation."[57]
2. Another strategy sees the Bible becoming authoritative in the interplay between the ancient world that produced the text, the literary text itself, and the modern reader of the text. This position, as proposed by Sharon Ringe, rejects any criteria extrinsic to the biblical text for evaluating the various biblical texts, believing instead that the Bible contains its own critique. For example, the principle of "no harm" can be gleaned from Isaiah 11:6–9.
3. A third strategy, called a hermeneutics of *correlation*, recognizes that the Bible does not explicitly articulate a critical feminist norm. Theologians such as Rosemary Radford Ruether express such a norm, for example, "the full humanity of women," and then correlate it with a biblical principle such as the prophetic dynamic in the Hebrew Bible.
4. A fourth strategy suggests, in effect, canonizing women's experience as a kind of third testament.[58]

Schüssler Fiorenza suggests a third alternative to the conservative and "canon within a canon" approaches. In both of these approaches, authority is located in the text. Her approach sees authority located in what she calls woman-church, essentially the feminist women and men who seek or experience God's liberating presence in the midst of the struggle for liberation.[59]

She writes: "A critical feminist hermeneutics of liberation therefore abandons the quest for a liberating canonical text and shifts its focus to a discussion of the *process of biblical interpretation* [emphasis hers] that can grapple with the oppressive as well as the liberating functions of particular biblical texts in women's lives and struggles."[60] She says that this approach includes four "key moments": a hermeneutics of suspicion, a hermeneutics of historical interpretation and reconstruction, a hermeneutics of ethical and theological evaluation, and a hermeneutics of creative imagination and ritualization.

The hermeneutics of suspicion "scrutinizes the presuppositions and interests of interpreters, and those of biblical commentators as well as the androcentric strategies of the biblical text itself."[61] The hermeneutics of historical interpretation and reconstruction attempts to reconstruct history in such a way that marginalized and subordinated "others" can be visible. The hermeneutics of ethical and theological evaluation "assesses the oppressive or liberatory tendencies inscribed in the text as well as the functions of the text in historical and contemporary situations."[62] The hermeneutics of creative imagination and ritualization "retells biblical stories and celebrates our biblical foresisters in a feminist/womanist key."[63]

The authority of the Bible is both a personal, emotional issue and an intellectually demanding one. Some feminists have rejected the Bible's authority because of its androcentrism. Many others have sought ways in which the liberating messages of the Bible may be heard without accepting the sexism found in significant parts of the Scriptures. None of the methods has won universal acceptance. Ultimately each of us accepts as authoritative those texts that ring true within the context of our experiences.

METHODS OF INTERPRETATION

Related to the issue of the authority of Scripture is the question of what methods feminist interpreters use in approaching the texts. The vast majority of feminist biblical scholars are trained in what is called the historical-critical method. Although we can debate, using the words of the African American poet Audre Lorde, whether her master's tools can dismantle her master's house, the consensus is that these tools are essential, if not sufficient.[64] Within the historical-critical method, Katharine Sakenfeld delineates three approaches.[65] These methods are not rigidly separated. They are sometimes used in combination.

The first approach is literary criticism. Trible is the best-known practitioner of this approach. Her type of literary criticism is called "rhetorical criticism." The literary critic studies the text to determine what the words and combinations of words mean.[66]

There are many forms of literary criticism. Among them are narratology and speech-act theory, utilized by literary critic Mieke Bal. This very technical kind of literary approach is difficult to summarize briefly. The results of Bal's work will be included in the chapters below, but a description of her method is beyond the scope of this book. Poststructural literary theories emphasize the reader's response to the text rather than either the author's (or the editor's) intention or the text itself.[67]

The second method Sakenfeld calls "culturally cued literary reading." This approach reads the text in its social context. In contrast to the first method, which looks at the text without much reference to the historical or social setting in which it was written, this second approach is acutely aware of the need to interpret texts in the context of the social world that gave rise to them. Esther Fuchs and Renita Weems favor this method,[68] which is widely used today. Gale Yee's sociological methodology also fits into this category.[69]

The third approach focuses more on historical inquiry than on literary study. Using archaeological evidence, data from other ancient cultures, and comparative sociological and anthropological models, scholars such as Carol Meyers and Phyllis Bird try to reconstruct an accurate picture of women's lives in ancient Israel.[70] Eleanor Ferris Beach, who begins with iconographic evidence, and Susan Ackerman also belong here. Of the three approaches, this has the fewest practitioners, in part because the data is so limited and the training more technical than in other approaches.

Because the Hebrew Bible is written in an ancient Semitic language, biblical scholars must concern themselves with philology, or what the words mean. Determining the correct meaning is not always easy, because biblical Hebrew is a dead language (as is the Koine Greek in which some of the apocryphal stories are written, as well as the New Testament), and many words occur only a few times, some only once. Context and comparisons with similar words in other related languages sometimes provide clues. Several important studies by feminist scholars involve a philological approach.

Other disciplines of biblical studies are sometimes used, such as textual criticism, which is the study of the ancient texts that underlie the translations used in churches and synagogues. In addition, because many feminist biblical interpreters are persons of faith and some are ordained ministers, theological and ethical approaches are often combined with any or all of the above.[71] Some interpreters also apply various types of psychological models to the stories.

Because many of the stories of the biblical characters are probably a mixture of history and fiction, most feminist biblical scholars do not attempt to reconstruct the historical persons. Most restrict their efforts to studying the stories from a literary perspective, with more or less reference to what is known of the history and culture of the period. Those who approach the material historically usually are trying not so much to reconstruct individuals as to understand women's roles at various points in the history of ancient Israel.

WOMEN'S STATUS IN ANCIENT ISRAEL

Most of what we know of women's status in ancient Israel comes from laws and stories in the Hebrew Bible. Before we turn to the biblical stories about women, it will be useful background to look at what the biblical laws tell us about women's status.[72]

Biblical law is very different from modern law. There are several collections of laws, from different historical periods and of different types. None of these collections is comprehensive. A common ancient Near Eastern culture (including southwest Asia and north Africa) is assumed, including patrilineality (descent traced through the father), patrilocality (the wife moving into the household of the husband's family), extended family, polygyny, concubinage, slavery, and the double standard. However, biblical laws exact harsher penalties for sexual transgressions than their counterparts in other ancient Near Eastern law. Similarly, laws that sought to maintain the exclusive worship of Yahweh were quite severe.

Most of the apodictic laws, those written in direct address, such as the Ten Commandments, were written to and for males. "You shall not covet your neighbor's wife" is clearly not addressed to women. The casuistic laws similarly began usually with the phrase "If a man ['îš = male] does X . . ."

The basic unit in Hebrew society was the family, headed by the father; it was called "the father's house." The religious community in turn was made up of adult males, all those who had been circumcised. These are the people Israel, who are also the warriors. This community shaped the laws that aimed to preserve the integrity of the family, where the family is frequently identified with its male head. Laws protected the man's rights against external and internal threats. Sometimes laws were concerned with dependents' rights.

The woman's primary responsibility was to bear children for her husband. Adultery by a married woman was punishable by death. Infidelity by the husband was not considered a crime, unless it was with a married woman. Brides were supposed to be virgins. If found to have committed fornication, they could theoretically be executed. However, a man who violated an unmarried woman had simply to marry her. Prostitution was tolerated, although female prostitutes were outcasts. Divorce was practiced, but only as a male prerogative.

Normally, property was passed from father to son. Ordinarily, only when no sons were available could daughters inherit, and then they were required to marry within their clan. As a result, the property would remain within the

clan. Their sons would eventually inherit the property. A related legal institution was levirate marriage. In this arrangement a (sonless) widow mated
with her brother-in-law to obtain heirs for her dead husband.

Before marriage, a woman was dependent on her father for support. After
marriage, she relied on her husband. If her husband died and they had no
children, the property would revert to the husband's clan. The widow was
then expected to return to her father's house. This apparently was not always
possible. As a result, widows were often the subject, along with orphans and
sojourners, of prophetic pleas for aid.

Only men could be priests. Only males were required to attend the
three annual pilgrim feasts. Women were also frequently prohibited from participation because of ritual uncleanliness from menstruation and childbirth.
The period of impurity observed after a son was born was seven days, but after
a daughter, fourteen days. Other laws placed greater monetary value on men
than on women. For example, Leviticus 27:1–8 lists the different amounts of
shekels required to release males and females of different ages from vows relating to religious service. It must be recognized, however, that because of men's
greater physical strength they were able to contribute more labor than women
or children could. In the contemporary world, children and senior citizens are
often charged lower prices at restaurants or theaters, but this does not mean
that they are considered either less or more valuable.[73]

On the positive side, children were told to honor both father and mother.
Most of the laws about impurity were egalitarian in theory, if not in practice.
Laws that dealt with major ethical, moral, and cultic sins did not discrimi-
nate on the basis of sex. Both men and women could undertake binding religious obligations. However, a father or husband could annul the vow of a
daughter or wife if "family" interests dictated.

The legal situation for ancient Israelite women was not very attractive.
Bird summarizes as follows:

> The picture of woman obtained from the Old Testament laws can be
> summarized in the first instance as that of a legal non-person; where she
> does become visible it is as a dependent, and usually an inferior, in a male-
> centered and male-dominated society. The laws, by and large, do not
> address her; most do not even acknowledge her existence. She comes to
> view only in situations (a) where males are lacking in essential socioeco-
> nomic roles (the female heir); (b) where she requires special protection
> (the widow); (c) where sexual offenses involving women are treated; and
> (d) where sexually defined or sexually differentiated states, roles and/or
> occupations are dealt with (the female slave or captive as wife, the woman
> as mother, and the sorceress). Where ranking occurs she is always inferior
> to the male. Only in her role as mother is she accorded status and honor

equivalent to a man's. Nevertheless she is always subject to the authority of some male (father, husband or brother), except when widowed or divorced—an existentially precarious type of independence in Israel.[74]

If the legal situation of women in ancient Israel makes your blood boil, take a few deep breaths. Some of the stories we will consider will make these laws appear to be generous. Yet we should not be quick to judge. The modern world and ancient Israel are so different that it is easy to condemn. It is more difficult, but more helpful, first to understand. Then we may be in a position to evaluate.

THE EVERYDAY LIVES OF HEBREW WOMEN
BEFORE THE MONARCHY

One voice that has been raised in this direction is that of archaeologist and Hebrew Bible scholar Carol Meyers.[75] She sees the emphasis on women's maternal roles as deriving from economic necessity. The Hebrews needed to produce many children to survive in the primitive agrarian society that existed in the early years of their community. She argues for the existence of much greater equality between the sexes in the premonarchic period than later. She suggests that changes in women's status may have been caused by the centralization of monarchy, which was in turn precipitated by external threats.

On the basis of archaeological finds, some biblical data, and a cross-disciplinary approach to interpreting the various data, Meyers paints a picture of a decentralized society, in which a little new technology made subsistence in the highlands of Palestine possible. Cisterns were used to catch scarce rainwater. Hillsides were terraced to prevent erosion and preserve as much moisture as possible. Both women and men had to contribute to the huge amount of labor needed to build and maintain the terraces and to sow, cultivate, and reap the crops. In this situation, lots of children were needed to increase the labor supply. A high birthrate was also a hedge against frequent losses to disease and war. As a result, women spent a large amount of time and energy in childbirth and related activities. Nevertheless they still provided around forty percent of the labor, not counting their work in childbearing and infant nurture, which also contributed to the economic viability of the community.

In this decentralized society, the split between domestic and public life that later occurred was nonexistent. Men and women worked side by side interdependently to survive. Meyers depicts a life of hard work, but of much greater equality than we might have expected in this early period in biblical history.

THE EVERYDAY LIVES OF WOMEN
DURING THE MONARCHY

The social-scientific literature about women's lives during the monarchy is meager. It may be that women lost power and status during this period of more centralized government. This is the view of Naomi Steinberg.[76] Carol Meyers believes that because most people continued their agrarian life style, the changes from the premonarchic to the monarchic period may not have been dramatic.[77] Women transformed crops into edible forms, produced clothing, and nurtured children, all time-consuming work.[78] Some women also worked "outside the home," weaving fabric, working for the palace as cooks, bakers, couriers, and perfumers, and in the arts as singers, dancers, and poets.[79]

THE EVERYDAY LIVES OF WOMEN
AFTER THE MONARCHY

The postexilic period has generally been thought of as a low period for women. This is largely because of the negative attitudes expressed especially toward foreign women in the books of Ezra and Nehemiah. However, Tamara Eskenazi disagrees. On the basis of evidence from Elephantine, a Jewish colony in Egypt, she writes:

> These documents from Elephantine begin to sketch legal and social roles for women that we do not normally ascribe to biblical or postexilic communities. They show women in the Jewish community who are able to rise from slavery to a position in the temple, to divorce their husbands, hold property, buy and sell. The documents also confirm the fact that daughters inherit even when there is a son. Consequently, these documents compel us to revise some typical assumptions about women's roles in the postexilic era.[80]

Eskenazi believes further that a similar legal situation may have obtained in Jewish Palestine. Her belief is based on one important supposition. Eskenazi and a number of scholars suspect that the real opposition to foreign marriages in the postexilic community was economic and political, even though the language used is religious and ethnic.

> Accordingly, ethnic purity may be an excuse for a more pragmatic economic and social concern about loss of inherited land. This explanation for the opposition to mixed marriages is appealing. Its strongest support comes, in my opinion, not from the sociological or linguistic analyses, but

from Elephantine documents such as the ones we have discussed. *The fear of mixed marriages with their concomitant loss of property to the community makes most sense when women can, in fact, inherit* [emphasis hers]. Such loss would not be possible when women did not have legal rights to their husbands' or fathers' land.[81]

Eskenazi also finds references in Ezra-Nehemiah to women playing important roles. She notes that in Nehemiah 8:2–4, at the climax of the restoration of the temple, when the Torah is read publicly, both men and women are present. Unlike the first giving of the law at Sinai, when it is not clear that women were present, here they clearly are.[82]

THE INTERSECTION OF SEX AND RACE IN THE HEBREW BIBLE

Many feminist interpreters have studied women's stories in the Hebrew Bible over the last thirty years. A few black biblical scholars have focused on issues of race and ethnicity in the Judeo-Christian Scriptures. Leading the way is African American New Testament scholar of Howard Divinity School Cain Felder, with his best-selling book *Troubling Biblical Waters*[83] and its sequel *Stony the Road We Trod*.[84]

There are even fewer black female biblical scholars than black male biblical scholars in this country. Renita Weems has done pioneering work in this area.[85] Both Felder and Weems point out that racial prejudice does not exist in the Scriptures.[86] In the Song of Songs (also called the Song of Solomon) 1:5 the woman says, "I am black and beautiful." Modern prejudice, however, has been imposed on the biblical material. The passage just quoted has often been translated, "I am dark, but comely" (KJV) or the like, and understood to be a negative comment on people of African descent.[87] The context, however, suggests that she is ashamed of her sunburnt complexion, not of her natural hue. Song of Songs 1:6 says, "Do not gaze at me because I am dark, because the sun has gazed on me."

Although racism as we know it today is a modern phenomenon, alien to the world of the Bible, the ancients were certainly aware of ethnic differences and experienced tensions that are not entirely dissimilar to modern problems. Nevertheless there was no animosity in ancient times toward people with darker complexions. To the contrary, Africans were highly regarded.[88]

Therefore it is important that we not read into the biblical texts racist assumptions that are alien to the Bible. This is an excellent example of how important it is to be aware of our assumptions. Without such awareness, it is likely that we will transfer our modern attitudes back into the ancient texts and thus misread the texts. Most white Americans assume that the biblical characters looked like them. This is evident in the pictures in children's Sunday school literature and even in adult material. For example, on the cover of Edith Deen's *All of the Women of the Bible*, three women, all obviously northern European, are depicted. Where is Hagar, the daughter of Pharaoh, or the Queen of Sheba? Even the matriarchs should not be depicted as though they were what we call white.

Beyond the biblical women who were clearly African, we know that the Hebrew people were mixed ethnically. Abraham and Sarah left their homeland in Mesopotamia and journeyed to Canaan. Because of famine, however, their descendants went down to Egypt, where they stayed for four hundred years, intermarrying with the Egyptians.

Joseph married an Egyptian woman by the name of Asenath. From that union were born Manasseh and Ephraim, two of the eponymous ancestors of the Israelite tribes. Moses himself was recognized as an Egyptian by his Midianite father-in-law's daughters. His name, as well as a host of other famous biblical characters, was probably Egyptian.[89] He was married to a Cushite, that is, a black woman (Num. 12:1). The crowd that left Egyptian bondage is called "mixed" by the Bible (Exod. 12:38).

Thus we may describe the Hebrews as Afri-Asiatics.[90] Today we would be more likely to call them black or mixed than white. The representations of the Hebrews presented in so many Sunday school booklets as white Europeans simply will not do.

Some years ago I saw a beautiful coffee table book of color photographic portraits of men who had been chosen by the author as modern-day representatives of the disciples of Jesus. Each portrait was accompanied by written text about the disciples. Of course, we don't know what the disciples looked like. Nevertheless I was intrigued by the attempt to depict what the disciples might have looked like. Following that model, I ask the reader to picture women as they may have looked in biblical times. These imagined portraits should not look like women of primarily northern European descent. Biblical women are people of color. If a picture is worth a thousand words, perhaps these portraits will help as much as the many words in this book to change the image of biblical women that we moderns carry in our heads. Although the ethnic mixtures of Hebrew women were not the same as contemporary African Americans, since they had more Asian and less European ancestry than most African Americans, they were certainly people of color.

As we study the women of the Hebrew Bible, we will take note of those whose ethnic identity is clearly African. We will also celebrate the ethnic diversity that is present in the ancient Hebrew community. This is important as one small way we can lay the foundations for the multicultural world into which we are moving.

SELECTION CRITERIA

Although this volume includes many feminist biblical interpreters, not every author or every book and article could be included. My choices are based on a number of criteria. First, I have included authors and their works that have been historically significant, even if their views are no longer widely accepted. My choices are not limited to interpreters with doctorates. Serious lay commentators as well as credentialed biblical scholars are included. I have tried to be inclusive of groups that have traditionally been marginalized. The work of men who share feminist principles and also the work of some women who may not be comfortable with the label "feminist" are included. I do not know personally all the authors I discuss. Few explicitly label themselves feminist or antifeminist. My choices are based on the content of their work. A few unpublished papers are included that I have heard at scholarly meetings when I felt the work was important and not covered by anything already in print. Inevitably, some feminist interpreters and their work have been left out. I hope that I have included enough, however, to give a good overview of this ever-expanding field.

HELPMATES, HARLOTS, AND HEROES: A WORD ABOUT THE TITLE

The title of this book describes many of the types of women we find in the Bible, but not all. "Helpmates" comes from the Revised Standard Version (RSV) of Genesis 2:18. It refers to the role of woman as a helping mate or wife. For our purposes we will broaden the concept to include the role of mother, since wives were usually mothers as well. The term "harlots" is used here for the prostitutes of the biblical world.[91] We think of Rahab and of Tamar, daughter-in-law of Judah, who played the harlot with Judah to obtain offspring for her dead husband. "Heroes" includes the Miriams, Deborahs, Ruths, Esthers, Queens of Sheba, and all the Hebrew women who stand out as acting independently or valiantly.

As inclusive as these three terms are, they do not quite cover everybody. They do not include Tamar, David's daughter, who is raped. Neither do they cover Jephthah's daughter, who is sacrificed by her father because of a thoughtless vow he made to God. Unfortunately, no appropriate term beginning with the letter *h* exists in English to cover such cases. We could call these women the harassed or the harmed, but these words are not strong enough terms. We need a word that means victim, the object of brutal behavior.

In an ironic way it is perhaps appropriate that the Hebrew women who were brutally victimized remain invisible in our title. The appropriateness lies in the reality that too often such victimized women are invisible. We do not notice them in the Bible or in the modern world. We do not like to hear about their stories or to think about them. In spite of their omission in the title, they will not be omitted in this book. Their stories need to be heard.

Eve's story is so important that an entire chapter is devoted to her. Interpretations of her story have been incredibly influential. They have powerfully shaped the negative views of women in the Western world. The feminist interpretations that have developed over the last twenty-five years have provided much more positive readings of this pivotal story.

The women of the Hebrew Bible who are presented to us in historical narratives are considered in chapters 3 through 7. These stories read like history, and many readers assume they are history. Most biblical scholars, however, believe that these stories are a mixture of fiction and nonfiction. Ancient historians went about their task in a very different way from modern ones. Historical accuracy was not nearly as important to them as telling a good story and making an important moral point. The modern reader can rarely be certain how much of a story is historically accurate and how much is literary fiction. For the most part, feminist biblical interpreters do not seek the historical Sarah or Rebekah or Rachel. Most feminists concentrate on interpreting the literary characters that we meet in the biblical texts, rather than trying to determine their historicity.

The stories of the women presented in each chapter are briefly retold to refresh the reader's memory. Then the more significant feminist and womanist interpretations of the characters are presented.

In chapters 8 and 9, I stretch the term "women's stories" to include some prophetic reinterpretations of early Hebrew women and the personified female figure Wisdom.

In chapter 10, women characters in what many scholars believe to be purely fictional stories are presented. Here we find the stories of Ruth and Esther. The stories of Susanna and Judith are also included, even though they are not in the Hebrew Bible or in the Protestant Old Testament (though the Apocrypha was originally printed in a separate section in the King James Version). They are in the Roman Catholic and Orthodox Old Testament and are similar in many ways to Ruth and Esther.

The final chapter summarizes and reflects. Although the main purpose of this book is to present the most important feminist interpretations of the most important women in the Hebrew Bible, a secondary goal is to evaluate both the biblical material and the feminist interpretations of it. There is both positive and negative material in the first testament as regards women, and some material may be seen as either positive or negative, depending on the perspective adopted.

It is my belief that the biblical short stories involving female heroes—Ruth, Esther, Susanna, and Judith—are the most subversive of patriarchy. These stories are probably among the most recent material in the Old Testament. Although the movement in the Old Testament is not uniformly in the right direction, the end of the story is the best part from some feminist perspectives. It is part of the foundation for what follows in the New Testament. But that is another story.

Not covered in this book are feminist interpretations of feminine imagery of God, of other feminine imagery with exceptions noted above in chapter 8, or of men's stories. The reason for these exclusions is primarily that this book is focused on women's stories. In addition, I have not included much material on the ways the stories of biblical women have been interpreted through the centuries in literature, art, film, or music. Space simply did not permit entry into this fascinating work.

Another area not included here is work on possible feminine authorship of biblical stories. The reason for this exclusion is that few feminist authors have written much on this matter, probably because it is difficult to determine the gender of authors with any degree of reliability.

The best-known work on this subject, *The Book of J*,[92] is hardly a feminist book. Harold Bloom argues that the author of one of the strands of the Pentateuch (first five books of the Bible), described as J by biblical scholars, was a woman. That sounds good, but the subtext of the book is a subtle putdown of biblical scholars in general and feminist scholars in particular. In one of the few reviews of Bloom's book written by a woman, Adrien Bledstein casts her review in the form of a letter to the author. She writes: "While readers may delight in your thesis that J is an ironic woman, part of your purpose is clearly blasphemy. You tweak the noses of biblical scholars; you tease feminists by presenting the greatest storyteller of the bible as a woman who in her urbane sophistication cares little about issues of injustice and oppression; you bait believers."[93] Although Bledstein disagrees with Bloom at many points, she likes his idea that J may have been a woman.[94] Most feminists generally suspect that the majority of the biblical authors and editors were probably men. However, Athalya Brenner and Fokkelien van Dijk-Hemmes have devised a new approach to the question of the gender of authors. Recognizing that most biblical literature has undergone an extensive oral and written transmission, they suggest that to speak of authors at all is misleading. Rather, they propose looking for the F (feminine) and M (masculine) voices that can be discerned in the text. Examples of F voices include victory songs, wisdom speeches, love songs, prayers, birth songs, and naming songs. Brenner and van Dijk-Hemmes's work breaks an impasse in feminist biblical scholarship.[95] Nevertheless, it is still probably true that the Hebrew Bible reflects many more M voices than F voices. For the most part, it is an androcentric book filled with stories reflecting M concerns. In many ways it was a man's world. But some of us find in these stories a glimmer of something that transcends the androcentrism. Thus we reenter that story world, focusing on the stories about women. We read these stories again in hopes of finding a word to liberate us from the past and to open the door to a better future.

DISCUSSION QUESTIONS

1. How do you feel about feminism? If you consider yourself a feminist, which type of feminism do you prefer—the one aiming for equality and reconciliation, or the one seeking the ascendancy of women? Do you believe that women are inherently different from men (other than biologically)? morally superior to men?

2. Do you believe the Bible is sexist? If so, what is your attitude toward sexism in the Bible? Do you accept the authority of the Bible and want to find ways to rehabilitate it? Or are you so unhappy with the androcentrism of the Bible that you are moving away from it as a source of authority in your life?

3. Is either feminism or womanism attractive to you? Why or why not? Bear in mind that womanism is a term that womanists prefer not be adopted by people who are not African Americans. Do you feel a common bond with your sisters (or brothers) from other ethnic groups?

4. Which of the three methods of interpretation is most congenial to you: literary criticism, culturally cued reading, or historical investigation? (You may want to save this question until you have read part 2 and have seen a number of examples of each method.)

5. Where do you believe religious authority is located: in the individual believer, in the community of believers, in the Bible, or in some combination?

Part 2
A Story about Stories

2

The Story of Eve

There are two creation stories in Genesis, in l:1–2:4a and in 2:4b–3:24. The first story belongs to the P source, for Priestly. It is the later,[1] more sophisticated story of the creation of the world in seven days. In this story humans are created last. In Genesis 1:27 we read, "So God created humankind (*ha'adam*)[2] in his image, in the image of God he created them; male and female he created them." The two genders are equal, though the male is listed first, perhaps indicating primacy.[3]

The second story is the familiar one of Adam and Eve. It is a much earlier story, in the J, or Yahwist, tradition (in German the *Y* is read as *J*).[4] This creation story is much earthier and focuses on different issues. The first story emphasizes the orderliness and goodness of God's creation. The second story tries to answer questions about how humans ended up with so much work to do, how men and women came to be attracted to one another, and how life became disharmonious.

Adam and Eve need not be understood as historical individuals. They represent humanity. The name Adam is used both as the name of the first human in Genesis 2–3 and as a term for the human species. Eve means something like "mother of the living" (Gen. 3:20).

Of all the stories of women in the Hebrew Bible, the story of Eve, more than any other, has been used as a theological base for sexism. Surprisingly, the creation stories in Genesis are not referred to and reworked by later writers in the Hebrew Bible the way, for example, the exodus story is. Repeatedly in Deuteronomy, the prophets, and the psalms, the wonderful story of liberation from Egyptian captivity is told, retold, and made the center of Hebrew identity.[5] The stories of the beginnings, however, are not developed similarly.

In the intertestamental period, between the writing of the Old and the New Testaments, however, the story of Adam and Eve began to be used by the authors of extrabiblical material. There are two classes of this literature. The Apocrypha consists of books that did not make it into the Hebrew canon. These books had been translated into Greek and used by the Greek-speaking Jewish and Christian communities. They are part of the Roman Catholic and Eastern Orthodox Old Testament, but not of the Protestant Old Testament, which is based on the Hebrew canon (though included in a separate section in the King James Bible and considered by the Anglican community as suitable for study). The Pseudepigrapha is the name given to a group of writings, most of which did not make it into any canon.

In apocryphal and pseudepigraphical literature, in a few New Testament books, and in some rabbinical and early Christian writings, the story of Adam and Eve is interpreted and shaped in ways that have had a lasting influence on Western understandings of women's status and roles. Because these materials have shaped our understanding of the biblical story, it will be helpful to consider the history of interpretation that precedes feminist studies of the story. This will make it easier to read the familiar lines without the tinted glasses given to us by centuries of use and misuse.

The first reappearance of Eve is in the second century BCE (before the common era) in an apocryphal work known as Ecclesiasticus, or the Wisdom of Ben Sira:

> From a woman sin had its beginning,
> and because of her we all die.[6]

Although Eve is not named, she is implied. At the time Ben Sira wrote this, he was bucking current opinion. The consensus in his day was that sin originated with Adam or with the fall and cohabitation of evil angels with women. Nevertheless his new idea was to prove to have an amazing staying power.[7]

About one hundred years later, Eve surfaces again in an even more negative light in the pseudepigraphical works of the *Life of Adam and Eve* and the *Apocalypse of Moses*. In both cases, Eve speaks of her sin in the first person, castigating herself for her terrible deed.[8]

This approach to Eve became quite common in Judaism in the last centuries before Jesus' birth. It made its way into the New Testament in passages such as 1 Timothy 2:13–14: "For Adam was formed first, then Eve; and Adam was not deceived, but the woman was deceived and became a transgressor" (though Adam is blamed in Rom. 5:14–21). In the centuries following Jesus' life, this view of Eve as the source of sin showed up frequently in religious literature. Eve was often associated with sin and sexuality, viewed in a negative light. Thus women were thought to be in need of domination by stronger, more virtuous men.[9]

Not only were negative commentaries on Eve common. Jerome's translation of the Adam and Eve story in the Vulgate also involved subtle anti-Eve shadings. The emphasis on woman's sin and inferiority found in religious texts also made its way into art and literature. The most important example is John Milton's *Paradise Lost*. Many people's mental image of the Eden story is based at least as much on Milton's version as on the original biblical text. Milton's worldview was hierarchical, with God at the top, followed by angels, men, women, and so forth.[10]

Phyllis Trible has articulated the prefeminist consensus about Adam and Eve. Her list of beliefs reveals the challenges that face feminist interpreters:

—A male God creates first man (Gen. 2:7) and last woman (2:22); first means superior and last means inferior or subordinate.

—Woman is created for the sake of man: a helpmate to cure his loneliness (2:18–23).

—Contrary to nature, woman comes out of man; she is denied even her natural function of birthing and that function is given to man (2:21–22).

—Woman is the rib of man, dependent upon him for life (2:21–22).

—Taken out of man (2:23), woman has a derivative, not an autonomous, existence.

—Man names woman (2:23) and thus has power over her.

—Man leaves his father's family in order to set up through his wife another patriarchal unit (2:24).

—Woman tempted man to disobey, and thus she is responsible for sin in the world (3:6); she is untrustworthy, gullible, and simple-minded.

—Woman is cursed by pain in childbirth (3:16); pain in childbirth is a more severe punishment than man's struggles with the soil; it signifies that woman's sin is greater than man's.

—Woman's desire for man (3:16) is God's way of keeping her faithful and submissive to her husband.

—God gives man the right to rule over woman (3:16).[11]

With this consensus in mind, we turn to the contemporary feminist readings of the material.

PHYLLIS TRIBLE

The work of Phyllis Trible on the story of Adam and Eve marks the beginnings of modern feminist biblical criticism. Her most developed statement about the story of Adam and Eve is in *God and the Rhetoric of Sexuality*, in the chapter entitled "A Love Story Gone Awry."[12] Her study uses a method called rhetorical criticism, a form of literary criticism that looks at the way passages are structured and how words are used and images developed.

The focus of the story of Adam and Eve in Trible's interpretation is the creation of *eros*, the Greek word for sexual love. Scene 1 (Gen. 2:4b–24) is called "Eros Created." In her reading of the story, Trible understands Adam to be a sexually undifferentiated human, and so she translates the Hebrew *ha'adam* as "earth creature." This earthling is neither male nor female, but *ha'adam* neuter, until sexuality is created.[13]

Then God decides that it is not good for the earthling to be alone and that he will make a companion corresponding to it (Gen. 2:18). The word translated "companion" is the Hebrew *'ezer*. It is traditionally translated as "helpmeet," "helpmate," or "helper." Trible translates "companion" to avoid the negative connotations of these traditional translations, since the Hebrew word does not have domestic or demeaning nuances.[14] David Clines disagrees,[15] but I do not find his arguments persuasive.

Animals are then created and brought to the earthling for naming, signifying his power over them (Gen. 2:19). However, none of the animals is up to the task of being the earthling's companion (Gen. 2:20). So God decides to operate on the earthling. A rib is taken as raw material. From this rib God creates woman, much in the same manner that God created the earthling from the raw material of dirt (Gen. 2:21–22). Now not only is a second earthling created, but the first earthling has also been changed. A rib is taken away. That is all the text says explicitly. However, in place of a sexually undifferentiated being, now there are two beings, a male and a female.[16]

Remarking on the new situation, the male declares, "This shall be called woman (*'iššâ*) because from man (*'iš*) was taken this" (Trible's translation of Gen. 2:23). This statement is different from the naming of the animals. The naming of the animals used the formula "to call the name" and involved domination. Here the male exclaims in wonder and joy, as he notices for the first time the power of eros. There is mutuality, equality, solidarity.[17]

Trible's scene 2 (Gen. 2:25–3:7) is entitled "Eros Contaminated." It begins by telling us that Adam and the woman were naked (*'arûmmîm*) and not ashamed (Gen. 2:25). Then the serpent is introduced as the sliest (*'arûm*) of creatures (Gen. 3:1). Unlike the puns in scene 1, which stressed the positive, this pun suggests that the serpent will undo eros.[18]

With this brief introduction, the narrative moves directly to the theological debate that the serpent starts with the woman (Gen. 3:1–5). Eve speaks well, explaining and interpreting for the snake God's commands to Adam (Gen. 3:2–3). She understands these commands to be her responsibility as well.

The wily serpent tells Eve that eating the fruit will not result in death but will make her like God, knowing good and evil (Gen. 3:4–5). Eve believes the snake, takes a piece of fruit, and eats. She then gives some to Adam, who is with her, and he eats (Gen. 3:6).

It is only at the end of the narrative (Gen. 3:6) that we discover that Adam is with Eve. Throughout the whole conversation between the serpent and Eve, Adam is there, listening, but not speaking. He has ample opportunity to enter the debate, to challenge the snake, but he does not. Eve is his representative. His silence can be interpreted as agreement. When Eve offers him fruit, he can say no. Because her words with the serpent represent him as well, however, this would not make sense. She is active; he is passive (a pattern that will be repeated surprisingly frequently, as for example with Rebekah and Isaac and Samson's parents). However, both make the choice to disobey.[19]

In the final scene, "Eros Condemned" (Gen. 3:8–24), God confronts Adam and Eve with their actions. The couple is hiding (Gen. 3:8). God asks Adam, "Where are you?" (Gen. 3:9). Adam answers only for himself: "Your voice I heard in the garden, and I was afraid because I was naked and I hid myself" (Trible's translation of Gen. 3:10).[20]

God then asks, "Who told you that you were naked?" and "Have you eaten from the tree of which I commanded you not to eat?" (Gen. 3:11). Adam's response involves betrayal of Eve, accusation of God, and finally acceptance of responsibility. He says, "The woman whom you gave to be with me, she gave me fruit from the tree, and I ate" (Gen. 3:12). The solidarity between the pair has been broken. Nevertheless Adam does not say that she tempted him, as many later commentators have suggested. He says simply that she gave him the fruit to eat and he ate.[21]

At this point God turns to Eve and asks her what she has done (Gen. 3:13a). Like Adam, she accepts responsibility only after blaming another. "The serpent tricked me, and I ate" (Gen. 3:13b). Unlike Adam, however, she does not blame God, nor does she implicate her partner. She speaks only for herself. However, in this speaking only for herself, the solidarity between the pair is again broken.[22]

In the judgment that follows, the serpent is cursed. Neither Eve nor Adam is directly cursed, though Adam is cursed indirectly, because the earth which he is to work is cursed (Gen. 3:14–19). Trible understands the judgments to be descriptive rather than prescriptive. Thus what happens to Adam and Eve is a natural outgrowth of their actions. Their fate, according to Trible, is not God's prescribed punishment.[23]

Trible follows the traditional understanding that the woman's predicament will be pain in childbearing as well as desire for a husband who dominates her.[24] Adam's condition will be unrelenting and unsatisfying toil. After the judgment, Adam names Eve, using the same naming formula he used before for the animals. This reduces her to the status of the animals, creatures that he controls and dominates.[25] Her name, which is interpreted to mean "mother of the living" (Gen. 3:20), might have been a positive one. In this context, it becomes intertwined with her inferiority and subordination.[26]

The final blow to the couple is the expulsion from the garden (Gen. 3:23–24). Adam alone is named. Trible interprets this as a generic reference to the human couple.[27] Otherwise Eve is not expelled, which is clearly not the author's intention.

Trible's analysis of the Adam and Eve story has been extremely influential. However, other feminist scholars have also made significant contributions. We turn now to some of these voices.

MIEKE BAL

Mieke Bal's interpretation of the story of Eve in *Lethal Love*[28] is similar in some ways to Trible's.[29] Both Trible and Bal use the method of literary criticism. Trible is an Old Testament scholar who uses literary criticism, while Bal is a literary critic who has turned her attention to the Bible. Bal's work is among the most difficult for even trained biblical scholars to understand. She uses technical literary critical jargon that is almost like a foreign language. Nevertheless, the effort taken to read her interpretations is usually rewarded.

Like Trible, Bal sees Adam as a sexually undifferentiated creature. She does not, however, view the term *ha'adam* as a proper name but as a species identification. She calls Adam "clod."[30]

Bal's reading of the story focuses on the way individuals gradually become characters. The move is from a single sexually undifferentiated "clod" to two sexually differentiated creatures, a man and a woman (*'iš* and *'iššâ*). They develop awareness and the ability to make choices. In the final stage of development, they are given separate sex roles, and the woman receives a new name.[31]

Bal suggests two ways of dealing with Adam's declaration: "she shall be called woman (*'iššâ*) because from man (*'iš*) she was taken" (Bal's translation of Gen. 2:23). After the operation, Adam, now male, projects his masculinity retrospectively into his past. Bal defends this on psychoanalytical grounds. She suggests that we attribute to our past those parts of our present selves that are so much part of us that we cannot imagine life having ever been different. The other way of dealing with Genesis 2:23 is not psychological but semantic. The woman was not literally taken from the man. Rather, she was differentiated from him.[32]

Bal agrees with Trible that the results of the disobedience are not punishment but a description of life in the real world. Unlike Trible, though, she does not see the action of eating the fruit as sin. Rather, Bal views the woman's choice to eat as a way to gain the wisdom that will make her like God. Ironically, her choice also fulfills God's intention of humanity made in the divine image (Gen. 1:27).[33]

By choosing to eat and gain knowledge, including sexual knowledge, the woman makes the continuance of the species possible, even though the individual will not be immortal. Her choice is a choice for reality. Her choice puts an end to the fantasy of individual immortality. It opens up reality as we know it.[34]

For Bal, the problems do not really begin until sex roles are defined in Genesis 3:16, where the woman's childbearing responsibility and the man's food-producing work are specified. She notes a possible solution to the problem of the man's domination of the woman offered by Jarich Oosten and David Moyer. They suggest that a couplet from Genesis 4:7 fits better at the end of Gen. 3:16. In this verse, the Lord explains to Cain why he has rejected his sacrifice and says:

> and unto you [shall be] his desire
> and you shall rule over him. (Bal's translation)

The phrase doesn't make much sense in its biblical context. It fits well at the end of Genesis 3:16, where it would provide an attractive symmetry. This is an example of a feminist scholar using the discipline of textual criticism in conjunction with her primary method, in this case literary criticism. Whether or not one accepts this alteration of the text, the difficulty remains that sex roles have been established. This has been a problem for feminists ever since.[35]

SUSAN LANSER

The readings of Trible and Bal view women in a relatively positive way. However, not all feminist interpreters are sanguine about rehabilitating from sexism the text of the Adam and Eve story. A good example is Susan Lanser.[36]

She disagrees with interpreters such as Trible and Bal, on the basis of a different theory of how language operates:

> They are able to refute standard interpretations because they assume a theory of language as formal code, in which meaning is a function of surface propositions and their semantic and grammatical properties. The more traditional rendering of Genesis 2–3, on the other hand, is consistent with the model of communication proposed by speech act theory, whereby meaning always depends on specific contexts of language use in which the process of inference plays a powerful role.[37]

Lanser believes we have to look at more than what the words mean by themselves. We have to look at context for the inferences that readers make. She offers the following example:

> ALAN: I have a headache.
> JOAN: I have an aspirin.

Alan can infer from Joan's statement that she is offering him medicine for his headache. The words don't say that explicitly, but in the context the inference can reasonably be made.[38]

In the Adam and Eve story, the text allows us to read Adam as a sexually undifferentiated being. Because humans are normally male or female, however, the reader is likely to assume that Adam is one or the other. His name has masculine gender, and thus the inference that he is male is logical and natural. The text does not lead the reader to think otherwise. After the woman is created, Adam continues to be called Adam. He is not often called '*īš*, "man," to correspond to '*iššā*, "woman." Adam becomes a word for both generic humanity and masculine man, thus "erasing woman and designating her as Other."[39]

Trible claims that Adam's words in Genesis 2:23, "This one shall be called Woman," are not the same formula that is used for the naming of the animals, which involves the words "call the name of." Therefore Adam is not dominating her in the same way that he dominates the animals. Lanser suggests, however, that the words used in 2:23 are shorthand for the longer formula and may mean the same thing.[40]

Trible and Bal call the judgments that God makes on Adam and Eve descriptive rather than prescriptive. Lanser counters that in the context of God's warning not to eat of the tree of the knowledge of good and evil, the divine pronouncements after the disobedience may be inferred to be God's punishment.[41]

Lanser asks finally, why, if Adam and Eve sinned equally, should the result be Adam's domination of Eve?[42] This is a serious problem, which we will revisit when we turn to the work of Carol Meyers.

Many of the objections to the "positive" interpretations of the Adam and Eve story that Lanser raises appear to be correct. Yet she herself notes a tension. The tension lies between the positive interpretations that are possible when the text is read excluding the inferred meanings and the more negative interpretations that result from including the inferences. She writes:

> But perhaps texts like Genesis 2–3 continue to rivet us precisely because of the complex and problematic relationships between their formal codes and their structures of inference. Perhaps it is not simply in the interplay, but in the tension between code and speech context—between form and use—that the most exhilarating feminist readings of Genesis 2–3 are to be found. For

to the extent that Bal and Trible have identified formal features which other readings have not adequately explained . . . they create apertures in the reading that is produced by my own theory of inference. Might not the tension between inference and form signify a deep ambivalence on the part of the Jahwist writer or his society about the place of woman? Might such a disease not signify the dissonance within early Judaism between the status of woman in traditional patriarchal society and the theologically egalitarian impulse manifested more openly in the later Genesis 1? Might this not make Genesis 2–3 the document of a patriarchy already beginning to be uncomfortable with itself? If so, I envision a third kind of feminist reading built upon the uneasy relation of context and code, made possible by, but not coextensive with, either Bal and Trible's formalism or the wholly inferential approach which I have opposed to it. It is this third reading, one that negotiates garden and wilderness, for which the feminist critic would indeed be a theoretical pioneer.[43]

How do we assess this approach? In addition to Lanser's arguments, we may note that the second human, who is created from Adam's rib, or side, is female and that Adam becomes male in the operation. This suggests that even though it might be logical to think of Adam as sexually undifferentiated before Eve's creation, he is nevertheless a protomale. We have not inferred from the context. It is a logical part of the way the story is structured.

Furthermore, at the end of the story it is Adam, now clearly a male, who is expelled from the garden. Eve is not even mentioned. Her invisibility at this point suggests again that the story is told from an androcentric point of view. It is, however, possible to view *ha'adam* here as a reference to humanity, and not simply to the male half of the couple.[44]

Feminist interpreters have not responded to Lanser's challenge to develop a kind of reading that negotiates between Trible's and Bal's formalism (pure literary criticism) and Lanser's inferential approach (culturally cued reading). Instead, other approaches have emerged.

DAVID FREEDMAN

We turn now to three interpreters whose readings of the Adam and Eve story are more positive from a feminist point of view than Lanser's but are different from Trible's and Bal's. Based on philological arguments, David Freedman proposes a different translation of the word normally rendered "helper" or the like. In an article entitled "Woman, A Power Equal to Man,"[45] he proposes to translate '*ezer* as "power." The translations "helpmeet," "helpmate," "helper," and "companion" are all based on the Hebrew root '*zr*. The meaning of '*zr* is "to rescue" or "to save." Another Semitic root *gzr*, meaning "to be strong," is represented in Hebrew by *'zr*. Around 1200 BCE the two sounds of ' (the ayin) and *ġ* (the *ġayin*) began to be written using the same sign. (The same situation exists in English where the letter *g* stands for the sound g as in "girl" and the sound j as in "George.") As a result, *'ezer* could come from either *'zr* = *'zr* or *'zr* = *ġzr*.[46]

Of the twenty-one occurrences of *'ezer* in the Hebrew Bible, eight come from the root *'zr*, meaning "rescue."[47] The other usages mean "strength."[48] When the woman is created, she is not intended to be Adam's savior or rescuer. Rather, she is created to be a strength or power equivalent to Adam.[49]

The second Hebrew word in the phrase *kenegdô*, usually translated "fit for him" or the like, appears only here in the Bible. In later Mishnaic Hebrew, *neged* means "equal." That is the meaning needed here, once *'ezer* is understood as "power" or "strength." This understanding of *'ezer kenegdô* harmonizes well with the statements in Genesis 1 that God made humanity, male and female, in the image of God.[50]

MARY CALLAWAY AND ADRIEN BLEDSTEIN

Freedman's point is supported by Mary Callaway's and Adrien Bledstein's interpretations of Genesis 2–3. Callaway sees the story as an attempt to demythologize the feminine power of giving birth. She writes:

> The curious story of woman coming from man rather than man being born from woman uses ancient mythological motifs in the service of a new theological statement: it was not a mother goddess, but the living power of Yahweh which brought man into being. The motif of the rib, echoing the Sumerian goddess of life, "the Lady of the Rib," and the naming of the woman *hwh* [Eve] with its interpretation as "the mother of all living," indicate that the woman once played a more significant role in the story of the creation of man. For the Yahwist's audience in the tenth century the message that woman is not a representative of the mother goddess but is rather an *'zr kngdw* must have been startling.[51]

Callaway does not translate *'ezer kenegdô*, but her point supports Freedman's emphasis on the equivalence between male and female human beings, albeit from the opposite direction.[52] Callaway's approach is culturally cued reading because it takes into consideration the larger cultural context, including the theological context in which the ancient Hebrews lived.

The views of Adrien Bledstein, a Jewish biblical scholar, are similar to Callaway's, but broader. Her reading is another example of culturally cued reading. She states:

In Hebrew thought, men are reduced from heroic, godlike beings to earthlings. Females are no longer divided into life- and death-dealing goddesses, on the one hand, or slavish menials of men on the other hand. Man and woman are equally human and each aspires to be as the gods and goddesses of mythology. Oppression, misery, slavery, disease, hard work, pain, all are attributed to the human tendency to confuse knowledge with wisdom, to act like gods and goddesses in shifting blame to another for any threat to their self esteem.[53]

She concludes with these reflections:

Why, then, has Torah been read for proof of woman's inferiority? Why did earliest rabbis see Adam as so beautiful that Eve was an "ape" in comparison? What mutual human frustrations pricked Maimonides to conclude that "the wife should wash her husband's hands and feet and serve him at table or be beaten"? What happened in history to prompt the predominating tradition of post-Biblical Judaism to distort the triumph of Hebrew monotheism in desexualizing Divinity and humanizing woman and man? Are we ready yet to appreciate the Hebrew version of the genesis of humans—a radically humanist and feminist statement both in its time and for our time?[54]

Bledstein has picked up some positive elements of the text, but they seem to have blinded her to its more androcentric features. Her reading of the story as the human confusion of knowledge with wisdom is reminiscent of some Christian "fall from grace" readings. We will return to this issue below.

LYN BECHTEL AND ELLEN VAN WOLDE

In the Feminist Companion to the Bible series, Lyn Bechtel presents a feminist reinterpretation of the Adam and Eve story that challenges some basic Christian assumptions about the story.[55] She is a structuralist, a kind of literary critic. Her point of departure is the problems inherent in the traditional Christian "sin and fall" approach. For example, she asks, why, if humans were created immortal, were they also created sexual? If they were created immortal, why were they made of finite clay? Why after eating the fruit do the humans fear their nakedness rather than death? Why is it considered punishment for Adam to be sent into the world to be a farmer, when Genesis 2:5 tells us that humans were intended to cultivate the ground?

Bechtel interprets the Adam and Eve story as the story of human maturation.[56] In this respect Bechtel's interpretation is similar to Bal's, but Bechtel's reading goes farther. In the first state of human development, Adam names the animals. Adam is not aware of sexual differentiation at this point. He is learning to differentiate himself from the outside world. The naming process does not indicate control over the animals, only his awareness of difference. He is a very young child. In the next stage of development, when the female is created, Adam becomes aware that there are boys and girls, but no sense of shame is present. In Genesis 2:25, Adam and the female human are naked and not ashamed. They are children, with a dawning awareness of sexuality. Later, they become aware of their nakedness (Gen. 3:7). Now they are adolescents. They have not fallen; rather, they have moved toward full human consciousness, freedom, maturity, socialization, and individual identity in relation to the group.

The tree of life represents a child's view of life, a view that cannot comprehend death. The tree is fine for children but not for adults. That is why the tree is not prohibited for the children Adam and Eve. Once they have matured, they cannot go back to the immature understanding of life. It would not be healthy.

The tree of knowledge of good and evil, which represents the beginning of the maturation process into adulthood, is prohibited only for children. God commands the children Adam and Eve not to eat of it, with the warning that the consequences will be death. We usually interpret this to mean that immediate death will follow, but that is not what happens when Adam and Eve eat. Thus it is better to interpret this to mean that those who eat will become aware of the reality of death. That is what gradually happens as we mature.

In traditional interpretations, the snake is a symbol of evil. In the ancient Near East, however, the snake had many positive associations. It symbolized wisdom and the human potential for discernment. The snake in Genesis is shrewd, but not in a negative sense. The snake is streetwise. It corrects the humans' misunderstanding of God's words about the consequences of eating of the tree of the knowledge of good and evil. It tells them they will not immediately die, and it is right. The snake emphasizes the positives of eating, that is, knowledge like God's, and it is right.

After the humans mature, they are ready to enter the world where they will take up their life's work, the work God intended them to do from the beginning. Although Bechtel sees the story as androcentric, she does not believe it is sexist. In addition, her reading has the advantage of placing life in the real world in a positive light. It is not a punishment for sin, but the world God created for mature men and women to share as partners.

One question that often arises from Christians who are accustomed to the "fall from grace" approach is how disobedience against God can be viewed as positive. Dutch scholar Ellen van Wolde discusses this problem in her treatment of the Adam and Eve story, which is similar to Bechtel's. She sees the clue to the whole story in Genesis 2:24: "Therefore a man leaves his father and his mother and clings to his wife, and they become one flesh." She writes:

> As man leaves his father and mother to become independent, so man, male and female, leaves YHWH God by means of his transgression of the prohibition in 3:1–7 to become independent. . . .
> The realization that verse 2:24 presents man's process of development in a nutshell and the realization that a similar behavior can be observed in man's attitude towards YHWH God, makes the reader aware of the fact that Gen 2–3 is really one extensive description of this growth.[57]

Van Wolde sees the transgression as a necessary disobedience, because freedom is the one thing that God could not build directly into the universe. Freedom cannot be conferred. It can only be grasped.

How one reads Genesis 2:24 is important. Trible and Bledstein believe that once woman is created, Adam and Eve consummate their "marriage." Bechtel and van Wolde believe that Adam and Eve are not mature enough for an adult relationship at this point. They see Genesis 2:24 as pointing toward the future rather than being descriptive of what is presently happening. Both readings are possible. If we read Genesis 2:24 as descriptive of present reality, then the "fall from grace" interpretation makes sense. Adam and Eve move from a perfect adult relationship to a broken adult relationship. However, if we read Genesis 2:24 as descriptive of future reality, then the maturation interpretation makes more sense. Adam and Eve change from immature children to mature adults. At this point it is difficult to choose between these approaches. The next interpreter, however, will provide some additional material with which to judge how to read the story of the garden.

CAROL MEYERS

Carol Meyers, one of the most important recent interpreters of the Adam and Eve story, treats Genesis 2–3 as a narrative of human origins, as a story that explains why certain human conditions are as they are, and as a parable or wisdom tale.[58] Like Bal, Bechtel, and van Wolde, she rejects traditional interpretations that view sin as the central theme of Genesis 3.

> Postbiblical interpretations interfere with our appreciation of the meaning and function of the story, and we must seek first to dismantle some of those obstacles. The introduction to this chapter suggests that the focus on Eve as the source of sin is not rooted in an intrinsic component of the Eden tale. It is time now to look more closely at the textual basis for our assertion that the focus on sin and punishment in the traditional exegesis of Genesis 3 is a distortion. Disobedience and its consequences clearly figure

in the story of the first human pair; this is the characteristic way for a creation story to suggest that the assertion of independence from any authority is a feature of first (= all) human life. But to allow the theme of disobedience to be of paramount importance to our interpretative eyes is to oversimplify a rich and powerful narrative. Even worse, letting the idea of disobedience dominate our conceptual field means obliterating other features of the story that were equally important, and perhaps even more significant, for the ancient Israelites.[59]

Meyers then explains that the primary reason for rejecting sin as the central theme of Genesis 3 is that there is no explicit reference to it. The act of eating the fruit of the forbidden tree is presented, but it is not explicitly judged as sinful in the text. Furthermore, the Hebrew Bible never associates any later sinful actions with Adam and Eve's disobedience in the garden.[60]

Like Bal, Bechtel, and van Wolde, Meyers suggests that Genesis 3 is not primarily about sin. Unlike them, she understands the story to be about etiology, or why things are as they are. Her explanation for dissenting from traditional sin-centered interpretations is more compelling than Bal's and is similar to Bechtel's.

The very fact that the serpent is held accountable along with the woman and the man diminishes the truly human theme of disobedience to God's word. The participation of the serpent as a creature equally responsible for obeying God's word (which had not been directed toward it) and equally capable of transgression brings the etiological dimension to the fore. Here we have a sample of how people coped with their abhorrence or fear of a certain order of mysterious, apparently self-regenerating, and sometimes dangerous reptiles. No animal could "naturally" be so awesome and awful; it must have "done" something to end up that way. Similarly, humans should not naturally have such difficult life conditions as they did in ancient Palestine, where the tale originated. The etiological workings of the human mind suggest that something must have happened to have produced such a state. The act in question, the eating of a forbidden food, is appropriate for a folk explanation but hardly has the same force as does murder, in the Cain story, as a paradigm for human sinfulness.[61]

Meyers also views Genesis 3 as a parable or wisdom tale because it is about a wise agent, the serpent, and the conferring of wisdom.

The prominent role of the female rather than the male in the wisdom aspects of the Eden tale is a little-noticed feature of the narrative. It is the woman, and not the man, who perceives the desirability of procuring wisdom. The woman, again not the man, is the articulate member of the first pair who engages in dialogue even before the benefits of the wisdom tree have been produced. This association between the female and the qualities of wisdom may have a mythic background, with the features of a Semitic wisdom goddess underlying the intellectual prominence of the woman of Eden. Be that as it may, the close connection between woman and wisdom in the Bible is surely present in the creation narrative, although it is hardly limited to the beginning of Genesis.[62]

Must we choose between Meyers's reading and Bechtel's and van Wolde's readings? Bechtel and van Wolde read the story as a story of human maturation. That is similar to Meyers's reading of the story as a wisdom tale. Meyers's interpretation is grounded in ancient southwestern Asian culture. Her approach at this point is culturally cued reading. Bechtel and van Wolde also sometimes utilize insights that are cultural but their approach is more purely literary critical. Their reading of the story as that of human maturation is intriguing. The one difficulty is that there is nothing in the story that provides direct evidence that at various points Adam and Eve are infants, children, adolescents, and so forth. This has been inferred. Nevertheless it makes such wonderful sense out of the story that it must be taken very seriously. There is nothing in Bechtel's and van Wolde's readings that contradicts Meyers's interpretation or vice versa. They complement each other.

One of the most fascinating aspects of Meyers's work on Genesis 3 is her translation of verse 16. The NRSV translation of this verse reads:

> To the woman he said,
> "I will greatly increase your pangs in childbearing;
>   in pain you shall bring forth children,
> yet your desire shall be for your husband,
>   and he shall rule over you."

These lines are poetry. The most basic element of Hebrew poetry is parallelism: one line parallels a second line. If we label the lines of the verse as printed above 1–4, then we may say that lines 1 and 2 are parallel to each other as are 3 and 4. Parallelism takes many forms. In its simplest form, one line repeats the meaning of the previous line with the same grammatical structure. However, the second line does not have to mirror the first. It can also develop the thought of the first in some way.

In line 1 there is a subject-verb-infinitive cluster and two objects. The subject-verb-infinitive is "I will greatly multiply." The objects are "pangs" and "childbearing," assuming the traditional translations of the Hebrew words for the moment. The two objects may be taken separately or together in what is called a hendiadys. (Because Hebrew has few adjectives, two nouns linked by a conjunction can be understood as modifying each other; this is called a hendiadys. For example, in Genesis 1:2, where we read *tohû wabohû*, "formlessness and emptiness," the meaning is a "formless void.") Most translators assume that the two objects in line 1 of Genesis 3:16 form a hendiadys. The NRSV translates, "I will greatly increase your pangs in childbearing." Normally in a hendiadys, the first word describes the second. The result in our line would be "I will greatly multiply your painful childbirths." It is not clear, however, that the second word cannot describe the first. Thus, most translators read, "I will greatly multiply your childbearing pains," or the like.[63]

Before trying to resolve the issue of whether or not to read the two objects as a hendiadys, Meyers studies the meaning of the words themselves. The word often translated "childbirth" (*heron*) does not mean childbirth; rather, it means "conception" or "pregnancy." This meaning, however, does not go well with the other object, usually translated "pain." Pain is associated with childbirth but not with conception and pregnancy.[64]

A closer look at the word translated "pain" ('*issabôn*) suggests that a better definition for it is "toil." In Gen. 3:17, Adam is told that he will eat of the fruit of the ground only through '*issabôn*. Thus Meyers translates line 1 as "I will greatly increase your toil and your pregnancies." The two objects of the verb are understood to be separate from each other rather than a hendiadys.[65]

As a result of being expelled from the garden, Eve will have to work a lot harder and she will experience many pregnancies. The reason for the former is obvious enough. Outside the lush garden everyone must work the ground constantly to produce enough food. Adam cannot accomplish enough alone. Everybody will have to participate.[66]

The reason for the second object may not be as obvious to modern Westerners, but it would be to people living in agrarian situations. To provide enough labor to work the ground, children are needed. In addition, the ravages of disease and war also require many pregnancies. These are the hard realities of life outside the garden in early Hebrew culture.

Line 2 is parallel to line 1. Meyers translates, "(Along) with travail you shall beget children." The word she translates "travail" ('*eseb*) is from the same root as the word translated in line 1 as "toil." The meaning is closely related but includes more of the idea of the emotional stress of very hard work. The verbal root translated "beget" (*yld*) can mean to bear or beget children as well as the more abstract notion of becoming a parent. It is the abstract notion that is wanted here. Meyers tries to convey this by using the masculine word "beget" of Eve. The thrust of this second line is that Eve's life will be hard because of the double burden of hard work and parenting.[67] Though the verse is descriptive of the plight of early Hebrew women in a subsistence agrarian economy, many a contemporary woman can nevertheless identify with the general concept.

In lines 3 and 4, Meyers finds fewer translation problems. Instead, she focuses on how lines 3 and 4 relate back to the first two lines. Line 3 states that a woman's desire shall be for her man. Because of the heavy work load of agricultural labor on top of bearing and nurturing children, women might well be inclined to avoid having so many children. The way around this problem is given in line 3. Her natural reluctance will be overcome by her sexual desire.[68]

There is no evidence that ancient Israelite women wished to avoid pregnancy; to the contrary, biblical texts uniformly depict Hebrew females as desiring children. Sons especially were a woman's social security in the event that her husband died, and they gave her status in the community due to the need for labor in an agrarian economy. Nevertheless, Meyers may be correct that line 3 explains one reason women would be willing to go through all the various types of labor that pregnancy entailed.

The last line is most difficult. Here Meyers translates, "he shall predominate over you."[69] The idea is not that the man will dominate the woman, rule over her, or have authority over her in all matters. Rather, if we keep in mind that line 4 is parallel to line 3, the field is limited. In the area of sexual relations, the man's desire for intercourse will overrule the woman's reluctance. Read this way, line 4 is not giving divine sanction to male chauvinism. Rather, it states the way enough children for the survival of the community will be ensured.[70]

Adrien Janis Bledstein translates line 4 as "he can rule over you" rather than "he will rule over you." The Hebrew allows for either reading.[71] This makes male dominance a possibility rather than an inevitability.

GALE YEE

Carol Meyers reads the story of Adam and Eve as reflecting the conditions of ancient Israel before the rise of the kingship. Gale Yee, an Asian American biblical scholar, using a materialist sociological analysis, situates the story in the pre-exilic monarchic period, when the Israelites were in transition from the more family/kinship-oriented economy of the tribal period to the centralized economy of the monarchy in which peasants were taxed to support royal projects. She suggests that on a symbolic level Adam (understood only as a male human and not as generic humanity) and Eve are like the peasants who used to have free reign in the "garden," but now must be banished to hard work in the real world. Similarly, their relationship to authority (God/human leadership) has become more distant in the monarchic period than it was when they were in a loosely organized, kinship-dominated tribal arrangement. In addition, marital bonds become stronger than kinship, since the man leaves his parents to join his wife (Gen 2:24), which facilitates the movement away from kinship-based tribal organization to more centralized monarchy.[72]

For Yee, the snake represents forces antithetical to the monarchy. When the snake focuses Eve's attention on God's prohibition rather than God's generosity, the implication is that God is unreasonably restrictive. By wanting more than is allowed by God (but also by the king in this reading), Eve (and Adam) increase the gulf between humanity and authority. The result is the legitimization of Adam's subsistence level and Eve's dependence on Adam (Gen. 3:16b).[73]

Although Yee's placement of the story in the transition from tribal confederacy to pre-exilic monarchy is plausible, it would be equally plausible to situate it in this time period and to see Adam as representing humanity as well as male humans (admittedly an androcentric perspective), and the woman's role as combining the labor of farm work and bearing children. In any case, Yee's reading is another version of a maturation theme. In her perspective it is the story of a society "maturing" from the tribal stage to a more centralized monarchy.

CONCLUSIONS

The work of Phyllis Trible on the Adam and Eve story broke important new ground. Her reading of the results of Adam's and Eve's actions as something other than divine punishment was the first in a series of feminist steps away from the traditional Christian "fall from grace" interpretation. Bal's reading of the narrative as the story of human maturation took another step in that direction. Lanser and others criticized Trible and Bal for missing some androcentric features of the text. Bechtel and van Wolde went even farther than Trible and Bal in their move away from the "fall from grace" approach. Meyers presented the most compelling evidence for an approach to this story that dissents from the "fall from grace" theme. Yee views the story as legitimizing a kind of fall from grace, the "grace" of the old kinship tribal confederacy, out of which the ancient Israelites moved into monarchy, with all its difficulties for the lower classes, but in some respects this is another version of a maturation myth.

With the exception of Meyers and Yee, these interpreters are primarily literary critics. Meyers uses a combination of literary criticism, philology, and historical investigation. By combining methods, she was able to go farther than any other interpreter of this story to date. Yee uses literary criticism, historical investigation, and sociological analysis, from which she develops an understanding of the story of Adam and Eve that explains the way the story may have functioned at the point at which it might have been written down, but seems overly reductionistic.

Freedman's work has not been utilized a great deal by feminists, though it should be. Callaway's and Bledstein's approaches are somewhat outside the mainstream of feminist work. Interpreters who do not share the view that the biblical material is problematically androcentric often have difficulty getting a hearing. Nevertheless, both Callaway and Bledstein should be taken more seriously. Some of their insights complement Meyers's work.

At the end of this review of feminist interpretations of the story of the garden of Eden many Christian readers may be wondering if most feminist biblical scholars reject the traditional Christian "fall from grace" understanding. My own position involves at least two layers of meaning. Many biblical passages have been reinterpreted and sometimes dramatically reshaped by later biblical authors for their own time. Perhaps the best-known example is Matthew's application of Isaiah 7:14 to Jesus in Matthew 1:22–23. Isaiah's prophecy, which originally spoke of a young woman ("virgin" comes from the Septuagint, the Greek translation) who was already pregnant with a son whose name would be Immanuel, is reinterpreted to foretell Jesus' virgin birth.

In a similar way, the story of Adam and Eve may have been reinterpreted as a story about the human fall from grace. Even the compilers of the Hebrew Bible placed it in a series of stories of human disasters that lead to the flood.[74] Although I do not believe that the "fall from grace" interpretation is the original meaning of the story, it does explain how life became so disharmonious. It also provides one way to deal with Genesis 3:16b. Men's domination of women can be explained as a result of sin, rather than God's intention for humanity.[75] Traditional Christian feminists then find the solution to this problem of male dominance in Christ, the second Adam, who redeems fallen humanity, with Mary as the second Eve. The fall from grace interpretation, however, as brought to us by Tertullian, Jerome, and Augustine, also views women and women's sexuality as the primary source of sin. Thus many feminists do not want to go near this road. Adrien Janis Bledstein's reading of Genesis 3:16d as "he can rule over you" is a more comfortable choice. It acknowledges the reality of the male tendency to dominate, without suggesting that it is inevitable.

The story of Adam and Eve is a bit like a hologram. What you see depends on the angle from which you view the story. This is one of the reasons the story is so rich, and so difficult. Whichever interpretation(s) one prefers, the feminist reader is confronted with the question: Is it sexist? The story itself does not depict women as inferior or as the origin of evil. Such depictions are the product of the sexism of the commentators. The story is certainly androcentric. Is it intrinsically sexist? That is the question each reader should consider.

DISCUSSION QUESTIONS

1. How have the traditional interpretations of Eve affected your understanding of women?

2. In what ways has the popular image of Eve as temptress influenced your picture of male-female relationships?
3. To what extent has the unholy trinity of inferiority, temptress, and sexuality, often associated with Eve, shaped your conception of women's sexuality?
4. Has the traditional understanding of Genesis 3:16a—that women will bear children in pain or naming Eve the "mother of the living" in the judgment scene—influenced your feelings about motherhood?
5. How has Genesis 3:16b, which declares that a woman's man will (or can) rule over her, affected your understanding of marriage?
6. How do you feel about Trible's belief that Adam was originally a sexually undifferentiated creature?
7. Does the knowledge of feminist interpretations of Eve change your view of women? of the Bible?

The Women in Genesis

The principal "historical" women of Genesis are Sarah, Hagar, Lot's daughters, Rebekah, Rachel and Leah, Dinah, Tamar, and Potiphar's wife. When we say that these women are historical, we do not mean that all the details of their stories are historically accurate. The ancients' concept of history was very different from ours. They were more concerned to convey their theological convictions than to report events.

Today we are aware of the impossibility of total objectivity in reporting any occurrence. What is told and what is left out can powerfully affect the way the event is understood. Nevertheless we value objectivity. We aim for historical accuracy. The ancients did not share this value. Thus the stories of the women of Genesis are colored by various political, social, and theological agendas, some more obvious to us than others.

In addition, most biblical stories have a complex oral and written prehistory. Several written sources are sometimes edited together to make a new whole. By using source, form, and redaction criticism, scholars are able to make intelligent guesses at the nature of the prehistory of the stories. These approaches dominated biblical scholarship during the first half of the twentieth century.

During the second half of the century, the focus gradually shifted. Without denying the results of the earlier approaches, biblical scholars devoted more energy to analyzing the finished product. Thus literary criticism has taken on new importance. This is especially true of feminist interpretations of biblical women's stories. Literary critics do not presume, however, that the stories they analyze are historically objective. Kernels of historical reality may underlie the stories. Determining which parts of the stories represent these kernels, however, is not the focus of most feminist interpreters. Though often unstated, the distinction between the literary characters and the historical persons is assumed.

In several important instances, feminist interpretations of Eve's story involve correcting inaccurate translations of key words or phrases. This is less the case with the women who follow Eve in Genesis. The focus of feminist and womanist interpreters in these stories is in three areas. Some consider how to evaluate the characters of the women. For example, biblical scholar Sharon Jeansonne uses narrative criticism to determine the attitude of the narrator toward the women, which in many cases is more favorable than the assessments of modern nonfeminist interpreters.[1]

Others are concerned with possible connections in the women's stories with institutions and customs in ancient southwest Asian and north African culture. In her study of the motif of the barren woman, for example, Mary Callaway notes that in the Code of Hammurabi provision is made for the husband of a priestess who could not bear children. He could marry a lay priestess who could bear children, or his wife could give him a female slave to produce offspring. Callaway also points out that the Nuzi tablets include a marriage contract that states that if the wife was unable to bear children, she would provide her husband with a surrogate. Finally, Callaway indicates that an Egyptian text from 1100 BCE sanctioned the use of a female slave as surrogate mother.[2] These documents shed light on the stories of Sarah and Hagar, as well as those of Rachel and Bilhah and Leah and Zilpah.

Still others contemplate how certain Israelite legal provisions apply to the women of Genesis. In particular, the story of Tamar involves the institution of levirate marriage, in which a widowed, childless woman had the right to mate with her brother-in-law in order to produce heirs for her dead husband.[3]

Many of the studies focus not on individual women but on patterns that can be discerned in the ways the stories are told[4] or on sociological matters.[5] Indeed, many of the women of Genesis are frustrating to study as individuals, because they are not developed very well as characters. Esther Fuchs describes the problem as follows:

> None of the biblical mother-figures matches the depth and complexity of father-figures like Abraham, Jacob, Jephthah, and David. Only father-figures are shown to experience conflict between, for example, parental love and the exigencies of divine authority (Abraham and Jephthah). Only they demonstrate the complexity of a situation in which a parent is called upon to scold his most beloved son, or to hide his love for fear of sibling revenge (Jacob). Only they exemplify the human conflict between love for and fear of one's own child (David). The parental role played by the father-figure constitutes only one aspect in the character, one that contributes to the depth and many-sidedness of this character. It does not eclipse his other

qualities. This is the difference between a multifaceted, well-developed literary character and a type, or a role model. . . . Although motherhood is the most exalted female role in the biblical narrative, the biblical mother-figures attain neither the human nor the literary complexity of their male counterparts. The patriarchal framework of the biblical story prevents the mother figure from becoming a full-fledged *human* role model, while its androcentric perspective confines her to a limited literary role, largely subordinated to the biblical male protagonists.[6]

With these considerations in mind, we move to the stories themselves. Most of the women of Genesis are helpmates, that is to say, wives and mothers. The importance of motherhood is a theme that runs through the stories of these women, as well as of the women of the Hebrew Bible in general.[7] Eight of the ten women are clearly mothers (Sarah, Lot's daughters, Hagar, Rebekah, Rachel, Leah, and Tamar). The parental role of one of the ten is not specified (Potiphar's wife).[8] One is precluded from marriage and legitimate family because of an illicit sexual encounter (Dinah). Three are initially barren (Sarah, Rebekah, and Rachel). Later they conceive and bear children, but only after two of them have given their handmaids to their husbands to produce offspring (Sarah and Rachel). Tamar pretends to be a harlot.[9] Her story centers on male denial of the ancient custom of levirate marriage. Hagar, Lot's daughters, and Dinah are victims.

One issue that comes up repeatedly is deception.[10] Of the ten women considered here, six of them are portrayed as tricksters (Lot's daughters, Rebekah, Rachel, Tamar, and Potiphar's wife). Biblical scholar Susan Niditch puts this issue in a broader context:

One of the biblical authors' favorite narrative patterns is that of the trickster. Israelites tend to portray their ancestors and thereby to imagine themselves as underdogs, as people outside the establishment who achieve success in roundabout, irregular ways. One of the ways marginals confront those in power and achieve their goals is through deception or trickery. The improvement in their status may be only temporary, for to be a trickster is to be of unstable status, to be involved in transformation and change. In Genesis, tricksters are found among Israelites sojourning in foreign lands, among younger sons who would inherit, and among women.[11]

Another dynamic in two of the stories involves power plays between women. In one case, the rivalry is between relative equals (Rachel and Leah).[12] In the other, it is between unequal partners (Sarah and Hagar).[13] One woman is depicted as a temptress (Potiphar's wife). Two of the women are clearly foreigners (Hagar and Potiphar's wife). The ethnic identity of one is uncertain but is probably Canaanite (Tamar).

With the exception of the temptress, the women of Genesis are portrayed by the narrator relatively sympathetically. For reasons that are not entirely clear, however, interpreters over the centuries have often assessed the characters of these women in more negative terms than the narrator. Having surveyed the women of Genesis in general terms, we can now look at them individually.

SARAH

Sarah is the first matriarch of the Bible. Her story is found in Genesis 12–21. She is described as beautiful (Gen. 12:11), so beautiful that twice Abraham passes her off as his sister to save himself (Gen. 12:11–20; 20:1–18). The narrator does not tell us how Sarah feels about these arrangements.

Sarah is the first in a line of barren women who through God's power finally have a male child.[14] Before Sarah conceives, though, she gives her Egyptian handmaid Hagar to Abraham to produce an heir (Gen. 16:1–3). When Hagar does become pregnant, problems develop between Sarah and Hagar (Gen. 16:4) that lead to Sarah's abuse of Hagar. As a result, Hagar flees to the desert (Gen. 16:6). The story leaves a lot of unanswered questions. Sarah blames Abraham for being the cause of the problems (Gen. 16:5). He does not deny the accusations but gives Hagar into Sarah's control (Gen. 16:6). He appears passive; Sarah comes across as cruel.

After Ishmael is born to Hagar, the divine announcement of Sarah's impending pregnancy is given, not to her, but to Abraham (Gen. 17:1–16; 18:10). When Abraham laughs in disbelief, he does not incur divine judgment (Gen. 17:17–21). When Sarah overhears the news in the tent, she also laughs incredulously. Then she is reprimanded (Gen. 18:15).

After Isaac is born to Sarah (Gen. 21:1–5), the rivalry between Sarah and Hagar continues (Gen. 21:9). As a result, Sarah finally sends Hagar and Ishmael away permanently. Although Abraham is concerned, Sarah has her way (Gen. 21:10–14). Again, Abraham appears to be passive, while Sarah appears jealous and cruel. Neither stands out as the role model we might have expected. Finally, when Abraham takes Isaac out to sacrifice him, he does not consult Sarah at all (Gen. 22:1–19).

The characters in this drama are painted as imperfect human beings. There are no heroes. Neither are there any villains. Sarah is old, but still beautiful, and desperate to have a son. She can be jealous and cruel. Nevertheless she is not vilified in the text.[15]

Feminist commentators react to her in a variety of ways. According to Esther Fuchs, biblical mothers, including Sarah, are depicted in ways that advance the interests of patriarchy, in particular the man's desire to control women's sexuality and reproductive capacity. Fuchs believes that Sarah is marginalized throughout the Abraham-Sarah sequences. She appears only in contexts where her sexuality or reproductive ability comes into play, and even then her role is limited. This is particularly evident in the annunciation scene, in which she is literally sequestered in the tent, where she can only overhear the birth announcement.[16]

Tammi Schneider reads Sarah's story in a more positive light, viewing Sarah as morally superior to Abraham. For example, many feminist interpreters are concerned that God reprimands Sarah for her laughter after she has heard the announcement that she will have a child (Gen. 18:15), but Schneider argues persuasively that it is not God who criticizes Sarah, but rather Abraham.[17]

In a fascinating article that focuses on Hagar but inevitably also involves Sarah, Pamela Tamarkin Reis suggests that when Sarah offers Hagar to Abraham "to be built up," the idea is not that Sarah will adopt the child as her own (which she never does), but that through her willingness to share the marital bed, her own fecundity will be stimulated.[18] At the point at which Sarah makes this offer to Abraham, God has promised Abraham numerous offspring, but Sarah has not been named as the mother, so Sarah is not showing lack of faith as some commentators have suggested.

Reis argues that the sexual relationship between Abraham and Hagar is supposed to last only long enough to produce a child. After Hagar becomes pregnant, she no longer should have access to Abraham's bed. In Genesis 16:5, the plot thickens:

> Then Sarai said to Abram, "May the wrong done to me be on you! I gave my slave-girl to your embrace, and when she saw that she had conceived, she looked on me with contempt. May the LORD judge between you and me!"

The Hebrew word translated "wrong," *hamas*, is a very strong word, even stronger than the English word "outrage." Aviva Zornberg says that it means "violent robbery with undertones of sexual rapacity."[19] Most interpreters do not understand what Abraham has done that should elicit such a strong response from Sarah. A failure to protect Sarah from Hagar's contempt hardly would seem to merit such a scolding. The fact that the second person pronoun in the last line, "May the LORD judge between you and me!" uses the Hebrew consonantal feminine spelling (though vocalized as a masculine form by the Masoretes) means that the line was probably spoken to Hagar rather than to Abraham, and shows that Abraham and Hagar were together when Sarah was speaking, first to Abraham and then immediately afterward without a pause to Hagar. This feminine pronoun, along with the use of the Hebrew word *hamas*, makes it likely that Sarah caught the couple in bed together and was therefore justified in her anger at both of them.[20] This reading changes Sarah from an irrationally angry woman who is quick to blame others into one whose anger and reproach are quite understandable and reasonable. Reis, nevertheless, does not believe that Sarah's response of treating Hagar harshly, or afflicting or oppressing her—however the Hebrew verb should be translated—is justified.[21]

Sarah does not impress most feminist readers as a positive role model. Womanist theologian Delores Williams suggests that Sarah "has been viewed as the haughty (white? Jewish?) slave owner seemingly unconcerned with her role as victimizer."[22] We will return to the issue of her ethnic identity in the discussion on Hagar. Some commentators, however, view Sarah as almost as much a victim as Hagar. Fuchs sees the problem as an ideological one. The narrative subtly suggests that because women can't get along with one another, sisterhood is not a viable alternative to patriarchy.[23]

How, then, do we assess Sarah? Is she victim or victimizer? The text depicts Sarah as a strong woman, but hers is not a modern egalitarian marriage. Her literary role and focus are limited to the important business of children. As presented in the text, she is a victimizer of Hagar, but she also suffers at the hands of her husband, who twice passes her off as his sister to save his own skin and who possibly cheats on her with Hagar. In addition she is also a victim of a value system that valued women primarily for their reproductive capacity, as economically necessary as it may have been.

Sarah's story is replayed wherever and whenever the oppressed oppress those who have even less power. Sarah is not a hero. She is someone with whom we can perhaps empathize, if we are honest. Some of the students at Howard University identify more with Sarah than with Hagar. Whatever our ethnic group, Americans and Europeans are privileged far beyond our sisters and brothers in many other parts of the world. Maybe Hagar can remind us that even as we seek justice for women, we must be careful not to do it at the expense of others, especially those whose position in society is more marginal than our own.

HAGAR

Hagar, Sarah's handmaid or servant, or what we might call a live-in domestic employee, is Egyptian. Her story is found in Genesis 16 and 21. In Genesis 16:1–3, Sarah gives Hagar to Abraham as a temporary wife to produce offspring. Hagar conceives and when she becomes aware of her pregnancy, looks down on Sarah (Gen. 16:4). If Reis is correct, Abraham and Hagar are sleeping together. Sarah blames Abraham, who tells her to do with Hagar as she pleases. She abuses her so badly—though the nature of the abuse is not stated—that Hagar runs away (Gen. 16:5–6). While she is in the wilderness,

God's messenger finds Hagar and tells her to go back to Sarah, because God intends to make a numerous people from her son, whom she is to name Ishmael (Gen. 16:7–12). Then Hagar names God *'el ro'i*, meaning "God who sees me" (Gen. 16:13). Hagar gives birth to a son, and Abraham names him Ishmael, "God hears" (Gen. 16:15).

The story of Hagar continues in Genesis 21 after Sarah has given birth to Isaac. Sarah notices Ishmael doing something with Isaac that commentators debate—perhaps playing, perhaps mocking, perhaps imitating, perhaps being drunk.[24] It enrages Sarah to the point that she demands that Abraham drive Hagar (whom she now calls a slave rather than a handmaid) and Ishmael away so that Ishmael will not share Isaac's inheritance (Gen. 21:9–10). Abraham is distressed, but God tells him not to worry, because Isaac is the one whose descendants will bear Abraham's name, but also God will make of Ishmael a great nation (Gen. 21:11–13). The next morning Abraham sends them away with a loaf of bread and a skin of water, and they begin to wander aimlessly (Gen. 21:14–15). Soon the water is used up, and Hagar puts Ishmael under a shrub a distance away from herself, because she cannot bear to watch him die. She begins to cry (Gen. 21:16). God hears Ishmael's (!) cry. God's messenger calls to Hagar and tells her that God has heard the boy's cry and reminds her that Ishmael is to become a great nation (Gen. 21:17–18). Then God opens Hagar's eyes and she sees a well of water from which they drink and fill their skin (Gen. 21:19). God is with Ishmael as he grows up in the wilderness and becomes an expert archer. Hagar finds a wife for him from her native Egypt (Gen. 21:21).

The story of Hagar is the story of a servant and her mistress, or in modern terms an employer and employee. It is the story of struggle for status. It is sadly also the story of abuse and exile. With the exception of the sexual component of the relationship, it is debatable whether the relationship can fairly be called any more economically exploitative than the relationship between a contemporary middle-class woman and a live-in domestic employee (or even a cleaning service worker). The modern domestic worker may be technically, legally free, but economically probably has few options. Modern readers should not be so quick to pass judgment without considering contemporary parallels that implicate us.

If Hagar was supposed to be a surrogate mother, it reminds us that surrogate motherhood is a thorny issue for legal and psychological reasons today. In the case of Hagar, however, although most interpreters believe the child she bore was supposed to belong to Sarah legally, Sarah never claimed Ishmael. If Reis is correct, Sarah never intended to adopt Ishmael. Even if Reis is correct, however, Hagar apparently had no choice about entering into a sexual relationship with Abraham. The text gives us no indications of her feelings in the matter. In the end, Hagar and her son became free, independent persons.

Hagar may have been fired from her "job," but she gained the economic security of a male descendant and the social status of being the mother of the Ishmaelites, or in modern terms the Arabs.

The story of Sarah and Hagar is also the story of two women of different ethnic identities in conflict. It would be easy to read into their relationship modern American racial tensions; it would also be wrong. Womanist Hebrew Bible scholar Renita Weems reminds us in her essay on Hagar that racism as we know it today did not exist in the ancient world.[25] Nevertheless she writes: "Theirs is a story of ethnic prejudice exacerbated by economic and sexual exploitation. Theirs is a story of conflict, women betraying women, mothers conspiring against mothers. Theirs is a story of social rivalry."[26] What kind of ethnic prejudice Weems has in mind is not clear. There was no prejudice against Africans at the time, as Weems herself makes clear. Indeed, Hagar's Egyptian nationality probably meant that in some senses her social class was higher than that of Abraham and Sarah, who were wandering nomads.

Trible's assessment is similar to Weems's, although she is careful not to speak in racial or ethnic terms. "Read in light of contemporary issues and images, her story depicts oppression in three familiar forms: nationality, class, and sex."[27]

African American biblical scholar John Waters raises many questions about the usual readings of Hagar's story. He notes that there are actually two different portraits of Hagar in the biblical text. The first portrait, found in Genesis 16, is mainly a product of the J, or Yahwist, writer. In this version Hagar is a proud woman who will not allow herself to be treated harshly. The second portrait, in Genesis 21:8–21, is considered by traditional source critics to be a product of the E, or Elohist, writer. Here Hagar is much more submissive.[28]

Most people who read Hagar's story are so gripped by the horror of Hagar's plight that they have difficulty focusing on any positive notes. Trible points out, however, that Hagar is the first person—not the first woman, but the first person—in the Bible who is visited by a divine messenger. She is the only biblical character who dares to name God.[29] She is the first woman who receives a divine promise of descendants. She is the first woman in historical Israel (excluding Gen. 1–11) to bear a child.[30] Her child becomes the father of a great nation.

These positives, however, do not erase the suffering. Neither do they answer our questions. Why does God send Hagar back to Sarah's oppression, when Hagar flees into the desert? Elsa Tamez responds to this question.

> The angel of the Lord counsels Hagar to return and subject herself to Sarah, her old mistress from whom she has been liberated. Indeed! Counsel of the Lord! God on the side of the oppressors, she might think, and so might we. Understood in this manner, it simply doesn't go with the text.

God's plans are not for Hagar to return to the oppression. . . . What God wants is that she and her child should be saved, and at the moment, the only way to accomplish that is not in the desert, but by returning to the house of Abraham. Ishmael hasn't been born. The first three years of life are crucial. Hagar simply must wait a little longer, because Ishmael must be born in the house of Abraham to prove that he is the first-born (Deut. 21:15–17), and to enter into the household through the rite of circumcision (chap. 17). This will guarantee him participation in the history of salvation, and will give him rights of inheritance in the house of Abraham.[31]

Along similar lines Delores Williams makes a distinction between (usually male) black liberation theology and womanist, Hagar-centered survival, quality-of-life traditions. She identifies three areas of theological importance in the Hagar story: a continuity of tradition about God between the Bible and African American experience, a new methodological level of interpretation that is different from, but complementary to traditional historical-critical exegesis, and a connection between faith and politics.[32]

Niditch again puts this story in broader perspective. She writes:

The motif of the exposed, endangered, and delivered child is as common in the stories of great heroes as that of their mothers' unusual, difficult conceptions. Compare Moses' origins (Ex. 2:1–10). The motif occurs also in Greek narratives about Oedipus and about the Persian king Cyrus. Embedded in the Israelite tale of origins is thus another related people's story of its hero's youth, and on some level Abraham and Sarah are its necessary villains. God is the god of those deserted in the wilderness, of those on the fringes, who are usually in the Hebrew Scriptures not Ishmaelites but Israelites.[33]

Nevertheless we cannot ignore the human side of the story. Trible and Weems challenge us to take this story to heart. Trible concludes her essay on Hagar with these words: "All we who are heirs of Sarah and Abraham, by flesh and spirit, must answer for the terror in Hagar's story. To neglect the theological challenge she presents is to falsify faith."[34]

Weems concludes:

Finally, out in the wilderness, overcome with grief, the bitter, distraught, banished Egyptian slavewoman set her child down and went off a short distance to weep alone. She could not bear to watch her son suffer.

This time, instead of an angel, the Lord appeared. However, it was not the mother's weeping which caused the Lord to speak. Rather, it was the child Ishmael's tears that moved the Lord to intervene on behalf of the mother, Hagar.

"But the Lord heard the voice of the lad" (Genesis 21:17).

Just as Ishmael must have wept for the senselessness of Hagar, Sarah, and Abraham's ways, maybe it will take our children weeping on our behalf—our children weeping for the sins and prejudices and stubbornness of we [sic] their mothers and fathers—to convince God to intervene on our behalf. Perhaps as a global community we will be saved—if we are to be saved at all—because of the little children whose innocent tears will prostrate heaven.

Though their tears have not always moved us, hopefully they will move God.

God have mercy on us.[35]

Who was Hagar? Her story is the story of cruel abuse. It is also the story of a woman who sees and names God and is the mother of a great nation. It is not the story of a black woman oppressed by a white one. Whatever ethnic tensions underlie this story, they are not the ones familiar to people living in the United States. The kinds of questions this story raises for modern readers are how privileged women, the primary readers of this book, relate to the women who serve them, whether as domestics in their homes, in public establishments such as restaurants, dry cleaners, and nail salons, or, at an even greater distance, in third-world countries.

THE DAUGHTERS OF LOT

Though unnamed and therefore considered unimportant by the biblical editors, the daughters of Lot are important for two reasons. First, they are saved from being substituted by their father for his male guests whom his neighbors intended to rape (Gen. 19:1–11). Second, through incest with their father, they bear the sons Moab and Ammon (Gen. 19:30–38), whose descendants become enemies of Israel.

Feminist interpreters debate the implications of the near gang rape episode. Some believe it was viewed as a reprehensible action by a reprehensible man.[36] Others believe it is indicative of the extremely low status of women in ancient Israel.[37] There is probably truth in both positions. Lot is no hero. The fact that he even considered such a solution to the problem that faced him, however, is an indication of women's low status. Though Lot is depicted as a selfish, thoughtless man, he is often exonerated by male interpreters. They condone his behavior on the ground that he was doing what hospitality customs required.[38]

After Lot's daughters are saved by the visitors who turn out to be angels (Gen. 19:10–11), Lot and his wife and daughters escape before Sodom is destroyed (Gen. 19:15–16). Then Lot's wife is turned into a pillar of salt for looking back (Gen. 19:26). It is not clear whether this story has a moral, not to disobey God or not to look back, or whether the story developed simply to explain an unusual rock formation that looked a bit like a woman.[39] Next, Lot takes his daughters to live in a cave (Gen. 19:30).

Lot had not been able to convince his prospective sons-in-law to leave Sodom (Gen. 19:14). How hard he tried is not clear. Since the angels had to urge him repeatedly to leave (Gen. 19:15–16), perhaps he did not impress upon them very strongly the urgency. In any case, the sons-in-law are destroyed along with all the other inhabitants of Sodom.

Thus Lot's daughters believe there are no men left to marry (Gen. 19:31). Desperate to bear children, they commit incest with Lot by getting him drunk on two successive nights (Gen. 19:32–35). To conceive children they commit two "sins": deception and incest. Ironically, they sexually manipulate the man who would have allowed a crowd to have their will with them. The text does not explicitly condemn them for their actions.

But what are we to make of this story of deception and incest? In a delightful article, Melissa Jackson counters the usual feminist tendency to read this story in a somber and pessimistic fashion. For example, Gail Corrington Streete sees the problem in the text not being the sin of incest, but the fact that the daughters have taken the initiative sexually; the result of this boundary crossing is tainted sons—the eponymous ancestors of Israel's enemies the Moabites and the Ammonites.[40] Similarly, Janice Nunnally-Cox suggests that the daughters are shamed, even as the Moabites and Ammonites are mocked.[41] Jackson, however, sees this story as an example of a comic trickster narrative. The daughters use their wits and achieve their ends, subverting the usual power relationships along the way. One of their sons, Moab, is even an ancestor of David. Jackson concludes:

> The writers of the patriarchal narratives invite us to step in with them and dream our own dreams of a world turned upside-down. Maybe in this reality patriarchy was not the status quo, men were seen as fools for behaving as if they were in total control, and women were valued for motherhood and also for their intelligence, courage, inventiveness, creativity.[42]

REBEKAH

Rebekah is the second matriarch in the Israelite genealogy. Her story is found in Genesis 24–27. Genesis 24 is the story of Abraham sending a servant to his homeland in search of an appropriate wife for Isaac (Gen. 24:1–9), the servant's "chance" meeting with Rebekah (Gen. 24:10–16), her passing the test the servant has devised by which to know whom God has chosen (Gen. 24:17–27), gift giving and discussion (Gen. 24:18–54), Rebekah's agreeing to go with the servant (Gen. 24:55–61), and finally Rebekah's marriage to Isaac (Gen. 24:62–67). Rebekah is depicted as beautiful, virginal, generous, and independent. Isaac finds solace after his mother's death in his love for Rebekah (Gen. 24:67). Rebekah's feelings about Isaac are not described.

The next episode in Rebekah's story concerns the birth of Esau and Jacob. She is initially barren, but Isaac prays to God and Rebekah conceives (Gen. 25:19–21). The pregnancy is difficult, so Rebekah consults with God, who tells her that she will bear twins and that the older will serve the younger (in the usual translations of Gen. 25:22–23). The twins are born—first red, hairy Esau and then Jacob. Esau becomes a hunter and is preferred by Isaac; Jacob keeps to his tents and is preferred by Rebekah (Gen. 25:24–28). One day when Jacob is cooking a stew, Esau comes in from the field famished. In exchange for his birthright, Esau buys a bowl of Jacob's stew (Gen. 25:29–34).

A famine forces Isaac to move into the territory of Abimilech (Gen. 26). There he tells people that Rebekah is his sister, because he fears he might be killed on account of her beauty (Gen. 26:1–7). One day Abimilech sees Isaac fondling Rebekah. Abimilech angrily rebukes Isaac for his lie and warns his people not to molest either Isaac or Rebekah (Gen. 26:8–11).

The final episode recorded about Rebekah is her deception of Isaac concerning the blessing. Isaac is old and blind. He calls Esau to him and tells him to catch some game for him and fix it so that Isaac can bless him (Gen. 27:1–4). Rebekah overhears this, calls Jacob, and tells him to bring to her two kids, which she will prepare. Jacob objects that Isaac will be able to tell that he is not Esau, because of his smooth skin, and will curse him rather than bless him. Rebekah tells him that she will bear any curse (Gen. 27:5–13). Jacob obeys; Rebekah fixes the meal, dresses Jacob in Esau's clothes, puts the kids' skins on his arms and legs, and sends him with the dish to Isaac (Gen. 27:14–17). Isaac is suspicious, because Jacob cannot disguise his voice, but in the end Isaac is convinced by the smell of the clothes and blesses Jacob (Gen. 27:18–29). When Esau comes with the meal he has prepared, he is so angry with Jacob that he is ready to kill him (Gen. 27:30–41). Rebekah, fearing for Jacob's life, sends him to her brother Laban's to sit out Esau's anger (Gen. 27:42–46).

Like Sarah, Rebekah is initially barren.[43] Unlike Sarah, she quickly conceives after Isaac prays to God (Gen. 25:21). Like Sarah, she is also passed off by her husband Isaac as his sister (Gen. 26:1–11). Again, the narrator does not tell us how Rebekah feels about this arrangement. Biblical scholar Alice Laffey writes of this incident:

> From a feminist perspective, this story more closely resembles Gen 12 than Gen 20. Isaac lied, risking his wife to secure his own well-being. He was more important than her, and if one should suffer, quite logically it

should be the woman. Isaac is not punished for his lie. On the contrary, Abimelech is grateful that none of his people has followed through on the implications of the lie, violating Rebecca whom, because of Isaac's lie, they understood to be fair game. That would have been a grave offense against Isaac, and the patriarchal culture, and would have resulted in misfortune for Gerar. Rebecca never speaks, never has a choice, never makes a decision. She is a passive character, passed between men, a tragic example of patriarchal culture.[44]

Bledstein sees this incident in a different light. She believes that Isaac, whom she calls Trickster, and Rebekah, whom she calls Binder (from the Hebrew root *rbq*, meaning "to tie fast"), cooperate with each other. She writes:

> Trickster and Binder cooperated in outwitting a powerful man, Abimelech king of Gerar (Gen. 26). As Abraham and Sarah had before, the couple presented Binder as Trickster's sister to keep the husband alive among covetous strangers. Later, however, in view of the monarch's window, Trickster was seen *mesaheq* [= *meṣaḥeq*], fondling Binder. . . . This deception/undeception in Gerar won the couple royal protection.[45]

It is impossible to determine which of these largely literary readings is "right," because they both make inferences from the text that are plausible but impossible to prove. Laffey is correct, however, in her statement that Rebekah is a passive character in this scene. She does not speak at all.

Rebekah displays no cruelty in her character, nor does she spar with any other female character. Her "sin," according to many readings, lies in deceiving Isaac into blessing Jacob, the younger son. However, Christine Allen counters the usual criticism of Rebekah by pointing out that God reveals to her in a dream that Jacob is the one who will carry on the family traditions. Allen argues that Rebekah, more than Isaac, is the spiritual link between Abraham and Jacob:[46]

> Rebekah then chose an alternative which used deceit. Another holy woman, Judith, later on used deceit to murder an enemy. Rebekah's deceit was to fool Isaac into believing that Jacob was his elder son Esau. Can it be that God asked this particular deceit of her? . . . In this case, Rebekah would not merely be acting on her own to fulfill the prophecy during her pregnancy, but she would be responding to a specific call to help the divine plan. Had not Abraham been asked to sacrifice Isaac? Could she not be asked to sacrifice her marriage trust? Had not Isaac been given back? Could not the marriage be reunited? Would not God "suspend the ethical for teleological reasons"?[47]

Even if Rebekah is exonerated, as Allen advocates, she is still the subordinate female who must maneuver around the male structures to achieve her mission.

Again, Bledstein has a somewhat different view. She agrees that Rebekah acts because of the information she received in her dream. Bledstein does not believe, however, that Isaac was really deceived. He was too much of a trickster himself to be tricked by someone else. Instead, he sets up the situation to test which son is most fit to receive the blessing.[48] This is an interesting theory that is not inconsistent with the text. Nevertheless we would be more comfortable with this approach if more explicit clues in the text pointed in this direction.

Although Rebekah is often viewed as a positive character from a feminist point of view, she is not well liked by male interpreters. The reason perhaps lies in the psychological realm. Biblical and modern women are often stereotyped as constantly fighting among themselves. The jealousy and fighting between Sarah and Hagar, for example, are seen as typically feminine. If a man is involved in the rivalry, and especially if the woman wins the fight, the situation is evaluated differently.[49] Sarah's behavior toward Hagar was cruel and far worse than Rebekah's deception of Isaac. Nevertheless, in the eyes of many, Sarah is the more ethical character. Abusing a woman servant is acceptable; deceiving a man, even to achieve God's mission, is not.

Allen concludes:

> If we view the complete circumstances of Rebekah's life in the above way it is clear that her sanctity was evident in a most profound way. Not only does she serve as a model of courage, immediate acceptance of grace, long-suffering and willingness to die for God, but she can also be seen as the first woman in the Bible to be a saint. In this way she stands on her own, regardless of the role she plays as mother or wife. Her primary significance is her own response to God. In addition, however, she is also the mother of the faith. As Abraham became the father of the faith through meeting the test, so Rebekah became the mother of the faith. More concretely, she is the mother of Israel. Jacob was told: "Your name shall no longer be Jacob, but Israel, because you have been strong against God, you will prevail against men" (Gen. 32:28). And if one could break the chain of patriarchy a more proper blessing would be "in the name of Abraham, Rebekah and Jacob."[50]

Another reading of Rebekah comes from students in a Women in the Old Testament course at Howard Divinity School.[51] Their concern is Rebekah's favoritism. How can a mother favor one child over another? How can a mother who would do this be lifted up as a role model? These questions, however, must be paired with another question: What moral choices and compromises might we make if we lived in the world of the ancient Israelites, where it was assumed that one male child would be the primary inheritor?

Who was Rebekah? Was she a strong and virtuous woman who responded to God's call, as Allen believes? Was she a mother with a favored son whose interests she selfishly promoted, as some of the students wondered? However one answers these questions, a few matters are clear. Rebekah was a character who had difficult choices to make, choices that were severely limited by her social context. Were her choices honorable? The narrator presents her in a positive light, giving her actions a divine mandate. Oppressed people often resort to what the dominant group considers deception to survive. How should we assess Rebekah?

RACHEL AND LEAH

Rachel and Leah are the third generation of Hebrew matriarchs. Their story is found in Genesis 29–35. After Jacob arrives at Laban's, he meets Rachel and falls in love with her (Gen. 29:1–14). He agrees to work for Laban for seven years in exchange for marrying her. Laban deceives him by placing Leah in his tent on the night of the marriage rather than Rachel, claiming that the older daughter had to be married first (Gen. 29:15–26). Jacob agrees to work another seven years to earn Rachel (Gen. 29:27–30).

Like Sarah and Rebekah, Rachel is barren (Gen. 30:1–2).[52] Like Sarah, she waits many years before she has a child. The narrator does not inform us how Sarah feels about being childless for so long. Rachel is distraught over her situation, and her long wait for children is made more vexing by the fertility of her sister. Before she is able to have children, she gives her handmaid to Jacob (Gen. 30:3–8), in the same way that Sarah gave Hagar to Abraham. Even though Leah is successful in having many children, she also gives her handmaid to Jacob (Gen. 30:9–13). Unlike the story of Sarah and Hagar, however, there are no evident problems between the sisters and their handmaids, though the sisters have troubles with each other.

In her ongoing struggle to have children, Rachel buys from Leah some mandrakes, supposed fertility enhancers. In exchange for them she provides Leah access to Jacob (Gen. 30:14–18). This is an interesting story in two respects: although Rachel and Leah are jealous of each other, they cooperate to achieve their goals; and they are able to determine Jacob's sleeping arrangements. Rachel is finally successful in having two sons (Gen. 30:22–24; 35:16–20). Leah must content herself with having many children, for she never wins Jacob's love.

Jacob is not content with Laban's attitude toward him, so he plans to return home (Gen. 31:1–13). He consults with Leah and Rachel who also feel that their father has cheated him (Gen. 31:14–16). They proceed to leave while Laban is busy shearing sheep. Rachel takes the household gods without telling Jacob (Gen. 31:17–19). Three days later Laban returns home from shearing sheep to discover that Jacob's family is gone. He catches up with them, upbraids Jacob for stealing away, searches for the missing gods unsuccessfully, and finally is reconciled with Jacob (Gen. 31:22–54). Jacob, Leah, Rachel, and their children and goods leave (Gen. 32:1–2). Rachel dies in childbirth after reaching Canaan (Gen. 35:18–20).

The story of Rachel and Leah is, on one level, the story of the rivalry between two sisters for the love of one husband. Beneath the rivalry is the story of the struggle for self-esteem. Leah is not as beautiful as Rachel. Her eyes are described as *rakkôt*, usually translated "weak," but the more basic meaning is "tender" or "soft."[53] Perhaps Rachel is more outwardly beautiful, but Leah is more sensitive and kind.[54] All the children she produces for Jacob cannot make him love her. Rachel enjoys Jacob's love but for a long time lacks the one thing her society requires for a woman to gain respect. Although tension mars the relationship of the sisters, they are united in their hatred of their father (Gen. 31:14–16). They despise him because he has put them in this awkward position of being married to the same man (Gen. 29:16–28) and because he has cheated them (Gen. 31:14–16).

The story of Rachel and Leah is, finally, the story of another deceptive act. Rachel steals her father's household gods as her family departs from Jacob's compound (Gen. 31:19). Although no motive is expressed, one possibility is that anger at her father is the reason for the theft.[55] Another possibility not inconsistent with the first is that the gods represent leadership of the family.[56] Ilana Pardes cites the Nuzi documents as evidence for this belief.[57] Another view is heard from Cheryl Exum, who, following Nancy Jay, believes that the gods represent the line of a descent reckoned through the mother. Thus Rachel's theft would signify her claim that her son Joseph was the one through whom descent should be determined.[58]

When Jacob comes looking for the idols, Rachel is sitting on them. She claims that she "has the way of women" (Gen. 31:34–35), evidently meaning that she is having her menstrual period. For this reason she cannot rise. Jacqueline Lapsley points out that there is an ironic double edge in her words. She cannot rise to confront her father in a legal action ("rise" being the verb used of a legal confrontation), because she is a female who is not allowed such independent action. Thus she will follow the "way of women," which means being a trickster.[59] In a fascinating discussion of Rachel's story, Pardes sees Rachel's life as paralleling Jacob's in important ways, but ultimately Jacob's dream is fulfilled, whereas Rachel dies in childbirth. Pardes says:

> Rachel's dream, however, is not doomed to total frustration. In a remarkable manner she has always managed to gain much admiration for her daring aspirations and compassion for her tragic failures. . . . She has never ceased to be the favorite matriarch in Jewish tradition. This is already evident in Jeremiah, who selects Rachel, and not Leah, as the mother of the nation, as the one who is best suited to accompany Jacob in his position as the eponymous father.[60]

We will return to this matter in chapter 8.

Who were Rachel and Leah? To what degree were they victims? To what degree was Rachel a strong woman fighting against either a selfish father or a patriarchal system or both? Most modern feminists will feel that Rachel and Leah were victimized by their father and a social structure that valued women primarily for their ability to bear children and secondarily for their beauty. Whether Rachel was consciously fighting patriarchy is another matter, a matter that cannot be proved. Was Rachel morally justified in stealing her father's gods? The humor in the story suggests that the narrator's answer is yes.

DINAH

Dinah's story is found in Genesis 34. She is Jacob's only daughter mentioned in the Bible. Her mother is Leah. Dinah's story is a sad tale of a woman who dares to leave the safe confines of her tent. She dares to go out to meet the local women in Shechem, where her family has settled (Gen. 34:1). She has a sexual encounter (usually described as rape, but see below) with Shechem, the son of Hamor, whose family inhabits the land (Gen. 34:2). He falls in love with her and asks to marry her (Gen. 34:3–4). He ends up murdered, along with the rest of the Shechemites, when Dinah's brothers Simeon and Levi act duplicitously (Gen. 34:5–24) and take revenge (Gen. 34:25–29). When Jacob hears of the sexual encounter, he waits until his sons return from the field to respond to the situation (Gen. 34:5). Just as his sons are returning, Hamor comes to negotiate (Gen. 34:6–7). They agree to a plan that requires the Shechemites to be circumcised in exchange for the right to intermarry with the Israelites. Simeon and Levi have no intention of keeping their side of the bargain (Gen. 34:13–17). Rather, they take advantage of the vulnerability of the Shechemites while they are healing from their circumcision to slaughter them (Gen. 34:25–26). We never learn Dinah's feelings about any of this, unless the phrase "spoke tenderly to her" (Gen. 34:3), literally "he spoke to her heart" (*wayedabber 'al leb*), suggests a reciprocal feeling.[61]

In a thought-provoking study of Dinah, Ita Sheres, a native of Israel, draws parallels between the story of Dinah and the Israeli-Palestinian conflict. Levi and Simeon are like some modern Israelis who will use any excuse to annihilate the Palestinians. Dinah is like the Israeli doves, mostly women, who would like to talk with the Palestinians, the people of the land. Like Dinah, they are quickly silenced.[62] Sheres seeks to make connections between the past and the present. Her work is imaginative and bold. It dares us to apply the texts to the crises of our time.

Working as a team, biblical scholars Danna Fewell and David Gunn challenge the interpretation of the Dinah story by another influential biblical scholar, Meir Sternberg.[63] Fewell, Gunn, and Sternberg are all literary critics, but they read the story of Dinah very differently. For Sternberg, Levi and Simeon are the heroes of the story who stand for idealism and rights. Fewell and Gunn disagree both with Sternberg's heroes and with his sense of morality. They believe the narrator elicits sympathy for Shechem when he falls in love with her. They believe that Jacob's slowness to act is not passivity but prudence. He waits until his sons return home so that they can consult together. He cannot do much alone. Fewell and Gunn read the brothers' angry reaction as the selfish outburst of men whose honor has been tarnished. They see no concern for Dinah. Fewell and Gunn see the brothers' agreement with the Shechemites as a good one. Jacob apparently approves the plan as the best possible under the circumstances. Little does he know the deceit that is involved. Finally, they understand the killing of the Shechemites to be way out of proportion with the crime. It endangers the whole family and leaves Dinah without matrimonial prospects.[64]

Fewell and Gunn summarize:

> Our discussion has run its course. What have we argued?
>
> First, that where Sternberg's reader sees admirable principles, our reader sees culpable neglect of responsibility. If Simeon and Levi are Sternberg's heroes, they are certainly not ours.
>
> Second, that where Sternberg's reader expresses contempt for the characters Jacob, Hamor, and Shechem, our reader expresses a measure of sympathy for them, not as heroes but as complex characters making the best of a flawed world.
>
> Third, that where Sternberg's reader sees Dinah as a helpless girl to be rescued, our reader sees a young woman who could have made her own choices—limited though they might have been—had she been asked.[65]

In conclusion Fewell and Gunn express their concerns about the risks in their reading of Dinah's story:

> Justice, we want to say, cannot be served in a society where men, men's rights, and men's honor control women's lives. To advocate a woman's marrying her rapist might itself seem to be a dangerous and androcentric advocacy. And so it would be if the story world offered other liberating alternatives.
>
> But for there to be a whole other way there would have to be a whole other world.[66]

When I first read Fewell and Gunn's interpretation, I found it persuasive in many respects. However, Sternberg's response reveals serious problems with their reading, even from a feminist perspective.[67] For example, the evidence that "he spoke to her heart" indicates a reciprocal feeling on Dinah's part is not convincing. One can whisper sweet nothings; how the hearer hears them is another matter.[68] This might seem a trivial detail, but in fact it is important to Fewell and Gunn's interpretation, as Sternberg points out:

> Thus, Fewell and Gunn end by sadly avowing that to urge "a woman's marrying her rapist might itself seem to be a dangerous and androcentric advocacy" (p. 211). Now, if even a Dinah supposed to find her redress in such marriage can get the supposers into trouble with feminism, then a Dinah hustled into marriage while herself uncommitted, possibly averse to the idea, would scandalize most people. At the very least, though nothing can quite save the redress and its endorsers from the taint of sexism, the prospective bride *must* be made a consenting, sentimental party. But how, given that she rarely appears in action, never in speech and thought? So the passing reference to her "heart" must serve for heartfelt consent . . . turning inside Dinah's mind the outside view of Shechem's utterance to her.[69]

The debate between Sternberg and Fewell and Gunn, one of the most gripping to appear in the *Journal of Biblical Literature* for many years, goes beyond the interpretation of this story to broader questions of the possibility of objective, or what Sternberg calls "foolproof" interpretation. Without entering here that broader debate, which is considered in the introduction to this book, I agree with Sternberg that Fewell and Gunn's interpretation of the Dinah story has both linguistic and feminist problems.

Another feminist interpreter approaches Dinah's story in a different way. Her conclusions are similar to Fewell and Gunn's, but her methodology is different. Rapists do not fall in love with their victims. This story does not "feel" like a story of rape. Did Shechem really rape Dinah?

Using a philological approach, Lyn Bechtel argues that what happens between Dinah and Shechem is not rape but an illicit sexual liaison in which there was mutual consent. There is no specific word in Hebrew for rape. The Hebrew root used here that is usually translated "rape" is 'nh. Bechtel believes that here this word has the meaning of "shame." To her, the sexual union between Shechem and Dinah was considered shameful to Dinah because Shechem and Dinah were not from the same group, but it was not what we call rape. This interpretation is supported by the last sentence of the story. Simeon and Levi say, "Has he [Shechem] made our sister like a harlot?" Bechtel writes:

> Harlots engage in sexual relations for business purposes, so there is mutual consent. Harlots are not raped. They are women with no bonding or obligation to a family unit; they do not fit into the central social structure. By saying that Dinah has become like a harlot, Simeon and Levi

show that Dinah has not been raped. Instead, she has crossed the tribal boundary and acted like a harlot without bonding or responsibility to the family or the community.[70]

Dinah's family believes that she has been shamed because she has consorted with an uncircumcised outsider. Even after Shechem asks to marry Dinah and he and his group agree to circumcision, Levi and Simeon still feel vulnerable and thus retaliate by killing the Shechemites while they are still healing from their circumcision. Jacob reprimands his sons because their behavior has jeopardized the group.[71]

Bechtel concludes:

> Dinah, Shechem, and the tribal patriarch, Jacob, are mediating figures in the story. Dinah and Shechem actively engage one another and bond sexually. . . . In light of this bonding Jacob tries to bond with and cooperate with the Canaanites in another way. . . . Yet, both attempts at unity/bonding are thwarted by Simeon and Levi, who place the concerns of the individual over the well-being of the community. So the tribes of Simeon and Levi are removed from the central social/political structure.
>
> In the story Dinah is not "raped"; the Canaanites are, but we can only understand what is going on in this story when we understand group-orientation and the dynamics of group bonding and obligation.[72]

One of the problems with the story of Dinah and Shechem is that if their encounter was not a rape, then what happened? It is hard to imagine that it was the ancient equivalent of modern free love. Anita Diamant suggests in her novel *The Red Tent* that Dinah meets the prince of Shechem (who is called Shalem) while helping her mother Leah, a midwife who is delivering a baby of the king of Shechem's concubine. Dinah and Shalem fall in love; the queen of Shechem likes Dinah and arranges for a return visit, playing matchmaker. Dinah and Shalem end up in bed together, and the story follows the biblical plot, at least for a while, before diverging again.[73]

Although the novel is historical fiction, with an emphasis on the word fiction, anthropologists indicate that in many societies, something called marriage by abduction was practiced up to relatively recent times—and in some cases perhaps down to the present. Although this sounds like rape, and sometimes it involved force, in other cases it was consensual and was actually arranged by friends or family members when the more usual marriage arrangements by fathers could or would not be made. Usually, after the fact the more formal financial negotiations occurred, although sometimes violence was the aftermath. Thus, it is possible that Dinah and Shechem's encounter was of this consensual, though nonnormative type, and they were among the unlucky ones for whom the relationship ended violently. The fact that Shechem was of a different, uncircumcised ethnic group probably contributed to the problems, making the story an ancient version of *Romeo and Juliet* or *West Side Story*.

From a modern Western individualistic perspective the story of Dinah is disturbing because no one seems to be concerned with Dinah's rights, including what we would view as her right to have a voice in decisions that affect her life. The story is also disturbing because the revenge seems completely out of proportion with the alleged crime. However, here our sense of discomfort may be shared by the narrator. Finally, the story is disturbing to us because we do not know what Dinah's feelings were concerning all the events in the story and what became of her. We would like the biblical authors to have answered these questions, but they were not interested in them. They were more interested in the group dynamics. It is hard to assess whether their lack of interest in the individual Dinah is a result of their androcentrism or simply their group orientation, but my guess is the latter.

Dinah was a victim, not of rape, but of brothers who were overzealous in their concern for what they mistakenly believed was good for their group. Although the modern Western perspective differs in many ways from the ancient one, at least on this one conclusion we may agree.

TAMAR

Tamar's story is told in Genesis 38. She marries Er, the eldest son of Judah, one of the eleven sons of Jacob. Er dies soon after he marries Tamar (Gen. 38:7), leaving her a childless widow. The rule of levirate marriage then comes into play, allowing her to mate with her husband's brother to produce heirs for the deceased (Gen. 38:8). Onan spills his seed, however, to avoid his responsibility (Gen. 38:9). God kills him in punishment (Gen. 38:10). Judah is afraid to give his only remaining son, Shelah, to Tamar. He tells her to return to her father's house until Shelah is older (Gen. 38:11). Nothing comes of Judah's promise.

Meanwhile, Judah is widowed (Gen. 38:12). At sheep-shearing time Tamar removes her mourning clothes and puts on a veil. Her goal is to obtain from Judah what he would not provide through his son (Gen. 38:14). Not recognizing her behind her veil, he arranges to hire her (Gen. 38:15). She requires him to give her his seal, cord, and staff as guarantees that he will later pay her (Gen. 38:16–18). When Judah sends a friend to pay her, however, no harlot[74] can be found (Gen. 38:20). Three months later, when Tamar is evidently pregnant, Judah wants her burned. Then she produces the evidence that he is the father. He pronounces her more righteous than he (Gen. 38:24–26). She bears twins, Perez and Zerah (Gen. 38:27–30).

Tamar is clearly a woman who takes charge. Feminist interpreters have pointed out the positive light in which she is cast. Johanna van Wijk-Bos (formerly Bos) writes:

> The story of Tamar points in the direction of a gynocentric bias. The men in the story are wrongheaded irresponsible bunglers, who don't see straight. They are shown up as such by Tamar, who notices correctly and who causes Judah such an "eye-opener" that his view of reality is restored. The tone in which the men are discussed, summarily dispatched by God, or acting as if they were in charge and all the while making fools of themselves, points to a gynocentric bias as well.[75]

The methodology of van Wijk-Bos is literary criticism. She is aware of the androcentric aspects of the story. These include the failure of the narrator to condemn Judah and Tamar's victory, consisting of the birth of two sons. In spite of these elements, van Wijk-Bos believes that the woman's point of view is dominant in the story.[76] In a similar fashion Melissa Jackson views Tamar's story as a comic trickster narrative. She invites us to

> study, think, and then choose how to interpret Scripture. Thus, we may choose not to perpetuate a tradition of utterly somber scriptural study. Instead, we may opt to stand in the subversive tradition of inviting the comic to break upon us, revealing to us our true selves—and in so doing, revealing a transcendent reality that can be the inspiration for our work and the substance of our dreams.[77]

Other interpreters have focused on the way the story functions in the larger narrative. It is sandwiched between the sale of Joseph by his brothers in Genesis 37 and the attempted seduction of Joseph by Potiphar's wife in Genesis 39. Chronologically the story of Tamar must come after the story of Joseph and Potiphar's wife, for at this point Judah is still a young man. Literary critic Mieke Bal suggests that the placement of Tamar's story warns the reader not to be too concerned about Joseph's problem with Potiphar's wife. The message of the story of Tamar is that women are not the lethal creatures that some, like Judah, might mistakenly believe them to be.[78] If this interpretation is correct, both the content of the story and its placement are subversive of sexist attitudes toward women.

Like many other biblical women, Tamar must use deception to achieve her ends. Like many other biblical women, she must become a mother to have a place in society. Nevertheless, in a culture that came to be fearful of women and especially of foreign women, Tamar's story is a ray of hope.

POTIPHAR'S WIFE

The story of the attempted seduction of Joseph by Potiphar's wife is told in Genesis 39. After several unsuccessful attempts at seduction, Potiphar's wife tries again. Joseph once more declines and flees, leaving a piece of his garment behind in her hand (Gen. 39:7–12). She then turns the tables on Joseph, accusing him of trying to seduce her. Ironically, she uses the torn garment as evidence (Gen. 39:13–18). Potiphar believes her and has Joseph thrown in jail (Gen. 39:19–20). There Joseph uses his skills as an interpreter of dreams. He so impresses Pharaoh that he is freed to become Pharaoh's second in command (Gen. 41:14–46).

Potiphar's wife is as undeveloped a character as Dinah. Unlike Dinah, however, she is a subject rather than an object. Potiphar's wife is hardly a victim, although she does not accomplish her goal of seducing Joseph. Athalya Brenner calls her a negative temptress and a negative foreign woman.[79] She contrasts with Tamar, who is a positive temptress, and Hagar, who is a positive foreign woman.

Susan Hollis points out that the story of Potiphar's wife uses an old folk motif. In this motif the apparently destructive actions of a woman result in a man's positive transformation.[80] The happy endings to these stories, however, do not change the negative portrayal of the women in general or Potiphar's wife in particular. Her intentions have nothing to do with the final outcome.

She is a seducer and a negative deceiver. Unlike Rebekah's deception of Jacob and Tamar's deception of Judah, the deceptive behavior of Potiphar's wife is self-serving, spiteful, and hypocritical. Potiphar's wife is the stereotypical sexually potent, evil woman. Unlikely to be historical, she represents a real masculine fear. This fear is perhaps neutralized by the male victim's surviving and even benefiting from the confrontation with the evil woman. In addition, although Potiphar's wife succeeds in having Joseph punished, she vanishes from the text afterward. In contrast, Joseph's story continues. He is remembered as hero. She is barely remembered, a flat character who moves the action along.

Heather McKay tries to flesh out the flat character of Potiphar's wife, whom she calls Rahpitop—Potiphar spelled in reverse. Joseph is brought in and usurps Rahpitop's role as manager of the household for reasons that are never explained. Because Potiphar is called a eunuch, McKay suggests he is sterile and assumes that Rahpitop is desperate for children. Thus Rahpitop tries to seduce Joseph, but when she fails, she lashes out against him, claiming that he tried to seduce her. Potiphar, who in McKay's retelling runs a prison, transfers Joseph there where he works his way up the employment ladder, thus resolving the crisis. This reading does paint a somewhat more sympathetic portrait of Potiphar's wife than the traditional one. The reading is not inconsistent with the biblical text.[81]

In an unexpected sequel to the story of Joseph and Potiphar's wife, Joseph marries an Egyptian woman named Asenath, daughter of Potiphara (Gen. 41:45). This warns the reader that not all foreign women are evil. Although the names Potiphar and Potiphara are not the same, the similarity suggests the possibility of reconciliation. We would like to imagine Potiphar, his wife, their daughter Asenath, and Joseph sitting around laughing about the past together.

Joseph's marriage to Asenath also tells us that one of Jacob's sons married an Egyptian and that his children were ethnically mixed. How many of Joseph's brothers also married Egyptian women we have no way of knowing. It is likely that many of them did. When the Hebrew people left Egypt, "a mixed crowd also went up with them" (Exod. 12:38). They were Afro-Asiatic.

CONCLUSIONS

How these stories are read depends in part on what methodology is used. The feminist readings of women's stories in Genesis vary widely. Literary critics look primarily at the texts, but there are enough gaps and enough unanswered questions that different interpreters read the texts differently. Those who use the culturally cued reading approach are more aware of the cultural context of the texts, but they do not always emphasize the same cultural phenomena. Those who seek to investigate these texts historically often must base their conclusions on less than concrete evidence. In spite of the variety of interpretations, some conclusions can be drawn.

The women of Genesis run the gamut from helpmates to harlots. The only missing category is heroes. One might argue that Rebekah, Rachel, and Tamar are heroes, but they are rather limited in their accomplishments. We would prefer to reserve the title of hero for those like the midwives Shiprah and Puah in Exodus, who defy authority, and those like Deborah, Jael, and Esther, whose heroism is more public. Or is that an androcentric bias?

Our invisible category of victim is well represented by Hagar and Dinah. Although the women of Genesis include a wide variety of individuals, they share a lack of structural power. Each must work through and around the patriarchal structures of father, father-in-law, or brother. When Sarah and Rebekah are passed off by their husbands as their sisters, it suggests that women were vulnerable to being acquired by the strongest man. Although the focus in these stories is on the potential harm to their husband, the implications for the women are clear.

Rebekah's efforts to ensure that Jacob is blessed reveal her lack of authority in inheritance decisions. The story of Rachel and Leah shows how little their feelings mattered in the marriage arrangements. Similarly, Lot's daughters are totally dependent on their father, who is not a good provider. Tamar's right to levirate marriage means little when her father-in-law chooses not to offer his third son to her. Her only resort is effective, but indicates just how weak her position is.

Hagar is doubly weak as a woman and a servant. Her feelings are not consulted about surrogate motherhood, nor does she have any right not to be abused. As powerful as Potiphar's wife is, even she must convince her husband that Joseph has tried to seduce her before Joseph is sent to prison.

In spite of their lack of structural power, the women of Genesis are portrayed as active, strong women. They are depicted as women who find ways to achieve their goals. With the exception of Potiphar's wife, these goals are characterized as honorable. Nevertheless the determination of a woman's worth by her ability to bear children is a shadow over all these stories. The lack of feminine authority and structural power made many of the women resort to trickery. It also resulted in too many of them becoming victims.

Finally, we cannot read these stories without being aware of the fear of women's sexuality. This comes through especially in the stories of Tamar and Potiphar's wife.

The women of Genesis are characters out of a distant past. Yet their stories continue to touch our lives, affecting the way women perceive themselves and the ways in which societies where the Bible is an important cultural influence perceive women. And these stories, though put in final form long ago, are never really finished. In subtle ways readers retell and reshape the stories to speak to each new generation in search of meaning.

DISCUSSION QUESTIONS

1. To what degree do you identify with Sarah? With Hagar?
2. How important is motherhood, in your self-image if you are a woman, or in your estimation of women in general?
3. Is deception ever acceptable behavior? If so, in what circumstances? Try to be specific.
4. Is surrogate motherhood morally acceptable in any circumstances? If so, under what circumstances?
5. How do you feel about hiring another person to help you with domestic responsibilities? Does it make a difference if that person has a different ethnic origin from yours? Does it matter whether the person is an illegal immigrant, and is it important whether the employer pays the required taxes?

6. Are women more likely than men to have difficulty getting along with each other?
7. Can you imagine a situation in which prostitution might be morally acceptable?
8. Does the stereotypical seductive woman exist in today's world?

4

The Women in Exodus and Numbers

At the beginning of Exodus comes the story of the birth of Moses (Exod. 1:8–2:10). Five women are instrumental in his birth and survival. They are the midwives Shiphrah and Puah, Moses' mother Jochebed and sister Miriam, and Pharaoh's unnamed daughter. In the first section of this chapter we will discuss these five women.

One of these women, Moses' older sister Miriam, becomes a leader, along with Moses and their younger brother Aaron.[1] Problems develop between them concerning Moses' leadership and his marriage to a Cushite, that is, an Ethiopian (Num. 12:1). Whether this Cushite wife is the same person as Zipporah, Moses' Midianite wife, is unclear. It is possible, however, that the two are one and the same. In the second section of this chapter we will focus on the women in Moses' adult life.

Finally, the third section will consider the case of the five daughters of Zelophehad: Mahlah, Noah, Hoglah, Milcah, and Tirzah. Their story is found in Num. 26:33; 27:1–11; and 36:1–13. Zelophehad produced no sons, so his daughters were allowed to inherit their father's property, but with a proviso. They could marry only within their father's tribe. We will consider whether this new legislation represented an advance in women's rights.

THE WOMEN OF EXODUS 1:8–2:10

Cheryl Exum analyzes the roles of the five women who disregard Pharaoh's order to kill all Hebrew male infants (Exod. 1:22).[2] The narrative divides into three sections, each dealing in a progressively more severe way with the problem of Hebrew population growth.[3] In the first section (Exod. 1:8–14), Pharaoh has the Egyptians press the Hebrews into even harder service than before. In spite of this oppression, they continue to thrive and increase in numbers.[4]

The solution that Pharaoh proposes in the second section (Exod. 1:15–22) involves the midwives. They are supposed to kill the male babies. Although the pharaoh is unnamed, the midwives who defy his order are named, indicating their significance. Shiphrah means something like "beauty," and Puah means "girl."[5]

In the Hebrew text, they are ambiguously described as Hebrew midwives. This could mean they were not Hebrews themselves but Egyptians. Their names are Semitic rather than Egyptian, but this is not conclusive.[6] In the Greek and Latin versions, they are understood to be midwives to the Hebrews.

Their defiance of Pharaoh to save Hebrew babies might suggest they were Hebrew. Pharaoh's own daughter disobeys him, however, so even this evidence proves nothing. It might seem odd for Pharaoh to order Hebrew midwives to murder the babies of their own people, but Pharaoh is portrayed throughout as inept. Again, we cannot be sure.

Whether Hebrew or Egyptian, Shiphrah and Puah not only defy Pharaoh. They also cover up their defiance with a witty response to his accusatory questioning. They tell him that "the Hebrew women are not like the Egyptian women; for they are vigorous and give birth before the midwife comes to them" (Exod. 1:19). Apparently Pharaoh is taken in by their deceptive words[7] and does not punish Shiphrah and Puah. Instead, he decides to try a third solution to his problem. In the first section (Exod. 1:8–14), the Egyptian people cooperate with Pharaoh when he asks them to make the Hebrews work harder. Although they cooperate, the Hebrews continue to thrive. In the second section (Exod. 1:15–22), the midwives do not cooperate, and the Hebrews continue to expand. In the third section (Exod. 1:22–2:10), Pharaoh again turns to the people for help, demanding that they expose all male babies on the Nile.

In the third section, Moses' mother is introduced as "a Levite woman" (Exod. 2:1). In Exodus 2:5, Pharaoh's daughter is introduced, but she is never named. Moses' mother hides Moses for three months, but then it becomes impossible to hide him any longer. She makes a little boat or ark and covers it with pitch. She places Moses in it on the Nile. Although she appears to be obeying Pharaoh's order, in reality she is defying it as much as the midwives.[8] She has not even left Moses alone in his little boat, for in Exodus 2:4 his sister is stationed nearby.

Phyllis Trible points out that the introduction of Moses' sister at this point is surprising. It was implied earlier that Moses was the firstborn child. His birth announcement follows immediately the announcement of his parents' marriage (Exod. 2:1–2). Unlike Moses' birth, his sister's birth is not heralded. She appears without introduction. The difference in the way the two siblings enter the text elevates one at the expense of the other.[9]

In Exodus 2:5, Pharaoh's daughter sees the ark in which Moses is lying and has her maid get it. Then she looks inside and sees Moses. She can tell that it is one of the Hebrew children and has compassion on the crying infant. Moses' sister then asks Pharaoh's daughter whether she can go and get a Hebrew woman to nurse the child. Pharaoh's daughter agrees, and Moses' sister goes and finds Moses' mother. The mother returns and is instructed by Pharaoh's daughter to nurse the child in return for wages that she will pay. The child becomes the son of Pharaoh's daughter through some form of adoption.[10]

Pharaoh's daughter names him Moses (Exod. 2:10), a name that scholars agree is Egyptian. Pharaoh's daughter gives a Hebrew etymology for the name: "I drew him out of the water" (*mešîtihû*). On the basis of this statement, one would expect the name to be *mašuy*, "the one drawn out of the water." Instead, we have *mošê*, "the one who draws out."[11]

One interpreter believes that Pharaoh's daughter is being ridiculed for her inadequate command of Hebrew. Exum disagrees. Origins of names in the Hebrew Bible are not always precise. Moses' name, understood as Pharaoh's daughter interprets it, points forward to Moses' role as the one who draws his people out of their oppression. In addition, the compassion of Pharaoh's daughter makes her a very sympathetic character in the story.[12]

Exum points out that many women appear in this story but that men are strikingly absent. Even Moses' father is not mentioned after Exodus 2:1. Nevertheless, although it is women who act, they are all focused on one male character. Moses is named at the end of the story and becomes the central focus of what is to follow.[13]

In a subsequent article, Exum has articulated feminist concerns with Moses' birth narrative. She believes that the literary method she first used was deficient because it remained inside the ideology of the text, rather than standing outside in order to critique it. She also suggests that although she was aware of the problem of the women's absence after the first four chapters of Exodus, she did not give adequate consideration to the relationship between the women's presence at the beginning of the story and their absence later, in terms of gender politics.[14]

Exum now believes that women are allowed a significant role in the opening chapters of Exodus because their involvement with an infant fits in with traditional gender roles, that the ability of even women to outwit Pharaoh makes him look particularly bad, and that the story serves to manipulate women hearers/readers into staying in their socially acceptable place. She writes,

The women in Exodus 1 and 2 are literary creations, male constructs—and they are powerful. They outwit and overcome men. Patriarchy fears women's power and seeks to circumscribe and control it. Precisely because women have power that they can use to subvert authority, they present a threat to patriarchal society. It is therefore in the interest of those who maintain the social and symbolic order to represent women characters as using their power in the service of patriarchy.[15]

There is much truth in Exum's critique. However, it is not entirely fair to assess an ancient culture through modern lenses. In a time before the advent of modern methods of birth control, the rise of technologically advanced food production, and other innovations of the last century, the biologically based division of labor between men and women was probably necessary for the survival of the entire group. Everyone, men and women alike, in whatever century we live, live within the constraints of our time and place.

Thus we can still celebrate that the most important story in the Hebrew Bible begins with women determining events. We can still affirm that it begins with God using the weak and lowly to overcome the strong. We can acknowledge that it begins with women who act courageously, defying oppression, and that it begins with women who are life-affirming, women who are wise and resourceful in tough situations. Without these women, there would be no Moses to liberate the Hebrews from bondage.

THE WOMEN IN MOSES' ADULT LIFE

Moses' sister has a significant role in saving her brother. However, she drops out of view during the pivotal events of the struggle against Pharaoh and the exodus out of Egypt. Trible notes that it is Moses, sometimes assisted by his brother Aaron, who dominates this part of the narrative. She contrasts the ways the women and men accomplish their ends. "In quiet, secret and effective ways, these women, Hebrews and Egyptians, have worked together. By contrast, Moses makes noise, attracts attention and becomes *persona non grata* to both Hebrews and Egyptians."[16] The women are suppressed in the story, but Trible finds bits and pieces of the buried story at the end.

After the events of the exodus, the narrative tells us that Moses sings a song to the Lord, along with the sons of Israel (Exod. 15:1). The poem begins with this jubilant verse:

> I will sing to the LORD, for he has triumphed gloriously;
> horse and rider he has thrown into the sea.

The song continues at length, proclaiming God's power. Then the text surprises us. After what would seem to be the climax of the story, there is an anticlimactic recapitulation in Exod. 15:19:

When the horses of Pharaoh with his chariots and his chariot drivers went into the sea, the LORD brought back the waters of the sea upon them; but the Israelites walked through the sea on dry ground.

Even more strangely, Exodus 15:20–21 reads:

Then the prophet Miriam, Aaron's sister, took a tambourine in her hand; and all the women went out after her with tambourines and with dancing. And Miriam sang to them:

"Sing to the LORD, for he has triumphed gloriously;
horse and rider he has thrown into the sea."

After this brief song, the story moves on to the wilderness experience, leaving Miriam's verse as the finale of the exodus narrative. Yet her song gives a sense that something is wrong. Her one-verse song is identical with the beginning of Moses' song. In addition, she is named here for the first time. She is called Miriam, the sister of Aaron. Her sibling relationship with Moses, however, is not mentioned.

Miriam is also called a prophet. Indeed, she is the first person—not the first woman, but the first person—in the Hebrew Bible given this title in its general sense.[17] Aaron is earlier called prophet, but only in the sense of spokesperson for Moses.[18]

Trible asks why the Miriamic ending survived, overpowered as it is by the Mosaic one. Some scholars believe that Miriam was the author of the entire Song of the Sea, not just the first verse. Later, in the process of elevating Moses, the song was attributed to him. Trible suggests that the Miriamic tradition was so strong, however, that it could not be squelched. As a result, the much-shortened version was appended. So Miriam was both preserved and diminished in importance, even as Moses was elevated. Ironically, Moses originally resisted accepting the call to leadership because he was inarticulate. In the hands of the biblical editors, he becomes a poet and a song leader.[19]

Fokkelien van Dijk-Hemmes, noting the work of M. Brenner, who believes that the whole song complex of Exodus 15:1–21 is a literary unit that developed relatively late, during the Second Temple period, states that perhaps all that can be said is that Miriam founds a women's song tradition. She also notes that even if this is true, Miriam's song has been placed in the shadow of Moses'.[20]

J. Gerald Janzen suggests a particularly interesting perspective on the relationship between Miriam's and Moses' songs. He suggests that Exodus 15:19 uses a literary device known as analepsis, in which vital information is delayed and presented later. The outline of events is as follows:

Exod. 14:26–29 God commands Moses to stretch out his hand over the sea; Moses complies and the sea returns, overthrowing the Egyptians, whereas the Israelites had gotten across on dry land.

Exod. 14:30–31 Theological reflection on God's saving activity

Exod. 15:20–21 Miriam led the women out and *sang to them*:

"*Sing to the LORD*, for he has triumphed gloriously; [note the imperative]
horse and rider he has thrown into the sea."

Exod. 15:1–18 Moses and the people respond to Miriam and the women:

"I will *sing unto the LORD*. . . ."

Exod. 15:19 Recapitulation of Exod. 14:26–29

The picture that emerges is that Miriam and the women sang each couplet and Moses and the people repeated it. But why the analepsis, the change in presentation of chronological events? Janzen suggests that the song itself is understood, not simply as celebrating the event, but as being part of the event and thus is linked directly with it, a more powerful presentation than one in which the parts played by the various participants in the liturgy are presented in chronological order.[21] Janzen's analysis does not address the issue of how old or historically accurate the songs are, but it does restore Miriam's role as the song leader and provide a plausible explanation other than malicious misogynist machinations for how her role seems to have been diminished.

Thus, both the beginning and the end of the exodus story belong to women. Miriam, Moses' sister, has an important role to play in both parts of the story. Trible writes: "The mediator has become percussionist, lyricist, vocalist, prophet, leader and theologian."[22] Rita Burns concludes her 1980 dissertation on Miriam with these words: "It can be said that the primary characteristic of the biblical portrait of Miriam is that she was a leader in the wilderness. In addition, it can be said that, although the texts do not yield a single role designation of her leadership position, they do firmly reflect traditions which regarded Miriam as a cult official and as a mediator of God's word."[23] Susan Ackerman, in an important article in the *Journal of Biblical Literature*, punctures this upbeat picture, suggesting that the only reason Miriam could be remembered as a prophet was that the historical period in which she is portrayed was a liminal one, that is a confused, marginal, transitional time between more ordinary events.[24]

There is one more episode in the story of Miriam. Again Moses is involved. After the exodus, the Hebrew people move into the wilderness period. It is a difficult period, and conflicts develop between leaders. Moses feels overburdened and seeks shared leadership. Seventy elders are chosen to help, but they are subordinate to Moses (Num. 11:16–25). When two other men begin to prophesy, some are opposed, but Moses is pleased (Num. 11:26–30). Tension remains.

Then Miriam enters the picture, with Aaron in a supporting role. Miriam challenges Moses because of the Cushite woman he married (Num. 12:1). This challenge raises more questions than it answers. Who is this Cushite woman? Cushite could refer to inhabitants of an area broader than present-day Ethiopia.[25] Zipporah is referred to as Midianite (Exod. 2:15–21; 3:1; Num. 10:29) and Kenite (Judg. 1:16; 4:11). If the Kenites, a subgroup of the Midianites, had migrated from Cush, then it is possible that Moses' Cushite wife is Zipporah.[26]

Why did Miriam object to Moses' Cushite wife? Renita Weems suggests that personal rivalry between sisters-in-law was the source of the conflict.[27] Burns points out, however, that there is nothing in the story that supports this view. Because Miriam was a public figure, Burns believes that the issue was a public one rather than a private one.[28] A number of male commentators, including some prominent African American interpreters, have suggested that racism was the basis of the complaint.[29] The suggestion is based on the nature of Miriam's punishment, being struck with leprosy. Many translations read that she became "white as snow," but what the Hebrew actually says is that she became "leprous as snow." It is not clear that any contrast is being made between Moses' black wife and Miriam's whitened skin. The name Miriam is perhaps Egyptian,[30] and she may have been a native of Kadesh.[31] Thus it is likely that she was a dark-skinned woman. This, coupled with the lack of racism in biblical times, makes it highly unlikely that Miriam's complaint against Moses' Cushite wife was racially motivated.

Then what was her motivation? The Bible does not tell us, but whatever the original source of controversy, it seems that the story may have been included to justify Moses' marriage to a foreigner. Centuries after Miriam and Moses' time, the marriage of Hebrew men to foreign women became a major issue.[32]

Irmtraud Fischer, in an interpretation related to the issue of foreign wives, takes her clues from Jewish tradition. Based on the idea that when Moses sent Zipporah away (Exod. 18:2), he had in effect divorced her and was no longer sleeping with her due to his prophetic activity, the complaint in Numbers 12:1 can be understood as a concern that Moses was not fulfilling the commandment to be fruitful and multiply.[33]

Fischer goes on to focus on the postexilic origin of the story, suggesting that it is not an early text transmitting an early story, but a late text that actually deals with religio-political issues hundreds of years later. Moses corresponds to the dominant postexilic group, with Ezra and Nehemiah in the leadership, who opposed mixed marriages of Jewish men and foreign women. Aaron represents the priests, and Zipporah stands for one of the prophetic groups who were opposed to the xenophobia of the dominant group of rigorous enforcers. Fischer concludes that Miriam's position, really the position of the postexilic antixenophobes, was substantially correct, only not in the case of Moses, due to his extraordinary relationship with God. Fischer's reasoning is that Moses was released from conjugal activity due to his unique prophetic role. This in turn means that Ezra's and Nehemiah's rule against mixed marriages should not be applied to everyone. At the same time Fischer believes Numbers 12 originated with the rigorists, those like Ezra and Nehemiah who rigorously enforced the rules, contrary to the more democratic spirit of Moses, who in Numbers 11 is eager for everyone to prophesy. That is why Miriam had to be punished.[34]

Fischer's reflections on the implications of this text for today are worth quoting:

> Despite all the injustice that leaps out at us at first reading, the story of Numbers 12 could be read even as a text of political realism, of empowerment for us women in patriarchally constituted religious communities. When we rise up in a discussion to make an intervention and assert that God speaks also to *us*, we may well be right, but still be punished, treated with contempt for a while and excluded from the community. I do not want to trivialize the injustice of such events. Obviously, it is the case that patriarchal, hierarchical religious communities reach for the weapon of humiliating their members, even when it is acknowledged that such members were right in what they were presenting. After all, the divinely legitimated authority of hierarchy is under no circumstances to be questioned in principle!
>
> As women, we must sometimes ask ourselves what is of greater value to us: our own reputation or the issue we have come to judge right before God. Just like secular communities, religious communities are marked by power relations. I do not argue that existing power relations be upheld when, as a Catholic woman at the end of the second millennium, I maintain that sometimes the way that is practicable in the perspective of political realism is better, particularly when we do not lose sight of the overall picture. Numbers 12 offers us at least this one consolation: the people will refuse to move on, the seven days will pass and the issue settled as we had proposed. But, during this Exodus from oppressive and inadequate structures, we ought not to let the nostalgic longing for the fleshpots of Egypt overtake us with the maxim: Better unfree but without worry about survival.[35]

Although we can only speculate about what the original nature of the conflict was,[36] a few clues may be gleaned from what we know of Zipporah. She was the daughter of the priest Jethro and performed one seemingly priestly function that is recorded in the Bible in a very strange text.[37] When Moses is on his way back to Egypt to begin his struggles with Pharaoh, we read: "On the way, at a place where they spent the night, the LORD met him and tried to kill him. But Zipporah took a flint and cut off her son's foreskin, and touched Moses' feet with it, and said, 'Truly you are a bridegroom of blood to me!' So he let him alone. It was then she said, 'A bridegroom of blood by circumcision'" (Exod. 4:24–26). Why God would want to kill Moses at this crucial moment is hard to understand. Why Zipporah cuts off her son's foreskin and touches Moses' feet, a euphemism for genitals, is also unexplained. Alice Laffey suggests that God is angry with Moses because Moses is uncircumcised and that the action of touching Moses' genitals with his son's foreskin is the equivalent of circumcision.[38] What is important is that Zipporah performs the ritual action, which later is done only by male priests. By her action, she saves Moses from God's wrath.

Drorah Setel concurs: "Although the specific meaning of Zipporah's action may remain a mystery, the elements of which it is composed clearly suggest ritual sacrificial significance. If that is so, this text is unique not only within a biblical framework but within the context of the ancient Near East as a whole, where there is no other evidence that women performed acts of blood sacrifice."[39]

Perhaps before the Israelite priesthood was set up officially as an all-male group, priestly functions were performed by women such as Zipporah.[40] Or perhaps, according to Ackerman, during a liminal period a woman could serve as a priest.[41] If Zipporah had cultic responsibilities, Miriam's objection to her could be related to her cultic role.

Miriam's conflict with Moses is not simply about his Cushite wife, whoever she is. It is also about prophetic authority. Miriam believes that God has spoken not only through Moses but also through herself and Aaron. Gene Rice suggests that when Moses married the daughter of the priest of Midian, he was strengthening his spiritual leadership credentials. That would explain the connection between Miriam and Aaron's concern about both the Cushite wife and authority (has the Lord spoken only through Moses?). Thus, the complaint was not because Zipporah lowered Moses' stature, as those who see racism at work would have it, but rather because it increased it.[42] It is possible that this was the original issue in the story, but that it later came to be interpreted as supporting those who were opposed to mixed marriages.

After Miriam (and Aaron) have spoken up to Moses, God summons the threesome (Num. 12:4). The ordering of the names suggests Miriam's diminution, according to Trible.[43] God declares to Aaron and Miriam a hierarchy of leadership with Moses at the top (Num. 12:6–8). God is exceedingly angry with them for their conflict with Moses on the issue of prophetic authority (Num. 12:9). The concern over the Cushite wife, however, is not answered directly one way or the other.

Although God has put down both Aaron and Miriam, it is Miriam who is punished. She is covered with leprous scales (Num. 12:10). Ackerman suggests the reason for the disparity: now that the Israelites have left Egypt and are no longer in liminal, marginal space, Miriam can no longer function as a prophet. In addition to complaining about Moses, she has overstepped gender boundaries.[44] After the punishment is inflicted, Aaron turns to Moses and asks him to intercede with God to remove the leprous condition (Num. 12:11–12). In making this request, he is acquiescing to the hierarchy that God has established. Moses agrees and petitions God (Num. 12:13). God confines Miriam outside the camp for seven days. The people show their loyalty to her by not setting out on the march again until she returns (Num. 12:14–15). After this, we hear no more of Miriam until her death notice in Numbers 20:1.

Trible points out that beyond the exodus and wilderness experience, fragments point to a trinity of leadership in which Miriam was the equal of Aaron and Moses.[45]

> For I brought you up from the land of Egypt,
>   and redeemed you from the house of slavery;
> and I sent before you Moses, Aaron, and Miriam.
>   (Mic. 6:4)

Another fragment is found in Jeremiah 31:4, where the prophet uses memories of the exodus experience in envisioning the restoration of Israel after the Babylonian exile:

> Again I will build you, and you shall be built,
>   O virgin Israel!
> Again you shall take your tambourines,
>   and go forth in the dance of the merrymakers.

Trible believes that the imagery can be read in two directions. It both recalls Miriam at the Reed Sea and predicts her restoration.[46] Although Miriam is not specified, the reference in the first line to "virgin Israel," a female figure, suggests that the allusion in the second line is to Miriam rather than to Moses.

Miriam emerges from the bits and pieces as a multifaceted character: mediator, cultic figure, prophet, musician, beloved leader, strong, even threatening personality. That she can be reconstructed at all from the fragments in Scripture is cause for celebration. That she has been diminished by these same

Scriptures is cause for concern. Yet her story is not unusual, in the Bible or in history. How many women's lives have been diminished or buried, their accomplishments attributed to others? We can never know, of course. We can sharpen our investigative skills, however, to be alert to the bits and pieces that point to stories yet hidden, remaining to be reconstructed.

THE DAUGHTERS OF ZELOPHEHAD

In Numbers 27:1–11 and Numbers 36 we find the story of the five daughters of Zelophehad: Mahlah, Noah, Hoglah, Milcah, and Tirzah. Zelophehad had no sons, only five daughters. He had died in the wilderness, and now his daughters are petitioning Moses to allow them to inherit their father's property to perpetuate their father's name. Moses hears their petition and takes it to God, who answers favorably. Later the leaders of Zelophehad's tribe, Gilead, come to Moses. They are concerned about the potential loss of property to their tribe if Zelophehad's daughters marry outside the tribe. Again Moses responds to the concern brought to him. This time he communicates the word of the Lord directing that Zelophehad's daughters must marry within their father's clan to preserve the tribal property.

Sakenfeld presents three interpretations of this story, each one using a different interpretive method.[47] The first approach is a purely literary one. The five daughters are seen as strong. They take the initiative to obtain greater rights than women previously had. They use the concern about their father's name as a means to their end. Unlike Miriam, who was punished for challenging Moses, the daughters of Zelophehad are rewarded; their petition is accepted. They are restricted in their choice of marriage partners, however. Sakenfeld concludes: "The story as a whole is a story of great celebration of women who inherit the promise, and of their own initiative in securing their future. Yet the story ends on a more somber note of reminder of the limits of those gains."[48]

The second approach to this story Sakenfeld calls "culturally cued reading." She points out that the major concern in the story is a problem faced by men, that of the loss of family name. The text makes a connection between land and name. Although it is not clear precisely how, the story assumes that when the daughters inherit their father's land, his name is preserved as well. In the second part of the story, the concern is loss of property to the tribe. Here it is the men of the Gileadite tribe who are concerned with economic loss. Although the alleged concern is with tribal land, the women are restricted to marrying not simply within their tribe but more narrowly within their clan. This restricts the number of male contenders for these women and their land, which no doubt made them highly desirable marriage partners. They are little more than pawns in a potential land dispute. Everything works out well, since the daughters of Zelophehad comply with Moses' decision. Decision making is assigned to God, but it operates through the male power figures of the community.[49]

The third interpretation focuses on historical inquiry. The two texts support certain inheritance and marriage laws. Four insights into the place of women in Judean culture are possible to discern. Each needs to be carefully evaluated.[50]

First, Numbers 27 shows that ordinary women were able to go directly to male authority figures to make their claims. It was unnecessary to go through a male who would make their appeal for them. The story of the two harlots who appear before King Solomon (1 Kings 3:16–28), as well as that of the two "cannibal" mothers who petition King Jehoram (2 Kings 6:26–31), supports this suggestion. However, we cannot be sure whether such direct access may have been limited to women who were not under the authority of a male relative.[51]

Second, Numbers 27 reveals that, at least for the historical period in question, women were able only under very limited circumstances to inherit and own property. Third, Numbers 36 shows that at least for this period, daughters who inherited property under these circumstances were limited in choice of marriage partners.[52]

Finally, Numbers 36 offers hints about marriage customs. The text does not add to our limited knowledge of how marriage partners were chosen. However, the emphasis is on marriage close to home. Marriage between a man and the daughter of his father's brother was allowed under Leviticus 18 and 20. This type of marriage is the practical outcome of Numbers 36. Thus, this story does not introduce a closer than usual exception to the incest rules in other legislation.[53]

Each of these approaches to the story of the daughters of Zelophehad tells us something important. The interpretations are not contradictory, although there is tension between the first two. The first celebrates the initiative of the daughters, while the second focuses on the androcentric basis of the new rules. The only possible difference is in the motivations of the daughters, which the text does not state. Were they primarily interested in obtaining greater rights for themselves? Did they use the concern for their father's name as a means to their end, as the first interpretation suggests? Or was their primary motivation the preservation of his name, as the second interpretation suggests?

There is no way to answer this question definitively. It seems, however, that their real motivation was that of preserving their father's name. Inheriting his land was probably only a temporary measure. Once they were married to another member of the clan, the land was probably considered to belong to the husband. Even if this was not the case, the land certainly would have been passed to the sons. At most, the inheriting daughter was a kind of stopgap in a patrilineal inheritance scheme.

Whatever the motivation of the daughters, the reason the story was included in the canon was surely concern for continuance of the father's name. Sakenfeld writes:

> But why was this story preserved in the canon? The drama of the story and the courage of the sisters are not sufficient explanation. It seems probable that the story survived because the basic point at issue was the preservation of the father's name (v. 4). The storyteller presumes an intricate connection between possession of land and preservation of family name. The women themselves are pictured as taking action for the sake of their father's name, not for the sake of their own opportunity to possess land. This story could be heard even in ancient Israel as a story of comfort for women who would not be left destitute, but it was preserved primarily as a story of comfort for men who had the misfortune not to bear any male heirs—their names would not be cut off from their clans.[54]

CONCLUSIONS

The women of Exodus and Numbers are a feisty lot. We begin with the five women who collaborate to save Moses from an early death. Each in her own way defies Pharaoh and succeeds. We move on to the story of the grown Miriam. In spite of diminution by the biblical text, she can be reconstructed as a multifaceted, strong character. She begins her literary life as a mediator and part of the Pharaoh-defying women who save Moses. She emerges as an adult who has cultic, prophetic, and musical leadership in the life of the Hebrews in the wilderness period. She confronts Moses and loses, is punished by God, and is silenced. In the eyes of the people, however, and later in the voices of the prophets, she is celebrated.

Then there is Zipporah, Moses' wife, about whom we know little. Yet what we do know is tantalizing. Daughter of a Midianite priest, exercising priestly functions, circumcising her son to save her husband, Zipporah is a woman we would like to know better. Is she the Cushite woman of Miriam's complaint? Possibly so.

Finally, we reflect on the five daughters of Zelophehad. They dare to appeal to Moses for inheritance rights, and they win. In the process, they also find that their choice of husbands is severely limited.

Among the women of Exodus and Numbers, we find two helpmates: Moses' mother Jochebed and Moses' wife Zipporah. There are no harlots in these stories.

There are quite a few heroes. All five of the women who save Moses may be considered heroic. The midwives Shiphrah and Puah, who both defy Pharaoh and use their wit to save Hebrew babies, are certainly heroes. Moses' mother Jochebed and his sister Miriam, who work together, are somewhat heroic as well. Pharaoh's daughter is also a hero; she goes against her own father's decree (of which she was presumably aware) and even adopts as a son a child her father had ordered killed. Miriam emerges as a leader in the wilderness and therefore is doubly a hero, in spite of her punishment by God.

There are happily no victims in these stories. The daughters of Zelophehad both gain and lose, but they are not victims.

The women of Exodus and Numbers are unusual because so few of them are identified primarily by their relationship with a male figure. Shiphrah and Puah are not associated with men explicitly at all. Moses' mother is called a daughter of Levi and her husband is mentioned, but neither man plays an important role. Miriam's father is likewise mentioned, but if Miriam is ever married, that information is not given. Pharaoh's daughter is obviously identified as her father's daughter, but she acts independently of him. Zipporah's role as helpmate to Moses is more central to what little we know of her, but she still is presented as an independent person. The daughters of Zelophehad are of course identified with their father, but their initiative, even if it is for his sake, shows them to be strong women.

Counterbalancing the independence of the women of Exodus and Numbers is the towering figure of Moses. Compared to Moses, the women are all minor figures. That is the literary reality. The historical reality may have been different.

DISCUSSION QUESTIONS

1. Have you ever been in situations where it was necessary to defy authority to save life or, less dramatically, to promote life-affirming values?

2. Midwives still function to this day. They are often called nurse practitioners. They give excellent care at much lower prices than medical doctors. Have you had any experience with modern midwives or know anyone who has? Is this ancient practice, of women midwives' (rather than men's medical) involvement with the birth process, one that feminists should celebrate? Why or why not?

3. When have you had to use your wit or witnessed someone else using his or her wit to accomplish goals that were not sanctioned by the persons in power?

4. Have you ever accomplished something that was then attributed to someone else? Do you know of others who have had this kind of experience?

5. Were you ever party to a conflict in which your side lost and some of those involved were treated more leniently than others? If so, how did you feel?
6. Have you experienced a situation like that of the daughters of Zelophe- had, in which you achieved a hoped-for advance, only to discover that you had paid for your advance in another area?
7. Which of the women in Exodus and Numbers do you especially admire? With which do you identify? About which ones would you like to know more?
8. Given the suspicion that Miriam's role has been diminished in the bib- lical text, what do you think Miriam actually accomplished?

5

The Women in Joshua and Judges

The books of Joshua and Judges are filled with unusual women. Rahab, the first bona fide biblical harlot, is also something of a hero. Manoah's wife, the mother of Samson, is a strong character. Delilah is a fascinating woman. She is not easily characterized by any of our three H words—helpmates, harlots, and heroes—nor is she a victim. Deborah and Jael are among the strongest heroes in the Hebrew Bible. In contrast, Jephthah's daughter and an unnamed victim, the Levite's concubine, are brutalized by men.

The period of history covered by Joshua and Judges was a wild time. Perhaps it was a bit like the West in the pioneer days of the United States. "Justice" was often carried out by those who had the physical strength or weaponry to enforce their idea of law and order. Women played more parts than they were destined to fulfill in later, more "civilized" times. The narrator puts it this way in Judges 21:25, the last verse of the book: "In those days there was no king in Israel; all the people did what was right in their own eyes."

In such a time, unusually good and unusually bad events were likely to happen. That terrible deeds could be done was used as part of the rationale to push for a king. That unusually strong and good leaders like Deborah and Jael could emerge was perhaps not considered in the desire for a king. Maybe they were even viewed as indicative of a need. Some might be uncomfortable unless men were always the military leaders and women stayed in their places in domestic roles. We cannot tell, but we can learn a lot from the stories of the women recorded in these chaotic times.

RAHAB

Rahab's story is found in Joshua 2. Two Israelite spies come to Jericho to see the land they are planning to attack. They stop at the house of Rahab the harlot and spend the night (Josh. 2:1). While they are there, the king of Jericho hears about them and sends orders to Rahab to turn them out (Josh. 2:2–3). Instead, she hides them and claims they have already left (Josh. 2:4–7). She strikes up a bargain with the spies. In exchange for her saving them, they will save her and her family when the Israelites take over, for she discerns that God is on their side (Josh. 2:8–14).

Some commentators suggest that Rahab's portrayal as a hero means that harlots were really accepted members of society. Phyllis Bird believes otherwise.[1] First she defines harlots. They are prostitutes, women who offer sexual services for money. In Hebrew society, harlots were outcasts who were tolerated but not held in honor. They were free women, not under the protection or authority of a husband. They wore different clothing, inhabited different parts of town, and did their business under cover of night.[2] Prostitution is typical of urban society, especially urban patriarchal society. It flourishes wherever there is an unequal distribution of power, and status and sexual roles are not symmetrical. Harlots result from the desire of men (who were usually married at a relatively young age) for exclusive possession of their wives and simultaneous access to other women sexually. Thus, harlots in Hebrew society were desired but shunned.[3]

In addition to the ordinary types of harlots, many scholars used to believe (and some still accept) that in Canaanite religions there were also female cult functionaries, sometimes called cult prostitutes.[4] This issue has generated much heat, in part because sexuality is involved. Feminists have generally been suspicious of the claims of traditional (mostly male) scholarship that cult prostitutes were a reality in Canaanite religions, because of the paucity of evidence. Some commentators have suggested that Rahab was a cult prostitute, but whatever one may think about the question of the existence of cult prostitutes in general, there is no evidence whatsoever that Rahab was depicted as anything other than an ordinary harlot.[5]

The obvious question that the story raises is, why would the Israelite spies be consorting with a prostitute? Perhaps they hoped to overhear the talk of the town at the brothel. At such a place, strangers would not be particularly conspicuous or suspicious. Perhaps they might have thought a harlot would be more open to outsiders than other citizens of Jericho.[6] Danna Fewell suggests an earthier motivation:

The spies go directly to a brothel and "they lay there." The verb "lie" is loaded with sexual overtones, and the context suggests that the spies are not above mixing business with pleasure. The common argument that a brothel would have been the best place to secure information about the city only accents the fact that the spies neither ask questions nor eavesdrop on many conversations.[7]

If the spies hope to go undetected, their plan is not successful. The king of Jericho receives word of their presence. Now we wonder why Rahab lies to protect the spies and hides them on her roof. Has she been harassed before by the authorities, so that she has no love for the king? Did she fall in love with one of the spies? Perhaps she identifies with them. They come from a marginal people (albeit a group that will become dominant in this land), just as she is probably marginal in her own society. These motivations would fit in with a leading theory of how the Israelites conquered Canaan. Norman Gottwald argues that what happened was not so much a military takeover by outsiders as a peasant revolution against the Canaanite overlords who were oppressing them.[8] If these are Rahab's motivations, however, they are not stated in the text.[9]

What the story does tell us is that Rahab discerns that God is with the spies and their people. This involves a reversal of expectations. Harlots were viewed as very low members of society, lacking in wisdom, morals, and religious knowledge. A certain amount of self-interest may have been involved in Rahab's decision to protect the spies. However, that is not her only motivation, according to the narrator. She takes a big risk in protecting the Israelites. The story shows her doing this because of her faith. Bird often investigates texts historically, but here utilizes a literary-critical method: "But if the harlot as heroine involves a conflict of expectations, it is also a recognizable subtype of the harlot in literature (and presumably also in life), a romantic antitype to the dominant image: the whore with the heart of gold, the harlot who saves the city, the courtesan who sacrifices for her patron."[10]

Rahab is a hero because she protects the Israelite spies. She is also heroic because she is a woman of faith who takes risks based on that faith. In addition, she is clever, like the midwives of Exodus. She outwits the king of Jericho, ignores his death-affirming command, and acts in a way that affirms life—for herself and the Israelite people.

Naomi Franklin believes that the story functioned metaphorically in the exilic community. She writes:

> The message, although not explicit in the text, is that as Rahab was a harlot, so was Israel. Rahab turned and confessed YHWH as the Almighty, so could Israel. Rahab kept her promise and was faithful, so should Israel. If they were faithful, they and their families would be allowed to partake

in the Promise as did Rahab and her family. This may be one of the reasons that the texts regarding Rahab were preserved and edited by the Deuteronomic Redactor and included within the canon.[11]

Franklin's approach highlights the way many scholars believe biblical texts functioned in various periods in biblical history. The stories were preserved not primarily because they happened, or even because they were important expressions of faith, but because of the way they could be used to provide hope in the present.

Rahab's story is interesting to modern feminists because prostitutes are rarely heroes, in ancient times or in the contemporary world. In religious circles in which sexuality is often suspect, even in far more respectable expressions, the story of Rahab is something of an embarrassment. That she is included in Matthew's genealogy of Jesus (Matt. 1:5) only compounds the problems.

Judith McKinlay reads the story of Rahab from another perspective. As a New Zealander of European descent, whose ancestors migrated to the Pacific island assuming it was theirs to take, she perceives colonialist undertones in the narrative. Rahab is part of the hated "other" group of Canaanites, who by siding with the Israelites legitimates their takeover.[12]

Similarly, Musa Dube, reading from a South African perspective, suggests that Rahab's story is a kind of prism through which other texts can be read to determine whether they have imperializing tendencies.[13] A third voice in this chorus, Lori Rowlett, compares Rahab to Disney's Pocahontas and concludes:

Both Rahab and Pocahontas are in a sense cartoon figures. Neither is allowed to speak in a truly indigenous voice. The colonizing powers telling the story have given her words to speak in praise of themselves as conquering heroes. She is supposed to be grateful because she is allowed into their society. In both cases, the woman is regarded as worth saving and assimilating because she recognizes the specialness of the conquerors, making her the mirror which magnifies their own glory. She becomes the medium for transmitting the colonizing power's arrogance in its representation of itself to itself.[14]

DEBORAH

Deborah's story has elicited a variety of interpretations from feminist interpreters, from questioning its historicity (how could such female leadership have existed in a patriarchal world?) to celebrating Deborah's leadership (women can and did do everything) to condemning her participation in warfare (women shouldn't participate in violence because it's patriarchal). Her story is found in a prose version in Judges 4 and in a poetic version in Judges 5. Deborah is a judge. She sits under a palm tree, called the palm of Deborah, and settles disputes for people (Judg. 4:4–5). She is either married to a man named Lappidoth or, according to another understanding of the Hebrew, a woman of torches, that is, a fiery, spirited woman.[15] Since Barak, the general she summons, means lightning, the latter understanding seems more likely.

Deborah calls Barak and tells him that God needs him to lead an army against the Canaanites (Judg. 4:6–7). Barak responds that he will go if Deborah accompanies him (Judg. 4:8). Deborah agrees, but warns him that the enemy, Sisera, will be given into the hands not of Barak but of a woman. Barak acquiesces and they go off to war.

Although Deborah accompanies Barak and the troops, it is not clear whether she actually goes into battle.[16] The battle goes badly against Sisera and he flees. His death by a woman is described in the story of Jael (Judg. 4:9–22).

Four feminist interpreters comment on what strikes most modern readers as the unusual nature of Deborah's multiple roles. Denise Carmody interprets the story theologically: "No matter how patriarchal the culture of her time, it could not deny the Lord's use of her. When God chose, patriarchalism had to give way."[17]

Mieke Bal approaches the issue from a literary-critical perspective: "It is perhaps not a coincidence that the only judge who combines all forms of leadership possible—religious, military, juridical, and poetical—is a woman."[18] Bal believes that Deborah could fulfill all of these roles because (1) poetry and prophecy go together; (2) mothers were noted for their words and actions that memorialized people and events; (3) poetry was related to the military-political and juridical business of judging, as seen in songs of judgment such as Deborah's song; and (4) one way of bringing order out of chaos, the judge's business, was by means of the spoken word.

Jo Ann Hackett writes from a historical perspective:

> There seems to be a reluctance on the part of some commentators to see Deborah as a true judge, alongside the other deliverers in the book. This reluctance probably lies behind the acceptance by some modern commentators of the old theory that Lappidoth (Deborah's husband according to Judg. 4:4) and Barak were the same person, and that Deborah, therefore, derived her status from her marital relationship with Barak, who is seen as the real judge in this episode. Granted it is Barak who is mentioned in the New Testament book of Hebrews (11:32, along with other Israelite heroes), and probably Barak who is meant in 1 Samuel 12:11 in the list of deliverers, rather than the unknown Bedan. We might conclude from this

substitution that some later Israelite historians, like many of their modern counterparts, had trouble accepting the notion of a female judge. But the text itself (Judg. 4–5) is clear that Deborah was a judge and there is really no reason to doubt the text here. In fact, our analysis of the society in Israel at this time, as well as analogies from other cultures, suggests that such a situation is entirely appropriate and believable.[19]

Hackett is not surprised by Deborah's leadership, because this period of Israel's history was one in which centralized forms of government did not exist, the line between the public and private sectors was not well defined, and serious social dysfunction existed. In such periods women's leadership often comes to the fore more than in more "normal" periods.[20] Hackett's analysis is both historical and sociological. She considers what is known of Hebrew society at the time and compares this information with what is known about similar societies.

Hackett's approach to the question of why in a patriarchal society a woman could rise to such a high leadership position is more scientific than Carmody's or Bal's theological or literary approaches. Her analysis is convincing because it is based on historical and sociological analysis. Hackett's results, however, are not inconsistent with Carmody's theological interpretation. God works in many ways. God perhaps could use Deborah in part because the social setting at this time allowed for the rise of a woman in a way that it may not have allowed in other periods. Nevertheless, Carmody's theological approach is a bit naive in that she does not ask why, if God broke through patriarchy to bring Deborah forth as a leader, God did not make such breakthroughs more regularly. Hackett's analysis provides an answer for this question.

Susan Ackerman offers two different solutions, the second somewhat reversing her earlier position. In her earlier article she is not as sanguine as Hackett about the historicity of Deborah's story. She finds it too discordant with the dominant division of gender roles in Israelite society. In *Warrior, Dancer, Seductress, Queen: Women in Judges and Biblical Israel*, published in 1998, her explanation is that the story reflects the Canaanite myths of the war goddess Anat and the god Baal, and that woman warriors such as Deborah and Jael involve a kind of demythologizing of such myths.[21] In a subsequent article published in 2003, in which she frequently mentions the work of archaeologist and biblical scholar Carol Meyers, Ackerman suggests that the story of Deborah could possibly reflect the historical reality that "women in early Israelite villages actually assumed Deborah-like leadership positions in their community's military assemblies."[22]

What do we learn from Deborah? Guatemalan Julia Esquivel reflects on Deborah's story:

It [Deborah's story] breaks the tradition of submission and calls on us to place our bodies before the machine guns. It observes that we continue to talk instead of taking our liberation concretely into our own hands while thousands of our people are being massacred. It breaks through the false understanding of pacifism that masks the face of God, reducing God to ineffectual neutrality in the face of injustice and oppression.[23]

Expressing the opposite point of view a Jewish writer, Lillian Sigal, is concerned with the bellicosity of Deborah:

As a Jewish feminist, I pay special attention to the presentation of women in the Bible with regard to the theme of compassion versus retribution towards one's opponents. In their zeal to identify strong female role models in the Bible, feminists often cite female characters who exercise power aggressively, proving that they are not wimps. . . . The tone of vengeance that pervades the poem of Deborah makes me wince.[24]

Similarly, Danna Fewell and David Gunn are concerned about the way the story of Deborah justifies the authority of violence. They write: "Deborah appears, by the song's end, to be more trapped—trapped in the very value system which we imagine her to be subverting."[25] The value system they seem to have in mind is a patriarchal one that approves of the use of force. The value system they believe she supports is apparently a version of feminism that is pacifistic. They write: "In reality, however, it is the authority of violence that is justified. And in the face of that authority, the woman, Deborah, has offered no real alternative. A woman in a man's world, her voice hardening, merging with a man's voice, defines that world by oppositions and so finds her place in it."[26] Fewell and Gunn imply that there is something wrong with a woman's voice hardening, something wrong with a woman warrior.

Not all violence is immoral, nor is violence an appropriate activity only for men. Nevertheless not all violence is acceptable. Fewell and Gunn point out an often-ignored detail in Deborah's story. The Israelite army destroyed Sisera's entire army (Judg. 4:16). The song, however, mentions captives (Judg. 5:12). Who could these be, other than the Canaanite women and children? By mockingly imagining the Canaanite women thinking their men are delayed because they are busy taking female captives (Judg. 5:28–30), the Hebrew poets Deborah and Barak justify the Israelites' doing the same. That may have been standard conduct in war in those times. Its ancient acceptability, however, does not make it any more acceptable to modern sensibilities. Nevertheless, even as I write, the newspapers are full of the horror stories of thousands of women in Darfur being raped and murdered along with their male counterparts. This too is shocking, yet not so shocking that anything effective is done to stop it. If anything, the modern world is more brutal than the ancient one. At least for Deborah and Barak, Sisera's mother imagined him taking females captive, to become wives, concubines, or slaves to be sure, but not to be raped and murdered, as is sometimes the case today in places like Darfur and Iraq.

Most of the reactions to Deborah come not from the violence against Canaanite women but from Deborah's prominent role as military leader. The reason that feminists can respond in such opposite ways to Deborah is that Deborah is what Gale Yee calls a liminal figure. Since warriors were usually male, the woman warrior was a woman acting like a man. Speaking about feminists' responses to the story of Deborah, Yee writes:

> Some found in the metaphor a source of female empowerment; others rejected the metaphor as a model for women because of its association with male martial values. It is precisely the liminality of the woman warrior, her anomalous position neither inclusively male nor totally female, that permits the metaphor to support, denounce, modify, or otherwise express various facets of gender meanings and relationships.[27]

Yee goes on to consider the historical situation. Like Hackett, she believes that the nature of social organization in premonarchic Israel, when public and private responsibilities were not strictly separate, made it not unlikely that women would occasionally become military leaders. She also stresses that this would not have been the norm. The nature of warfare also facilitated women's participation in warfare. The clans used small defensive forces rather than large professional armies. They were not equipped with bows and chariots. Instead, they relied on guerrilla tactics, which meant the use of cunning, surprise, deception, and diversions.[28]

Yee sees two ways in which the woman warrior metaphor is used in Judges 4. The first she calls the shame syndrome. According to Yee, Barak and Sisera are both shamed by Deborah's and Jael's leadership. Certainly, Sisera's death at the hand of a woman was considered ignominious. Barak is overshadowed both by Deborah, to whose call he responds, and Jael, who kills Sisera (though not so much that some commentators still suggest that Barak was the judge rather than Deborah!). Whether this overshadowing is tantamount to shaming may be debated. The text gives no explicit clues. Yee calls the second way in which the woman warrior is used the voracity syndrome. This comes into play only in the story of Jael, which will be discussed below.[29]

Finally, Yee considers the history of the interpretation of Deborah. Deborah has been seen as the avenger of wrongs perpetrated against women, as a woman deferring to a man, as a model of cooperation between men and women, as a woman calling men to their responsibilities, as a womanly protector of her people, as a model of courage on our personal battlefields, and paradoxically as a model for women against war![30] There is truth in most of these perspectives.

How are we to assess Deborah? As the reader considers this question, it is important to remember that Deborah's actions are a response to twenty years of cruel oppression under the Canaanite King Jabin and his commander Sisera (Judg. 4:2–3).

JAEL

The story of Jael's murder of Sisera in Judges 4:17–22 is grisly. Despite its gruesome character, it shows the overpowering of the strong by the weak. Jael is portrayed as a Kenite. Susan Ackerman argues that she was some sort of religious functionary and that her tent was a kind of sanctuary.[31] The Canaanite Sisera thought he would be safe in her tent, but her loyalties were not what he expected.

Sisera's death at the hand of a woman is ignominious. Just as Barak is shamed by Deborah taking the lead, Sisera is shamed by losing his life in a woman's tent. In addition to the shame syndrome, Yee also sees the voracity syndrome at work in Jael's story. The woman warrior embodies sexual license and unbridled lust. Although it is not obvious in many English translations, there are strong sexual allusions in the Hebrew text. Sisera is not only killed in Jael's tent; he is also unmanned.[32] In Judg. 4:20, Sisera tells Jael to stand at the entrance of the tent and if anyone comes and asks if a man is there, she is to answer negatively. By the end of the story there is no (live) man in the tent, and Sisera's death by penetration of a tent peg figuratively turns him into a woman.

Over the years women have reacted variously to Jael's actions. Harriet Beecher Stowe, author of *Uncle Tom's Cabin*, related Jael's gruesome work to an incident in her own late nineteenth century:

> Let us remember how the civilized world felt when, not long since, the Austrian tyrant Heynau outraged noble Hungarian and Italian women, subjecting them to brutal stripes and indignities. When the civilized world heard that he had been lynched by the brewers of London—cuffed, and pommelled, and rolled in the dust,—shouts of universal applause went up, and the verdict of society was "served him right."[33]

Elizabeth Cady Stanton had a very different view in *The Woman's Bible*:

> The deception and the cruelty practiced on Sisera by Jael under the guise of hospitality is revolting under our code of morality. To decoy the luckless general fleeing before his enemy into her tent, pledging him safety, and with seeming tenderness ministering to his wants, with such words of sympathy and consolation lulling him to sleep, and then in cold blood

driving a nail through his temples, seems more like the work of a fiend than of a woman.[34]

Many contemporary male commentators concur with Stanton. Jael is described as deceitful, a coward, and an assassin. Her lack of hospitality is denounced.[35]

We may ask, however, what kind of man did Jael see coming toward her tent? Judges 4:3 tells us that Sisera had nine hundred chariots and oppressed the people cruelly for twenty years. In Judges 5:28–30, Sisera's family is depicted as waiting anxiously for his return. His mother wonders what could be delaying him. Her companions conjecture that Sisera is busy "finding and dividing the spoil . . . A girl or two for every man." Presumably Jael knows what kind of man Sisera is. Van Wijk-Bos writes:

> So Jael does what not many of us would have the courage to do. She invites a known rapist into her tent, and then, without hesitation, using what she has and what she knows, with skill and determination, she kills him. Not a "nice" story, but then the times were not nice, and Sisera was not a nice man. Talking about desert hospitality in the face of this reality is inappropriate.[36]

Fewell reads Jael's story less idealistically:

> Though her thoughts are never revealed, she is clearly a woman caught in the middle. The Israelites have obviously won. They cannot be far behind Sisera, and they are unlikely to take kindly to a family that has allied itself with the enemy—especially if found to be hiding the Canaanite commander. Jael does what she has to do. She offers Sisera a seductive welcome, treats him with maternal care, and when he falls asleep assured of his safety, drives a tent peg through his mouth (*raqaq* = "parted lips," often translated misleadingly as "temple"), severing his spinal column, leaving him to die a convulsive death.[37]

Ackerman suggests a third perspective. Because she views Jael as a religious functionary, she believes that Jael discerns that it is the Lord's will that Sisera be killed, and thus she violates the conventions of religious sanctuary for a higher end.[38]

Whether the idealistic reading (van Wijk-Bos), the "realistic" reading (Fewell), or the historically based reading is more accurate is impossible to determine. The Hebrews were not as interested in Jael's motivations as in the results of her action. We are interested because our assessment of her character depends in large measure on her motivation. Nevertheless we can only guess, because the text does not tell us clearly.

In contrast to our inability to evaluate Jael for lack of information, and to modern (male) commentators' negative assessments of Jael, the poets of

Judges 5 praise her. They call her "most blessed of women" (Judg. 5:24). Their praise is presumably based on results rather than motivations. The phrase "most blessed of women" is used elsewhere in the Bible only of Mary, Jesus' mother, and Judith in the Apocrypha, who also murdered an enemy. Jael used deception and she murdered in cold blood. This does not matter to the poets of Judges 5 and perhaps not to us. Jael killed an oppressor. Some condemn Jael. All peace-loving folk will find the violence of her actions disturbing. If her story is one of self-defense, there is nothing to denounce, nor is there a hero to celebrate. However, if her motivation went beyond saving herself, then this is a story many can celebrate.

In an article dealing with the diverse responses of women to Deborah, Jael, and Sisera's mother, Katharine Sakenfeld concludes with this story:

> A group of Korean women were expressing some enthusiasm for Jael's exploits, and I commented that most women I knew—white, middle/upper-class North Americans like me—had trouble with this story. I suggested certain roots for our difficulties with the story: we are too accustomed to not having to defend our homeland. Many of us are also influenced by the Christian theme of "turning the other cheek." I asked these Koreans what they could offer out of their setting that might be of help to me. After a brief pause, there came a bold reply from the far end of the table. "If you American women would just realize that your place in this story is with Sisera's mother, waiting to collect the spoil of your interventions across the world . . ." I did not want to hear that. I did not want to be reminded of the negative effects of first-world colonialism and military might in which I participate by my citizenship. But as I have reflected longer about it, I wonder whether I did not hear God's prophet as that woman spoke. That thought and that exchange remain among the most disturbing and the most profound moments of my Asian journey, a time of hearing the Bible as word of God through the voices of those not like myself.[39]

THE WIFE OF MANOAH

The unnamed[40] wife of Manoah gives birth to Samson in Judges 13. An angel of the Lord appears to her and tells her that she will bear a son and that she is to drink no wine and eat nothing unclean. When the son is born, no razor is to touch his head, because he is to be consecrated. He will begin to deliver the Israelites from the Philistines (Judg. 13:2–5). Manoah's wife tells her husband that a man of God has visited her, and she reports his words. Manoah then prays that the visitor will return to instruct them on what they should do for the boy (Judg. 13:6–8). God answers Manoah's prayer and reappears to his wife. She runs to get him, and the angel tells Manoah what he has already told his wife. Manoah then tries to persuade the messenger to stay for a meal, but he declines. However, he tells Manoah he may offer a holocaust to the Lord. Not realizing the messenger is an angel, Manoah asks his name. The angel answers that it is mysterious (Judg. 13:8–18). Then Manoah offers a kid and a cereal offering, and as the flame goes up, the angel ascends with it. Manoah and his wife bow to the ground. Manoah is terrified, believing that since they have seen God, they will die (Judg. 13:19–22). Manoah's wife points out that if God had wanted them to die, God would not have accepted their holocaust and cereal offerings, nor would God have told them or shown them what they had heard and seen (Judg. 13:23). Manoah's wife bears a son, whom she names Samson. He grows up and is blessed by God (Judg. 13:24).

Although Manoah's wife is not named, she is clearly the stronger human character in this story. It is she who primarily interacts with the angel and she who recognizes the angel as an angel. The story makes Manoah look foolish and his wife wise.

Thus Cheryl Exum writes: "Good theologian that he is, Manoah recognizes that seeing the deity brings death (v. 22). His wife, it seems, is a better theologian, for it is she who calls attention to a divine purpose behind the events (v. 23)."[41] Nevertheless, Exum later suggests that the narrator depicts Manoah's wife acting on behalf of and in subordination to her husband, undermining her positive portrayal.[42] Susan Ackerman agrees, stating that "Deuteronomistic notions about a woman's ability to exert religious power eventually appear more transitory than real, and this suggests in turn that the degree of *actual* religious authority ancient Israelite women could exert during all but the earliest eras of the Israelite cult was very restricted indeed."[43] And yet in this story, Manoah's unnamed wife is clearly the more discerning of the two human characters. The fact that this story appears in a text that was probably canonized in the postexilic period suggests that the Deuteronomistic editors were comfortable including a text that highlighted a woman's superior religious discernment. These same editors also depicted King Josiah turning to a woman, the prophetess Huldah, to ascertain the authenticity of the book of the law found in the temple during renovations.

DELILAH

The story of Samson and Delilah is found in Judges 14–16, with the portion involving Delilah occurring in Judges 16. But first, against his parents' wishes but with their acquiescence, Samson decides to marry a Philistine woman from Timnah. As part of the wedding festivities, he tells a riddle to his bride's male friends, promising to give thirty linen garments and thirty festal garments to the one who correctly solves it, but demanding the same from the group if none can come up with the right answer. When they cannot figure it out, they pester her to find out the solution from Samson, threatening to burn down her house if she does not succeed.

She then begs him to tell her until he finally breaks down. She then gives them the answer, they tell Samson, and he is furious. He kills thirty men from the Philistine town of Ashkelon and gives their garments to the group, then returns home. The bride's father then gives her to the best man, thinking that Samson has rejected her. After a while, Samson decides to go visit his wife and is livid when he discovers what her father has done, so he ties torches to the tails of thirty foxes and lets them loose through the fields, burning the wheat, olives, and vineyards. In retaliation, the Philistines burn the woman and her father. Samson swears revenge and for the next thirty years "judges" Israel, wreaking havoc among the Philistines (Judg. 14–15). Samson then has a brief liaison with a prostitute before falling in love with Delilah (Judg. 16:1–4).

The lords of the town each promise to pay Delilah eleven hundred pieces of silver, an enormous sum of money, if she can find out the secret of Samson's strength (Judg. 16:5). So Delilah asks Samson how he could be bound so that one could subdue him. He responds that if they bind him with fresh bowstrings, he will become weak. Delilah tells the lords, and they provide her with fresh bowstrings with which she binds Samson. They come upon him from hiding places, but he easily snaps the bowstrings (Judg. 16:6–9).

Delilah chides Samson for mocking her and asks him again. This time he tells her that they must bind him with new ropes. The earlier scenario is repeated, with similar results (Judg. 16:10–12). Again Delilah chides Samson and asks him his secret. His story this time is that they must weave his hair into a web. A third time she follows his instructions, the Philistines come out of hiding, and Samson easily breaks free (Judg. 16:14). Finally, after Delilah tells Samson that he doesn't love her and nags him for several days, Samson tells Delilah the real secret of his strength. If his hair is cut, he will become weak (Judg. 16:15–17). Again Delilah calls the Philistines, and while Samson sleeps, a man cuts off Samson's hair. When Samson awakes, the Philistines descend upon him and he is captured. They gouge out his eyes and shackle him in bronze fetters and put him to work at the prison mill (Judg. 16:18–22). Of Delilah we hear no more.

Delilah is often viewed as among the most evil women in Scripture. She is depicted as beautiful, but seductive, unfaithful, and treasonous. Many feminist interpreters have noted the theme of love as betrayal in the standard readings of this story.[44] Betsy Merideth writes:

> I would like to suggest that the story is at least as much about Samson's pride and pretensions to immortality as it is about Delilah's harm to him. One

problem with the application of the concept of betrayal to Judges 16 is that it emphasizes Delilah's role in Samson's capture by the Philistines, at the expense of any acknowledgement of his own responsibility for the outcome. Quite simply, a reading that finds "betrayal" or "deceit" in Delilah's actions is unconvincing because Samson is depicted as knowing what is going on and is thus an active participant in the events, not merely a victim.[45]

It is clear that Delilah did harm Samson and that she betrayed his love for her, but it is equally clear that he was blinded by his love for her. In addition, if we assume that Delilah was a Philistine,[46] from the Philistine point of view, Delilah would probably be viewed as a hero.[47] Similarly Rahab, if described by her fellow citizens in Jericho, would undoubtedly be vilified.

Mary Cartledge-Hayes relates the story of Samson and Delilah to previous events in Samson's life. In particular, she ties in Samson's marriage with a woman from Timnah, who is burned to death as a result of the chain of reactions beginning with Samson telling the solution to his riddle to his wife (Judg. 14:1–15:8). She writes:

> After thinking about this story, I was very angry. Samson, by any recognizable standard, is a jerk. Loved by God he undoubtedly was, but what of the woman of Timnah? She was one leg of a hate triangle—and the leg most easily broken.
>
> Her life was ruined because one day some guy happened to walk by and notice her. Imagine her alarm when thirty men surrounded her, demanding she conspire with them. Imagine her fear when she was handed off to some other man, her horror when Samson returned to destroy her people's livelihood. And imagine her terror when the thirty Philistines came back to break their promise.
>
> I imagined it all, and I came up furious and filled with rhetorical questions. Who hushed up this story? Who decided Samson was a hero? Who weighed Samson's cruelty and Delilah's sneakiness and proclaimed Delilah the villain? This was a plot, I decided, a deliberate, nasty plot to degrade women, with coconspirators numbering in the millions. . . .
>
> My sympathies lodged squarely with Delilah, creating a new dilemma. I no longer hated her, but what was there of value in her story? Samson's wicked behavior neither excuses nor justifies hers. Besides, I was conditioned to despise her. How could I break that old habit of judging?
>
> I followed my thinking around corners and up trees and through the woods until it came out the other side. On that other side was a possibility. What if Delilah knew of Samson's exploits in Timnah?[48]

If Delilah knew of Samson's failed marriage and the horrible events that led to his wife's death, then her actions would be explainable not only as patriotic but also as retributive justice. Samson's behavior in Timnah had resulted in the fiery death of an innocent woman and her family. If Delilah was aware of this, then she might well have been eager to see this criminal brought to justice. This is all speculation, of course, yet by filling in the motivational gap in this manner, a much more sympathetic picture of Delilah emerges.

Whether Delilah was a real person we cannot be sure. Whether she was real or purely literary, however, modern readers want to understand her motivations perhaps more than ancient readers did. Another reading understands Delilah's motivation to be financial security. Danna Fewell writes:

> Delilah's identity is not bound to any man. Introduced simply by name, she is a woman who takes care of herself. She conducts her love affair with Samson and her business affairs with the lords of the Philistines without any father, brother, or husband acting as mediator. The narrator says that Samson loves Delilah. How Delilah feels about him is not revealed. Some degree of ambivalence is probable since she readily agrees to the Philistine proposal that she seduce Samson and discover the source of his strength. Eleven hundred pieces of silver from each Philistine nobleman are promised in exchange for information on how Samson might be subdued. Doubtless, as a woman alone, Delilah finds that the love of a wanted man is no match for the security of wealth.[49]

Nevertheless, Carol Smith perceptively notes that Delilah, the independent woman who owns her own sexuality and uses it for her own ends, "represents a particular view of women that has been castigated by the patriarchal establishment and feminists alike and that sits uneasily in a feminist context. Postfeminists might be much more comfortable with Delilah's behaviour."[50]

Cheryl Exum analyzes the way the stories of all the women related to Samson (his mother, the Timnite woman, the prostitute from Gaza, and Delilah) function to uphold patriarchal values. Men fear women's sexuality and thus in the story it is controlled in various ways. Samson's mother's ability to conceive is granted by God. Alone she is incapable of having a baby. The Timnite woman is controlled by the Philistine men who threaten her if she does not find out the answer to Samson's riddle. Delilah is controlled by the offer of a large sum of money. If greed is what motivates her, as the story subtly suggests, then although she is the means by which Samson is destroyed, the initiators are Philistine men. The sexual ideology encoded in these stories assures fearful men that women may be dangerous, but they can be controlled—by threat, by reward, and, of course, by God.[51]

Carol Smith disagrees that the story of Samson and Delilah is primarily about gender politics, suggesting that it is both more subtle and simple than this. For Smith, the narrative reflects the values of the patriarchal culture in which it arose, but does not reinforce those values so much as leave open the possibility that they may be questioned:

My own suggestion is that although the text clearly *reflects* a patriarchal society, far from "justifying" it, in many places it makes men appear ineffectual, even in their traditional roles as rulers and fighters. Even the powerful Philistines are incapable of conquering Samson, who is, after all, only one man, except with the help of a woman; and she has to be bribed heavily to do it. It is true that what starts out as a "reflection" of a situation can later be used as a justification for it, but that is not the same as suggesting that the writer of Judges was using the story of Samson and Delilah to make polemical points about the status of women.[52]

Delilah is a controversial character who elicits strong reactions from feminist and nonfeminist readers alike. Her independence is laudable, but her use of her sexual attractiveness to manipulate a man and bring him down makes many uncomfortable, even when it is admitted that she did so openly and without pretense.

JEPHTHAH'S DAUGHTER

The story of Jephthah's unnamed daughter found in Judges 11 has been the subject of a large number of interpretations by feminist biblical scholars.[53] It is also one of the most horrifying stories of victimization in the Hebrew Bible and, in fact, in all literature read in the Western world.

The story begins when the reader is told that Jephthah is the son of Gilead by a prostitute[54] and as a result he cannot inherit any of his father's property. His half-brothers drive him away. Because he is a warrior, however, and the Israelites need someone to fight the Ammonites, Jephthah is pressed into service. He agrees to serve on the condition that if he is victorious, he will become the head of the Gileadites (Judg. 11:1–10).

Then Jephthah summons the Ammonites to war (Judg. 11:11–28). He makes a vow to God that if God gives him victory, he will sacrifice whoever or whatever (the Hebrew can mean either) comes out of his house to meet him first (Judg. 11:30–31). Jephthah is victorious. When he returns home, his daughter comes out to greet him with timbrels and dancing, as was the custom (Judg. 11:34–35). Jephthah is chagrined. His daughter tells her father to do as he has vowed. She asks only to go with her friends to bewail her virginity on the mountains for two months first (Judg. 11:37–38). At the end of the two months, she returns home and her father fulfills his vow (Judg. 11:39). A custom develops in which for four days every year the Israelite girls go out to lament Jephthah's daughter (Judg. 11:39–40).

Feminist interpreters comment on this sad tale in a variety of ways. Cheryl Exum notes that the message in the story is that daughters are expected to submit to their fathers, regardless of the consequences. Because Jephthah's

daughter is a "good" daughter, submitting as expected, she is remembered.[55]
Esther Fuchs shows how the use of language tends to make Jephthah look as
good as possible in a situation in which his actions are really horrifying.[56]
Peggy Day reflects on the nature of the annual festival that was established.[57]
Renita Weems points out the deceptiveness of the story:

> On the surface, the story is about religious integrity: a man spares noth-
> ing to honor a vow he has made to the Lord. . . . But in the story of Jeph-
> thah and his daughter, somewhere nobility turns into a nightmare,
> devotion turns into death. Somewhere the quest for honor and duty, in
> the face of a young woman's senseless death, becomes a gross distortion of
> justice.[58]

The one positive note Weems finds is in the women's solidarity: "Thus,
the story of Jephthah's daughter which began as a story about a man's radical devotion to God ends as a story of women's radical devotion to one
another—and to the whole truth. It is a story of women once again taking
the only weapon they have—their tears—and craftily cultivating a new song
for themselves."[59]

Phyllis Trible, the first feminist biblical scholar to highlight this story,
notes the contrast between this story and that of Isaac who is spared at the
last moment.[60] She also notes the way the Scriptures have handled this story:

> The earliest evidence is in the conclusion of the Jephthah cycle of stories.
> It shifts attention from the private crisis of sacrifice to a public confronta-
> tion between tribes (12:1–7). Challenged by armed Ephraimites, Jephthah
> leads the Gileadites to a resounding victory. The mighty warrior prevails
> uncensored; the violence that he perpetrated upon his only daughter stalks
> him not at all. In the end he dies a natural death and receives an epitaph
> fit for an exemplary judge (12:7). Moreover, his military victories enhance
> his name in the years to come. Specifically, the prophet Samuel proclaims
> to Israel that "Yahweh sent . . . Jephthah . . . and delivered you out of the
> hand of your enemies . . ." (I Sam. 12:11, RSV).[61]

In the New Testament in the book of Hebrews, Jephthah is praised as one who
through faith did great things (Heb. 11:32–34). His daughter is forgotten.[62]

Alice Laffey compares this story with the account of Saul's vow that his
son Jonathan violates in 1 Samuel 14:

> Though Saul is willing to have his vow fulfilled, that is, to allow his son
> to die (vv 39, 44), the people are not. In the first place, they protest the
> appropriateness of Saul's vow (vv 24–26); second, they do not allow
> Jonathan to become its victim (v 45). In contrast, the companions of the
> daughter of Jephthah do not protest. Rather, they too are submissive.

They support the victim by their presence, but they do not challenge the girl's fate.

The episodes narrated in Judg 11 and 1 Sam 14 both involve vows made to God. They both involve consequences for their children. Both fathers are willing to have their vows fulfilled. What distinguishes the two stories are the responses of the children's constituencies and the stories' outcomes. The female companions of the daughter of Jephthah are typical products of patriarchy; the "sons of Israel" are also, but differently! One response leads to life; the other to death. Interestingly enough, there is no penalty placed on the people for obfuscating Saul's vow and securing Jonathan's life. May we conclude similarly that no penalty would have ensued had the girl's companions had the courage to challenge Jephthah?[63]

Danna Fewell also considers God's deliverance of Isaac and Jonathan. Although she sees one possible conclusion as the lower value of women, she also suggests another. "Perhaps, too, the death of the daughter, the silence of God, and the absence of the people are but signs of something rotten with the state of Israel."[64]

Choosing between these two views—that the story of Jephthah's daughter is a reflection of the low value of women and that it is a sign of something rotten in Israel—is difficult. Certainly part of the purpose of Judges is defense of kingship. By telling horrible stories, the narrator solicits support for the royal institution. Nevertheless we must ask whether it is a coincidence that the horrible tales involve so many female victims. However, even this coincidence can cut both ways. Are women the victims because their value is lower, or are they the victims because through their victimization greater sympathy for kingship is elicited? This latter suggestion, however, may be based on a modern assumption that should not be read into the ancient text. Thus, it seems most likely that women are depicted as victims in Judges because that is the way it was. Women were less valued and physically weaker and therefore were vulnerable to victimization. That does not mean that these stories are perfect reflections of historical reality in every respect. Nevertheless it is probably safe to assume some correspondence between literary and historical reality. In the final analysis, however, both Laffey and Fewell could be right. The story of Jephthah's daughter could reflect women's low value and also the rotten state of affairs in Israel at the time.

How are we to assess Jephthah and his daughter? Surely Jephthah's vow is rash.[65] Surely he is too eager to win the battle and thereby regain standing in his community. Surely he is either stupid or thoughtless not to consider who is likely to come out of his door to greet him. Yet, in spite of these problems, he is not explicitly condemned in the Bible. Rather, he is praised. That he could carry out such a vow at all is chilling. That he could be praised suggests the low status of women in ancient Israel and early Christianity.

What of his daughter? Is it fair to wish that she had put up more of a protest? What were her choices? Was there anywhere or anyone to whom she could flee for safety? Perhaps not. Perhaps she acted in the only way possible. Perhaps she made the most out of a horrible situation. But we cannot help wondering whether there was not some way out. What would the midwives Shiphrah and Puah have done, or the harlot Rahab? To thoughts such as these Mieke Bal responds:

> The critic who suggests Bat's [Jephthah's daughter's] anonymity is a deserved punishment for her submission to the father's desire, instead of protecting herself as was her duty, . . . misses the point of the story as it is interpreted here. The daughter cannot but submit, but within the limits assigned to her by patriarchy and the unlimited power over the daughter it assigns to the father, she exploits the possibility left open to her. Using oral history as a cultural means of memorialization, she makes her fellow-virgins feel that solidarity between daughters is a task, an urgent one, that alone can save them from total oblivion. Although she can only be remembered as what she never was allowed to overcome, as Bat-Jephthah [daughter of Jephthah], it is she, not the man who does have a proper name, who is made immemorial. She is remembered as she was, in submission to the power of the father, a power over life and death, exclusive possession, which he decided to exercise until death did them part.[66]

Finally, we return to Weems's reflection: "The story of Jephthah's daughter is deceptive because it is about something graver than honor, integrity, and obedience—for too often noble ideas are corrupted in the hands of extremists and the insane."[67] It is ironic that biblical women often were forced to resort to deception to accomplish godly ends. In the process they were denounced by subsequent commentators. In Judges 11 the narrators use a much more subtle form of deception. They paint a stupid, self-serving vow as the action of a faithful man. They also diminish the grave consequences of that act.

Their deception has not been completely successful, however. They have been found out. Jephthah can no longer be thought of as a hero. At best he comes across as a man who, blinded by his own lack of self-esteem, cruelly sacrifices his own daughter and with her his future. Perhaps there is a lesson we can learn from this sad tale. We must be careful to discern the difference between genuine piety and self-serving, ersatz versions that destroy rather than build up. If we can learn this lesson, then perhaps Jephthah's daughter did not die in vain.

Perhaps, even Jephthah's daughter was trying to say something like that. So Fewell suggests that her coming out the door was suicidal. She writes:

> An unknown character who had no option but obedience is not, however, the only possible reading. Jephthah's vow was most likely made at Mizpah and not necessarily in secret. The daughter could very well have known

the substance of her father's bargain. Indeed, when she responds to her father, she seems quite aware of what his vow entails. Rather than reading her answer as innocent submission, one might hear a tone of ironic judgment: "My father, you have opened your mouth to Yahweh. Do to me that which has gone forth from your mouth. After all, Yahweh has given you vengeance over your enemies, the Ammonites" (11:36).

Perhaps Jephthah had intended that his daughter hear the vow, to warn her against coming out first. Perhaps he had in mind forfeiting a servant or a bodyguard left behind to protect his home. In that case the daughter intends her greeting. She is one of Jephthah's troublers because, as she steps forth, she takes the place of someone whom he has considered expendable. She thereby passes judgment on her father's willingness to bargain for glory with the life of another. Her action condemns his priorities, and perhaps those of all Israel.[68]

Valerie Cooper, a womanist scholar, reads the story in almost the opposite fashion, in a way that seems historically more plausible. Noting that Jephthah was unfairly marginalized by his brothers because of his mother's status as a prostitute, she identifies with Jephthah's daughter as a person doubly marginalized by gender and social standing, who also needed to express solidarity with her father: For Jephthah's daughter, the choice was between death and dishonor. For Bat-Jephthah, to accept her father's words meant certain death, but to reject her father's rash vow meant to declare a fool the man all of Israel had once before rejected and then to run, with no place to hide. Bat-Jephthah held in her hands not only her own honor but her father's. For many black women today, the same choices define their conduct as they barter their silence for the prestige of the men they love.[69]

Again we are faced with the impossibility of determining with any certainty the motivation of a character in a text. Yet in the text Jephthah's daughter is alive enough for us to be horrified by her story. Reflecting on that horror can perhaps lead to something better in the future.

AN UNNAMED WOMAN, THE LEVITE'S WIFE

Judges 19 has another text of terror that is remarkably similar to the story of Lot's daughters in Genesis 19:1–11. Unfortunately the story in Judges 19 does not end so well. In this story of a Levite from Ephraim and his wife (usually translated as concubine, but see below), the woman has either played the harlot (Hebrew text) or become angry with the Levite (the Septuagint) and left him, returning to her father's house.[70] The Levite from Ephraim journeys to Bethlehem to be reconciled with his wife, who is staying with her father. After several days of feasting, the pair start for home along with a servant. They do so late in the day, however, making it impossible to complete the journey before nightfall.

They stop in Gibeah in the territory of the tribe of Benjamin and stay with an old Ephraimite man. They think they will be safe because both he and the Levite are from Ephraim. The men of the city, however, demand to have intercourse with the Levite. The host offers instead the Levite's wife and his own virgin daughter. They do not accept this offer. Nevertheless the Levite (or the Ephraimite host) takes his wife, puts her out, and they rape and abuse her throughout the night.

As light dawns, she comes and falls at the door of the man's house. When the Levite is ready to leave, he finds her on the doorstep. He tells her to get up, but she does not respond. So he puts her on his donkey, sets out toward home, and once there takes a knife, cuts her into twelve pieces, and sends them throughout Israel.

In Judges 20 the tribes of Israel gather to attack Benjamin in retaliation. They are so successful that only six hundred men escape to the wilderness. This creates another problem, because none of the other tribes wants to give their daughters in marriage to the remaining Benjaminites.

So in Judges 21 the tribes discover that Jabesh-gilead did not send anybody to help with the fight against Benjamin. Thus, a force is sent to Jabesh-gilead, and its inhabitants are killed. Four hundred virgins are spared to become wives for the Benjaminite men, but more are needed. Next, the tribes decide to get the remaining wives by telling the Benjaminites to abduct them from the annual festival at Shiloh.

Thus the story of the rape and murder of the unnamed woman becomes the story of the destruction of an entire tribe. The men, women, and children, minus six hundred men, are all killed. This story is also about the destruction of the town of Jabesh-gilead, with the exception of four hundred young virgins. It is finally about the abduction of two hundred more young women from the festival at Shiloh.

Before we comment on this atrocious story, the nature of the relationship between the Levite and his woman should be considered. She is called his *pîlegeš*, a Hebrew word normally translated "concubine," meaning slave used for sexual purposes. Mieke Bal suggests that she is rather his wife, but has been living with her father rather than with her husband. When the Levite takes her from her father's house, he is trying to change the nature of their relationship.[71] Exum argues that the woman is a legal wife of secondary rank. She disagrees with Bal on the grounds that Bal's definition does not fit most biblical occurrences of *pîlegeš*.[72]

Phyllis Trible deals with this story in *Texts of Terror*.[73] She notes the various responses to the woman's rape and murder:[74]

1. The tribes respond by going to war against Benjamin. They justify further violence, which includes violence against innocent women and children as vengeance.[75]

2. The editor of the book of Judges repeats the opening words of Judges, "In those days, there was no king in Israel" at the end of the book. He adds the words, "Every man did what was right in his own eyes." The editor is using the violence in the book of Judges to promote monarchy. Ironically, Israel's first king, Saul, is a Benjaminite. He establishes his first capital at Gibeah. He also delivers Jabesh-gilead from the Ammonites. The editor may here be undercutting Saul in preparation for promoting David. However, David's reign has its own horrors: his killing Uriah to win Bathsheba; Amnon's rape of Tamar; and Absalom's violation of his father's concubines.[76]

Trible writes: "In those days there was a king in Israel, and royalty did the right in its own eyes. Clearly, to counsel a political solution to the story of the concubine is ineffectual. Such a perspective does not direct its heart to her."[77]

3. A third response comes from the order of the books. In the Hebrew order, the story of Hannah follows; in the Greek order, the story of Ruth follows. The absence of misogyny, violence, and vengeance in these stories makes a positive contrast with the story of the unnamed woman.[78]

4. From the prophets, specifically from Hosea, two passing references suggest that the memory of all the violence of this story does not quickly disappear.[79] Hosea writes in announcing punishment:

> They have deeply corrupted themselves
>   as in the days of Gibeah;
> he [God] will remember their iniquity,
>   he will punish their sins.
>   (Hos. 9:9)

> Since the days of Gibeah you have sinned, O Israel;
>   there they have continued.
> Shall not war overtake them in Gibeah?
>   (Hos. 10:9)

5. From the rest of Scripture the response is silence. Trible writes: "The biting, even sarcastic, words of the prophet Amos on another occasion capture well the spirit of this response:

> Therefore, the prudent one will keep silent about such a time;
>   for it is an evil time.
>   (Amos 5:13, RSV)

Silence covers impotence and complicity. To keep quiet is to sin, for the story orders its listeners to 'direct your heart to her, take counsel, and speak' (19:30; 20:7)."[80]

6. Finally, there is a place for a sixth response, our own response. How will we direct our hearts to her, what counsel will we take, how will we speak and what will we say? Trible concludes:

> First of all, we can recognize the contemporaneity of the story. Misogyny belongs to every age, including our own. Violence and vengeance are not just characteristics of a distant, pre-Christian past; they infect the community of the elect to this day. Woman as object is still captured, betrayed, raped, tortured, murdered, dismembered, and scattered. To take to heart its ancient story, then, is to confess its present reality. The story is alive, and all is not well. Beyond confession we must take counsel to say, "Never again." Yet this counsel is itself ineffectual unless we direct our hearts to that most uncompromising of all biblical commands, speaking the word not to others but to ourselves: Repent. Repent.[81]

Stuart Lasine agrees with Trible that the story promotes monarchy, but unlike Trible he believes that the narrator subtly but powerfully condemns the Levite. He shows how elements from Genesis 19 and 1 Samuel 11 provide contrasts that reveal the narrator's perspective:

> The use of material from Genesis 19 allows the reader to contrast the situations at Gibeah and Sodom so that he can see how the old host inverts Lot's hospitality into inhospitality, and how the action of the Levite-guest is the inverse of the action taken by Lot's divine guests. Similarly, the deliberate contrast between the Levite dismembering his concubine (Judg. 19.29) and Saul dismembering the oxen (1 Sam. 11.7) demonstrates the difference between the way a disaster is avenged by an irresponsible, callous, and self-absorbed man who lives at a time in which there is no king in Israel. Comparison of Judges 19–21 with Genesis 19 and 1 Samuel 11 allows the reader to recognize that a world in which there is no king in Israel and every man does what is right in his own eyes (Judg. 19.1; 21.25; cf. 17.6) is an "inverted world" where actions are often ludicrous, absurd, and self-defeating.[82]

As in other biblical stories, we are again confronted with two interpreters who share a feminist perspective but who read the story differently. They agree that the story is horrible. They agree that it is propaganda for monarchy. But the one reads the story as implying no condemnation of the terrible acts, and the other sees subtle condemnation in the contrasts with other stories. I agree with Lasine that the context of the story implies condemnation.

Koala Jones-Warsaw criticizes Trible for setting up a simplistic dichotomy of wicked men vs. innocent victimized women, whereas many men as well as women suffer in this story. The Levite's wife is raped and murdered, but all the men, as well as the women and children of the tribe of Benjamin, also die, with the exception of six hundred men. All but four hundred young women from the city of Jabesh-Gilead are killed because they refused to become involved in the fight against Benjamin. In addition, not only are the two hundred virgins of Shiloh abducted and victimized, but their families also lose economically and emotionally when their daughters are stolen from them.

> By reducing the problem of victimization to gender, she [Trible] victimizes the other characters with a silencing technique comparable to that used by the narrator. One may arguably posit that the narration represents the view of the dominant class, which favored the institution of kingship. This entire story functions within the Deuteronomistic history to justify the establishment of kingship in ancient Israel. Likewise, Trible's feminist perspective, rooted in the dominant culture and the middle-class, contributes to her propensity not to acknowledge other types of victimization beyond that which white middle-class females experience (that is, from male domination).[83]

Warsaw-Jones's critique of Trible involves an important reminder that although we may use various lenses to study biblical narratives, we should avoid simplistic, dichotomous thinking that tends to see all women as powerless victims and all men as powerful oppressors.

Finally, Jacqueline Lapsley agrees with Lasine that the biblical narrator condemns the violence and with Warsaw-Jones's concern that violence against a single woman escalates into violence against many men and women. She goes on to indicate, however, that concern in the West about the living conditions of women under the Taliban in Afghanistan was the background of media coverage of research suggesting that in particular societies there is a connection between higher status of women and lower levels of violence generally, as well as greater economic and social stability.[84]

CONCLUSIONS

The women of the books of Joshua and Judges present us with stark contrasts. The heroes Rahab and Deborah are praised by the biblical narrators and modern commentators. The hero Jael receives positive marks from her biblical reviewers but often negative ones from contemporary interpreters. Manoah's wife, a strong, if somewhat minor character, is generally liked by all. Delilah is a villain in the eyes of the Bible and of most modern readers, but some feminist critics assess her more positively. These women are all strong characters who are understood to be heroic by at least some interpreters. None of them can be considered victims. The fact that at least two of them are helpmates (Manoah's wife, Jael, and perhaps Deborah) and another is a harlot (Rahab) is interesting, but these roles are not the most important information given about Manoah's wife, Jael, Deborah (?), and Rahab. What is important is that they are depicted as strong women who act independently and in a positive fashion.

In contrast to these strong women are Jephthah's daughter and the Levite's wife. These women are victims. They are relatively passive characters, at least as they are presented in the Bible. Feminist interpreters are not in total agreement on how to assess these stories. All agree, however, that they are among the most atrocious stories of victimization, not only in the Bible but anywhere. That this is true is cause for concern.

DISCUSSION QUESTIONS

1. Reflect on prostitution as it exists in your community. Does Rahab's situation parallel what you know of modern-day harlots? Is her depiction as a hero plausible? If so, why? If not, why not?
2. Was Delilah an evil woman? With whom do you sympathize more, Samson or Delilah?
3. How do you feel about Deborah's involvement in military aggression?
4. Does Jael seem to you to be a positive or a negative character?
5. Would Barak have dealt any better with the Canaanite women than Sisera was expected to deal with the Israelite women?
6. How do you feel about the way Jephthah's daughter handled the terrible situation in which she found herself? Can you think of modern parallels?
7. The story of the Levite's woman brings to mind contemporary stories of gang rapes and murders, with their cycles of violence. What can we do to stop the violence in our own society?

6

The Women in 1 and 2 Samuel

The books of 1 and 2 Samuel include the stories of Hannah, the woman of Endor, Saul's concubine Rizpah, the three most important wives of David (Michal, Abigail, and Bathsheba), David's daughter Tamar, the wise (?) woman of Tekoa, and the wise woman of Abel. Five of these are helpmates (Hannah, Michal, Abigail, Bathsheba, and Rizpah). Three of these helpmates are also victims (Michal, Bathsheba, and Rizpah). Tamar is a victim.

The women of Endor, Tekoa, and Abel are, as far as is known, independent women. Nevertheless, their stories are told because of their relationships to David and Saul. Indeed, all of these women except Hannah are remembered because of their relationship with one of these two kings. Hannah gives birth to Samuel, who anoints Saul and David. There are no harlots in this group, though Bathsheba is sometimes condemned as a seductress. Nor from a modern perspective are there any heroes, although the narrator depicts Abigail heroically. Although the period of David's reign is often cast by later generations of Israelites as a golden era, it was not golden for the women who were most closely associated with the king.

HANNAH

Hannah's story is told in 1 Samuel 1:1–2:10. In some ways it is the typical Hebrew birth of the hero story. Like Sarah, Rebekah, and Rachel, Hannah is initially barren (1 Sam. 1:2).[1] Her plight is exacerbated by the fertility of Elkanah's second wife, Peninnah, who provokes Hannah and makes life miserable for her (1 Sam. 1:7). Their rivalry recalls that of Sarah and Hagar, as

123

well as the conflict between Rachel and Leah. However, unlike these pairs of women, Hannah does not display any jealousy or hostility toward Peninnah.[2] Hannah's husband Elkanah is depicted as loving Hannah but not being particularly troubled by her barrenness, asking if he is not more devoted to her than ten sons.[3] His attitude can be read as positive from a feminist perspective because he does not value her based on her ability to bear him sons. Read in the historical context, however, he does not understand that his love for her does not make up for her lack of sons in a culture where her future economic security may depend on them and where her status in the community is largely determined by them. His lack of empathy, although in a different sphere from Abraham's self-centeredness, Isaac's passivity, and Jacob's lack of sensitivity toward Rachel's barrenness, is nevertheless reminiscent of their shortcomings in key areas. The similarities end there.

In one key sense, Hannah is unlike the two barren matriarchs of Genesis whose husbands are involved with God in their efforts to get children. Abraham receives the revelation of the conception of a child. Isaac prays to God asking for children. Here, however, it is Hannah, rather than Elkanah, who takes the lead and prays to God an anguished prayer (1 Sam. 1:9–18). God hears her prayer and she conceives Samuel (1 Sam. 1:19–20). She then dedicates him to God as a Nazirite (1 Sam. 1:24–28), according to the vow she had made in her prayer (1 Sam. 1:11).[4]

Finally, Hannah prays a beautiful prayer (1 Sam. 2:1–10). Mary's Magnificat (Luke 1:46–55) is modeled after Hannah's prayer. The prayer in its canonical form cannot have been composed by Hannah on the occasion of the dedication of young Samuel to God. The phrase "he [God] will give strength to his king" in 1 Samuel 2:10 must have been written after Samuel had become a man and anointed King Saul. Perhaps the prayer was attributed to her because of the reference in verse 5 to the barren having borne seven children. Nevertheless it is a prayer with profound sentiments that could have been written by a woman. Anyone who has experienced oppression will feel the joy of the prayer, in which God is praised for toppling the mighty and helping the poor and needy.

WOMAN OF ENDOR

The woman of Endor, sometimes called the witch of Endor, is able to call forth the spirits of the dead. Today we would call her a medium. She appears briefly in 1 Samuel 28:3–25. Saul is desperate in the face of the Philistine army encamped and ready for battle against the Israelites. He consults her after all other means of inquiring of God's will have been unsuccessful (1 Sam. 28:3–7). He visits her in disguise (1 Sam. 28:8), because he himself has banned mediums from the land (1 Sam. 28:3, 9). She is quite concerned about practicing her art in the face of the ban (1 Sam. 28:9). Saul assures her, however, that nothing will happen to her (1 Sam. 28: 10).

When the spirit of Samuel appears, the medium realizes that the man who asked for him is Saul. She is again quite concerned (1 Sam. 28:12), but Saul tells her not to be afraid (1 Sam. 28:13). Samuel is not pleased with being called from the dead. He tells Saul that the Israelites will lose the battle the next day and that Saul and his sons will be killed (1 Sam. 28:15–19). Saul is terrified. He is also weak from not having eaten (1 Sam. 28:20). The woman of Endor and her servants urge him to eat. He initially refuses, but she finally persuades him. She kills the fatted calf and makes unleavened cakes (1 Sam. 28:21–24). Saul and his servants eat and then leave (1 Sam. 28:25).

The woman of Endor is an independent woman. Her business has been banned, but she seems to have sufficient wealth to live comfortably. She has servants and can prepare a feast on short notice. Her marital status is not clear: there is no mention of a husband.

Her concerns about not violating the ban against mediums indicate that she is prudent. Her willingness to practice her art in spite of the ban and with only the word of a man she does not know is harder to assess. Whether she acts out of compassion or some other motivation is not indicated. Her concern for Saul after he has received devastating news from Samuel is a sign that she has compassion for him. Admittedly, he is the king, but her concern for him seems to be more personal. There is no hint that she stands to gain anything by killing the fatted calf.

The narrator portrays her in a positive light. Although her art has been proscribed, the proscription is not because it is thought counterfeit. In all likelihood, Saul is not alone in breaking the rules. There is always a desire to know what the future holds. In ancient times, mediums were frequently consulted. The woman of Endor apparently is a respected member of society, but she must operate carefully because of the ban.

Janice Nunnally-Cox writes:

> The first thing to be noted is that the woman is nowhere called witch. Yet over the centuries she has commonly been referred to as the "witch of Endor." The Authorized Version describes her as "a woman that hath a familiar spirit"; the Revised Standard Version calls her a "medium." But the footnotes and page headings of these versions speak of "the witch," and many commentators label I Samuel 28:3–25 as belonging to the Witch of Endor.[5]

Nunnally-Cox goes on to quote Edith Deen's description of the woman of Endor: "A wise old person with gnarled hands, deep, penetrating eyes, course [sic], leathery skin, and dark hair falling over her stooped shoulders. Probably

she had resorted to fortune telling because it was her only means of liveli-
hood. . . . Many had gone to her cave home, seeking counsel."[6] Nunnally-Cox
responds:

> It is remarkable that this rather unassuming woman elicits such response.
> We do not know that she is old, we are not told that she lives in a cave,
> has stooped shoulders, and tells fortunes. She is a necromancer, but nam-
> ing her a witch is another matter. It seems that this somewhat ordinary
> woman has been maligned because of her unusual sight. What we do
> know is very little, but it can readily be seen that she is a kindly person,
> much more charitable than the caustic Samuel, who seems to delight in
> bearing ill tidings. The woman comforts Saul in his despair, and makes
> haste to give him the best of what she has: her calf and her bread. History
> has quite possibly judged her character harshly, and it would serve us well
> to view the woman of Endor with sympathy rather than suspicion.[7]

Nunnally-Cox is correct in her assessment of Deen's view of the woman of
Endor. Filling in gaps in the text is one thing. Rewriting the story is another.
Deen crosses the line.

RIZPAH

The story of Rizpah is told in 2 Samuel 3:7–11 and 21:8–14. She is identified in 2 Samuel 3:7 as having been Saul's concubine. Saul is now dead, and
the houses of Saul and David are at war. David is king over Judah, and Saul's
son Ishbaal is king over Israel. Abner is the head of Saul's army, which is losing strength. In 2 Samuel 3:7, Ishbaal complains to Abner. The complaint is
that Abner has had sexual relations with Rizpah. Abner responds angrily:

> "Am I a dog's head for Judah? Today I keep showing loyalty to the house of
> your father Saul, to his brothers, and to his friends, and have not given you
> into the hand of David; and yet you charge me now with a crime concern-
> ing this woman. So may God do to Abner and so may he add to it! For just
> what the LORD has sworn to David, that will I accomplish for him, to trans-
> fer the kingdom from the house of Saul, and set up the throne of David
> over Israel and over Judah, from Dan to Beer-sheba." (2 Sam. 3:8–10)

Abner is evidently using Ishbaal's complaint against him as a pretext for
changing sides in the struggle for kingship. He characterizes the complaint as
petty, when contrasted with his great loyalty to Saul's house. Probably Ishbaal
sees Abner's taking up with Rizpah as a grab for power. His concern probably has nothing to do with Rizpah's feelings, which are not divulged. If this
interpretation is correct, then Rizpah is a pawn in a dangerous game.

In the second incident that involves Rizpah, David is now king over all of Israel. He is busily wiping out Saul's family to prevent the possibility of any usurpation. Rizpah's two sons are killed, as are the five sons of Merab, Saul's daughter (2 Sam. 21:8–9).

Their deaths are grisly. Delivered into the hands of the Gibeonites, they are then impaled. Rizpah responds by taking sackcloth and spreading it on a rock for herself. She guards the bodies against the birds and wild animals from the beginning of the harvest until the coming of the rainy season (2 Sam. 21:10). When David hears about it, he is shamed into giving these bodies, as well as those of Saul and Jonathan, a decent burial (2 Sam. 21:11–14).

Rizpah is a sad figure, concubine of the king, pawn in a power struggle in which her husband's side loses, grief-stricken mother of two murdered sons. Yet, through her vigilant watch over her sons' bodies, she has the satisfaction of knowing that they receive a decent burial. This was important to the ancient Hebrews. After this success, she fades from history but not from memory.

MICHAL

The story of Michal, daughter of Saul and wife of David, is told in 1 Samuel 18:20–29; 19:11–17; and 2 Samuel 6:20–23. Michal loves David (1 Sam. 18:20), but David's motivation for marrying Michal is probably political. By marrying the king's daughter, he apparently puts himself in a better position to become the next king (1 Sam. 18:26).[8]

Using deception and wit, Michal helps David escape from her father, Saul (1 Sam. 19:11–17). Thus she chooses between father and husband. Ironically, in the process she loses David. He flees, with no plans to return to her. When he does return to meet with Jonathan and is in hiding for three days, he makes no attempt to see Michal (1 Sam. 20).

David picks up two more wives while roaming about (1 Sam. 25:42–43). In the meantime, we learn that Saul has given Michal to another man, Palti (1 Sam. 25:44). After Saul's death, David becomes king over Judah and is offered the opportunity to become king over the northern tribes. Then David demands Michal back (2 Sam. 3:13–16). Her new husband is very upset, but Michal's feelings are not stated.

However, when David brings the ark of the covenant to Jerusalem with much leaping and dancing, Michal despises him (2 Sam. 6:16). After the ceremonies are over, she confronts David with these words: "How the king of Israel honored himself today, uncovering himself today before the eyes of his servants' maids, as any vulgar fellow might shamelessly uncover himself!" (2 Sam. 6:20). David responds curtly: "It was before the LORD, who chose me in place of your father and all his household, to appoint me as prince over Israel, the people of the LORD, that I have danced before the LORD. I will make myself yet more contemptible than this, and I will be abased in my own eyes; but by the maids of whom you have spoken, by them I shall be held in honor" (2 Sam. 6:21–22). The narrator concludes by informing the reader that Michal remained childless (2 Sam. 6:23).

In analyzing Michal's story, Cheryl Exum points out Michal's negative portrayal as a jealous, bitter, and, worse yet, nagging woman. Part of the negative depiction of Michal lies in her contempt for the "servants' maids" ('*amhôt 'abadaw*, literally "the female servants of the male servants"), although precisely who is meant is not clear. What is clear is that Michal comes across as haughty and elitist. Her criticism of David is also made to seem harsh. Michal's anger with David for displaying himself immodestly, however, probably masks deeper issues.

On a political level, the domestic quarrel represents the battle between the houses of Saul and David.[9] On an emotional level, much is implied, but nothing is made explicit. David Clines, in the introduction to a volume devoted to a variety of interpretations of Michal's story, says:

> What lies behind Michal's aversion to his sexual display is harder to determine. Her whole story has been so freighted with sexuality that it comes as little surprise that this issue rises to the surface as her relationship with David comes to a bitter end. But of what frustration, jealousy, disappointment, outrage, desire her outburst is compounded we can only guess. Once again, the story of Michal demands that we tell another story, a more causally integrated story of Michal, but refuses to lend us its sanction. No one motivation can account for the course of this episode.[10]

Michal, symbol of the rivalry between her father and her husband, is a victim of their conflict. She dares to confront male authority. As a result, she is to remain childless, the literary near-equivalent of murder. In spite of her "murder," we can applaud her self-assertion in the face of unfair treatment. Katharine Sakenfeld concludes her treatment of Michal in this way:

> [I]n her actions . . . we see a woman who makes some effort to shape her future. She defies her father, rescues her husband, and eventually defies her husband. She is a woman of emotion, as is seen in her "love" for David and in her biting sarcasm to him as she exits the stage of the story. Yet we learn far less of her story than we might like. . . . I mourn with Palti over Michal's fate.[11]

On a personal level, we may also wonder whether any other options were open to her that might have led to a happier conclusion.

Although most feminist commentators write in prose, Shoshanna Gershenzon offers this poetic salute of Michal, entitled "Michal Bat Shaul" (Michal, Daughter of Saul):

> This was *his* city, taken from
> The Jebusites, and opened to
> Priests and short southern boys, sporting
> Scarves ripped from Philistine corpses.
>
> This was his home, rustling with younger
> Women and their children, who bowed to her and
> Scurried past towards laughter in the inner courtyards.
>
> This was his god, silent now after the leaping and the
> Carnival and the harsh street instruments and the cakes flung
> To the crowd by the kitchen boys; breathing darkness
> In the shut tent in the shut farm wagon.
>
>> She had loved the god that sang in the voices of the *nebiim* [prophets],
>> and blew through their sweet pipes, when they came down from the
>> high places, and her father always the tallest and the best, his arms
>> wide to catch her leaping body; she had loved the hill country and the
>> tall Benjamite warriors; they sang of women taken in battle, but she sat
>> safe on Saul's lap, gripping his chief's fringes.
>
> While his men roared and drank, she sat bathed
> In the great grief that poured from his face, and forgave
> All that he would do to her.
>
> A warrior's daughter. A warrior's prize. An heiress whose
> Patrimony was mumbled by scarred old men. A captive woman
> Of Benjamin dried by the southern sun, the desert always
> Blowing in the corner of her eye. She followed it to heaped stones
> Under the last tamarisk. An odor stung; a hand accepted
> Her coins and offered a rancid cup.[12]

ABIGAIL

If Michal represents the woman who rebels against injustice, Abigail may be characterized as the prudent woman, the "good" wife.[13] Her story is found in 1 Samuel 25:2–42. Abigail is married to Nabal, whose name means fool. She is beautiful and clever, he surly and mean (1 Sam. 25:3). As Nabal is shearing his many sheep out in the wilderness (1 Sam. 25:4), David's men come asking for provisions (1 Sam. 25:5–8). They apparently seek to exchange food for the protection they have provided during sheep shearing (1 Sam. 25:16, 21). Nabal refuses, and David prepares to fight (1 Sam. 25:10–13).

One of Nabal's men tells Abigail (1 Sam. 25:14–17). She prepares extravagant amounts of food and sends it to David. Then she herself follows (1 Sam. 25:18–20). She speaks ingratiatingly to him, dissuading him from violence (1 Sam. 25:23–31). She predicts that God will appoint David prince over Israel (1 Sam. 25:30). She asks that when this happens, he will remember her (1 Sam. 25:31).

When she returns home, she finds Nabal having a feast (1 Sam. 25:36). The next morning after the wine has worn off, she tells him what she has done and he is mortified (1 Sam. 25:37). Ten days later he dies (1 Sam. 25:38). David then marries Abigail (1 Sam. 25:39–42), and they have one son, Chileab (2 Sam. 3:3).

Alice Bach believes that Abigail is more subversive than her "good wife" image suggests.[14] Abigail speaks a great deal in this story, more than her husband and more than David. She constantly speaks of herself in very lowly terms, calling herself maidservant ('amhâ) and handmaid (šiphâ). These terms stand in contrast to the power she wields through her words. She effectively prevents David from attacking her husband and his men, and she links herself with David.

From the narrator's perspective, Abigail's prophecy concerning David's royal future is her most important utterance. She is wise, prudent, and psychologically savvy. Yet the unctuousness with which she ingratiates herself to David does not sit well with the modern reader. Nor are we happy with her spending so much of her energy on limiting men's foolish choices. We would prefer to see her in a more positive role. Nevertheless we must admit that she is more successful than Michal in securing what presumably was a happy life.

Abigail seems better suited to be wife of a king than wife of the foolish Nabal. Ironically, her marriage to David silences her voice literarily and perhaps in reality as well. While married to Nabal, she has a voice and power. As one of David's many wives, she produces one son, Chileab, who is not even a principal son.[15]

BATHSHEBA

Bathsheba's story is told in 2 Samuel 11–12. Walking on his roof, David notices a beautiful woman bathing (2 Sam. 11:2). He inquires who she is and finds out she is Bathsheba, wife of Uriah (2 Sam. 11:3). He sends for her and commits adultery with her. Then she returns home (2 Sam. 11:4).

She conceives and sends word to David (2 Sam. 11:5). Upon hearing this news, David sends for Uriah, who has been in the field with the army. David orders him home (2 Sam. 11:6–8). Uriah does not go home, however, out of solidarity with the troops (2 Sam. 11:9–11). So David tries a second scheme. He has Uriah eat and drink with him to the point of drunkenness, but Uriah still does not go home (2 Sam. 11:12–13).

David's third way of dealing with the problem is to write a letter to his general, Joab, telling him to put Uriah in the front lines. Joab is then to draw back and leave Uriah exposed (2 Sam. 11:14–15). Joab follows orders, Uriah is killed, and Joab sends a message back to David (2 Sam. 11:16–21).

When Bathsheba hears the news of Uriah's death, she makes lamentation. When the mourning time is over, David sends for her and marries her. She bears him a son (2 Sam. 11:26–27), who dies as punishment for David's sin (2 Sam. 12:1–23).

Although Bathsheba is often condemned as a seductress, there is nothing in the text that suggests her complicity in David's crime. Quite the contrary.[16] She appears to be an innocent victim of his lust. He sees her bathing in her own private area. He can see her, because he is standing on the roof of the palace. He finds out who she is and summons her. She has no way of knowing what is in store for her. How she feels about the rape, for that is what it may have been, we are not told.[17] How she feels about her husband's murder, again the narrator does not say. Indeed, Bathsheba does not speak directly until much later. In this part of the story, her only communication is sending word to David that she is pregnant.

Regina Schwartz points out that when the prophet Nathan comes to David with his story about the rich man stealing the poor man's ewe lamb (2 Sam. 12:1–15) which brings about David's repentance, Nathan compares Bathsheba with an animal. Schwartz writes:

> When Nathan the prophet tells David a didactic parable about the rich man taking the poor man's only ewe-lamb, he drives home the point that the king's adultery is a violation of a property right: Bathsheba is compared to an animal, a favored animal, to be sure, one that is like a daughter (alluding to the Hebrew wordplay on Bathsheba's name, *bath* = "daughter"), and the only one the poor man has; but the polluting of his woman is analogous to the slaughter of his animal.[18]

When the child of Bathsheba and David dies, we are not told how Bathsheba feels. Laffey notes that David was punished for his sin as was considered appropriate by Deuteronomistic theology. But few commentators notice that Bathsheba was equally punished—unjustly. From the perspective of the patriarchal producers of the text, however, no injustice was involved, because the wife belonged to her man and thus was expected to partake in his punishment.[19]

She does fare better than Michal and Abigail, in that her son Solomon becomes king, and she becomes queen mother. Nevertheless we do not really get to know Bathsheba. She remains a flat character.

A detail of Joab's message to King David after Uriah has been killed is intriguing. In 2 Samuel 11:19–21, Joab says:

> When you have finished telling the king all the news about the fighting, then, if the king's anger rises, and if he says to you, "Why did you go so near the city to fight? Did you not know that they would shoot from the wall? Who killed Abimelech son of Jerubbaal? Did not a woman throw an upper millstone on him from the wall, so that he died at Thebez? Why did you go so near the wall?" then you shall say, "Your servant Uriah the Hittite is dead too."

The allusion to the death of Abimelech by the hand of a woman (Judg. 9:53–54) requires explanation. Mieke Bal points out that whereas David victimizes Bathsheba, a woman victimizes Abimelech. The positions of the male and female actors are reversed.[20] Joab's allusion has something to do with his suspicion that a woman is involved in the orders he has received to have Uriah killed. It is possible, then, to see Uriah as the victim who is like Abimelech. Bathsheba is the cause of his death. On another level, David is the victim who is in danger because of a woman.[21] In both cases, Bathsheba is seen as the victimizer, even though in reality she is the victim. Bal writes: "It is possible that his anger with David about the bad strategy and the death of an innocent man imposed on him, an anger that, as a subordinate 'servant of the king,' he cannot afford, is directed against the intuitively appropriate scapegoat, woman in general."[22] It is a classic case of blaming the victim.

Bach points out the way each of the three named wives of David represents aspects of the wifely role: "Michal is the dissatisfied daughter/wife of divided loyalties; Abigail is consistently the good sense mother-provider, and Bathsheba, the sexual partner."[23] We are accustomed to the split between the nurturing, mothering wife and the sexy wife-mistress. To this duo is added the angry feminist, not content with subordinate roles.

Adele Berlin notes the ways in which David's three named wives are characterized. She finds three different approaches.[24] Michal is a developed character, Abigail is a type (the good wife), and Bathsheba is only an agent who moves the action along. (Bathsheba the queen mother is a developed character, but that role comes later, in 1 Kgs. 1–2.) Different as the characterizations of these three women are, they are alike in one sense. Indirectly, each throws light on the main character of the story, David. Berlin summarizes:

> The David stories have been woven into a masterful narrative in which all facets of the hero's complex personality are allowed to emerge. This is accomplished by highlighting him at times, and by showing him in the reflection of lesser characters at other times. This shift in focus and in clarity of presentation produces a narrative which has depth, which is credible to the reader, and which never fails to engage his interest.[25]

Even the best-developed female character is a pale shadow in comparison with the "hero" of the story. We would like to know about these women, because we are interested in their stories. Unfortunately the biblical narrators do not share our interest. They have used David's wives as means to characterize him, rather than to tell us something about the women themselves. When information about them is divulged, it is accidental rather than intentional.

TAMAR

Tamar's rape is chronicled in 2 Samuel 13. Tamar's half-brother Amnon lusts after her to the point of making himself ill. He knows he cannot do anything about his lust, since she is a virgin (2 Sam. 13:1–2). However, Amnon's crafty cousin Jonadab devises a plan (2 Sam. 13:3–5). Amnon lies down, pretending to be sick. When his father, King David, comes to visit, Amnon asks that Tamar make some cakes and feed them to him (2 Sam. 13:6). David orders Tamar to do as Amnon has asked (2 Sam. 13:7). She goes and does as commanded (2 Sam. 13:8), but Amnon refuses to eat. Amnon asks that everyone leave except Tamar, who is to come into his chamber and feed him by hand (2 Sam. 13:9–10). When she complies, he asks her instead to lie with him (2 Sam. 13:11). She answers: "No, my brother, do not force me; for such a thing is not done in Israel; do not do anything so vile! As for me, where could I carry my shame? And as for you, you would be as one of the scoundrels in Israel. Now therefore, I beg you, speak to the king; for he will not withhold me from you" (2 Sam. 13:12–13).

Amnon will not listen to Tamar. Instead, he rapes her (2 Sam. 13:14). Then Amnon hates her intensely (2 Sam. 13:15). He sends her out and her last words are, "No, my brother; for this wrong in sending me away is greater than the other that you did to me" (2 Sam. 13:16). Again Amnon will not listen. So he puts her out of his presence (2 Sam. 13:17).

Tamar puts ashes on her head, tears her long robe, and cries out (2 Sam. 13:18–19). Her full brother Absalom tells her not to "take this to heart" (2 Sam. 13:20), perhaps because he plans revenge (2 Sam. 13:23–32). Although King David is angry, he does nothing, because of his love for Amnon, his firstborn (2 Sam. 13:21).

Phyllis Trible analyzes this story in *Texts of Terror*.[26] She reflects on its relationship with another text, one from Proverbs 7:4–5, which is written for young men:

> Say to wisdom, "You are my sister,"
> and call insight your intimate friend,
> that they may keep you from the loose woman,
> from the adulteress with her smooth words.

In Proverbs, wisdom is personified as a woman who is to protect the young man from the dangers of "bad" women. The irony is that in the story of Tamar and Amnon, Tamar's words to Amnon are wise. She counsels him not to do the foolish thing. Just as the young man in Proverbs is counseled to call wisdom his sister, Amnon calls Tamar "my sister." His intimate friend, however, is Jonadab, whose insight is clever, but hardly wise. Amnon does not need protection from a "bad" woman. He needs protection from his own lust, and Tamar needs protection against it.[27] Trible concludes:

> Compassion for Tamar requires a new vision. If sister wisdom can protect a young man from the loose woman, who will protect sister wisdom from the loose man, symbolized not by a foreigner but by her very own brother? Who will preserve sister wisdom from the adventurer, the rapist with his smooth words, lecherous eyes, and grasping hands? In answering the question, Israel is found wanting—and so are we.[28]

Today there is an acute awareness of the high incidence of child abuse, much of it in the form of fathers' sexual abuse of daughters. Other forms, such as brothers raping sisters, are also common. Incest leaves deep scars on its victims. Women are also subjected to sexual abuse by men who are not family members but who are also not strangers. Date rape is so common that college students are receiving instruction about it as part of their orientation to college life. Tamar is not an ancient anomaly. She is all around us. If awareness can lead to change, let us remember Tamar's story and resolve that sexual abuse can and will stop.

THE WISE (?) WOMAN OF TEKOA

In the aftermath of Absalom's murderous vengeance on Amnon, Absalom stays in exile for three years. Then his father is consoled over Amnon's death (2 Sam. 13:37–39). Joab perceives that David is ready to see his son Absalom again. So he sends to Tekoa, where a wise (or shrewd) woman lives, and brings her to Jerusalem, He has her put on mourning garments and instructs her what to say to David (2 Sam. 14:1–3).

Her fabricated story is that she is a widow with two sons, one of whom killed the other. The rest of the family wants to kill the remaining son in revenge, but she protests that this would quench her one remaining ember (2 Sam. 14:4–7). After King David gives orders that will protect her son (2 Sam. 14:8–11), she says:

> "Why then have you planned such a thing against the people of God? For in giving this decision the king convicts himself, inasmuch as the king does not bring his banished one home again. We must all die; we are like

water spilled on the ground, which cannot be gathered up. But God will not take away a life; he will devise plans so as not to keep an outcast banished forever from his presence." (2 Sam. 14:13–14)

After further conversation, David heeds her words and allows Absalom to return to Jerusalem (2 Sam. 14:15–24). Two more years go by before Absalom and David are reunited. That is another story (2 Sam. 14:25–33). Our interest lies in the woman of Tekoa.

The narrator tells us that Joab puts the words in her mouth (2 Sam. 14:3). If all he needs is an actress, however, he doesn't need to find a wise woman. Denise Carmody wonders whether the woman of Tekoa may have had more of an authorial role in the plan than we are told.[29] She also notes that the woman of Tekoa is a champion of mercy, a role that women often play:

Women have inherited such a courageous, debunking, and accusing role as one of their socially sanctioned possibilities. . . . It is instructive for us to ponder what intercessions like that of the woman of Tekoa have accomplished throughout the ages. Again and again, they have been a way for antagonists to put aside ego, drop their demand for bloodlust, and be reconciled. Mothers mediating between fathers and sons, sisters mediating between brothers, teachers and nurses smoothing rough interactions—all have helped keep the world from becoming totally a war zone.[30]

What Carmody says is true up to a point. Nevertheless many feminists are uncomfortable with this perspective, because often women have fulfilled mediating roles and been teachers and nurses because society allowed them no other options.

Alice Laffey points out the patriarchal nature of the story the woman tells. A widow about to lose her only remaining son is in grave risk in that kind of society.[31] She continues by describing this text as an exception within patriarchal culture:

The narrative contains sexual reversals of the story contained in 1 Kgs 3. There it was King Solomon's wisdom which determined the real mother of the living son. Here it is the unnamed woman's wisdom which calls King David to again acknowledge his son Absalom. . . .

The narrator names the woman who secures Absalom's return as wise (v 2) while the woman herself asserts that the king (David) has wisdom "like the wisdom of a messenger of god" (v 20). One should not fail to observe the linguistic comparisons subtly being made here. The woman is like the king, not only in significant aspects of the content of her story, but especially in her possession of wisdom. But if the woman is like the king, she is also like the messenger of God—not only because she serves as a messenger, but especially because of her wisdom. She has a patriarchal script in

a patriarchal culture, but she is in no way portrayed as a victim of patriarchal prejudice. She is a notable exception.[32]

What Laffey seems to overlook is that the woman is merely playing a role
that has been scripted for her by a man. Although she is called wise, there is
a problem. Either her own work is attributed to a man, a real enough possibility, or she is not really wise. This problem brings us to our next interpreter.

Patricia Willey sees the story very differently from other feminist commentators. She calls her the importunate woman of Tekoa, a woman who is
more shrewd than wise. She notes the apparent similarities between this story
and the one in which Nathan indicts David for his adultery with Bathsheba
with a fabricated story. She writes:

> The desire to read the story of the Tekoite woman as an episode running
> parallel to the Nathan story in its intent and outcome has required inter-
> preters to discount textual difficulties, ignore syntactic and structural
> problems, overlook logical fallacies, and rationalize glaring non sequiturs.
> A more critical appraisal reveals that this story is very different from its
> counterpart in chapter 12. In fact, its outcome is almost the direct oppo-
> site of that of the Nathan story, gaining much of its effect from its clever
> parody of the contours of the previous story.[33]

Willey analyzes the Tekoite woman's speech. In contrast with Nathan's very
clear speech, the woman's speech is filled with grammatical and syntactical
problems. In spite of this, David grants Joab's request. Willey believes that
the woman from Tekoa has not convinced David but rather has shrewdly
manipulated him:

> [Her speech] makes certain veiled allusions for the king who has ears to
> hear them. On one level there are her frequent references to sin and guilt,
> coupled with her elaborate praise of the goodness and wisdom of the king,
> which neither he nor we, knowing his story, can swallow without chok-
> ing. These references which juxtapose hints of guilt with declarations of
> elaborate praise put the king in a very awkward psychic position, espe-
> cially since he does not yet know who sent the woman and whether or not
> she is in a position to know the damning details of his private life.[34]

David brings Absalom home, but because he has not really been convinced of the rightness of this action, he does not welcome Absalom. Absalom's return later leads to his bid for the kingdom and his death. Willey asks:

> So where is the wisdom of the wise? In the very most positive sense pos-
> sible, the word hakamah [= ḥakamâ, normally translated "wise"] can refer
> merely to the woman's ability to coerce the king while keeping her own

self safe, perhaps not a small accomplishment considering the mortality rate around the king. But more likely the narrator addresses us ironically, playing a joke on us. By setting up a tale similar to the Nathan tale, the narrator raises our expectations for a similarly luminous outcome, but then fails splendidly to deliver. This importunate woman reads not as a second Nathan, come again to set things straight, but as a parody of his methods, fit for a king doomed to moral confusion.[35]

Was the woman from Tekoa wise or merely shrewd? Was she compassionate or only concerned to protect her own interests? What was her motivation? Although we cannot be certain, Willey's careful reading of the Hebrew gives considerable weight to her view.

THE (TRULY) WISE WOMAN OF ABEL

In 2 Samuel 20, the Benjaminite Sheba has revolted against David, and the northern tribes have joined him (2 Sam. 20:1–2). Joab and Abishai are leading David's forces against the walled city of Abel, where Sheba is staying (2 Sam. 20:14–15). Then a wise woman calls out to Joab that she does not want to see her city destroyed. Joab tells her he is not interested in razing the city, only in stopping Sheba. She tells Joab she will have his head thrown over the wall (2 Sam. 20:16–21). She convinces the people of the town that it is better to give up Sheba than lose the whole town, so they kill him, throw his head over, and Joab returns to Jerusalem (2 Sam. 20:22).

Claudia Camp believes that the stories of the women of Tekoa and Abel provide evidence for a regular role of women, at least during the early part of the monarchy. She notes further that "[a]lthough the increasing political encroachment of the monarchy may have undercut the wider power of the village wise women, it is unlikely, however, to have eliminated their authority among their own people. Rather, the interests of the male court historians became focused more on urban life and male leaders than on life in rural communities."[36]

CONCLUSIONS

It is ironic that this chapter begins with Hannah, whose beautiful prayer praises God for empowering the weak and striking down the mighty. She sings of God's strengthening the king and exalting the anointed one. In the stories that follow, we see the failure of kingly power to break "the bows of the mighty" or help "the feeble gird on strength" (1 Sam. 2:4). Power changes hands, but the women most closely associated with kings Saul and David do not fare well. Weak already because of their gender, for the most part they lose what little power they have.

Rizpah is a pawn in the struggle between Saul's and David's houses for the kingship. Her two sons are brutally murdered. Michal is silenced and left childless. Abigail has one son who plays no major role, and we hear no more about her. Bathsheba is possibly raped, and her first child dies as punishment for David's sin; her son Solomon will become king; we will hear more of her in the role of queen mother in the next chapter of this book. Tamar is raped by her half-brother Amnon; David is irritated, but does nothing. The women of Endor, Tekoa, and Abel fare better. They are apparently independent women, however, who are wise to the ways of the world and of kings.

At the end of the book of Judges, the editor concludes, "In those days there was no king in Israel; all the people did what was right in their own eyes." He is suggesting that the acquisition of a king would solve the problems of wrongdoing. Perhaps we may call it progress that no stories as terrible as those in Judges are found in 1 and 2 Samuel or in the books of Kings. Nevertheless rape and murder continue and the voices of those like Deborah and Jael are no longer heard. The period of the reigns of Saul and David is not the golden age for women.

DISCUSSION QUESTIONS

1. Of all the women in the books of Samuel, with whom do you identify most? Why?
2. Have you had experiences of oppression? If so, have your attempts to find a solution been understood by others, as Hannah's prayer was by Eli?
3. What do you think about psychic phenomenon? Can the spirits of the dead be brought back by mediums?
4. Could Michal have found a more effective way to let David know that her feelings mattered? Would anything she said or anything she did result in the same silencing?
5. Did Abigail really need to be so oily in her praise of David to achieve her ends?
6. Was Abigail the "good wife" in terms of her relationship with Nabal? Why or why not?
7. How do you think Bathsheba felt when she discovered why she had been called to the palace? How do you think she felt about having her husband murdered and then becoming David's wife?
8. What do you think of the woman from Tekoa?
9. What modern-day women are like the wise woman of Abel?

7

The Women in 1 and 2 Kings

In the books of Kings we meet Abishag, old King David's "attendant."
Bathsheba plays a continuing role as queen mother during Solomon's reign.
Solomon follows in his father's footsteps in his weakness for women,
although very little is known about his wives and concubines. We learn of
Solomon's wisdom in discerning which of the two harlots who have come to
him is the true mother of a child. We also read about the meeting between
Solomon and the queen of Sheba. We find the stories of Queen Jezebel and
Queen Athaliah. We meet the two cannibal mothers whose dilemma shocks
King Jehoram of Israel.

In addition to these stories of women related to royalty, stories of several
women associated with Elijah and Elisha are told: the widow of Zarephath,
whom Elijah befriends; a woman whom Elisha helps; the Shunammite woman
who befriends Elisha; and finally, the prophetess Huldah.

ABISHAG

When David is very old, he cannot get warm, so a young, beautiful girl is
sought to be his attendant and to lie with him (1 Kgs. 1:1–2). Abishag the
Shunammite is found and brought to King David. She becomes his attendant but does not have sexual relations with him (1 Kgs. 1:3–4). We may
think this strange, but Gandhi did the same thing.

When David dies, Solomon becomes king. Adonijah (David's son by
Haggith) asks Bathsheba to get permission from Solomon for him to marry
Abishag (1 Kgs. 2:13–17). Bathsheba agrees, but Solomon sees the request as

tantamount to a coup d'état and refuses (1 Kgs. 2:18–23). He also decides to have Adonijah killed (1 Kgs. 2:24–25).

This story is reminiscent of Ishbaal's complaint against Abner for taking up with Saul's concubine Rizpah (2 Sam. 3:7–11). It was not explicit in that story that the concern was about power grabbing. Here the issue is more explicit. Solomon has reason to be concerned about Adonijah (cf. 1 Kgs. 1:5–10; see also below). Adonijah's request certainly provides a pretext to have a possible throne claimant removed. As usual, Abishag's feelings are not an issue. We do not know what becomes of her after this episode. We hear of her no more.

BATHSHEBA, THE QUEEN MOTHER

Before David's death, Adonijah attempts to have himself crowned as king (1 Kgs. 1:5–10). The prophet Nathan hears about it and goes to Bathsheba with the news. He advises her to tell David; then Nathan will confirm her report (1 Kgs. 1:11–14). They follow the plan (1 Kgs. 1:15–27). David immediately acts to ensure that Solomon becomes king (1 Kgs. 1:28–49).

The second incident involving Bathsheba has been discussed above in relation to Abishag. What is surprising about this incident is Bathsheba's willingness to ask Solomon for a favor for Adonijah, who had very nearly wrested the kingship from Solomon.

Adele Berlin explores the question of why Bathsheba agrees to make Adonijah's request of Solomon. She suggests that Bathsheba is naive but quickly dismisses this possibility as inconsistent with the experienced Bathsheba. Berlin's alternative explanation is that Bathsheba is really hateful. She wants to get Adonijah out of the way. She knows that Solomon will react negatively to the request. Thus she sets up the situation in which he will be killed.[1]

Berlin also speculates that Bathsheba may be a little jealous of Abishag and not want Solomon to have her. Having Abishag in the middle of a troublesome situation could be helpful to Bathsheba. Berlin concludes: "Bathsheba's part in the story ends here, but, no matter what motivated her, it is clear that she is a full-fledged character, important to the plot but with feelings and reactions developed beyond the needs of the plot. There is a different literary use of Bathsheba here from the one in 2 Samuel 11; there she was an agent, here she is a character."[2] Perhaps Bathsheba was putting Adonijah under obligation to her, playing a game of power politics. In any case, these episodes involving Bathsheba as queen mother show that she was thought to have a lot of influence with both King David and King Solomon. Her influence with David was perhaps personal. She was not his first wife or the mother of his first child. She was, however, apparently his favorite, since her son was his choice for successor. Whether her influence with Solomon was personal or institutional is harder to say, although Solomon certainly owed much to her for her role in his becoming king. Bathsheba's story begins sadly, possibly with rape, and with a murdered husband. She apparently makes the best of what begins very badly. She more than survives; she thrives.

THE WIVES AND CONCUBINES OF SOLOMON

In 1 Kings 3:1 we learn of Solomon's marriage alliance with Pharaoh, the king of Egypt, and his marriage to Pharaoh's daughter. The marriage is reported, with nothing unusual noted in the arrangement. As Renita Weems points out, modern racial prejudice is unknown in the Bible.[3] The marriage was more likely to have raised Solomon's social status than to have lowered it.[4]

Unfortunately, from the perspective of the narrative, King Solomon has his father's weakness for women. First Kings 11:1–3 reports that Solomon loved many foreign women. These include seven hundred princesses and three hundred concubines. In his later years, they reportedly turn his heart to the worship of Astarte, Milcom, Chemosh, and Molech. Beyond this, we know nothing of these women.

TWO UNNAMED HARLOTS

In 1 Kings 3:16–28 we find the famous, possibly fictional, very strange story of two harlots that sounds like an urban legend. Each has recently had a baby, but one has lost her child. She accidentally lay on it while sleeping, and the child died. Each harlot claims that the living infant is hers (1 Kgs. 3:16–18). The women seek King Solomon's assistance. Each presents her side of the story (1 Kgs. 3:19–22). Solomon suggests that the living child be divided in half and that each mother receive half. The mother of the living baby protests, preferring to see her child live with another mother than die. The mother of the dead infant is ready to accept the decision (1 Kgs. 3:23–26). Solomon then orders the child to be given to its mother, and he is praised for his wisdom (1 Kgs. 3:27–28).

The woman who is ready to let Solomon kill the baby rather than give it up is a very strange character. At first she fights for the baby; then when it appears that will be denied her, she becomes vindictive, not wanting the true mother to have the child if she can't have the baby herself. Is her crazed behavior a result of postpartum depression combined with grief over the loss of her own baby? Solomon's wisdom discerns the true mother, but for the modern reader this wisdom is overshadowed by the psychological condition of the bereft mother, if indeed the story can be believed.

Esther Fuchs reads the story ideologically:

> The motif of motherhood in the biblical narrative seems to be closely associated with the motif of female rivalry. The mother-harlot who steals her roommate's son away and encourages the king to kill him acts on the same motivation that drove Sarah to drive out Hagar and her son Ishmael (Gen 21:9–10). . . . By perpetuating the theme of woman's mutual rivalry, especially in a reproductive context, the narrative implies that sisterhood is a precarious alternative to the patriarchal system.[5]

But the two women who apparently live together and perhaps shared babysitting responsibilities are very much part of the patriarchal system. Their banding together is not an alternative to patriarchy, but a subset of it.

Claudia Camp sees the story in the light of Solomon's renowned wisdom. She writes:

> In Proverbs, the task of the sage is to discern one female figure—Woman Wisdom, who brings social order—from another who is portrayed in often similar terms, Woman Stranger or Folly, the promiscuous purveyor of social chaos. Significantly, these "women" are known by their speech: Wisdom's "mouth will utter truth" (Prov. 8:7), while the seductive Stranger's lips "drip honey and her speech is smoother than oil" (Prov. 5:3). Female sexuality that exists outside of male control functions as a metaphor for deceitful speech, and the character of the "harlot" thus poses the ultimate test of kingly wisdom. Solomon demonstrates his ability to bring social order by dividing from the chaos of female sexuality before him the "true speech" of the mother, the woman whose sexuality is controlled and thus acceptable.[6]

Camp is correct in seeing this story as functioning to highlight Solomon's wisdom. However, it is hard to understand how the sexuality of one of the harlots is controlled and therefore acceptable. They are both harlots and both mothers. Solomon's wisdom is in discerning which of the two women is telling the truth. The story does use the stereotype of bickering women to showcase Solomon's wisdom, and thus leaves modern readers with the same kind of discomfort we feel when someone tells a racially insensitive joke.

THE QUEEN OF SHEBA

Like Cleopatra, the Queen of Sheba is a spectacularly colorful woman. Her story is found in 1 Kings 10:1–13. She is very rich and comes from a distant country to see Solomon and test him with hard questions or riddles to see whether the reports she has heard of his wealth and wisdom are really true

(1 Kgs. 10:1–5). She learns that the reality surpasses the reports and gives Solomon many precious gifts (1 Kgs. 10:6–10). Solomon in turn gives to her "every desire that she expressed, as well as what he gave her out of Solomon's royal bounty" (1 Kgs. 10:13). Her story is included in the Bible to impress upon the readers how rich and wise Solomon is. If a great and very rich queen would travel many miles to meet Solomon, then Solomon is surely an impressive man.

Camp sees the Queen of Sheba as "Woman Wisdom," who comes to test Solomon's wisdom. He passes the test. However, Camp believes that

> this tale of verbal sparring only partly conceals an erotic subtext. The contest between Solomon and the queen is framed as a language game: a riddle match that Solomon wins, as he had solved the prostitutes' dilemma, by discerning the truth in the midst of trickery. While the narrative speaks of Solomon's victory of wits, however, later tradition will elaborate on its unspoken possibility of sexual relationship between the wise king and the foreign queen. In the foreground is the power of wisdom; in the background, a seductive strangeness that can be suppressed but not eliminated.[7]

We are fascinated with this rich queen who travels freely and interacts with Solomon as an equal. The most intriguing and difficult question about her is the location of her homeland. Where is Sheba? The Ethiopians and the Muslims claim her, both with some evidence to support their claims.

Most biblical scholars incline toward South Arabia on linguistic grounds, but African American New Testament scholar Cain Felder argues that the evidence is not conclusive. He believes that racial bias has tipped the balance toward South Arabia.[8] In favor of African provenance is the witness of the ancient historian Josephus, who calls the Queen of Sheba "the queen of Egypt and Ethiopia."[9]

South Arabia and Ethiopia were separated by only a narrow body of water. The South Arabians and the Ethiopians interacted culturally on a regular basis. Ethnically they were closely related.[10] We think of Africans and Arabs as very different, but they can be overlapping identities. If the Queen of Sheba was indeed a historical person and not just a legend, whether African or South Arabian, she was probably what we today would call black.[11]

JEZEBEL

Jezebel is the best-known Israelite queen. We don't know much about most Israelite queens—for example, how many others were foreign—but Jezebel stands out both because of the strength of her personality and her unwillingness to subordinate her religious traditions to those of her husband. She lived in a time of religious ferment that culminated in the victory of those who believed in strict Yahwistic monotheism. They are the ones who tell her story, not surprisingly with little sympathy for her convictions.

With Jezebel we hit the nadir of biblical women, at least from the perspective of the biblical narrator. We also confront the biblical character who vies with Eve for the position of most negative biblical female. To this day the epithet "Jezebel" is applied to women who are thought to wear too much makeup or jewelry, or sexually provocative clothing. Tina Pippin took an informal survey of college students, artists, and church members in her Southern context and generated the following list of phrases descriptive of Jezebel:

> everything negative; wicked; scheming; whore; cheap harlot; either promiscuous or a complete whore; female form of gigolo; the name has seductive connotations; biblical queen; wife of Ahab; gave her husband bad advice; evil and treacherous; two-faced; one who seduces men and leads them to destruction; a woman who gets around; not ashamed; bimbo; I didn't know what it meant until my roommate called me this; someone who is wild, free, and comfortable with her sexuality; uninhibited, some might say slutty; a beautiful name; a Southern belle with a mind and will and sex drive who is damned for not fitting the stereotype of a helpless, frigid woman; Scarlett O'Hara; Bette Davis in the red hoop dress in the 1938 film; condescending term used for African American women in the time of slavery; Gene loves Jezebel; you're a jezebel, a flirty girl, light, flighty, aloof or dirty slut; free spirit, happy, cute, very feminine; always a lady (but not always nice); slinky, powerful; ambitious; calculating; ruthless, eaten by dogs; taking pleasure from material things; self-centered; decorated woman; painted face; Cosmo clothes; sensual; she has been given a 'bad rep' by many scholars and people; she is famous for her badness; vamp, vampire, temptress, femme fatale, siren, witch—a woman who takes or ruins the life of another.[12]

Jezebel's story is told in 1 Kings 16:31; 18:13; 19:1–2; 21; and in 2 Kings 9:30–37. Except for 1 Kings 21, the story of Naboth's vineyard, and Jezebel's death description in 2 Kings 9:30–37, only a few verses are devoted to her. Yet these verses, especially combined with the tale of Naboth's vineyard, suggest a very terrible person.

The first mention of Jezebel is in 1 Kings 16:31, where we are told that King Ahab has married Jezebel, daughter of King Ethbaal of the Sidonians. As a result of this marriage, Ahab begins to worship Baal. In 1 Kings 18:13, Obadiah alludes to Jezebel's killing the prophets of the Lord.

Next is the famous contest between the God of Israel and Baal and Asherah. Baal and Asherah are silent, but the Lord sends fire to consume the sacrifice. Then Elijah kills all 850 of the pagan priests (1 Kgs. 18). When Jezebel hears about this, she vows to make Elijah's life like theirs (1 Kgs. 19:1–2).

Up to this point, Jezebel is portrayed as a strong woman. She is locked in a very serious battle with Elijah over whose religion will prevail. Mutual tolerance is not a possibility for either of them. Both are committed to a battle to the death. Although we may retrospectively prefer Elijah's God to Jezebel's, Elijah and Jezebel use the same means to accomplish their identical ends. Both are intent on wiping out the other's religion. Their lack of tolerance puts them both at odds with modern Western values.

The next episode of which Jezebel is a prominent actor is different. The story of Naboth's vineyard in 1 Kings 21 involves murder for land. Ahab wants Naboth's vineyard, but Naboth will not sell, because the land is part of his ancestral inheritance (1 Kgs. 21:1–3).

Ahab pouts (1 Kgs. 21:4), and when Jezebel asks him why (1 Kgs. 21:5), he tells her (1 Kgs. 21:6). Taking matters into her own hands (1 Kgs. 21:7), she writes letters in Ahab's name and sends them to the elders and nobles (1 Kgs. 21:8). She tells them to proclaim a fast and seat Naboth at the head of the assembly between two scoundrels. They are to accuse him of cursing God and then stone him to death, based on this fabricated charge (1 Kgs. 21:9–10).

The nobles and elders follow her orders (1 Kgs. 21:11–13) and report back to her (1 Kgs. 21:14). Then Jezebel tells Ahab to take the vineyard, because Naboth is now dead (1 Kgs. 21:15). Ahab does as she tells him (1 Kgs. 21:16).

Although this story is not pretty, it is no worse than what David does to Uriah when Bathsheba becomes pregnant, or for that matter what Jael does to Sisera (especially from a Canaanite perspective). Jezebel is not a model of morality, but she does not deserve to be the symbol of evil that she has become. Of the most disturbing aspect of Jezebel's story to modern readers, Camp writes: "Her brutal response to Naboth's refusal to sell his vineyard may be understood from her point of view as an appropriate royal response to insubordination, in contrast to Ahab's unconscionable weakness as a leader."[13]

Alternately, Judith McKinlay wonders whether Jezebel has been framed:

> Reading the penned role of Jezebel in the Naboth tale, and drawing on the analyses of postcolonial criticism, has led me to ask sharp questions. . . of the very 'itinerary of silencing'. For while in the text Jezebel does indeed speak, the words put in her mouth may well have been part of the mechanics of silencing an historical Jezebel. . . . as the ventriloquist's dummy, she now mouths a part by which, as Phoenician, she will be remembered by generations of biblical readers as the evil foreign murdering queen, not only involved in the theft of Israelite land, but finally responsible for the downfall of her Israelite husband's dynasty. If this is so, then I am reading the deliberate polemic of a religio-political movement within Israel or Judah or Yehud.[14]

The final story involving Jezebel is the notice of her gruesome death in 2 Kings 9:30–37. After Ahab's death and the death of Ahab and Jezebel's son, King Ahaziah, who had fallen through a window (2 Kgs. 1:2), Ahaziah's brother Jehoram (or Joram) becomes king of Israel. Jehu is anointed king of Israel by the prophet Elisha while Jehoram is still on the throne. Jehu kills King Jehoram (as well as King Ahaziah of Judah, not to be confused with Ahaziah, the former king of Israel) and then comes to see Jezebel. Expecting Jehu's visit, she paints her eyes, adorns her head, and looks out of her window (2 Kgs. 9:30). When she sees Jehu, she cries out, "Is it peace, Zimri, murderer of your master?" The question is rhetorical. She knows that Jehu has just been responsible for the death of her son.

By calling Jehu "Zimri," she recalls Zimri's murder of King Elah and usurpation of the throne. More important, she recalls Zimri's reign, which lasted only seven days (1 Kgs. 16:8–16). In so doing, she pronounces Jehu a usurper and predicts that his reign will be short. She is mostly wrong. Jehu is a descendant of David, though not a descendant of Ahab, and his reign lasts for twenty-eight years. Nevertheless she goes down fighting. Camp reflects that Jezebel shows remarkable strength, pride, and defiance, putting on her best clothes to meet her death, traits that modern readers would not question if the actor were a man.[15] Next, Jehu asks who is on his side. A few eunuchs look out of the window (2 Kgs. 9:32). He orders them to throw Jezebel down, and they proceed to follow his orders. Her blood spatters on the wall and on the horses who trample her (2 Kgs. 9:33). Eleanor Ferris Beach, in a scholarly based, but fictive retelling of Jezebel's story based on the common ancient Near Eastern image of the woman at the window, suggests that the biblical report of Jezebel's death is false.[16]

In the biblical story, after eating and drinking, Jehu orders that Jezebel be buried because she is a king's daughter. However, there is nothing left of her but skull and palms and feet (2 Kgs. 9:34–35). Upon hearing this, Jehu says: "This is the word of the LORD, which he spoke by his servant Elijah the Tishbite, 'In the territory of Jezreel the dogs shall eat the flesh of Jezebel [cf. 1 Kgs. 21:34]; the corpse of Jezebel shall be like dung on the field in the territory of Jezreel, so that no one can say, This is Jezebel'" (2 Kgs. 9:36–37).

Denise Carmody writes:

Jezebel finally came to a bad end, her flesh eaten by dogs. . . . In the sight of the biblical authors, her death was simple justice, as it was simple justice for priests of the false foreign gods to be slain. How much in these stories is genuine history and how much parable is hard to say. Jezebel died, though, as she had lived, a robust hater, and the biblical authors especially stigmatized her because she was a foreigner and a woman. Under both headings, they saw her a seducer. By the time the Deuteronomistic history entered the biblical canon Israel was trying to reconstitute its national life after return from exile. Foreign elements seemed to threaten its historic relationship with God, so the reformers Ezra and Nehemiah proscribed marriage with foreigners. Jezebel, like the foreign wives of Solomon, made useful propaganda. Representing femininity turning all its wiles against God and luring Ahab (her obvious inferior in intelligence and will) to his doom, Jezebel encapsulated in one word the worst scenario the reformers could envision. Thus, she greatly helped their cause.[17]

Jezebel is popularly thought of as a whore, but nothing in her story suggests that this was her sin. In 2 Kings 9:22, Jehu asks the sitting king of Israel, Jehoram, before he kills him, "What peace can there be, so long as the many whoredoms and sorceries of your mother Jezebel continue?" He is speaking metaphorically rather than literally, however. Nevertheless, this question, combined with the makeup Jezebel puts on before her death, has won for her a symbolism that continues to this day to wield a powerful negative influence on women.

ATHALIAH

In 2 Kings 11 is the story of the only woman who reigned as queen in her own right in Israel. She is the daughter of Jezebel and Ahab according to 2 Kings 8:18, but according to 2 Kings 8:26, Omri, Ahab's father, is Athaliah's father, although translations often call her his granddaughter. She marries King Joram (or Jehoram) of Judah, not to be confused with her brother of the same name who reigned in Israel. After the death of her son Ahaziah, the king of Judah (again not to be confused with her brother of the same name who once ruled Israel), at the hand of Jehu, Athaliah sets about killing the entire royal family (2 Kgs. 11:1). One young prince, Joash, is saved (2 Kgs. 11:2). He is hidden for six years while Athaliah is queen (2 Kgs. 11:3). In the seventh year of her reign, the priest Jehoiada has Joash crowned king (2 Kgs. 11:4–12). Athaliah is killed (2 Kgs. 11:13–16). That is all that is known about her.

Athaliah worships Canaanite gods, as did her mother, Jezebel, and as did many in Israel and Judah, alongside the Hebrew God, according to recent scholarship. After Athaliah's death, the priest Jehoiada makes a covenant with the people to worship the Lord. They tear down the temple of Baal and kill the priest. The people rejoice and the city is quiet (2 Kgs. 11:17–20).

Although the biblical narrators lead the reader to see Athaliah as an evil usurper, Claudia Camp views Athaliah in a more sympathetic light:

Although Athaliah's ruthlessness is shocking, her political position must be considered. Her power and position derived from two sources, her royal family in Israel and her status as queen mother in Judah. With the death of Jezebel and the rest of her blood kin, as well as that of her ruling son, she was suddenly cut off not only from her power bases but also from any means of retreat or escape. Like her mother, she responded with power rather than surrender. The complexity of the political situation is worth noting. On the one hand, Athaliah considered herself greatly threatened; on the other, she could not have then ruled for six years without support. Backing for the new female ruler would have come from the Jerusalem-based politicians who had promoted the Judean-Israelite alliance symbolized by Athaliah's marriage to Jehoram. The threat probably came from the so-called "people of the land." These were Judean nationalists, opposed to the alliance with the North. They are also adherents of exclusive Yahweh worship, appalled at Athaliah's religious practices, and thus later at Jehoiada's disposal.[18]

THE TWO CANNIBAL MOTHERS

Backtracking chronologically, in 2 Kings 6:26–31, during the siege of Samaria, the capital of Israel, by the Arameans, a woman approaches King Jehoram of Israel with a story that is reminiscent of the story the two prostitutes presented to Solomon, another urban legend. Two women had made an agreement. First they would kill and eat one woman's son, and the next day they would kill and eat the other. The first woman's son had been killed and eaten, but the second woman had hidden her son. The first woman asked the king's assistance. The king tore his clothes, revealing sackcloth beneath. Laying the guilt on Elisha because of a previous act of mercy that Jehoram believed was responsible for Samaria's predicament, the king then declared, "So may God do to me, and more, if the head of Elisha son of Shaphat stays on his shoulders today." Commenting on this sad tale and comparing it with the story of the two prostitutes, Camp writes: [I]n spite of the magnitude of her loss, we feel nothing but horror. Eat her child so she could survive! How could she! Our expectations of self-sacrificing motherhood, which so win us to the real mother in Solomon's case, turn us against the cannibal mother here."[19]

Another response to this story comes from Laurel Lanner, who empathizes with the cannibal mother who has been brought low by circumstances. She writes of a woman in her own New Zealand context who in 1997 killed her own baby. Although this woman did not eat her child, Lanner sees a parallel between the women. Lanner asks:

What can be done with a text like 2 Kgs 6:24–7.20? . . . Can we dismiss the influence of the story of the cannibal mother upon the judgment of the mother in Aotaeroa/New Zealand, even separated so radically by time, space and culture? I think not. Obviously, the Bible, and how it has been read, is embedded in many of our cultures. I suggest that this short episode cannot be passed over as an obscure and abject textual moment without consequence. While it may not be as well known as the story of Eve and Adam, the mother's story has no less potential power to influence and adds another negative image in the cumulative picture of women in the Bible.[20]

There have been quite a few stories of mothers killing their young children in the United States in the last few years, no doubt reflecting the stress and hardship of the role. Without more evidence, it seems unlikely that these women or the one in New Zealand were influenced by an obscure biblical story. However, these modern stories do have something in common with the ancient one. Under extreme duress, even mothers can be driven to kill their children. The perennial fascination with such horror stories suggests not so much a simple negative image of women as a deep concern that fundamental traditional feminine values such as women's nurturing roles may be at risk.

THE WIDOW OF ZAREPHATH

We turn now to three stories of a different kind, in which Elijah and Elisha interact with women. In 1 Kings 17:8–24, we meet the poor widow of Zarephath who feeds Elijah. He in turn performs miracles on her behalf. God tells Elijah to go to Zarephath to live, because he has asked a certain widow there to feed Elijah (1 Kgs. 17:8–9). Elijah does as told and finds a woman gathering sticks at the city gates. He asks her for water, but before she has a chance to get it, he asks her for something to eat (1 Kgs. 17:10–11). She tells him that all she has is enough meal and oil to make one last meal for her son and her before they die. She is gathering sticks for the fire, even as they speak (1 Kgs. 17:12).

Elijah asks her to make him a little cake first and then make one for her son and herself. Then he tells her that her jar of meal and flask of oil will not run out until God sends more rain (1 Kgs. 17:13–14). She does as he asks her. The jar and the flask remain full for many days (1 Kgs. 17:15–16).

Then her son becomes so ill that he isn't breathing. She remonstrates with Elijah, saying, "What have you against me, O man of God? You have come to me to bring my sin to remembrance, and to cause the death of my son!" (1 Kgs. 17:17–18). Elijah takes the boy to the upper chamber. He lays him on his bed and prays to God. He stretches himself out over the child three times and prays some more (1 Kgs. 17:19–21). God hears Elijah's prayer and revives the child (1 Kgs. 17:22). Then Elijah takes him downstairs and presents him to his mother, who exclaims, "Now I know that you are a man of God, and that the word of the LORD in your mouth is truth" (1 Kgs. 17:23–24).

This last exclamation is the reason the story is included in the Bible. We are interested, however, in the story in part because of what it may tell us about widows. Paula Hiebert analyzes the economic situation of biblical widows.[21] She notes that widows are often classed with orphans and sojourners as the most vulnerable members of Israelite society. Widows are defined differently in Hebrew society from the way they are defined in modern Western society, however. According to Hiebert, a biblical widow is a woman whose husband is dead and who has no living sons to support her.[22] Although the widow of Zarephath has a son, he is too young to support her, so she still fits the definition.

According to the story, a drought is making life difficult for the widow of Zarephath and her son. As a result, she believes they are about to eat their last meal and then die of starvation. Presumably their situation is worse than that of their fellow Israelites, who also must experience the effects of the drought. They can weather it better, however, because of more resources and larger reserves.

Jopie Siebert-Hommes points out that the widow in this story and Jezebel are both Sidonians. However, the two figures are presented in stark contrast with each other. The widow of Zarephath feeds Elijah, but Jezebel takes care of the prophets of Baal and Asherah and annihilates the prophets of the Lord. The widow pronounces that Elijah is a man of God, while Jezebel says no such thing and tries to kill him. The widow's son falls ill, and Elijah performs a miracle in an upper room to raise him from the dead. In contrast, Jezebel's son Ahaziah reportedly falls from an upper room to his death, and Elijah does not intervene. Rather he announces that Ahaziah will die.[23]

AN UNNAMED WIDOW

Another widow gets Elisha's help (2 Kgs. 4:1–7). This woman is desperate because her creditors are about to take her two children as slaves (2 Kgs. 4:1). Elisha performs a miracle similar to Elijah's miracle for the widow of Zarephath. He asks her what she has in the house. She answers that she has only a jar of oil. He tells her to get as many jars as she can from neighbors and pour oil into them (2 Kgs. 4:2–4). The oil keeps flowing, until she runs out of jars (2 Kgs. 4:5–6). Elisha then tells her to sell the oil to pay her debts, and live on what is left over (2 Kgs. 4:7). Again, the historicity of the story is questionable. The picture it paints, however, of a poor widow desperate over the possible loss of her children to slavery is quite plausible.

Johanna van Wijk-Bos suggests that this woman may have been a disciple of Elisha's. Instead of the usual translation of "wife of a member of the company of prophets" (NRSV) or the like, she translates, "a certain woman *from the women among the prophet's disciples.*"[24] The Hebrew reads literally "a woman (or wife) from the women (or wives) of the sons of the prophets" (*we'iššâ 'ahat minnešê benê hannebî'îm*). If the meaning was a wife of a member, we might rather expect to find "a woman (or wife) of a son of the prophets" or "a woman (or wife) of a man of the sons of the prophets." Van Wijk-Bos writes, "Since female prophets are mentioned four times in the Hebrew Bible, the disciples of Elisha may well have included women."[25]

In reflecting on the story, van Wijk-Bos speaks of the woman's need to name her pain and express it. She suggests that modern feminists also need to give voice and name to their pain as a first step in changing it. As long as they rationalize that things are not so bad, that they themselves are better off than others or that crying out is "negative," nothing constructive can happen.[26]

Van Wijk-Bos also notes that the Hebrew verb *ṣʿq* is more than a cry of pain. It implies a protest and a reproach; it is a cry of distress under oppression. It implies Elisha's responsibility toward her. What man of God will let one of his disciples (or disciples' wives) starve?[27]

Elisha's response is positive. He listens. Listening to cries of pain and protest is not easy. We have heard it before. We don't like to feel guilty again. But Elisha listens. Then he asks a question: "What shall I do for you?" He does not assume that he knows how to help. Next, he asks the widow what resources she has. Although she has only a jar of oil, that is the place where he starts. Change must begin where she is, with what little she has. Elisha is a prophet, not an administrator, a power broker, or a king. Those types are not likely to listen and discover a way to help. Elisha listens, asks questions, and uses the resources the woman has on hand to help her out of her predicament.[28] He is like Hawkeye Pierce, the archetypal sensitive male character in the 1970s and 1980s television series *M*A*S*H*, portrayed by Alan Alda.

THE SHUNAMMITE WOMAN

In 2 Kings 4:8–37, we find the rather strange story of a wealthy married woman in the town of Shunem. She feeds and houses Elisha. This story has certain elements in common with the story of the widow of Zarephath and Elijah. One day when Elisha is passing through Shunem, the Shunammite woman urges him to have a meal. After that, whenever Elisha is in town, he stops by (2 Kgs. 4:8). The woman suggests to her husband that they build a guest room for him (2 Kgs. 4:9–10).

The next time Elisha comes, he goes up to his room and lies down. He calls his servant Gehazi and tells him to summon the Shunammite woman. He wants to do something for her. She comes but resists the idea of having a word spoken on her behalf to the king or the commander of the army. Gehazi suggests that she and her husband are old and have no son. So Elisha tells her that she will bear a son (2 Kgs. 4:11–16). The prophecy is fulfilled.

Years later when the child is out reaping with his father, he complains of a headache. His father sends him in to his mother, who nurses him until noon, when he dies (2 Kgs. 4:17–20). She then asks her husband to send a servant and one of the donkeys so she can go to Elisha. He says, however, that she should wait until the new moon or the Sabbath. Instead, she saddles the donkey herself and sets out (2 Kgs. 4:21–25).

When Elisha sees her coming, he sends Gehazi to meet her. Gehazi asks how she and her family fare, and she tells him they are fine. When she reaches Elisha, however, she pours out the news (2 Kgs. 4:25–28). Elisha sends Gehazi with his staff to put on the child's face. The Shunammite woman will not leave unless Elisha comes with her, so he does (2 Kgs. 4:29–30).

Gehazi arrives first, puts the staff on the child's face, but nothing happens. When Elisha arrives, he enters the room, closes the door, and prays to God. He lies on the child, mouth upon mouth, eyes upon eyes, hands upon hands, and the child begins to get warm (2 Kgs. 4:31–34). Elisha gets up and walks about. The child sneezes seven times and opens his eyes (2 Kgs. 4:35). Elisha summons Gehazi and tells him to call the Shunammite woman. When she comes, he gives her back her son, and she bows low to the ground (2 Kgs. 4:36–37).

The Shunammite woman is a strong character, her husband a weak one. We are nevertheless surprised at his lack of concern for his boy's health. Elisha deals with the Shunammite woman primarily through his servant Gehazi. Whether this is simply easier or whether Elisha prefers maintaining distance from her, we cannot say.

When she is in distress, however, she does not want to deal with Gehazi but prefers to deal directly with Elisha. She doesn't believe that Gehazi will cure her son, even with Elisha's staff, and she is right. She is persistent. As a result of that persistence, she gets what she wants.

Fokkelien van Dijk Hemmes interprets this story using two different hermeneutic approaches; one that highlights the androcentric aspects of a story and one that is more optimistic and liberating. In the former approach, she notes that the Shunammite woman must become a mother, even though she has not stated any wish to be one; once she has a son and he becomes ill, she gratefully receives him back again once restored to life. On the other hand, it is through the initiative and persistence of the Shunammite woman that Elisha proves himself to be a man of God.[29] Van Dijk-Hemmes suggests that this woman deserves a name and calls her Gedolah, the great one, which is what the Hebrew text calls her (2 Kgs. 4:8).[30]

Mary Shields suggests that in some ways the independence, competence, and initiative of the Shunammite woman subverts Elisha's power, who mainly responds to her initiatives. On the other hand, the story still has a patriarchal feel. The woman is not named. In the end Elisha heals her child, and she bows low before him.[31]

HULDAH

The last important woman in the books of Kings is the prophetess Huldah. Her brief literary life is recorded in 2 Kings 22:14–20. During King Josiah's reign, the high priest Hilkiah finds the great book of the law, probably the core of the book of Deuteronomy (2 Kgs. 22:8). Hilkiah, Shaphan the secretary, and others consult with Huldah over the discovery. She is described as the wife of Shallum son of Tikvah, son of Harhas, keeper of the wardrobe. She lives in Jerusalem in the Second Quarter (2 Kgs. 22:14). When she examines the book, Huldah declares:

> "Thus says the LORD, the God of Israel: Tell the man who sent you to me, Thus says the LORD, I will indeed bring disaster on this place and on its inhabitants—all the words of the book that the king of Judah has read. Because they have abandoned me and have made offerings to other gods, so that they have provoked me to anger with all the work of their hands, therefore my wrath will be kindled against this place, and it will not be quenched. But as to the king of Judah, who sent you to inquire of the LORD, thus shall you say to him, Thus says the LORD, the God of Israel: Regarding the words that you have heard, because your heart was penitent, and you humbled yourself before the LORD, when you heard how I spoke against this place, and against its inhabitants, that they should become a desolation and a curse, and because you have torn your clothes and wept before me, I also have heard you, says the LORD. Therefore, I will gather you to your ancestors, and you shall be gathered to your grave in peace; your eyes shall not see all the disaster that I will bring on this place." (2 Kgs. 22:15–20)

Why Huldah was chosen to validate the book of the law, rather than Jeremiah, who may have been active at this time, is not clear. Some scholars do not believe that Jeremiah had received his call during Josiah's reign. It is also possible that Jeremiah was active, but either not well known yet or not popular. Diana Edelman suggests that perhaps Huldah was a prophet of

Asherah rather than the Lord. Josiah might have feared that inquiring through a Yahwistic prophet like Jeremiah might have further upset the Lord, whose law—if it turned out to be genuine—the people would have been violating. Later the Deuteronomistic editors might have painted her in more appropriate colors for their narrative.[32] The discovery of the book of the law was very important. Josiah's famous reform was based on it. It is intriguing to wonder whether Huldah may have prophesied much more than this one instance and whether many of her words have been lost to us. We wish that a book of Huldah had survived.

CONCLUSIONS

The books of Kings contain many more strong women than the books of Samuel. Jezebel and the Queen of Sheba stand out. Athaliah, the only Hebrew queen in her own right, is also a strong woman, although we know little of her. Huldah is a respected prophetess, whom we would like to know much more about. She must have been a strong woman to be a female prophet in such a society. Each in her own way, the women associated with Elijah and Elisha exhibit a quiet kind of strength.

We do not find here the kinds of stories we found in Judges, where individual women are victimized by individual men. Nevertheless the stories of the two widows reveal the problems inherent in the patriarchal society that existed in ancient Israel. Although Jezebel is not victimized in the normal sense, her portrait is probably unfair.

The period of Solomon's reign and the aftermath was a religiously and politically chaotic time (especially after Solomon). Judging from the stories of women that were preserved, women were not as badly victimized as they were during David's reign. Whether that is really true, or just a quirk of which stories were preserved, is hard to tell. However, if women fared worse under more centralized governments, and if Solomon's administration was even more centralized than David's, both of which seem likely, then it may well be that the appearance of less feminine victimization during Solomon's reign and the reigns that follow in the northern and southern kingdoms belies the historical reality.

DISCUSSION QUESTIONS

1. The name of Jezebel is emotionally charged. Does Jezebel deserve the bad press she has received? Why or why not? Can you think of anyone who is a modern-day Jezebel?

2. Compare contemporary widows with biblical ones. Which do you think fare better?
3. The unnamed woman cried out to Elisha and told him her need. What social ills need to be named and voiced today?
4. Fantasize about what kind of life, both personal and professional, the prophetess Huldah might have led. Who are the modern-day Huldahs?

8

The Women in the Prophets

In chapter 3 we noted how difficult it is to determine the historical accuracy of the characters in Genesis and in the other historical books of the Bible. Factual and fictitious elements are interwoven so deftly that the line between fiction and nonfiction is often quite fuzzy. The ancient authors were far more interested in making theological points than in writing an objective history. The women characters in this chapter and in chapters 9 and 10 are in some cases pure fiction, for example, the important figures of Wisdom and Folly, whom we will consider in chapter 9. No such human beings ever existed. But that does not make these two characters any less worth our attention. While Wisdom and Folly are clearly fictional, the character Gomer, Hosea's wife, may or may not have been a real human being.

In all the prophetic books, the woman who stands out is Hosea's wife, Gomer. Jeremiah does not marry, and Ezekiel's wife dies suddenly. In addition, a prophetess is mentioned in Isaiah 8:3, and an unnamed young woman is destined to bear the son Immanuel in Isaiah 7:14. Groups of women are condemned by various prophets, especially for their worship of goddesses.[1]

Ella Pearson Mitchell and Henry Mitchell write:

Perhaps the most telling evidence of Old Testament cultural bias against women . . . is to be found in the resounding silence of most of the prophets. The treatment of women simply was not even an issue. Isaiah 19:16 speaks figuratively of women, but they represent fear and cowardice, which is a put-down. Hosea's wife, Gomer, is certainly no credit to her gender, and Zechariah's female angels also represent evil (5:7–11). The preponderance of female figures is unmistakably evil.[2]

156

In the prophets, a great deal of feminine imagery is used, much of it in negative ways.[3] Because our focus is on women's stories, we will not consider this important material, with two exceptions. Ezekiel describes Samaria and Jerusalem as two sisters, whom he names Oholah and Oholibah. In Jeremiah and Second Isaiah (Isa. 40–55) the barren woman motif that we encountered in the stories of Sarah, Rebekah, Rachel, and Hannah is reinterpreted, and Rachel and Sarah are reenvisioned. Following up on these reinterpretations, Jerusalem is portrayed as a mother in Third Isaiah (Isa. 56–66).

GOMER

Gomer's story is found in Hosea 1–3.[4] Whether she is historical or fictional is uncertain, but most scholars incline to the former opinion. In Hosea 1:2, Hosea is told by God to take a "wife (or woman) of whoredom" ('*ešet zenûnîm*). The term is unusual. It is different from the normal term for harlot (*zonâ*), although it is from the same Hebrew root. It probably means "loose or promiscuous woman" rather than "professional prostitute,"[5] or even less likely "sacred prostitute."[6] Gomer as woman or wife of whoredom is intended to shock the audience, because wives were presumed not to be whorish; the outrageousness of Gomer is premised on an idealized, pedestalized theory of women, or at least wives. Hosea is given this strange order to marry a wife (or woman) of whoredom because "the land commits great whoredom by forsaking the LORD" (Hos. 1:2). Thus Hosea's scandalous marital situation is going to parallel and be a symbol of the spiritual situation of Israel.

In Hosea 1:1–9, Gomer bears three children to Hosea: Jezreel ("God sows"), Lo-ruhamah ("Not loved"), and Lo-ammi ("Not my people"). The chapter ends on a note of hope, when God declares, "Yet the number of the people of Israel shall be like the sand of the sea, which can be neither measured nor numbered; and in the place where it was said to them, 'You are not my people,' it shall be said to them, 'Children of the living God'" (Hos. 1:10).

At the beginning of Hosea 2, Lo-ruhamah has been renamed Ruhamah ("Loved") and Lo-ammi, Ammi ("My people"). They are told to plead with their mother to put away her sexual promiscuity (Hos. 2:2). Otherwise, Hosea will "strip her naked" (Hos. 2:3). He will also build a wall around her, so that she cannot pursue her lovers (Hos. 2:6). He complains that she believes she receives her bread, water, wool, flax, oil, drink, silver, and gold from her lovers (Hos. 2:5, 8). He asserts that they come from him (Hos. 2:8).

Subtly the imagery changes. It is now Israel that is being chastised for her activity with lovers, that is, the Baals:

I will punish her for the festival days of the Baals,
   when she offered incense to them
and decked herself with her ring and jewelry,
   and went after her lovers,
   and forgot me, says the LORD.

(Hos. 2:13)

This chapter also ends on a note of hope. God says that he will allure Israel into the desert and speak tenderly to her. She will respond as in the days of her youth, when she came out of the land of Egypt (Hos. 2:15). God will love Lo-ruhamah. To Lo-ammi, God will say, "You are my people." Ammi will respond, "You are my God" (Hos. 2:23).

Hosea 3, consisting of only five verses, may be a variant version of the story. Gomer is not mentioned by name, but Hosea is told to "love a woman who has a lover and is an adulteress" (Hos. 3:1). So Hosea buys her (Hos. 3:2). He tells her she must stay with him and not engage in any sexual activity. This parallels Israel's situation (Hos. 3:3). Israel is to remain many days without king or prince, sacrifice or pillar, ephod (some sort of cultic image) or teraphim (another type of cultic image) (Hos. 3:4). This chapter too ends on a positive note. Hosea says the Israelites shall return and seek the Lord and David their king. They shall come in awe to the Lord and to his goodness (Hos. 3:5).

Many feminist biblical scholars have commented on the Hosea-Gomer material, but several are singled out as having especially important readings here. The first feminist perspective on Gomer that we will review comes from Drorah Setel.[7] She considers the relationship between the sexual imagery in Hosea and pornography. Setel defines pornography as having the following characteristics:

(1) Female sexuality is depicted as negative in relationship to a positive and neutral male standard; (2) women are degraded and publicly humiliated; and (3) female sexuality is portrayed as an object of male possession and control, which includes the depiction of women as analogous to nature in general and the land in particular, especially with regard to imagery of conquest and domination.[8]

In contrast with the gender-neutral dictionary definition of pornography as eliciting sexual arousal, Setel defines the function of pornography as the "maintenance of male domination through the denial, or misnaming, of female experience."[9]

Setel then describes biblical attitudes toward female sexuality. During the early history of Israel, there was a preoccupation with women's reproduction capabilities. Later, during the early monarchical period, the all-male priesthood expanded. With it, the ritual system of "clean" and "unclean" states was developed.[10]

During much of women's life-bearing cycle, they were "unclean." This can be seen as an acknowledgment of their participation in divine power. It can also be understood as a male attempt to control female power[11] and, we might add, as a reflection of male awe or fear.

In addition, women's sexual activity is defined passively. Marriage is a property relationship in which the man takes a woman. Adulterous relationships violate the husband's property rights. Prostitution is tolerated, if not encouraged, as no man's rights are violated. The institution also provided men access to women's bodies.[12]

After consideration of the nature of pornography and of female sexuality in the Bible, Setel then turns to female sexual imagery in Hosea. She notes the implications of the representation of God as husband and the people as wife. First, marriage in ancient Israel was not an equal partnership. That God is represented by the husband and the people by the wife is no accident. Rather, it is a "reflection and reinforcement of cultural perceptions."[13] God has the authority to control people, just as the husband has the power to control his wife.

In addition, "in a dualistic division between the divine (spiritual) and human (material) spheres of experience, men are categorized as belonging to the former, while women are assigned to the latter."[14] God/Hosea is portrayed positively, while Israel/Gomer is depicted negatively. Israel/Gomer strays. God/Hosea takes the initiative to create reconciliation. Israel/Gomer is the passive recipient of the grain, wine, oil, silver, gold, and so forth, that God/Hosea provides (Hos. 2:8–9; Heb., 2:10–11).[15]

This part of the imagery ignores woman's normal role in processing the raw materials into palatable food and clothing. "The underlying implication is that males nurture females, a reversal of (at least certain aspects of) social reality."[16] Women's positive roles in reproduction are also denied.[17]

Through all of these means Setel believes Hosea degrades women. Whether Setel's definition of pornography should be accepted is debatable.[18] In addition, whether Hosea's *intention* was to degrade women is also questionable. His use of language certainly reflects ancient attitudes toward male and female roles. The final question Setel raises concerns the use of Hosea today:

A central issue for contemporary religious feminists is the extent to which the use of these (and other) biblical writings continues to so define women in our own societies. The use of feminist theory gives us a framework in which to discuss that issue constructively. For some, understanding the historical setting of prophetic texts may provide a perspective of "moral realism" which allows them to be read as sacred writing. For others, the "pornographic" nature of female objectification may demand that such texts not be declared "the word of God" in a public setting. In discussing these issues we will certainly emerge with new questions and challenges as well. As difficult as the process may seem, it is one that may allow us to redefine our relationship not only to the text but also to our own histories and communities in ways which fully acknowledge female experience.[19]

Renita Weems raises the issue of sexual violence in Hosea.[20] She writes:

Hosea's ingenious use of the marriage metaphor to describe the nature of the YHWH and Israel's relationship provides special insight into divine-human relations. While it functions as a very effective literary device, it raises serious hermeneutical problems for those who are concerned about biblical texts that may be interpreted as excusing violence against women. In the case of the Hebrew Scriptures, to the extent that divine retribution is based on the presumably sound theological notion that the deity has the right to punish the people, the image of a husband physically retaliating against his wife becomes almost unavoidable, and his right to do so unquestionable.[21]

The sexual violence that Weems refers to occurs in Hosea 2:

I will strip her naked
and expose her as in the day she was born,
and make her like a wilderness,
and turn her into a parched land,
and kill her with thirst.
                              (Hos. 2:3)

Therefore I will hedge up her way with thorns;
and I will build a wall against her,
so that she cannot find her paths.
                              (Hos. 2:6)

Therefore I will take back
my grain in its time,
and my wine in its season;
and I will take away my wool and my flax,
which were to cover her nakedness.
                              (Hos. 2:9)

Now I will uncover her shame
in the sight of her lovers,
and no one shall rescue her out of my hand.
                              (Hos. 2:10)

This threat of sexual violence functions in three ways. First, it is supposed to show the lengths to which Hosea is willing to go to get his wife back. Second, it makes the point that punishment precedes reconciliation. Third and most important, "sexual violence functions as a poetic device to relate the punishment to the crime."[22] Hosea claims that Gomer adorned herself with vulgar jewelry that flaunts her promiscuity (Hos. 2:13; cf. 2:3). He then threatens to strip her, not just of her jewelry, but down to nakedness. Weems writes: "One cannot help but wonder if the implication is that had Gomer only taken off the brazen apparel as Hosea had first ordered, she could have been spared public stripping and humiliation. *In other words, the punishment (public stripping) fits the crime (vulgar apparel)*."[23]

Weems recognizes the versatility and effectiveness of the marriage relationship as a metaphor for the divine/human relationship. Nevertheless she asks, "Does the fact that the marriage metaphor is '*only* a metaphor' and the motif of sexual violence '*only* a theme of the metaphor' insulate them from serious theological scrutiny?"[24]

The risk begins when the metaphor works so well that we forget that it is only a metaphor and we disregard the dissimilarities. Then the husband becomes God, not just a representative of God in the imagery, and his physical violence against his wife is permissible.[25]

All metaphors are limited. Each has strengths and weaknesses. The experience of the hearer influences how a metaphor is heard. Those who have been displaced militarily will not be sympathetic with the image of God as the divine warrior in the conquest narratives of Joshua. Those who have experienced harsh reigns by dictator kings will not feel positive about the imagery of God as king. Women who have suffered from domestic violence will not find Hosea's metaphor useful, in spite of its more positive aspects.[26] Weems writes: "To the extent that in our modern culture there are no circumstances under which physical punishment is acceptable in marriage, the violent measures Hosea takes to chastise Gomer (should) pose a problem for the modern hearer."[27]

Gale Yee uses sociological criticism in her critique of the Hosea-Gomer material. She suggests that Hosea's concern is not primarily about the worship of the Baals, but rather is a critique of the eighth-century Israelite elite's economic and political oppression of the masses. In summary Yee writes:

Hosea reacts against an oppressive mode of production, embodied in the cult of eighth-century Israel. This mode of production involved: (1) an intensive agribusiness producing grain, wine, and oil for export by the elite classes; (2) a volatile political situation coupled with a reckless foreign policy; (3) an intertwining of cult, kingship, and priesthood with foreign policy; and (4) an unpolemical monolatry whose male cultic veneration of Baal legitimated elite interests. Previous scholarship on Hosea 1–2 isolated Israelite cult from state interests and imagined licentious fertility cults of Baal that infected a pure Yahwism. In the rest of the book, however, Hosea's "lovers" are the foreign nations (as in Jeremiah and Ezekiel) with whom the elite are economically and politically entangled. Hosea thinks that the nation's aristocracy forgot that God freed Israel from oppression in Egypt to worship YHWH alone in a self-sustaining tribal fellowship. Instead, the elite administer an exploitative state that violates the very theological principles of their origins.[28]

Yee suggests that by identifying Israel's elite with a shamed woman, Hosea simultaneously reinforces the lower status of women. Even more unfortunate is the fact that over the years what readers have heard in the story of Hosea and Gomer is not the conflict between the prophet and the male aristocracy, but rather that between a faithful male God and a faithless female Israel.[29]

On a more positive note, Helen Schüngel-Straumann suggests that the gendered imagery of Hosea 1–3 is reversed in Hosea 11. She argues in a close reading of the Hebrew text that God is depicted in Hosea 11 as a gentle mother to her son Israel, in contrast to the Hosea-Gomer story of Hosea 1–3, where God is violent husband and abusive father, and the people Israel are wife and children. She translates the first four verses of chapter 11 as follows:

1 When Israel was young, I loved him;
   out of Egypt I called my son.
2 But when I called them
      they ran from me,
   and they sacrificed to the Baals,
   and they sent up incense to images.
3 But it was I who nursed Ephraim,
      taking him in my arms.
   Yet they did not understand
   That it was I who took care of them.
4 I drew them with cords of humanity,
      with bands of love.
   And I was for them like those
   who take a nursling to the breast,
   and I bowed down to him
   in order to give him suck.[30]

Even if Schüngel-Straumann is correct in her reading of the divine imagery in Hosea 11, the image of God that opens the book of Hosea is a bad taste that is hard to get out of the contemporary reader's mouth, even with a sweet piece of cake.

NO WIFE FOR JEREMIAH

The message that Jeremiah receives from God is doom for Judah. As a result he is instructed not to marry. This will save him the anguish of seeing the death of his wife and children (Jer. 16:1–7).[31] Since Jeremiah uses much imagery that portrays women negatively (especially in chapters 2, 3, and 5), we may wonder whether there was a human explanation for Jeremiah's failure to marry as well as a theological one. Although Israelite culture displayed at times a fear of women's sexuality, perhaps Jeremiah had internalized this fear more than most Israelite men. Or perhaps he was what we would call gay.

THE DEATH OF EZEKIEL'S WIFE

Ezekiel is told that his wife will die suddenly and that he is not to mourn for her (Ezek. 24:15–18). The reason for these strange instructions is that when Judah is taken into exile, there will be no time for mourning. Ezekiel's lack of mourning for his wife is a symbol of things to come. He obeys God, and when his wife dies, he goes about his business and does not mourn for her in any public way. The poignancy of the instructions not to mourn for his wife contrasts with negative feminine imagery in Ezekiel 16 and 23.

In Ezekiel 16, the two capital cities are depicted as sisters who behave lewdly. In Ezekiel 23 Jerusalem and Samaria are again depicted as two sisters, but this time they are named. Samaria is Oholah (perhaps "Her Tent") and Jerusalem is Oholibah (perhaps "My Tent Is in Her"). The tent is a traditional symbol of God's presence and probably refers to a sanctuary. The name Oholah suggests that Samaria is apostate.[32] Oholah and Oholibah are described as the Lord's lovers (vv. 4–5), the mothers of his children (vv. 4, 37). Their sexual behavior is said to be lewd and whorish (vv. 21, 29, 35, 48–49). They are stripped, raped, stoned, put to the sword, their survivors burned, and their homes destroyed (vv. 9–10, 22–35, 45–46).

WOMEN AND WORSHIP

Although women were second-class citizens in the religion of Israel, they sometimes participated in pagan religions involving the worship of goddesses. The biblical authors, primarily priests and prophets, depict priestly and prophetic religion as normative. There is evidence, however, that religious practice was more diverse than implied and that such diverse practice was accepted as legitimate.

One such practice was the worship by women of sixth-century Judah and Israel of the Queen of Heaven (Jer. 7:16–20; 44:15–19, 25). Jeremiah denounces the women for their worship of the Queen of Heaven. Nevertheless they devote themselves to her, baking cakes in her image as offerings (Jer. 7:18; 44:19) and pouring out libations to her (Jer. 44:15, 19).

Susan Ackerman suggests an identity for this goddess and reasons for her worship.[33] She notes that scholars propose various identifications for the Queen of Heaven: the great East Semitic goddess Ishtar, Ishtar's West Semitic counterpart Astarte, the West Semitic goddess Anat, and the Canaanite goddess Shapsu. Some say that there is no way to ascertain her identity. Still a third group conjecture that she is a syncretistic combination of Ishtar and Astarte. That is Ackerman's view.[34] She argues that one of the things about the cult of the Queen of Heaven that attracted women was that it allowed them active involvement in the cult.[35] This cult seems not only to have been popular in the domestic spheres of home and family but also among kings and queens.[36] She concludes as follows:

> Since it is winners who write history, the importance of this women's cult in the history of the religion of Israel has been obscured by our sources. The ultimate "winners" in the religion of early sixth-century Judah, the Deuteronomistic historians, the priest-prophet Ezekiel, and the prophet Jeremiah, were men. The biblical texts these men wrote malign non-Deuteronomistic, non-priestly, and non-prophetic religion, and in the case of the cult of the Queen of Heaven they malign the religion of women. But fortunately for us, the sources have not completely ignored some women's cults. The losers have not been totally lost. If historians of Israelite religion continue to push beyond biblical polemic, we should hear more and more the voices of the women of Israel witnessing to their religious convictions.[37]

Judith Hadley is less sanguine about the possibility of discovering the identity of the Queen of Heaven. She writes:

> [I]f the text of Jeremiah derives from a much later time in the post-exilic period, it may be that exactly which deity the people were worshipping was not a matter of interest to the author, since by that time all of the duties of any other deities would have been absorbed into Yahwism, and Yahweh was the only deity needed. It is even possible that precisely which deity was responsible for what in those heady pre-exilic times was as confusing for the late post-exilic writers as it is for us today. Thus, all that was necessary for the writer to drive home the point was that there had been a time, generations ago, when the people worshipped the Queen of Heaven, who would represent, for the late author, *any* deity that was worshipped apart from Yahweh, be it in the past, the present, or, indeed, even the future.[38]

RACHEL IN JEREMIAH

In Jeremiah 31:15–22 Jeremiah uses Rachel as a symbol for the new community. The historical context is either the early part of King Josiah's reign (late seventh century BCE), when it was hoped that the former northern kingdom of Israel (destroyed in 722 BCE by the Assyrians) might be reincorporated into Judah, or the early postexilic period (the years following the destruction of Jerusalem in 587 BCE by the Babylonians). Rachel's lost children are either the lost northern tribes of Israel or the Judahite exiles in Babylon.

> Thus says the LORD:
> A voice is heard in Ramah,
>> lamentation and bitter weeping.
> Rachel is weeping for her children;
>> she refuses to be comforted for her children,
>> because they are no more.
> Thus says the LORD:
> Keep your voice from weeping,
>> and your eyes from tears;
> for there is a reward for your work,
>>> says the LORD:
>> they shall come back from the land of the enemy;
> there is hope for your future,
>>> says the LORD:
>> your children shall come back to their own country.
>>>>> (Jer. 31:15–17)

The poem then focuses on Ephraim, the repentant (male) child whom God has forgiven and upon whom God will have mercy (Jer. 31:18–20). Finally, in Jeremiah 31:21–22, God speaks to (female) virgin Israel, the faithless daughter, who is wavering in indecision, telling her to return to her cities. The poem ends (Jer. 31:22) with a cryptic line—"For the LORD has created a new thing on the earth: a woman [literally female] encompasses a man [Hebrew *gaber*, literally strong man)"—that has occasioned much debate. Phyllis Trible has pointed out the way the female encases the male, both in the final line of the poem and in the structure of the poem as a whole (Rachel weeps; Ephraim repents; Virgin Israel addressed). She also notes the feminine qualities of God's love, especially in verse 20, where God has compassion on Ephraim, using the same Hebrew root from which the word "womb" comes.[39] In any case, the figure of Rachel is a positive, albeit traditionally maternal character. She is an antidote to Gomer.

SARAH IN SECOND ISAIAH

In Isaiah 49:19–21; 51:1–3; and 54:1–3, Second Isaiah reinterprets the barren woman motif for the despairing Hebrews in Babylonian exile. Isaiah 51:1–3 explicitly refers to Sarah, the only text in the Old Testament outside the Pentateuch that mentions her:

> Listen to me, you that pursue righteousness,
>   you that seek the LORD.
> Look to the rock from which you were hewn,
>   and to the quarry from which you were dug.
> Look to Abraham your father
>   and to Sarah who bore you;
> for he was but one when I called him,
>   but I blessed him and made him many.
> For the LORD will comfort Zion;
>   he will comfort all her waste places,
> and will make her wilderness like Eden,
>   her desert like the garden of the LORD;
> joy and gladness will be found in her,
>   thanksgiving and the voice of song.

Mary Callaway sees in these verses a reinterpretation of the story of Sarah. Sarah is no longer just the mother of Isaac. Now she is the mother of the entire Hebrew people. Second Isaiah is instilling hope in the exiles by reminding them that it all started with one barren woman. If God could bring Isaac from her, he will bring many more people from the current group of exiles. They are her spiritual children. Moreover, the references to Eden make it clear that what God is doing in Second Isaiah's time is tantamount to a new creation.[40]

There is more to the reinterpretation than this, however. The barren woman motif derived from Sarah's story is applied to Jerusalem, personified as a woman. Zion (= Jerusalem) complains in Isaiah 49:14, "The LORD has forsaken me, my Lord has forgotten me." The Lord responds beginning with verse 15; the following are the important verses for our purposes:

> Surely your waste and your desolate places
>   and your devastated land—
> surely now you will be too crowded for your inhabitants,
>   and those who swallowed you up will be far away.
> The children born in the time of your bereavement
>   will yet say in your hearing:
> "The place is too crowded for me;
>   make room for me to settle."
> Then you will say in your heart,
>   "Who has borne me these?
> I was bereaved and barren,
>   exiled and put away—
> so who has reared these?
> I was left all alone—
>   where then have these come from?"

(Isa. 49:19–21)

Thus Sarah, the mother of Isaac, becomes Jerusalem, the mother of Israel.[41] Her bereavement has still to be explained. Who is Jerusalem's husband? It is none other than the Lord himself, whom many of the exiles thought was dead.

The imagery of Jerusalem as feminine and more specifically as the wife of the deity was inherited by the Hebrews from West Semitic mythology. In this mythology, capital cities were considered to be goddesses, the consorts of the god of the city. Much of this way of thinking was taken over by the Israelites, although it was not until the eighth century BCE that it took on a distinctly Israelite form.[42] Second Isaiah fused this Canaanite imagery with the barren wife motif.[43]

Second Isaiah depicts the Lord married to Jerusalem, the once-barren woman who will bear many children. He also portrays Jerusalem as a disgraced woman:

> Sing, O barren one who did not bear;
>   burst into song and shout,
>   you who have not been in labor!
> For the children of the desolate woman will be more
>   than the children of her that is married, says the LORD.
>
> (Isa. 54:1)

The word translated here as "desolate" (šômēma) refers to an unmarriageable woman, one who has been sexually defiled, such as Dinah or Tamar, David's daughter.[44] Callaway writes:

> The outrageous nature of the situation now becomes clear: Yahweh has taken for his wife a woman whose defilement could never be purified to make her marriageable; her position was defined as šmmh, and she was as one who is dead. To hear the words ḥpṣ ["delight in"] and b'l ["husband"] replacing šmmh must have jarred in the ears of Second Isaiah's audience, for she who was untouchable is now called by names of most intimate endearment. Second Isaiah has reminded his community of the old stories of the rivalry between the barren and the fruitful wives and how Yahweh visited the barren one to give her a son. But he then reinterprets the old story: what he did for Sarah and for Rachel who were barren was only done in days of old; now he is taking to himself Jerusalem, who is šmmh.[45]

The least acceptable person in human society, in this case the barren and sexually defiled woman, becomes the vehicle through whom God accomplishes the divine ends. Unlike the book of Hosea, where Hosea=God also takes a sexually impure woman (Gomer=Israel), here God as husband is not depicted as threatening sexual violence. From Gomer the wife or woman of whoredom who is threatened into line by Hosea (Hos. 1–3), to Rachel who weeps for her children and then morphs into the Virgin Israel— the wavering, faithless daughter—who is encouraged to return home (Jer. 31:15–22), to Sarah who is enjoined to sing in celebration of her new children (Isa. 51:1–3; cf. 54:1), we move steadily in a positive direction in terms of the depictions of symbolic females. To some degree this imagery counters the depiction of God as a violent husband seen in Hosea (1–3), Jeremiah (e.g., 2:20; 3:1–20), and Ezekiel (16, 23), though many contemporary readers will not feel that the more positive imagery totally rectifies the problem.[46] Yet this imagery, so infrequently noticed by feminist readers, could go a long way toward subverting the negative images in Hosea, Jeremiah, Ezekiel, and other biblical prophets, if it were not so often ignored.

ZION AS MOTHER IN THIRD ISAIAH

Third Isaiah draws on Second Isaiah's development of the imagery of personified Jerusalem as mother and takes it a step farther. He changes the metaphor from a barren woman made fruitful to a loving mother drawing her children to herself. The historical context is the period after the return from exile. The people are discouraged, because they are few and the task of rebuilding is enormous. We read:

> Rejoice with Jerusalem, and be glad for her,
>   all you who love her;
> rejoice with her in joy,
>   all you who mourn over her—
> that you may nurse and be satisfied
>   from her consoling breast;
> that you may drink deeply with delight
>   from her glorious bosom.
> For thus says the LORD:
> I will extend prosperity to her like a river,
>   and the wealth of the nations like an overflowing stream;
> and you shall nurse and be carried on her arm,
>   and dandled on her knees.
>
> (Isa. 66:10–12)

Here Zion is described as a nursing mother. The words that describe the satisfaction she gives are ordinarily used of the Lord. Callaway writes:

> This image of Zion giving birth miraculously and feeding her children from her own abundance is reminiscent of the ancient Semitic mother goddess, whose cult had never completely disappeared from Israel. The

emphasis on Zion's breasts would not have been missed by the prophet's audience, who still remembered and in some cases still possessed, figurines of the mother goddess holding her breasts in a gesture of invitation and of self-glorification.[47]

Third Isaiah was the first to adapt the great Mother image in a way that served the monotheistic Hebrew religion, rather than being in conflict with it.[48]

CONCLUSIONS

The prophetic corpus provides many difficult texts for feminists, especially the frequent use of women as representative of sinful Israel and Judah. However, a few bright spots also exist. Helen Schüngel-Straumann's interpretation of Hosea 11, Jeremiah's reinterpretation of Rachel, and Second and Third Isaiah's use of the barren woman motif provide us with intriguing positive readings of some imagery in the prophetic literature, literature that elsewhere often denigrates women.

DISCUSSION QUESTIONS

1. How do you react to the sexual violence in Hosea? Do you think it fits the definition of pornography? What can we do in our society to reduce the incidence of sexual violence? Can religious communities help? If so, how?
2. What image of women did the Hebrews of Hosea's time have that Hosea's depiction of Gomer would have shocked and disturbed them? Which image is more disturbing to you?
3. One of the possible implications of the worship of the Queen of Heaven is that when women are denied full participation in mainstream religious communities, they sometimes look elsewhere for spiritual sustenance. What might this mean for contemporary religious life?

9

The Women in the Wisdom Literature and the Song of Songs

The wisdom tradition in the Bible is an important one. The books of Job, Psalms, Proverbs, and Ecclesiastes are wisdom books. The Song of Songs, or the Song of Solomon as it is often called in English Bibles, is not a wisdom book, although it is attributed to Solomon. We will consider it here, however, because it can be interpreted in the light of wisdom thought patterns. Most scholars read Job as a fictional story. Nevertheless the nameless wife of Job is worth considering. The book of Job has no major women characters, but Job's wife does play an important, if small, part. His second set of daughters also is somewhat important, if for no other reason than that they are the only daughters in the Hebrew Bible who are named by their father.

In Proverbs we find the personification of Wisdom as a female character. The strange or foreign woman who is also sometimes called Folly, in contrast to Wisdom, is condemned. The good wife who may represent personified wisdom is also praised.

The Song of Songs is love poetry. The woman or women in these poems are probably fictitious, although the woman who calls herself black and beautiful in Song 1:5 has been understood to be the Pharaoh's daughter whom Solomon married.

JOB'S WIFE

Job's daughters and his wife do not play major parts in Job's story. Nevertheless Job's wife is an interesting character. Carol Newsom notes that her words to Job, "Do you still persist in your integrity? Curse God, and die" (Job 2:9), are radical and provocative. They echo God's assessment of Job in 2:3a, when God describes Job as one who persists in integrity.[1]

Ellen van Wolde points out that the Hebrew *berek*, which is usually translated "curse" in this line, can actually mean either "curse" or "bless." Its basic meaning in the Hebrew Bible is bless, but in the book of Job it is also used as a euphemism for curse, making it hard to determine exactly what Mrs. Job means.[2] She could either be saying that Job should bless God as long as he can hold on to his sense of integrity, despite the suffering that would suggest he has sinned. Then, having blessed God, he can die in peace.[3] Alternately, she could be saying that if he maintains his integrity, then his suffering is unjust. He should therefore curse God, and accept the consequences, that is, death.[4]

Newsom points out an ambiguity in the speech of Job's wife that centers in the word "integrity." A person of integrity is one whose behavior is in accord with moral and religious norms. Such a person is also an honest person, one without guile. The two senses of the word are, however, sometimes in tension with each other. Job's wife could be asking him whether he persists in his righteousness and suggesting that it has not gotten him too far. In this case, she would be encouraging him to give it up and curse God.[5]

But she could also be asking Job if he persists in his honesty and suggesting that he continue to do so even to the point of cursing God. Job was so honest that he could not admit he was aware of any sins grave enough to have brought upon him the suffering he experienced. In the end, God vindicates Job against his so-called comforters, who try to make him repent of sins he knows he has not committed. Part of the point of the story is that not all suffering is a result of sin. Some of it happens to the just and the unjust alike. This notion can be disturbing to those who believe that their prosperity is a result of their good works and conversely that those who suffer are responsible for their fate. Thus anyone who suggests that life is more complex often receives a less than enthusiastic response. Newsom writes, "Both in the original Hebrew book of Job and in many of the retellings of the story, Job's wife is the prototypical woman on the margin, whose iconoclastic words provoke defensive condemnation but whose insight serves as an irritant that undermines old complacencies."[6] Job's wife has no name; her loss of children is not the focus of the story; and even the birth of a second set of children for Job at the end of the story, of whom she is presumably the mother, occurs without any mention of her role.

Ilana Pardes also explores the role of Job's wife. Although she largely agrees with Newsom, Pardes notes that Job rebukes his wife and calls her foolish before doing in effect what she suggests. She also notes the way Job is transformed by the end of the book in terms of his relationships with women. He names his daughters, the only place in the Hebrew Bible where a father names his daughters. The names he gives them are not the pious names one expects he would have used before his transformation, but sensuous, beautiful names:

Bright Day (or Dove), Cassia (a kind of perfume), and Horn of Antimony (ancient eye shadow).[7] Pardes also notes that Job's daughters inherit property from him, a clear deviation from the law.[8]

In spite of these discoveries that will be pleasing to feminists, Pardes finds one less pleasing reality. She asks:

> But where is Job's nameless wife? She is conspicuously absent from the happy ending in which Job's world is restored. One may well ask why. While Job's dead children spring back to life, as it were, for he now has, just as in the beginning, seven sons and three daughters, his wife, who actually managed to escape death, is curiously excluded from this scene of familial bliss. Let me suggest that here too censorship is at work. It is no accident that Job's wife does not benefit from her husband's changed relation to femininity in the epilogue. Although in a sense her words give rise to Job's criticism of the ways of God, they remain far too antithetical to allow her reappearance. The challenge of the outsider—and woman is something of an outsider in divine-human affairs—seems far more threatening than a critique voiced from within.[9]

PROVERBS

Women figure prominently in the first and last parts of Proverbs. Carol Newsom writes: "A casual reader asked to describe Proverbs 1–9 might reply that it was the words of a father talking to his son, mostly about women."[10] Athalya Brenner argues that the instructor may be a mother rather than a father.[11] The parent and son should not be taken literally. Newsom writes, "All readers of the text, whatever their actual identities, are called upon to take up the subject position of son in relation to an authoritative parent."[12]

In Proverbs 1, personified Wisdom is introduced (Prov. 1:20–33). She is allied with the parent figure. In Proverbs 2, the son is told to accept the teaching of the parent and of Wisdom (Prov. 2:1–11), which will protect him from the crooked man (Prov. 2:12–15) and the words of the strange woman Folly (Prov. 2:16–19).

Who is the strange woman? She is described as "the adulteress with her smooth words, who forsakes the partner of her youth" (Prov. 2:16–17). Her "way [Heb. "house"] leads down to death" (Prov. 2:18). Why is she called "strange" or "foreign" (zarâ)? Her strangeness may be ethnic, legal, social, or some combination of them.[13] Brenner does not believe zarâ means "strange" or "foreign" in this context. Rather, she is persuaded that its basic meaning is "other" or "liminal." The "strange" woman is someone who does not fit into the socially accepted order.[14]

On the other hand, Gale Yee, in her sociological analysis, places Proverbs 1–9 in the postexilic period. When the exiles returned from Babylonian exile, they frequently married into the population that had remained behind in order to gain agricultural land. Generations later, the priestly elite encouraged endogamy rather than exogamy (marriage within the extended family rather than outside it), to keep land within the *golah* community of returned exiles. The strange woman in Proverbs, according to Yee, represents the women outside this in-group.[15] Although it is easy to see how Proverbs 1–9 could have functioned to support endogamy, there is enough concern in the text with adultery to suggest that the strange woman in these chapters cannot be limited to those outside the *golah* community.

The "strange" woman is a useful symbol for the author of Proverbs, because she is both frightening and attractive. Her words are "smooth," that is, slippery, suggesting both pleasure and danger.[16]

In Proverbs 3, Wisdom's benefits are described. They are income better than silver and gold (v. 14); long life, riches, and honor (v. 16); pleasant ways and peaceful paths (v. 17); and a tree of life and happiness (v. 18). The contrast between Wisdom and the "strange" woman, whose path leads to death, is striking.

Proverbs 4 gives further encouragement to the son to acquire wisdom and insight and not to forsake Wisdom. In Proverbs 5 and 6, the son is warned again about the dangers of the "strange" woman. For example, we read:

> For the lips of a loose [Heb. "strange"] woman drip honey,
>   and her speech is smoother than oil;
> but in the end she is bitter as wormwood,
>   sharp as a two-edged sword.
> Her feet go down to death;
>   her steps follow the path to Sheol.
> She does not keep straight to the path of life;
>   her ways wander, and she does not know it.
>
> (Prov. 5:3–6)

If the son disregards this advice, he will give his honor to others, his years to the merciless, and his wealth to strangers. At the end of his life he will groan, because he will be ruined in the public assembly (Prov. 5:7–14). With the use of the imagery of cistern, well, springs, and fountain, the son is encouraged to be satisfied with his wife and not be intoxicated by an adulterous woman (Prov. 5:16–23).

Toward the end of Proverbs 6, the parent returns to this theme. He/she tells the son to follow his/her commandments to avoid the evil wife and the smooth tongue of the adulteress (Prov. 6:20–24). The son is not to desire her beauty, nor should he let himself be captured by her eyelashes (Prov. 6:25). The prostitute is contrasted with the wife of another man:

> for a prostitute's fee is only a loaf of bread,
>> but the wife of another stalks a man's very life.
>>> (Prov. 6:26)

This line suggests that consorting with prostitutes is considered less of a problem than adultery. The rest of Proverbs 6 spells out the problems that adultery creates (Prov. 6:27–35).

In Proverbs 7 and 8, the attractions of the "strange" woman (chap. 7) and of Wisdom (chap. 8) are further described. The "strange" woman is depicted as "decked out like a prostitute" (Prov. 7:10), "loud and wayward" (Prov. 7:11), aggressively pursuing the young man physically and vocally (Prov. 7:12–21). Finally we read, "Her house is the way to Sheol, going down to the chambers of death" (Prov. 7:27). She symbolizes evil.

In contrast, Wisdom speaks truth (Prov. 8:7). Her words are straight and right, not crooked or twisted (Prov. 8:8–9). She is more valuable than all one can desire (Prov. 8:10–11). With Wisdom are good advice, insight, and strength (Prov. 8:14). Kings rule justly through Wisdom (Prov. 8:15). Those who follow Wisdom will become wealthy (Prov. 8:18–19, 21).

In Proverbs 8:22–31, Wisdom's role in God's creation of the world is described in terms that anticipate the opening words of the Gospel of John: "In the beginning was the Word [Gr. *logos*<*sophia* = Heb. *ḥokmâ*, "wisdom"], and the Word was with God, and the Word was God." Proverbs 8:22 reads: "The LORD created me at the beginning of his work, the first of his acts of long ago." After several more verses, we read:

> When he established the heavens, I was there,
>> when he drew a circle on the face of the deep,
> when he made firm the skies above,
>> when he established the fountains of the deep,
> when he assigned to the sea its limit,
>> so that the waters might not transgress his command,
> when he marked out the foundations of the earth,
>> then I was beside him, like a master worker;
> and I was daily his delight,
>> rejoicing before him always,
> rejoicing in his inhabited world
>> and delighting in the human race.
>>> (Prov. 8:27–31)

How and why this female figure emerged is difficult to say. Wisdom is feminine in gender in Hebrew, but that alone would probably not have been enough. Gerlinde Baumann suggests that in the postexilic era, when the Deuteronomistic philosophy, which viewed suffering as a result of sin, was being questioned (as for example in the book of Job), perhaps faith in YHWH tolerated or even required an additional transcendent figure who was linked to him in some not entirely clear manner. Proverbs 1–9

> allow[s] a certain range of interpretation of the Wisdom Figure: She can be seen as a goddess on a similar level to YHWH, or only as his subordinate creature. There are a number of parallels to YHWH-speech which support the first explanation, but the texts do not commit themselves to it, nor dictate it to their readers. It seems possible that the authors of Proverbs 1–9 intend to go beyond the contemporary boundaries of faith in YHWH in a somehow playful manner. Chapters 1–9 do not explicitly say anything that would not be acceptable to those who worship YHWH alone; to those who want to see it differently, though, the texts speak about a goddess-like figure at YHWH's side.[17]

Baumann also suggests that the prestige and authority of women must have been considerable in order for the figure of Lady Wisdom to emerge.[18] This is positive, but many feminists are disturbed by the fact that this figure embodies traditional feminine values. She is more intimate than YHWH, caring for her children (Prov. 8:17), nourishing them (Prov. 9:4–5), and teaching them.[19] In addition, the contrast between Wisdom, the playmate and helper of the Lord, and the "strange" woman, who drags men down to Sheol, is stark. How did woman come to symbolize both extremes? Newsom believes that it is because woman as man's other comes to represent both what is inferior and what is superior. She quotes Toril Moi, who develops Julia Kristeva's understanding of women's marginal position in patriarchal societies:

> If patriarchy sees women as occupying a marginal position within the symbolic order, then it can construe them as the limit or borderline of that order. From a phallocentric point of view, women will then come to represent the necessary frontier between man and chaos; but because of their very marginality they will also always seem to recede into and merge with the chaos of the outside. Women seen as the limit of the symbolic order will in other words share in the disconcerting properties of all frontiers: they will be neither inside nor outside, neither known nor unknown. It is this position that has enabled male culture sometimes to vilify women as representing darkness and chaos, to view them as Lilith or the Whore of Babylon, and sometimes to elevate them as representatives of a higher and purer nature, to venerate them as Virgins and Mothers of God. In the first instance the borderline is seen as part of the chaotic wilderness outside, and in the second it is seen as an inherent part of the inside: the part that protects and shields the symbolic order from the imaginary chaos.[20]

Newsom notes that analyzing Proverbs 1–9 is not simply an antiquarian exercise. She draws a parallel between the movie *Fatal Attraction* and the message of these chapters.[21]

Gale Yee is disturbed by the message that Proverbs 1–9 sends to female readers. She says:

> Given the erotic imagery that surrounds both Lady Wisdom and the *'iššâ zārâ* [strange woman], the most profoundly unsettling message that comes across particularly to the female reader is that only man pursues Wisdom like a lover, and it is a woman who seduces him away from her. How does one mitigate such imagery when it touches a person at the most elemental and symbolic level, e.g. the sexual? Proverbs 1–9 clearly have as their referent a father teaching his son in the ways of Wisdom and the dangers of the foreign woman. . . . The Proverbs 1–9 texts leave the female reader with questions that still need to be resolved: Can a woman ever seek and ultimately find Wisdom? Or does she simply suffer the fate of the *'iššâ zārâ* [strange woman], an object of aversion and ever condemned?[22]

Tikva Frymer-Kensky sounds a similar warning. She writes:

> Having a literary figure of Woman-Wisdom can reinforce the idea that women are wise. . . . Similarly, the later Jewish images of the sabbath Queen-Bride and the Torah are positive female images that can raise women's prestige and reinforce women's self-esteem. . . . Nevertheless, despite the obvious appeal of these images to women, when union with them is described as marriage, women are excluded from the symbolic relationship.[23]

Proverbs 31, the final chapter of the book, is the one remaining chapter to consider. Verses 10–31 begin, "A capable wife who can find? She is far more precious than jewels." Actually, the words translated "capable wife" literally mean "woman (or wife) of strength." It is odd that modern translations avoid a literal rendering. The poem goes on to praise her for her industriousness, long hours of work, and economically productive activity. She is also praised for domestic duties well done, charitable responsibilities, support of her husband who is known in the city gates, and her wise teaching. She is a mother whose children call her happy. With all of her virtues, one wonders what is left for her husband to do. The traditional Jewish answer, as depicted in the musical *Fiddler on the Roof*, that the man studies the Torah, will not make many feminists happy.

Denise Carmody notes the ambivalence with which this text leaves us. It acknowledges that competent management of the domestic sphere is no small accomplishment, but much of the woman's status is secondary.[24] Her work enables her husband to do his more public duties and her children to live well. That is not bad, but it is not reciprocal.

In addition, Proverbs 31:30 is disturbing. It reads, "Charm is deceitful, and beauty is vain, but a woman who fears the LORD is to be praised." Charm is not always deceitful and a good wife doesn't have to be plain. Underlying this verse is the same fear of woman that we have seen throughout. Carmody concludes:

> So give us fewer paeans to good wives, fewer dutiful acknowledgements of women's important and special gifts. . . . In their place, just a little courage, a little imagination, a little wit, and a little resolute honesty would be like fresh air from on high. Indeed, charm can be deceitful and beauty vain, but both also can be gifts of God. . . . Let us start judging and promoting all of the people of God, men and women alike, only by their fruits.[25]

On a more positive note, Ella Pearson Mitchell and Henry Mitchell, while acknowledging that the male is the dominant figure, point out that "this book . . . proposes that women engage in business (31:10–31), to an extent not found anywhere else."[26]

Although many interpreters have understood Proverbs 31:10–31 as a poem about the ideal wife, recent scholarship has generally taken a different view. Kathleen O'Connor writes:

> Rather than supplying the image of the correct marriage partner, this acrostic or alphabetic poem serves as a summary of the whole Book of Proverbs. Its central character is no typical woman but the Wisdom Woman herself. Drawing from images of the young man choosing between the Wisdom Woman or the Strange Woman found in Proverbs 1–9, this poem demonstrates what life is like once one has chosen to live with the Wisdom Woman.[27]

Another feminist interpreter who views the women in Proverbs in a more positive light is Carol Fontaine. She notes the possible connections between Proverbs and goddess worship:

> The significance of this book for women goes far beyond the positive and (mostly) negative comments about women encapsulated in the various proverbs. The figure of Woman Wisdom may be a survival of goddess worship within the monotheistic structure of Israelite theology, since the wisdom traditions of Mesopotamia and Egypt were sanctioned by tutelary goddesses.[28]

Although this may well be so, the figure Wisdom in the Hebrew Bible is in no sense a goddess. This is the conclusion of Claudia Camp. She writes: "it is clear that there is goddess-imagery at work in the presentation of female

Wisdom. It is also clear, however, that this imagery is in some way trans-formed."[29] In the intertestamental period, Wisdom is an important figure closely allied with God, and in the New Testament Hebrew *ḥokmâ* becomes Greek *sophia* and finally *logos,* the word of God incarnate.[30] For many femi-nists the female figure Wisdom is therefore extremely important.[31]

THE SONG OF SONGS

The Song of Songs, a book of love poetry, is an important book for feminists. It has sometimes been interpreted allegorically as referring to the love of God for Israel or the church. It has more frequently been ignored, perhaps because the imagery is foreign, perhaps because of discomfort with the body. For many feminists it is a bright spot.

Marcia Falk believes that the Song is not a structural unity but a compila-tion of lyrical love poems. In this case the love of a number of couples may well be the subject of the individual poems.[32]

Phyllis Trible sees this book as the redemption of the love story that went awry in Genesis 2–3. She writes:

Using Genesis 2–3 as a key for understanding the Song of Songs, we have participated in a symphony of love. Born to mutuality and harmony, a man and a woman live in a garden where nature and history unite to cel-ebrate the one flesh of sexuality. Naked without shame or fear (cf. Gen. 2:25; 3:10), this couple treat each other with tenderness and respect. Nei-ther escaping nor exploiting sex, they embrace and enjoy it. Their love is truly bone of bone and flesh of flesh, and this image of God male and female is indeed very good (cf. Gen. 1:27, 31). Testifying to the goodness of creation, then, eroticism becomes worship in the context of grace.

In this setting, there is no male dominance, no female subordination, and no stereotyping of either sex. Specifically, the portrayal of the woman defies the connotations of "second sex." She works, keeping vineyards and pasturing flocks. Throughout the Song she is independent, fully the equal of the man. Although at times he approaches her, more often she initiates their meetings. Her movements are bold and open: at night in the streets and squares of the city she seeks the one whom her *nephesh* [life force] loves (3:1–4). No secrecy hides her yearnings. Moreover, she dares to describe love with revealing metaphors. . . . Never is this woman called a wife, nor is she required to bear children. In fact, to the issues of marriage and procreation the Song does not speak. Love for the sake of love is its message, and the portrayal of the female delineates this message best.[33]

Danna Fewell evaluates the Song less positively:

[Trible's] reading, while powerful, depreciates the rather oppressive social structure that provides the backdrop for the poetic scenario: There are "brothers" who are overprotective of the "little sister"; there are watchmen who, upon finding the woman in the streets looking for her lover, beat her and strip her. Furthermore, Trible's reading overlooks the poems' suggestions that the male also "pastures his flocks" in other places besides the embrace of the female persona. Hence, the poetic garden of equity, intimacy and mutuality is not without its thorns.[34]

Cheryl Exum makes a list of ten things that every feminist should know about the Song of Songs, in an article with that title. The list begins with a warning that reading the Song can be "*hazardous to your critical faculties* [all emphasis hers], since it turns even the most hardened of feminist critics into a bubbling romantic."[35] The second item on the list is a notice that "*the immediacy of the Song is an illusion*,"[36] that even though there is no obvious narrator, this does not mean that there is no narrator. Third, Exum reminds feminist readers that "*there are no real women in this text*,"[37] it is fiction, a literary creation. The fourth warning is a corollary: "*The woman, or women, in this text may be the creations of male authors.*"[38]

Exum's fifth item is similar to Fewell's concern: "*There is no gender equality.*"[39] The sixth warning, which is related, is that "*bad things happen to sexually active, forward women*,"[40] like being beaten by watchmen (Song 5:7). Item seven is that "*the female body is on display.*"[41] Exum acknowledges that the male body is also on display, but it may not be the same.[42] The eighth warning is that "*there is something wrong with the body,*"[43] by which is meant that the woman is a collection of body parts rather than a whole body. Warning nine is like the first, that "*the poetry of the Song is seductive.*"[44] Finally, Exum's tenth item is slightly more cheerful: "*feminists don't have to deny ourselves the pleasure of the text.* All we need to do is misread it."[45]

In a more upbeat manner, Carol Meyers analyzes the gender imagery in this book and concludes:

Gender was not a constraint on power in the world of the gods. Nor . . . was gender a constraint on power in the intimate world of a couple in love. From a social perspective, the domestic realm is the setting for such love, and therein exists the arena in which female power is expressed. Luckily for feminists, who often despair of discovering meaningful material in the man's world of the official canon, a single biblical book has preserved this non-public world and allows us to see the private realm that dominated the social landscape for much of ancient Israel's population.[46]

O'Connor is not as sure as Meyers that the poems reflect the private realm as it actually existed. Seeing connections between the Song of Songs and the strong woman in Proverbs 31, she states:

For a woman of the ancient world she [the woman in Song of Songs] is completely out of character. In these love poems the actual relationships between men and women in Israelite society are reversed, as they are in the Poem of the Strong Woman in Proverbs 31.

Marriage as a symbol of the intimate connection between the Wisdom Woman and her disciple is the subject of Prov 31:10–31. Life in union with Wisdom is meant to be as close as a love affair or a marriage. Moreover, the language of love appears elsewhere in Proverbs to encourage the disciple to love her, to embrace her, to hold her fast, to live with her (for example, Prov 3:15–18; 4:6–8; 8:17–21).[47]

This understanding of the Song may explain some of the thorns that Fewell notices. If the women in the poems represent Wisdom, many forces might stand in the way of the lovers attaining their hearts' desire.

O'Connor does not see the connection between the women in Song of Songs and the woman in Proverbs 31:10–31 as being the only level on which the Song of Songs should be interpreted, however. Rather, she sees the relationship between these two parts of Scripture as providing

a poetic coloring for the love poems, an additional layer of meaning in connection with the wisdom traditions. If this interpretation is correct, not only is the sexual arena blessed as good in itself, the Song also serves as a metaphor for wisdom's relationship with human beings. To live with Wisdom, to pursue her and to be pursued by her, is to enter into a love affair set in a garden of paradise where true human desires will be realized. It is a relationship which itself expresses the harmony and blessedness of the universe.[48]

Whereas O'Connor sees a relationship between the Song and Wisdom, Ilana Pardes finds connections between the Song and the use of women as symbols for Israel in the prophetic literature. She writes:

Hence the antipatriarchal model of love in the Song could be made to function as a countervoice to the misogynist prophetic degradation of the nation. It could offer an inspiring consolation in its emphasis on reciprocity. For once the relationship of God and His bride relies on mutual courting, mutual attraction, and mutual admiration, there is more room for hope that redemption is within reach.[49]

Nevertheless Pardes does not see the Song as totally depatriarchalized. She sees many tensions within the text. The question she tries to answer is how the Song made it into the canon. Referring to the guards in the Song, she concludes:

According to the midrashic interpretation, the keepers of the walls are "the keepers of the walls of the Torah" (Shir HaShirim Rabbah v. 7). Using this allegorical reading as a springboard, let us return to the opening question. Why was the Song canonized? Let me suggest that the canon-makers, those who set limits to the sacred corpus, were in fact not unlike the keepers of the walls in the Song. Just as the guards in the Song are neither omnipotent nor innocent of forbidden desires, so the watchmen of Holy Writ could not fully prevent the admission of ideologically alien voices within the canon, especially those other voices which filled (unconscious) needs in the biblical array. And the Song too played a role in the drama. If this deviant text could have circumvented the keepers of the walls, it is probably because the Song is not entirely antagonistic to the Law. Like the Shulamite, the Song simultaneously challenges the Law and accepts it, reveals and conceals its otherness.[50]

One other point needs to be made. Returning to Song of Songs 1:5 and assuming that the man is not primarily of African descent, we have here the love poetry of an ethnically mixed couple. This is probably more subversive today than it was in its original context, when various shades of skin color coexisted without any sense that this was unusual.[51] It is odd that so few feminist or womanist interpreters have commented on this.[52]

The Song of Songs is a biblical book that we can celebrate on two counts. Although the setting of the Song is not without its problems, it nevertheless depicts the love of men and women who are much more equal than men and women in much of the Hebrew canon. It also portrays a lighter-skinned individual and a darker-skinned individual who have high self-esteem and deep affection for each other. Much in the Hebrew Bible may strike us as archaic and oppressive. Here is a model that challenges us to live up to its poetry and its politics.

CONCLUSIONS

The Wisdom literature contains much that is problematic for feminists, but also much that is the source of hope. The figure of the "strange" woman in Proverbs is the most disturbing, and the dichotomy between the good and bad women, Wisdom and Folly, is very difficult for many feminists. On the other hand, the figure Wisdom is the source of much feminist theology. In addition, women in Job, although they play small roles, are important and for some feminists positive. The Song of Songs is generally viewed as one of the most feminist of the books of the Hebrew Bible, although it is not without some problems. Nevertheless there is much in this book of love lyrics that provides feminists with palatable food for thought.

DISCUSSION QUESTIONS

1. How do you feel about Job's wife?
2. The dichotomy between the safe wife and the smooth, other woman is very much a part of our society today, as shown by the movie *Fatal Attraction*. If you saw the movie, discuss the imagery there; or think of other examples of the dichotomy in our culture. How does this way of thinking affect women's self-esteem?
3. What are the characteristics of a truly good wife and of a truly good husband?
4. What/who is Wisdom and how is it/she related to God?
5. How do you feel about interracial relationships?

10

Subversive Women in Subversive Books:
Ruth, Esther, Susanna, and Judith

The stories of Ruth, Esther, Susanna, and Judith convey the most liberating messages for women of any of the stories of women in the first testament. Most modern readers miss the subversive points being made, because we are not part of the ancient culture out of which these books arose. Thus the purpose of this chapter is to help the modern reader see these stories in a new light.

RUTH

The story of Ruth and Naomi is a perennially popular one. It is often characterized as sweet: a story of loyalty and tragedy turned into triumph. It is the story of Naomi, whose husband Elimelech and two sons Mahlon and Chilion die while they are living away from their Israelite homeland in Moab. It is also the story of Orpah, one of Naomi's two daughters-in-law, who heeds Naomi's advice and returns to her mother's house, and of Ruth, the other daughter-in-law, who decides to return to Israel with Naomi (Ruth 1). Ruth meets Boaz, a relative of Naomi, as she gleans in his field, and he praises her for her loyalty to Naomi (Ruth 2). Ruth 3 describes Naomi's plan for Ruth to present herself to Boaz where he is sleeping and Ruth's execution of the plan. Boaz again praises her, but this time for choosing him rather than a younger man. In Ruth 4, the final chapter, Boaz works out the legal arrangements for redeeming a field of Naomi's and marrying Ruth. A son, Obed, is born, who becomes the grandfather of King David, according to the story.

Much has been written about Ruth. Phyllis Trible was the first modern feminist Hebrew Bible scholar to offer an interpretation. She sees the story as that of two women, loyal to each other, struggling to survive in and transform a patriarchal world.[1] On the other end of the feminist spectrum, Esther Fuchs believes that Ruth and Naomi are considered biblical heroines because they voluntarily and actively support the patriarchal institution of the levirate, which ensures the patrilineage of the deceased father.[2] Between the ends of the spectrum that Trible and Fuchs represent, four other feminist authors—one male, one female, and one male-female team—have contributed especially important understandings of the book of Ruth.

Although the book of Ruth is set in the period of the judges, André LaCocque argues for a late date of composition, after the Babylonian exile.[3] He believes the book is not historical but is a novella, or short story.[4] He writes: "At stake in the discussion of date are diametrically opposed interpretations of Ruth. Either the tale is a preexilic apologue [story with a moral] or it is a postexilic parable. Apologue sets an ethical model; its purpose is edification and confirmation of world. Parable questions ideology; it subverts world."[5] How is Ruth subversive? Ruth's primary subversiveness lies in her ethnic identity. Ruth is a Moabite (Ruth 1:4, 22; 2:2, 6, 21; 4:5, 10). She is not just a foreign woman. She is from Moab, one of Israel's most hated enemies. The beginnings of the hostility go back to the period of Israel's wilderness sojourn. At this time Numbers reports that the women of Moab tried to corrupt the Israelite men (Num. 25:1–5). As a result, Moabites are prohibited from ever being part of the Israelite community (Deut. 23:2–6). This exclusion of the Moabites was reaffirmed in the postexilic period by Ezra and Nehemiah (Ezra 9:1–10:44; Neh. 13:1–3).[6]

Even more scandalous than having a Moabite woman as the hero of the story is that the law of levirate is applied to her. This law allowed an *Israelite* widow without heirs to mate with her deceased husband's brother to produce an heir. The custom was intended to preserve Israelite families and property. Here it is applied to the Moabite daughter-in-law of an Israelite widow.[7] Worse yet, Ruth is praised for her *ḥesed*, her steadfast love and loyalty. Such a term was not normally used for a Moabitess.[8]

Part of the subversive effect of the book of Ruth comes from the parallels between it and the story of Tamar and Judah (Gen. 38). Ruth is the new Tamar. The unnamed man who forfeits his "rights" when he does not agree to redeem Naomi's field and marry Ruth (Ruth 4:1–6) corresponds to Shelah in Genesis 38 and the third son whom Judah withholds from Tamar. LaCocque writes: "Thus, by artistic transpositions, Tamar the Canaanite becomes Ruth the Moabite, and Judah's sons or Judah himself become 'So and so' [the unnamed kinsman who refuses to buy Naomi's field]. The symbolism is transparent; the postexilic Judahites of the exclusivist party in

Jerusalem are put on a par with Shelah or with Onan. They sterilize history."[9]
In other words, the ruling elite situated in Jerusalem, who wanted to exclude
from the Israelite community all foreigners, are being subtly mocked. In contrast, Ruth's role brings Naomi back to life. The story shows that the tension
created by the introduction of the repulsive Moabite outsider will be resolved
not by her expulsion, but rather by her marriage to Boaz.[10]

If we read the story of Ruth this way, it is no longer a sweet story, appropriate for children's bedtime reading. It is a story with profound, subversive
intent, which will be especially pleasing to both feminists and ethnic minorities. Reading the book of Ruth is like hearing the message of Sojourner
Truth. Although the specific concerns about Moabite women are not issues
today, there are modern parallels. Nonwhite women in American society
have double problems. They are marginalized in subtle and not so subtle
ways. But, like Ruth, they are needed for the vitality of American culture. We
will return to this issue below.

Mieke Bal analyzes the story of Ruth from a literary perspective.[11] Her
approach is not inconsistent with LaCocque's. Rather, they complement
each other. She challenges the traditional reading, in which Boaz is seen as
the generous, rich man who allows the poor women another chance at life.
Bal's reading turns on Boaz's response to Ruth at the threshing floor in Ruth
3:10: "May you be blessed by the LORD, my daughter; this last instance of
your loyalty (ḥesed) is better than the first; you have not gone after young
men, whether poor or rich." Boaz is not just a nice old man who helps poor
young Ruth out of a bad situation. He is an unmarried man, perhaps a wid-
ower, possibly even a childless one. He is pleased to have been chosen by an
attractive, younger woman.[12]

Bal is especially interested in the allusions in the text, especially those in
Ruth 4:11–12:[13]

> Then all the people who were at the gate, along with the elders, said, "We
> are witnesses. May the LORD make the woman who is coming into your
> house like Rachel and Leah, who together built up the house of Israel.
> May you produce children in Ephrathah and bestow a name in Bethle-
> hem; and, through the children that the LORD will give you by this young
> woman, may your house be like the house of Perez, whom Tamar bore to
> Judah."

Rachel's childlessness and Leah's lack of access to her husband are solved when
the two of them work together. Leah gives Rachel the mandrakes and Rachel
gives Leah access to Jacob. In so doing, they break out of the narrow situation
in which their father and husband have placed them. Thus Bal sees their story
as subversive. She writes: "The elders, in Ruth, comment upon that story by
acknowledging afterwards the rightness of the women's subversion when they

equate Ruth to the position of Rachel and Leah together. The equation 1 + 1 = 1 . . . restores the unity of the two aspects of femininity [beauty and fertility] that were separated by the men."[14]

The second comparison is between Boaz and Perez, the son of Judah and Tamar. Bal writes:

> As the son of his mother, he [Perez] is a transgressor of rules. His name means "break." Breaker of rules, he represents also the "brèche vers une latence" [break toward a latency] of the cure. Boaz the perfect citizen is compared to him. How can he be compared with the fruit of Tamar's wit and Judah's double standard? Integrating the two laws [levirate marriage and redemption of property], Boaz is transgressing as well. . . . When Boaz goes to court at the city gate, he identifies with Parez [sic] the transgressor of rules, son and grandson of Judah, who is like himself a mediator. Boaz becomes the mediator, between generations, sexes, classes, and people, between law and justice, the public and the private, economy and history.[15]

In other words, Boaz bends the rules to establish a higher justice.

Thus the book of Ruth can be read not only as subversive of one particular law excluding Moabites from participation in the Israelite community. By setting justice higher than law and higher than charity, it implies a whole different way of determining religious truth. It is subversive of every narrow reading of biblical law, especially biblical laws that oppress.

This point of view is taken up by Jesus in the New Testament. He was quick to throw out old rules that no longer fit. The book of Ruth, understood this way, provides us with a biblical precedent to interpret and reinterpret the ancient stories and laws that have shaped, and have been shaped by, our spiritual forebears.

At many points Fewell and Gunn's reading of Ruth echoes those of LaCocque and Bal. Their understanding of the scene at the city gate is different, however. They note that when Boaz brings up the piece of land owned by Naomi, it is the first time we have heard about it. Boaz is using this probably worthless piece of land as a way of making himself look good. He wants to marry Ruth, but because she is a Moabite, his reputation in the community is likely to be lowered. So he publicly asks the next of kin if he will redeem land. The unnamed next of kin reluctantly agrees, because it is the honorable thing to do. But then Boaz tells him that on the same day that he redeems the field, Boaz will marry Ruth. At this point Fewell and Gunn are reading a slightly different text than most translators.[16] Their translation alters the picture significantly. Boaz's imminent marriage to Ruth means that Naomi may have an heir to whom the piece of land would ultimately revert. At this point the next of kin bows out. Boaz then magnanimously agrees both to redeem the land and to marry Ruth. His marriage announcement is couched in terms of levirate marriage, even though that institution doesn't apply to a Moabite daughter-in-law. By describing the marriage in terms of raising up an heir for Naomi's dead husband, he makes himself look good in the eyes of the men.[17]

Fewell and Gunn write: "Why the public confrontation? Because the essence of Boaz's operation here is public. He is in the business of effecting a dubious marriage in such a way as to make it a public triumph. He is a pillar of society and determined to remain that way. The name of the game is Public Relations and he is a master of it."[18] They conclude their consideration of Boaz with these words:

> So what is the measure of Boaz's faithfulness? His willingness to pay tribute to the patriarchy and subordinate all else to its rule? Viewed from one angle Boaz is as trapped by the patriarchy as Naomi, though he is trapped in privilege, she in dependency. Viewed from another, he is instrumental in mocking the system. He wishes to marry the Moabite woman and does so. His profession of commitment to the name of the dead is hollow. He cares no more for Mahlon and Elimelech than does the narrator. They are but weapons in his hand as he defeats one set of prejudices by wielding another. The measure of his faithfulness, then, surely lies somewhere else, somewhere in his offer of grain, and the spreading of a wing, in the exercise of *hesed* [= *ḥesed*] for mixed reasons, in a compromised world. Or is that too kind to Boaz?[19]

Like Bal, Fewell and Gunn see Boaz as a character who has mixed motives, as have all the characters in the story. They are all human, yet out of the tangle of human interactions God's redemption occurs. Nevertheless Ruth emerges in Fewell and Gunn's reading as the hero.

> Perhaps she [Ruth] was recognized by Naomi as the real redeemer in this story. Perhaps not. Perhaps the gate of Boaz's people did come to consider her a woman of worth—like the woman of worth in Proverbs 31, a woman subservient, and thus valuable, to the patriarchy. Perhaps they only thought of her as Obed's (surrogate?) mother. Or perhaps, just perhaps, a few saw her as a woman of great strength and determination, a redeemer, in her own right, deserving of her own story, a woman worth more than seven sons of Israel.[20]

How do we evaluate these diverse perspectives? Ruth is a story with many gaps. Depending on how these gaps are filled, different readings result.[21] One reading is not better than another. There is some overlap, but where there is contradiction, it results from the polyvalence of the text, rather than from one interpreter reading correctly and another incorrectly.

Ruth is a hero as understood by Trible, LaCocque, Bal, and Fewell and Gunn. Although they differ in significant ways in their understanding of the book of Ruth, on this there is general agreement.

In the years since the first edition of this book was written, two issues have become important. The first is the question of possible female authorship, or at least of female voices and culture being heard or reflected in the story. Athalya Brenner and Fokkelien van Dijk-Hemmes have raised this latter question especially clearly, but others have also contributed to the discussion.[22] Although it is impossible to be certain, it seems likely that women's interests are being communicated in the book of Ruth, at least indirectly. Nevertheless, given the androcentric nature of the larger culture, women's voices have also surely been filtered through the lens of patriarchy.

Given modern tensions over immigration and colonialism in many parts of the world, the second issue has to do with Ruth's status as an immigrant. The issue is partly economic and partly ethnic. Aware of the problems of foreign laborers in Israel, Athalya Brenner reflects on how marriage between a foreign worker and a native Israeli, though rare, enhances the position of the foreigner today, but does not allow full assimilation. Similarly, she writes: "Foreigners may be accepted; less so if they are of the underprivileged classes and women; and full integration, even in the case of Ruth, an exemplary female character in many ways, is in fact impossible. The variables of class, occupation and femaleness usually override those of foreignness and personal excellence—then and now."[23]

Judith McKinlay, a white woman from New Zealand, reads the story of Ruth in the context of the tensions between the dominant *Pakeha/Palagi* (non–South Pacific) culture and the indigenous Maori people. Given the fact that the Israelites, at least according to the biblical story, conquered Canaan, then Ruth may be compared to one of the Maori. She says: "My fear is that there is a seemingly coherent insider mythos of the book of Ruth that all too easily reinforces a sadly persisting and pervading colonial ethos. Moabite mothers beware! *Pakeha/palagi* women read very carefully."[24]

Laura Donaldson and Musa W. Dube have similar concerns, but they write from different social locations. Donaldson, of Cherokee Indian descent, and Dube, an African South African (her terminology for nonwhite, black, or indigenous South African), identify with Orpah, who refused to abandon her own people, rather than Ruth who assimilated with the then-dominant culture. Donaldson writes:

[M]y responsibility as a person of Cherokee descent and as an informed biblical reader transforms Ruth's positive value into a negative and Orpah's negative value into a positive. Such is the epistemological vertigo inspired by reading in the contact zone. . . . I can only hope that my indigenization of Ruth has located new meaning in the interaction between biblical text and American Indian context—a meaning that resists imperial exegesis and contributes to the empowerment of aboriginal peoples everywhere.[25]

Dube uses the genre of fictional letters between Orpah and Ruth to make her point. In this way she brings Orpah to life, who otherwise is silent after Naomi and Ruth return to Bethlehem. In one of her letters, Orpah explains to Ruth: "I had to return to my old widowed mother who, like Naomi, did not have any son or husband left. It was also right that I should return to my people and religion, for Naomi herself was returning to her people and religion. I have continued in this court, serving my mother and my country as the regent queen and priestess. . . . These are the true words of Orpah, who returned to her mother's house and to her Gods."[26]

Katharine Sakenfeld raises a concern related to those of Brenner, McKinlay, Donaldson, and Dube. From her travels in Asia and work with poor Asian women, she is concerned about the sexual exploitation of such young women. Reflecting on Ruth's risky initiative with Boaz, she writes:

> When marriage will not provide economic stability, however meager, or a husband is not available, women turn to some form of employment to support themselves and their families. All too often, the seeming best or only option is to sell their bodies. And in many cases, they are tricked into doing that even when it is their intention to take other employment, such as domestic work. The story of Ruth has a "happy ending" within its own cultural context, as marriage, security, and a boy baby are the outcome of Ruth's initiative. But women cannot always realistically count on such an ending.[27]

Sarojini Nadar, a South African Indian Christian interpreter, writes from the context of the Indian tradition of Sati, in which traditionally Hindu widows burnt themselves to death on their husbands' funeral pyres. Although this extreme practice is not practiced among the South African Indians, the mind-set has carried over in that widows often feel that their only hope of survival dies with their husband. Thus, Nadar sees in the story of Ruth a model of a widow who does not resign herself to destitution, but rather persistently and creatively struggles to survive.[28]

What can we make of such a diversity of voices? If the story was told in the postexilic period and its intent was to challenge those who objected to foreign women, then in that context it can be viewed as a progressive, positive story. In addition, the fact that women are the primary actors and, with the help of a cooperative man and presumably God, are able to turn their destitution into fullness may also be applauded. Nevertheless, from a contemporary perspective, the happy ending of the book of Ruth should not make us insensitive to concerns about the ways majority cultures often mute the voices of women and minorities and the continuing problems of sexploitation.

ESTHER

The book of Esther, like Ruth, is historical fiction. It was written in the post-exilic period, and the setting is the Persian court. Although the book is named after its female protagonist, the character Esther has not always fared very well in commentaries. The story is well known. King Ahasuerus (Xerxes) banishes Queen Vashti when she refuses to display herself with (only?) her crown on before his guests at a banquet (Esth. 1). After much preparation, Esther is chosen as the new queen (Esth. 2).

Meanwhile, Haman has been made the king's deputy and Mordecai, Esther's cousin, has refused to bow down to Haman. Haman then decides to get rid of all the Jews. He gets the king's permission to write a royal decree to this effect and seal it with his ring (Esth. 3). When Mordecai hears about it, he puts on mourning clothes and wails in the street (Esth. 4:1).

Mordecai then advises Esther to go to the king. She responds that she cannot without his invitation, but Mordecai encourages her with his famous lines: "Do not think that in the king's palace you will escape any more than all the other Jews. For if you keep silence at such a time as this, relief and deliverance will rise for the Jews from another quarter, but you and your father's family will perish. Who knows? Perhaps you have come to royal dignity for just such a time as this" (Esth. 4:13–14).

In Esther 5, Esther puts on her royal robes and stands at the inner court of the king's palace. The king, seeing her, bids her come in. She then invites him and Haman to a banquet that evening. At the banquet, the king asks her what she wants, and she invites them to yet another banquet the following evening.

Esther 6 describes the king reading the record books one night when he cannot sleep. He is thus reminded of how Mordecai had saved his life by discovering an assassination plot. So he asks Haman how he should honor someone, and Haman, thinking he is referring to himself, suggests lavish ceremonies. He is mortified to learn that the recipient is his enemy Mordecai and that he, Haman, is to carry out the honors that Mordecai is to receive.

In Esther 7 the second banquet sees Haman's downfall. Esther tells the king how Haman has planned the destruction of her people. Haman is sentenced to die on the same gallows that he has built for Mordecai. Esther 8 describes how a new edict is sent out under the king's seal. This edict allows the Jews to defend themselves against their attackers (the old edict cannot be revoked, as Persian laws were irrevocable). In Esther 9, the destruction of 75,000 anti-Semites is recorded. Then the biblical story concludes by saying that these days should be remembered in the annual festival of Purim, the word *pur* meaning "lot," since the lot had been cast against the Jews (Esth. 9:26–32).

Renita Weems considers the characters of both Vashti and Esther in her study of the book of Esther.[29] In thinking about Vashti's refusal to display herself before the king's banquet, she writes:

> The story of Vashti's reign stands as a valuable lesson about the enormous pressures, demands, and responsibilities upon women who live public lives. It is a memorial to the price often extracted of public women when they step outside of their prescribed roles. Nancy Reagan, Rosalynn Carter, Eleanor Roosevelt—wives of modern American presidents—come to mind.[30]

Weems says that it may seem old-fashioned to talk about women whose power and influence are based on their relationship with their husbands. However, some of the most important contributions made by women in our history have been made by wives of political and religious figures.[31]

Weems also suggests that the king's experience with Vashti may have softened him up a bit. When Esther appears at the door to his inner court, he is more open to listen to her. This suggests that we have a responsibility to remember and celebrate the female leaders who paved the way for others. Weems concludes:

> If the truth be told, we today are who we are—if we are anybody—because some woman, somewhere, stooped down long enough that we might climb on her back and ride piggyback into the future.
>   Ask Queen Esther.[32]

On the other hand, Susan Niditch believes that Vashti and Esther are being contrasted as wise and foolish.

> A number of modern feminist writers have, in fact, found their heroine in Vashti, their empathy with her, while regarding Esther as a weak collaborator with tyranny, an antifeminist. . . . For the writer of Esther, however, Vashti's foolishness is the foil for Esther's wisdom, justifies her dismissal, and indeed from a narrative point of view is the spark that commences the story.[33]

Sidnie Ann White notes that Mordecai is often thought of as a stronger character than Esther.[34] For example, Carey Moore writes, "Between Mordecai and Esther the greater hero is Mordecai, who supplied the brains while Esther simply followed his directions."[35] White argues just the opposite:

> The Jews in the Diaspora . . . are in the position of the weak, as a subordinate population under the dominant Persian government. They must adjust to their lack of immediate political and economic power and learn to work within the system to gain what power they can. In the book of Esther, their role model for this adjustment is Esther. Not only is she a woman, a member of a perpetually subordinate population, but she is an orphan, a powerless member of Jewish society. Therefore, her position in

society is constantly precarious, as was the position of the Jews in the Diaspora. With no native power of her own owing to her sex or position in society, Esther must learn to make her way among the powerful and to cooperate with others in order to make herself secure.[36]

White points out that although Esther's joining a harem sounds degrading to modern readers, in the period in which the story is set, it is an acceptable means of gaining power. The narrator does not intimate that Esther should be condemned for her willingness to try out for the position of queen.[37] In addition, oppressed people often must use whatever means are available to them to survive.

Although Mordecai is often hailed as the hero of the story, he initiates the crisis by his refusal to bow down to Haman. No reason is stated for his refusal. Perhaps it is because he is Jewish, but there are other examples of Jews bowing down to officials without condemnation. For example, Joseph's brothers bow down to him as ruler (Gen. 42:6). Mordecai appears foolish. He does not come across as the wise courtier.[38]

In addition, Mordecai's reaction to hearing about the edict to destroy the Jews is not helpful. The putting on of mourning clothes and wailing in the city streets (Esth. 4:1) reveals his panic. This is an acceptable way of expressing grief, but it does not solve the problem.[39]

When Mordecai informs Esther of the edict and tells her to go to the king, her reluctance is based on an objective understanding of reality. Going inside the inner court of the king uninvited means death. Nevertheless, when Mordecai sends his famous message, Esther springs into action. From this point on, she is in charge. Esther 4 ends, "Mordecai then went away and did everything as Esther had ordered him." Esther's plan uses indirect methods of persuasion common among oppressed people, including women. It works beautifully.[40] White concludes:

> Her conduct throughout the story has been a masterpiece of feminine skill. From beginning to end, she does not make a misstep. While in the harem, she earns the favor of Hegai [the chief eunuch], and follows his advice and the advice of Mordecai, both experienced in the ways of the court. She wins the king's heart, becomes queen and then, when danger threatens, skillfully negotiates her tricky course. She is a model for the successful conduct of life in the often uncertain world of the Diaspora. The fact that she is a woman emphasizes the plight of the Jew in the Diaspora: the once-powerful Jewish nation has become a subordinate minority within a foreign empire, just as Esther, as a woman, is subject to the dominant male. However, by accepting the reality of a subordinate position and learning to gain power by working within the structure rather than against it, the Jew can build a successful and fulfilling life in the Diaspora, as Esther does in the court of Ahasuerus.[41]

Thus White sees Esther not only as heroic but as a model for the Jews in the Diaspora.

LaCocque sees the subversiveness of the book of Esther in its implication that the fate of Israel lies with the fate of the dispersed Jews.[42] He makes several points that are of interest to us here. One of them has to do with the humor in the story. LaCocque notes the absurdity of the grotesque excesses: Vashti the queen is a mere sex object, Ahasuerus issues a royal edict that throughout his kingdom husbands will be masters of their homes, and the beauty contest for the new Miss Persia will deliver to the king the most beautiful woman in the kingdom, who after one night with the king will be sent to the harem where she will stay until the king desires her services. The book of Esther does not describe ancient reality; it is a satire.[43]

A contrast is made between the king, who appears very weak and stupid, and the edicts that issue from him, which are irrevocable. The point, however, is not simply to put down Persian law. It is to condemn a way of thinking about law that had become common at that time. LaCocque writes:

> [Esther] is the story of the clash between two laws and, beyond that, between two world views. One could also define the problem as a contest between two inviolabilities. The denouement of the story will show that what is inviolable is the Jewish people, not an abstraction such as the "Persian law" (6:13; cf. 4:14). When ideology prevails over humanity, the machine indiscriminately crushes friends and foes.[44]

Danna Fewell makes a similar point. She writes:

> One might also see in "the law that cannot be changed" a veiled reference to Torah. As authoritative scripture, Torah holds pride of place in Jewish tradition. As such its text must be preserved. On the other hand, texts that cannot change are stagnant texts. They become absurd, like those in the story world of Esther, creating massive instability despite their attempt to stabilize. One way to introduce change without changing the text itself is to add another voice to the dialogue. Esther, as it were, elbows its way into the canon of authoritative texts, demanding a hearing and making room for the new holiday of Purim. This text, like rabbinic commentary, keeps the canon from becoming a law that cannot change; it helps to keep the canon alive and talking.[45]

The points made by LaCocque and Fewell, like the one Bal believes is being made in the book of Ruth, are about the necessity of reinterpreting old laws. Bal's treatment of Esther, like that of Weems, considers the relationship between Vashti and Esther. However, her approach is different. She writes:

> Vashti is necessary to produce Esther. In the plot, the elimination of the former produces the vacancy necessary for the latter, hence, for the

unfolding of the plot. But there is more to this narrative status of the first queen. As an agent of ideological reflection she is eliminated for the sake of the ideology of male dominance. But she is eliminated only to reemerge in Esther, who takes her place, avenging her punishment by turning disobedience into access to power. Vashti's refusal to be an object of display is in a sense a refusal to be objectivized, hence, to be robbed of her subjectivity. Esther's insistence on appearing, albeit using the tools of display (5:1: "On the third day, Esther put on her royal robes . . ."), is the positive version of Vashti's negative act; she appears not for show but for action, not as sheer possession but as self-possessed subject, and to drive this continuity between Esther and Vashti home, it is now *she* who makes the king appear at *her* banquet.[46]

Bal is also concerned about the way the book of Esther acts as a mirror for the reader. In it we can see ourselves. The important task is not to seek the historical origin of Purim, the Jewish festival that the events in the book of Esther supposedly inaugurate. Rather, Bal concludes:

> When the lot has determined that another people is now subject to danger, the critic reading "Esther" cannot innocently submit to lots. For obedience was shown to be the wrong attitude. It is an ironic misreading of the mirror of "Esther" to see the scroll as only about the history of the Jews and one of their festivals. By reading the text as about reading-writing, one is led to reflect upon all the issues intricated with it: gender, power, and the state, genocide and otherness, submission and agency. In short, upon history.[47]

In other words, the book of Esther is about more than past history. It calls its readers to reflect and presumably act in the challenges to human dignity that confront us today.

Klara Butting agrees. She sees the book of Esther as having been written by women, who were rewriting the Joseph story, thus focusing not only on the oppression of the Jews, but also of women. In so doing, they encourage contemporary readers to follow in their paths:

> The authors testify with their procedure that the Bible wants to be an interlocutor, not an authority. They recognize the deity witnessed therein as a deity that invites examination of all transmitted texts, in order to determine whether their God talk legitimizes and reassures the suppression of women and men. In the dispute over biblical texts, the book of Esther is interesting for feminist hermeneutics. Feminists, in their discussion of the Bible, can go on from here. We are encouraged to find evidence of the liberating deity in biblical texts and, at the same time, stimulated to testify to this deity by telling the story anew and after a critical analysis of the existing record.[48]

Madipoane Masenya, an African–South African biblical scholar who calls her way of reading *Bosadi* (womanhood), finds disturbing elements in the story of Esther. Unlike Sidnie White, she believes that although the book bears Esther's name, it is really more about Mordecai than Esther. In addition, she is concerned that the upper-class nature of the story renders it unhelpful to most African women. Finally, and perhaps most importantly, from an African–South African perspective the story is troubling. The Jews, the foreigners, are God's chosen people and the indigenous Persians are the "other" group. The Jews are cruel to many innocent Persians in revenge for Haman's plan, which was never carried out; Esther even asks for a second day of killing. In the context where the indigenous South Africans were brutalized by Christian Europeans, Esther has painful resonances.[49]

The book of Esther gives us much to ponder: the nature of law, the ways in which women achieve their goals, especially in situations when they have little power, and the use of humor and satire to make important points. Esther is a much stronger, more positive character than she might at first appear to modern readers, though the story is not without some disturbing elements.

SUSANNA AND JUDITH

Although the stories of Susanna and Judith are not included in the Hebrew Bible or in the Protestant canon, they are part of the Roman Catholic and Eastern Orthodox Bibles, as well as being included in the Apocrypha in the King James Bible.[50] We do not know why they were omitted from the Hebrew canon. They are very similar to Ruth and Esther. They share the same literary genre, and their religio-political stands are perhaps no more subversive. Nevertheless Susanna's story is less subtle in its condemnation of the religious establishment.

Whatever the reasons for the exclusion of these stories from the Hebrew and Protestant Christian canons, they are worthy of consideration by Jews and Protestants. They are both wonderful stories that read well. Judith is the more feminist of the two stories, but Susanna is high drama and should not be missed.

Susanna

Susanna is a virtuous Jew from a well-to-do family. She is also very beautiful. Her name, which means "lily," occurs as a name nowhere else in the Hebrew Bible. The word "lily," however, occurs numerous times in the Song of Songs (also known as the Song of Solomon). Thus, Susanna is so-named probably to evoke the beautiful woman of the Song of Songs.[51]

Two elders see her walking about her garden daily and lust after her (Dan. 13:1–8). They then plot to satisfy their lust (Dan. 13:9–14). While she is in her garden, they confront her with the choice of sexual intercourse or, if she refuses, their accusation of the same (Dan. 13:15–21). The accusation of two elders would mean death.

Susanna refuses, is accused, and is being taken to her death, when the wise young Daniel intervenes (Dan. 13:22–46). He cross-examines the elders, asking them near which tree in the garden the alleged adultery took place. The elders give different answers, thus exposing their lie (Dan. 13:47–59). They are then executed (Dan. 13:60–62).

The story is undoubtedly modeled after the story of Potiphar's wife accusing Joseph of adultery (Gen. 39). Of course, here the sexes of accuser(s) and accused are reversed.[52]

LaCocque suggests that a story of a child teaching the guardians of tradition has to have had a subversive aim. The point is that religious authority does not lie simply in good exegesis, but in the Spirit. This becomes especially subversive when the bad guys in the story turn out to be not minor members of society, but elders on whose authority the community relies.[53]

Susanna is the hero of the story, but her role is sometimes considered to be secondary to that of Daniel. Certainly, compared to the elders, the villains of the story, she is a hero. Certainly Daniel, the young sage who saves Susanna, is a hero, without whom Susanna would be just another innocent victim. The impression that Daniel is the "real" hero of the story is created by the conclusion of the story, which focuses on Daniel. Toni Craven comments:

> The importance of Susanna's voice in the narrative's conclusion is not noted. To judge that she was found innocent only because the boy Daniel spoke in her defense would be comparable to saying that Daniel survived the lions' den in Bel and the Dragon [another apocryphal story] only because Habakkuk came to him (14:33–39). But twice the text says more. Before the judges, "Susanna groaned and said, 'I am completely trapped. For if I do this, it will mean death for me; if I do not, I cannot escape your hands. I choose not to do it; I will fall into your hands, rather than sin in the sight of the Lord.' Then Susanna cried out with a loud voice" (vv. 22–24a). Condemned to death, "Then Susanna cried out with a loud voice and said, 'O eternal God, you know what is secret and are aware of all things before they come to be; you know that these men have given false evidence against me. And now I am to die, though I have done none of the wicked things that they have charged against me!'" (vv. 42–43). So it happened that, "The Lord heard her cry. Just as she was being led off to execution, God stirred up the holy spirit of a young lad named Daniel" (vv. 44–45). She proved her inno-

cence and dedication to the law when she decided not to sin with the elders
(v. 23). Though seemingly trapped in a situation in which social convention
allowed men of age and rank to determine her fate, she found a voice to
refuse the elders and cry out to God. God heard her prayer. But in the end,
the narrative overlooks her and credits Daniel.[54]

Craven believes that to miss Susanna's central role in the story is a mistake.
After all, Susanna is the name by which the story is remembered.[55]

Amy-Jill Levine views the story more ambivalently. Although virtuous,
Susanna appears to be an upper-class woman with nothing better to do than
pamper herself. Compared with Esther, or even Ruth, she does not fare well.
Although she prays for help, she is not otherwise involved in her own rescue.
In addition, the taint of the charge of adultery clings to her, even after she has
been vindicated, as it does to many today who have been similarly charged.
She concludes:

> Susanna's exile from the peace and privacy of her own garden, the diaspora
> setting of the text, its problematic canonical history, and the marginaliza-
> tion of the modern Jewish woman engaged in analysis interweave around
> shifting borders. What may be celebrated from one perspective may be con-
> demned from another. Susanna's freedom from domestic responsibilities
> may indicate to some the economic success of the diaspora community; to
> others it signals complacency and indolence. For some she is a heroine
> whose righteousness is recognized by heaven; for others she is a weak figure
> unable or unwilling to protest her own innocence in the public sphere until
> seemingly too late. Recognition of class differences provokes an entry into
> the critique of Susanna-as-character and thereby allows exploration of inter-
> textually negative associations. Recognition of her marginalized position as
> a woman leads to the discovery of the relationship between the constructs
> of gender and ethnicity in Hellenistic Jewish narratives. Recognition of the
> value of her education, her piety and her prayer reinstates a more positive
> social role for Jewish women, which is often overlooked by those wedded to
> Christian or select rabbinic constructions. I have asked questions that arise
> from my own various, marginalized situations. The explorations they gen-
> erate and the tentative answers those explorations provide incorporate all
> fellow travelers across religious and sexual borders into the ongoing re-
> creation of Jewish history, of women's history, of human history.[56]

Susanna is a story that on some levels is emotionally satisfying. Truth
prevails, the hypocritical wrongdoers are punished, and the virtuous are
vindicated. In addition, there is created a tradition of cross-examination of
witnesses that can protect the weak and vulnerable. Nevertheless, feminist
readers will be uncomfortable with the fact that it is a woman who is lacking
in power and it is a man who has the wits to save her, thus leaving these

stereotypes in place. When Joseph is falsely accused by a woman, he goes to jail but eventually through his own God-given gifts is released. Susanna does pray to God and God answers her through Daniel, but we would be happier if the answer came through Susanna herself, or at least from another woman.

Judith

Judith is a much longer and more complex story than Susanna and one in which Judith is unquestionably the hero. Indeed, she is perhaps the strongest Hebrew hero in all of biblical literature. Again we are dealing with historical fiction. Nebuchadnezzar is depicted as king of the Assyrians. In real life he was the hated Babylonian king who exiled the Israelites. Holofernes is his general. In the first half of the story (Jdt. 1–7), Holofernes wins the allegiance of many cities and countries who then bow down to Nebuchadnezzar as God. On the way to Jerusalem, Holofernes arrives at the fictional Israelite town of Bethulia and cuts off their water supply. The situation is tense, and the council of elders has decided to hold out five more days. However, if God doesn't save them by then, they will surrender rather than all die.

At this point (chap. 8) Judith, a wealthy widow, appears on the scene, scolds the elders for their lack of faith, and declares she has a plan. After a long prayer (chap. 9), she goes to the Assyrian camp (chap. 10), persuades Holofernes to believe that she has defected (chap. 11), and succeeds in getting him to fall in love with her (chap. 12). While he is drunk, she chops off his head and returns to Bethulia (chap. 13). When the Assyrians discover the murder, they go crazy and the Bethulians kill a large number of them (chaps. 14–15).

They celebrate Judith, who lives to one hundred and five. She never remarries, although she has many suitors. Her only companion is her favorite maid, who was along with her when she killed Holofernes. In the end, she gives her maid her freedom (chaps. 15–16).

As in the story of Susanna, the primary point of this story is criticism of the establishment, but here the accent is a little different. The religious leaders are seen as too ready to compromise on important points and not flexible enough on lesser matters. In thinking about the roles of Judith, Esther, and Ruth in preserving and shaping tradition, Craven writes:

> Judith and her canonical sisters Esther and Ruth conserve ancient religious truth and preserve the life of the covenant community in ways suitable to their times. Each woman does her own kind of work in a man's world. In Ruth and Judith, women bind together for mutual support. Ruth has the counsel of Naomi; Judith has the help of her favorite maid. In Esther and Judith, political concerns motivate sexual involvements. Esther wins the favor of Ahasuerus as the most pleasing maiden in the

Persian empire; Judith dares much with Holofernes as a daughter of Israel feigning escape. Ruth, Esther, and Judith teach that certain conventions may be forced to give way so that tradition can be faithfully preserved. No unalterable set of prescriptions regarding appropriate female behavior forbids their participation in the process of modifying tradition. And no small debt is owed these women of scripture for their part in the hermeneutical process of continuity and change.[57]

Like Jael before her, Judith has sometimes been condemned for her deception and murder. She does use deception, but women and other characters who lack physical strength or structural power often must resort to devious means in order to achieve noble ends.

Judith is reminiscent of Jael. She also reflects quite a few other biblical women. LaCocque writes: "The book [Judith] is an anthology of texts about, and allusions to, other women in the Bible: Miriam, Deborah, Jael, Sarah, Rebekah, Rachel, Tamar, Naomi, Ruth, and Abigail, among others. Parallels with Esther and Susanna also are clear. In fact, the cumulative effect is striking; it amounts to a panegyric of the biblical woman."[58]

It is worthwhile to catalog the allusions. Judith is a rich widow (Jdt. 8:7). This is an unusual combination in Hebrew society. Her wealth indicates that she is a wise manager, like the "good" wife praised in Proverbs 31. However, she is also an independent woman. This puts her in the same category with Shiphrah and Puah, Miriam, Rahab, the woman of Endor, the Queen of Sheba, the wise woman of Tekoa, and Huldah. Like Abigail, Bathsheba, and Ruth, she is a widow. These widows are all related, one way or another, to David. LaCocque writes:

> The accumulation in the Judith story of lies, deceits, double entendres, assassinations, as well as the beauty of the woman, make one think not only of the episode of the rape of Dinah by the Shechemites [sic] in Genesis 34, but also of the triangle David–Bathsheba–Uriah in 2 Samuel 11. As to the beheading of Holofernes, the parallel with 1 Sam. 17:51, David drawing Goliath's own sword to decapitate him, is striking. As Judith brings back Holofernes's head to Bethulia and dedicates to God what she had taken from the general's tent, so had David done with the head of Goliath and the weapons that he brought "to Jerusalem," meaning that he dedicated the Philistine trophy to God. In more than one way, Judith is David in the feminine.[59]

But Judith is also a female version of a more recent Hebrew hero, Judas Maccabeus. Again, LaCocque writes:

> Judith is subversive by showing that a woman can take the lead and become the model of faith and martyrdom, while "elders" recoil in the holes of their complacency. Judith is not only a David redivivus of sorts, she is Judas Maccabee in the feminine; her very name says as much

(cf. 1 Macc. 3:1–9). At the time of the composition of Judith, it was surely not a trivial feat to feminize the hero of the day![60]

Judith never remarries. The church fathers were impressed with her chastity, but modern feminists are impressed with Judith for different reasons. Patricia Montley sees Judith as the archetypal androgyne. She combines elements of the soldier and the seductress that are culturally defined in the West as masculine and feminine. Montley writes, "Judith embodies yet somehow transcends the male/female dichotomy."[61]

Judith is a new kind of woman. She is independent, in need of no male protector. She uses both traditional feminine wiles and more masculine strategies. LaCocque believes that Judith "announces a new era."[62] She represents all the biblical women that have gone before her, and yet she is altogether a new creation.

Judith also has in common with Ruth self-sacrifice. Their sacrifices result in better lives for those whom they love. Naomi is too old to have the law of the levirate marriage apply to her, so Ruth substitutes for her. As a result, the story ends happily for everyone. Similarly, Judith substitutes herself for the elders who do not do their job properly. LaCocque writes:

> Judith substitutes herself, as a propitiatory sacrifice, to an establishment that has lost its head, much before Holofernes loses his for other reasons. When those in charge of the public protection are disheartened and thus expose their protégés, these must either undergo slaughter or take their fate in their own hands—thus, perhaps saving themselves *and* their appointed leaders. How they do that may take different forms. According to Isaiah and Zechariah, the Servant goes through substitutive suffering and death, and God only can change his failure into victory, his death into life. The book of Judith, influenced as it is by a Hellenistic world view, stresses instead heroic substitution, and Judith's victory is not postmortem, although it is in extremis. In both cases, the results are comparable and the premises similar. Of the two, Judith is perhaps to us more understandable and imitable than is the Suffering Servant—but, ultimately, Judith saves only Bethulia, whereas the Servant of YHWH redeems the world.[63]

The notion of self-sacrifice recalls a different sort of female sacrifice, that of Jephthah's daughter. Jephthah's daughter allows her father to sacrifice her, although she may not have had many practical alternatives. Nevertheless there is an element of acquiescence in the story. Her sacrifice probably served no real purpose and was the result of her father's stupid vow. Judith's self-sacrifice is the result of her own free choice. It is wise and careful. Furthermore, it preserves a whole Israelite town from destruction.

Thus Judith is a new woman in another sense. Not only is she independent. Not only is she able to act in ways that are thought of as feminine and masculine. She is also able to give of herself in ways that are public, constructive, and self-chosen. She gives of herself, not because it is her role to be the supportive wife and mother or because she has little choice. She gives of herself, not simply in the domestic sphere. She gives of herself, using her mind, her feminine charms, and her masculine military prowess. She gives of herself to achieve for the public good what no one else in her town dared to imagine. She risks much, both in terms of her virtue with Holofernes and her reputation back home, where her actions are most unusual. She comes out the victor and with her all her compatriots win.

Great danger to the public calls for citizens to risk their lives and their reputations. This is true even if our actions are not always understood or hailed, as Judith's were. Eileen Schuller notes that Judith's story is remembered and retold by Latin American women who are involved in the struggle to liberate their people.[64] Judith is a model, not just for women, but for everyone who would like to make an impact on the world. She teaches us courage, disregard for petty conventions, and vision. Where these three abide, hope for a better world cannot die.

The one fly in the ointment in Judith's story is the fact that after she has saved Bethulia, she withdraws from public life. If she had been male, we would have expected her dramatic rescue of her town to have been the beginning of a long and successful political career. Amy-Jill Levine writes:

> All that remains of the intrusion of Judith's otherness into the public realm is her 'fame' (16.23). That is, her deed become incorporated into public memory and public discourse, and it is thereby controlled. Yet each time her story is told, this woman who represented the community as well as exceeded that representation will both reinforce and challenge Bethulia's—and the reader's—gender-determined ideology.[65]

On the other hand, there are some modern male parallels to Judith's early retirement, notably George Washington. Rising to meet a community challenge, then returning to private life is perhaps a more noble pattern than the modern one in which politicians, both male and female, seek their own power and status more than what is truly good for the community.

CONCLUSIONS

Ruth, Esther, Susanna, and Judith are strong, virtuous women. They are role models, not just for women, but for people of faith regardless of gender. Although short in length, these stories go a long way toward providing a counterbalance to the many texts with which Jewish and Christian feminists struggle.

DISCUSSION QUESTIONS

1. The book of Ruth is about including the excluded, in this case a foreign woman. Who are the excluded in our society or in our religious
   communities who need to be included? In what ways do we expect
   them to change in order to be assimilated into our midst?
2. Women's friendships are very important to many women. Is there a
   difference in the value that women and men place on same-sex relationships? What about friendships that cross cultural and racial lines?
3. Based on your understanding of the books of Ruth and Esther, how
   should we deal with biblical laws that seem archaic and oppressive?
4. Did Vashti have any choice when she was summoned to appear before
   the king and his revelers "in her crown"? Have you ever been caught in
   a similar situation? (Be broad in your interpretation of "similar.")
5. How do you feel about the privileges and the responsibilities of
   women who are married to public officials?
6. Esther combines the sexual, spiritual, and vocational in her actions to
   save her people. How have the vocational, sexual, and spiritual
   aspects of your life related to each other? Is there a difference in the
   way women and men typically integrate these parts of their lives?
7. How do you feel about interracial marriage?
8. Have you ever been unjustly accused? Was there anyone who could
   come to your aid? In what ways could you or did you act to vindicate
   yourself?
9. How prevalent in the contemporary world are the "unjust judge" and
   the "unrighteous elder"? How should we deal with them?
10. Do the ends ever justify the means? If so, when and why?
11. Who are the Judiths, the new women, of today?
12. What are some of the petty conventions in our society that need to be
    bent or changed, and what are some of the fundamentals that should
    not be compromised?
13. Should the stories of Susanna and Judith be in the Hebrew and
    Protestant canons of Scripture? Why or why not?
14. Compare Judith with other biblical women like Jael and Jezebel. How
    are they similar and how are they different?

Part 3
Reflections

11
Summary and Conclusions

The end of this story about helpmates, harlots, and heroes, as well as victims, is rapidly approaching. We have reflected on the variety of feminist interpretations of these stories, and now, before we try to draw any conclusions, let us summarize the story.

At the outset, we defined feminism and womanism. Feminism is the conviction that women are fully human and thus entitled to equal rights and privileges, and the critique of patriarchy that flows from this conviction. Womanism is a term used by many black feminists for their own unique sense of identity and worth. Feminist and womanist biblical interpreters read the Bible with a special sensitivity to the androcentric and patriarchal nature of many of the texts.

A variety of approaches to interpretation have been taken, from purely literary to scientific. Included in some of the approaches are the disciplines of archaeology, sociology, and anthropology.

For many feminist interpreters the androcentric and patriarchal nature of the Hebrew Bible has raised the theological issue of the authority of Scripture. Again, a variety of responses have been articulated. They range from abandonment of the Scriptures as a religiously authoritative source; to the discernment of a subversive, liberating strand within Scripture by which the rest of Scripture may be judged; to locating the source of authority outside the Bible in the community of feminist men and women.

After a consideration of these philosophical and methodological concerns, our account moved to the story of the first woman, Eve. Source of much trouble for women, Eve has been interpreted and reinterpreted more than any other biblical woman. She has been viewed as the second, inferior sex and as the temptress responsible for humanity's downfall.

Phyllis Trible stirred the waters in the 1970s with her interpretation of Adam as a sexually undifferentiated earthling. This allowed for the emergence of male and female from Adam at the same moment in time. More recent interpreters have not been so sanguine about the ability of this story to be redeemed from androcentrism. Adam is a masculine name, and after the creation of Eve, Adam is masculine.

Thus Adam is at least a protomale before his "operation." In addition, when the first human couple is expelled from the garden, Eve is not even mentioned. However much one might like to discover that the sexism is in the interpreters, the current consensus is that the text is part of the problem. It may not be sexist, but it is androcentric.

Nevertheless the story of Adam and Eve was never as central in the Bible as it has become in the Christian tradition. Some interpreters question whether the "fall from grace" approach provides an adequate basis for interpreting the story. However one may decide that issue, within the Old Testament the foundational story is God's liberation of the Hebrew people from oppression through the exodus and the giving of the law at Sinai. These, rather than the traditions based on the story of Adam and Eve, are the theological themes that provided the Old Testament authors with the heart of their story.

From the story of Eve we moved into the rest of Genesis with its matriarchs and were pleased with the strength of some of the women characters, but disappointed to find many women who are not characterized as fully as we would like. Nevertheless we found women whose depictions are in most cases somewhat sympathetic. However, they are women who suffer literarily, and perhaps suffered in real terms as well, from the strictures of their society. Nevertheless we also were surprised at finding that they often fared better in the hands of the biblical narrators than of modern interpreters. Rebekah especially comes to mind. Perhaps the most positive female figure in Genesis, she is condemned by commentators because of her use of trickery.

We found that Sarah was cruel to Hagar. She herself was victimized by her limited power, pawned off twice to save her husband, or so he thought. Hagar doubly suffered because she was female and servant. Yet we can at least celebrate the vision of God that was given her and her unique position in the Bible as the only person to give God a name. Rebekah, much more than her husband Isaac, was responsible for ensuring that God's chosen Jacob would receive the blessing.

Rachel and Leah are pitiable, although we can celebrate their cooperation that led to Rachel's giving birth and Leah's access to Jacob. The events subsequent to Dinah's sexual experience with Shechem and the near gang rape of the daughters of Lot are disturbing. They serve as examples of the powerlessness and low status of women, as well as the group orientation of ancient Israelite society.

The story of the attempted seduction of Joseph by Potiphar's wife is somewhat balanced by the story of Tamar's clever plan to obtain offspring. This story sends the message that women are not lethal after all.

The situation looks up somewhat in Exodus and Numbers. Five women cooperate literarily to ensure Moses' survival. The midwives Shiphrah and Puah, Moses' mother Jochebed and sister Miriam, and Pharaoh's unnamed daughter all act in subversion of Pharaoh's order to kill Hebrew male babies. This is a story of female protagonists. Yet we must keep in mind that the goal is the birth and survival of a male hero.

Moses' wife Zipporah is an intriguing character about whom we would like to know more. The adult Miriam is a strong, independent woman and an early leader of the Hebrews. Her role has probably been reduced in the retelling of the stories.

The daughters of Zelophehad won the right to inherit their father's property in the absence of sons. They have been viewed by some as advancing women's rights and by others as mere place holders in a patrilineal inheritance scheme. Perhaps there is some truth in both positions.

There is more to celebrate in women's stories in Exodus and Numbers than in Genesis. Nevertheless none of the women receive the full character development that Moses receives. Biblical clues suggest that Miriam was of equal stature with Moses and Aaron. Nevertheless her importance has likely been reduced, while Moses' story has surely been glorified. Even her song seems to have been placed in Moses' mouth, and she has been left with only the opening lines. At least with the clues that are left, we can surmise that the historical reality was probably more favorable to Miriam than the historical memory of her.

In the stories in the books of Joshua and Judges, there is a considerable amount of violence. Also, there is a juxtaposition of strong women who act independently, such as Rahab, Deborah, and Jael, and unnamed women who are brutally victimized. In regard to the story of Samson and Delilah, Delilah is vilified somewhat unfairly by commentators, since Samson is blinded by love and Delilah does not pretend to reciprocate his feelings or hide her goals from him. Nevertheless the characterization of her is weak, and there are only a few clues about her feelings and motivations.

On the positive side, Deborah is one of the strongest female leaders in the Bible. Called both a judge and a prophet, she functions on many levels. She both calls the military leader Barak to prepare for battle (a traditionally masculine role) and sings a victory song (a traditional female role). She settles disputes under a palm tree (a judicial role) and foretells that a woman will get the glory in the upcoming battle (a prophetic role). Jael is also a strong woman, but one who fares better in the biblical text than in modern commentaries, both traditional and feminist. She is often condemned for her deception and lack of hospitality. Modern readers would like to know her motivations, which are not revealed in the text.

On the negative side, however, Judges contains more women's horror stories than any other book of the Bible. Here are the stories of the sacrifice of a young woman and the gang rape, murder, and dismemberment of a concubine, which leads to even more violence. Here is also the story of the fiery death of an innocent young bride and her family.

What is worse is that commentators have often glossed over these stories, as if they were peripheral details. Feminist interpreters have restored a proper "appreciation" for these tales of horror. With the beginning of a more organized society under the leadership of a king, we might have hoped for better lives for women. Unfortunately, the women in the books of Samuel fare only a little better than those in Judges. The extremes disappear. There are no sacrifices of virgin daughters, no gang rapes and murders of young women, no fiery deaths of young brides. But there are no leaders like Deborah or strong women like Jael.

In the books of Samuel, Hannah, the mother of Samuel, is shown as a positive character but not really a hero. The three named wives of David do not fare as well as they should: Michal is treated despicably; Abigail disappears as soon as she has fulfilled her role; and Bathsheba is perhaps raped (or, according to some, seduces David) and her husband is murdered before David takes her as wife. David's daughter Tamar is raped by his son, and David doesn't seem at all concerned about her. David is depicted as the great and glorious king of Israel and no doubt accomplished much politically. His personal life and relationships with women, however, leave his image rather tarnished.

In the books of Samuel, we meet three independent women: the medium of Endor, whom Saul consults; the woman of Tekoa, who confronts David with the need for him to call Absalom out of exile; and the wise woman of Abel, who saves the town of Abel by convincing the townspeople to surrender the rebel Sheba's head to Joab. Although we know little of these women, their independence is striking. This is especially so considering the literary and probably historical dependence of the other women who appear during the reigns of Saul and David.

The story continues in the books of Kings. Here we meet two strong women, both foreigners. The Queen of Sheba is a colorful, independent woman, whose primary function, however, is to make Solomon look good. Nevertheless she represents a tradition of female leadership that is largely alien to the Hebrew approach to royalty. Whether she was Arabian or African is unclear, but whatever her continent of origin, she was a dark-skinned woman.

The strange urban-legend-like story of the two prostitutes demonstrates Solomon's wisdom more than it reveals anything about these flat characters. Similarly, the story of the two cannibal mothers is probably a fictionalized account written to indicate the social chaos that reigned during a siege.

In contrast to the positive portrayal of the Queen of Sheba is the negative portrayal of Jezebel, wife of King Ahab and daughter of Ethbaal, a Canaanite king. She is a worshiper of Baal and Asherah and a zealous defender of her religious tradition. She locks horns with Elijah in a deadly fight. As a result, Jezebel has become a symbol of evil. Although the story of Naboth's vineyard suggests that she is no angel, her vilification is out of proportion with her behavior. She is condemned, probably at least in part, because she is a strong, foreign woman.

We also encounter in the books of Kings the widow of Zarephath, another unnamed widow, and the Shunammite woman. These women who relate to the prophets Elijah and Elisha are models of faith. In contrast is another negatively depicted woman, Athaliah, the only woman in Hebrew history to reign as queen in her own right. Finally, we meet the prophet Huldah, whose religious leadership is evident, but about whom we know very little.

Fortunately, in the books of Kings there are no victims such as we meet in previous biblical books. On the other hand, Jezebel's vilification is probably out of proportion to her crimes. We can celebrate the independence of the Queen of Sheba and the religious leadership of Huldah. In both cases, however, we would like to know more.

Next are the prophets. Here we meet Gomer, Hosea's allegedly whorish wife, Isaiah's unnamed prophetess wife, an unnamed young woman who is pregnant with a son to be named Immanuel, and Ezekiel's unnamed wife, after whose death he is told not to mourn, as well as women who worship the Queen of Heaven. Much of the prophetic literature is troubling with many negative feminine images, such as Samaria and Jerusalem being personified as two whoring sisters Oholah and Oholibah, but some pleasing passages to some degree mitigate the negative imagery.

In the Wisdom literature we find Job's wife susceptible of a much more positive interpretation than she normally receives. The twin figures of Wisdom and Folly in Proverbs disturb many feminist readers, but some find much positive material in the female personification of Wisdom. The women in the Song of Songs provide relatively pleasing images of sexuality and ethnically diverse relationships.

The short stories also provide a word of redemption and hope. The books of Ruth and Esther present generally positive images of women: Ruth and Esther, who are well-developed characters; women who act independently and creatively; women whose stories empower women and minorities; and women who effectively subvert opposition to women and foreigners.

These findings continue in the stories of Susanna and Judith. Judith is one of the strongest heroes in all of Jewish literature. She combines traditional piety with feminine beauty and masculine daring to accomplish what no other leader could. Although some commentators have been concerned with her use of deception to achieve her ends, her depiction by the narrator is positive. We wish these two books had made it into the Hebrew canon. They are clearly of a piece with Ruth and Esther. At least they have survived for us to enjoy and celebrate.

CONCLUSIONS

What can we learn from the new readings of these stories? First of all, there is not always a single feminist reading of a biblical woman's story. Many of the stories can be understood in a number of ways, although there are limits to how many plausible readings are possible. Nevertheless feminists do agree at many points.

We can learn from the positive role models, the women who had power and used it well and the women who had little power and accomplished important goals in spite of powerlessness. In the first regard we think especially of Deborah and Miriam. We remember Esther and Huldah as well. We celebrate the Queen of Sheba. Of the women who had little institutional power, Rebekah and Tamar, Judah's daughter-in-law, come first to mind. The five women who defied Pharaoh to save Moses provide wonderful role models. Here are women who took risks to accomplish important ends.

Judith and perhaps Jael likewise put themselves in jeopardy and as a result saved people from oppression. In a different way Ruth moved from powerlessness to security and acceptance through loyalty to Naomi, gumption, and courage. The daughters of Zelophehad made the most out of the situation in which they found themselves. Although our goal is total and complete equality, we must often move in that direction by taking whatever opportunities life offers.

We can also learn from the women who in various ways were victimized. In their stories we can see the parallels in contemporary society and can work for change. The list of abuses is long: Sarah's rejection of Hagar; the rape of Tamar, David's daughter; the sacrifice of Jephthah's daughter; the gang rape and murder of the Levite's concubine; the unfair treatment of David's wives Michal, Abigail, and Bathsheba; and the impoverishment of widows because of the patriarchal structure of society. Rape and sexual harassment, impoverishment and silencing are still the lot of more women in our society today than we would like to acknowledge.

We can learn from the tendency to make women look worse than they are, a tendency operative both within the text and in the work of many commentators. Jezebel is vilified by the biblical narrators. Although we cannot be sure, it seems likely that her negative portrayal goes beyond what the historical facts would merit. This may also be true of Athaliah.

Commentators condemn Eve, Rebekah, Tamar (Judah's daughter-in-law), Delilah, Jael, Bathsheba, and Judith. We find reason to praise them. They are courageous, smart, and resourceful. For all except Eve, their lack of physical prowess, economic power, and legal authority are compensated by their use of the tools at their disposal, sexual appeal and/or deception, or, to put it more positively, tricksterism.

Finally, we can learn from the biblical propensity to categorize women as very good or very bad. This dynamic is seen at work in the portrayal of Abigail as the good wife and Jezebel as the evil foreign woman. It is especially clear in the book of Proverbs, where women personify wisdom and folly. Life hasn't changed a great deal in more than two thousand years. The images of the good girl and the bad girl are very much with us yet.

As the end of this story approaches, we may ask whether we can detect any progress in the biblical stories. Strong women appear both near the beginning and near the end of the story. However, women probably had less-restricted roles in the early days than during the monarchy. After the exile the evidence is mixed. The books of Ezra and Nehemiah record opposition to foreign women. This may in part have resulted from women's increased legal rights. If women could inherit property, marriage to foreign women might result in loss of Israelite property.

In any case, it is in this postexilic age that we find the wonderful fictional stories of female heroes. These stories were probably written, at least in part, to subvert a misogynist tendency in that period. In these stories of Ruth and Esther, Susanna and Judith, one can find comfort and hope.

In addition, toward the end of the story we find evidence of a struggle to find ways to integrate the feminine into the Hebrew understanding of God in a manner appropriate to a monotheistic religion. There is some evidence of this in the prophets, where Rachel and Sarah are reinterpreted as metaphors of Israel, the bride of God, imagery reminiscent of Semitic goddesses. We find even more important evidence of this in Proverbs, where Wisdom, a divine attribute or even a way of thinking of God, is personified as a woman. Although the prophets and Proverbs contain much that is difficult from a feminist point of view, they also contain the seeds of a much more positive understanding.

At the conclusion of this story about stories, we need to reflect further on the various methods that feminist scholars bring to the task. We have seen examples of pure literary criticism, culturally cued reading, and historical approaches. We have also seen the important roles that the more technical disciplines of philology, textual criticism, form criticism, and even redaction criticism play. In addition, we have observed the use of archaeological and social-scientific methods.

Two interpreters using the same methodology may not necessarily read a text the same way. This is particularly true of literary critics who fill gaps in the text in diverse ways. Often the gaps are motives that modern readers are eager to understand but in which ancient writers seem to have had much less interest. When readers fill in these gaps, usually there is no one right answer. Thus a variety of equally plausible readings is possible.

Some of the purely literary readings that we have considered are fascinating. In general, however, the culturally cued readings seem more plausible. In a sense there is no such thing as a totally pure literary reading, because every reading is somewhat aware of the cultural setting. The more cognizant of the historical and social setting an interpreter is, the more likely she is to read the story in a way that is consistent with the original intentions of the author or editor.

Determining the original meaning of the story is not the only goal of feminist interpreters. Indeed, many interpreters deny the possibility of reaching that goal and focus their attention on the text or the reader, rather than on the author or editor. However, discerning the original meaning is an important goal for some feminist interpreters, even if we must admit that we can never be absolutely certain that we have succeeded.

This relates to the current debate over historical (supposedly value-free) objectivity versus (value-laden) advocacy. This debate is very important. We will probably ultimately end up on a middle ground. This middle ground acknowledges the importance of the search for the history behind the text and the original intended meaning of the text, even though that search will never be completely successful. It cannot be successful in part because lack of information about the past keeps us from having the whole picture and in part because the issues that face contemporary interpreters color the way we look at the past. Nevertheless this does not mean that we can know nothing of the past. Elisabeth Schüssler Fiorenza puts it this way: "A critical feminist version of objectivity recognizes the provisionality and multiplicity of particular knowledges as situated and 'embodied' knowledge. Knowledge is not totally relative, however. It is possible from the perspective of the excluded and dominated to give a more adequate account of the 'world.'"[1]

Some of the particularity and "embodiedness" of knowledge is good. For example, before women gained the tools to enter into the biblical scholarship debate, women's stories in the Hebrew Bible were largely ignored. Women brought a new creative perspective to the enterprise that has stimulated many new avenues of research.

But not all of the particularity is helpful. When we read modern values such as racism into the ancient texts, however, we distort their meaning. The entry into the field of academic biblical interpretation of a formerly largely excluded group, African Americans, has stimulated insights that have helped us become aware of the ways in which we were reading modern, racist assumptions into the biblical texts.

Interpreters from Asian countries may help us see other modern Western values that we unwittingly are reading in. A diversity of interpreters will help us to get as close to "objective reality" as is humanly possible. Thus I agree with the new consensus that objectivity is a myth, to the extent that I acknowledge that it is impossible. However, I do not reject objectivity as a goal. I want to know, insofar as is humanly possible, what happened, even though I admit that the questions I ask are shaped by who I am. I want to know what the ancient authors and editors intended, even though I realize that texts may say more than authors and editors intended and that again my interests will in subtle and sometimes not so subtle ways affect my understanding of the issues.

Even if one accepts objectivity as a reasonable goal, that does not mean that what one discovers is neutral in terms of values. There are values inherent in the text, values that we may or may not like. However, the Hebrew Bible is not all of one piece. Ilana Pardes warns against making the Bible better or worse than it is in terms of gender issues. Rather, she suggests that we "defy comfortable categorizings of the biblical stance on gender issues . . . [so that] unknown reaches of the past may open out before us, revealing faded figures of female precursors who, through their very otherness, have the striking capacity to add much color and intensity to our own lives."[2] She calls for a consideration of the heterogeneity of the biblical text. She writes:

In my effort to retrieve the biblical past, I oscillate between a disturbing suspicion that this well is quite empty insofar as female sources are concerned and a fascination with the unexpected ways in which antipatriarchal perspectives have been partially preserved, against all odds, in the canon. Accordingly, my analyses entail both an examination of the marks of patriarchal modes of censorship and an attempt to reconstruct, in light of the surviving remains, antithetical undercurrents which call into question the monotheistic repression of femininity. I try, in other words, to avoid an all too common tendency of feminist critics to turn the remote past into the fulfillment of current dreams. This does not mean that the present has no bearing on my endeavors. Quite the contrary. Like any hermeneutic pursuit, my own pursuit entails an attempt to make sense of the present in light of the past, to explore a distant mystery which includes our own. I try, however, to engage in a dialogue with the past without idealizing it. I strive to listen to the otherness of past voices, though I realize, with Stephen Greenblatt, that in our most intense moments of straining to listen to the dead, it is our own voices that we hear.[3]

We read ancient texts not simply to find out what happened, what the ancients thought, and what the texts meant. We read these texts because of the way past history and the ancients' thoughts interact with, shape, and challenge our contemporary views, even if it is not always easy to tell which is which. We read the Bible because of what it means to us today.

Thus what the story of Eve was really about in its original setting is important to us today. If Eve was not originally the terrible seductress responsible for the human fall from grace that she became in subsequent interpretation, that is important for us to know. Indeed, the implications of feminist interpretations of Eve's story go beyond the important issues of images of women.[4] They touch on very fundamental matters of Christian theology, built as it usually is on assumptions about the story of the garden.

If Jezebel was not the sexual flaunter that she has come to represent in modern Western culture, that too is important. Total objectivity is impossible, but reasonable certitude about some historical matters is possible and important. Historical facts, although in themselves morally neutral, may quickly be pressed into the service of various values. If Eve and Jezebel and a host of other biblical women characters, fictional and nonfictional, were not what we thought, either historically or literarily, these facts become powerful ammunition in the feminists' arsenal.

Another matter important for feminist biblical interpretation is the place of the traditional technical tools of the trade. My own academic training is in the field of Semitic languages. I spent years studying Hebrew and other related languages. Thus I confess a certain bias in the direction of interpretations that look closely at the Hebrew text. Philology, textual criticism, and form and redaction criticism are all powerful tools that we should continue to use in conjunction with newer literary approaches. Some powerful new readings come from scholars who use these older tools. Carol Meyers's reading of Genesis 3:16 is a prime example. Her careful scholarship has changed the way we read this important text. Fewell and Gunn's interpretation of Ruth 4:5 turns on a textual issue. It makes sense of a difficult part of the story in a way that few others have.

Not only are the traditional academic disciplines of philology, textual criticism, form and redaction criticism, and the like, important. Archaeology, sociology, and anthropology are also tools that feminists should learn to use. Again, Carol Meyers is the example that comes to mind. Her work on women's roles uses these tools brilliantly.

In the 1970s and '80s, feminist biblical criticism was dominated by Christian scholars who were in most cases trying to find a way to redeem the Bible from its androcentricity and patriarchal nature. In the 1990s came the reaction, and it became fashionable for feminists to look at the Hebrew Bible through the most negative lenses possible. The glass was half empty rather than half full. Victims were everywhere. Now in the early part of the twenty-first century, a reaction to that overly negative perspective is emerging. Victimological readings are giving way to a recognition of the economic and technological constraints of the ancient world.

In a largely rural, poor, agrarian economy with little that we today would call technology or medicine, survival required the birth of many children, only a fraction of whom would survive to adulthood. Women's lot in such a world was to produce as many children as possible before death in childbirth or through disease or the ravages of aging claimed them. This was the economic reality, not simply some patriarchal plot. In addition, poverty required that society be organized along communal rather than individualistic lines, this being the only way the majority of people in the group could survive. In such a world the strongest (usually males) and wisest—those who had lived the longest, that is, the patriarchs—were generally going to run the show. That so many women in the Hebrew Bible emerge as strong characters, with intelligence as well as fecundity, is all the more remarkable when we consider the constraints of their world.

No doubt men's greater physical strength and freedom from childbearing responsibilities allowed them to be the dominant players, and in many cases they clearly abused their power. That is the nature of power. Nevertheless, that the relatively weaker women were able to dominate the men in their lives in quite a few cases is rather amazing.

One question worth considering is how the theoretical differences in approach articulated by feminists of various persuasions and ethnic identities translate into practice. Surprisingly, I am unaware of any overarching differences among feminists that can be traced to their social location, ethnicity, or faith tradition.

This judgment may seem at first to be contrary to the assumption that one's social location influences one's interpretive stance. However, influence is different from control. We cannot tell in advance how a black woman is going to interpret a text any more than we can predict how a Catholic woman will read the same material. Women have much in common, especially those who have the necessary resources to have been published. However, each person is a unique individual whose interpretations are shaped by a multitude of factors, both obvious and subtle. The interplay of these factors results in the varied shadings of meaning that feminist biblical interpreters express in their work.[5]

Much is left to be done. We have only begun to consider the intersection of race or ethnicity and gender. I have touched on these matters in this book, but much more work remains. Much more remains to be done also in the area of women's status and roles, both in Hebrew society and in the related southwest Asian and north African cultures. Knowledge of the languages and facility in the disciplines of archaeology and various social sciences will be essential for filling in the lacunae in our knowledge.

Much work also awaits those who will spread the news of the work that has already been done. I have taken one step in this direction. Every time this material is incorporated into a seminary course, religious education class, or sermon, additional important steps are taken.

We have come to the end of our story. But the story goes on. In a sense it has just begun. Feminist interpreters have produced a large body of literature in the last forty years that is revolutionary. Only in the last few years, however, has their work begun to be recognized and respected. The story will continue. As more women become trained as biblical scholars and as more men are sensitized to the gender issues in the Hebrew Bible, new studies will take us to new understandings of familiar stories and of the issues that continue to challenge us in our own day.

DISCUSSION QUESTIONS

1. Considering all the biblical women whose stories you have studied, which give you hope?
2. Which stories hold the most promise for transforming contemporary society?
3. Which women do you identify with the most?
4. Which women give you the most problems?
5. Which women would you like to learn more about?
6. Considering other literature, history, films, and other media with which you are familiar, how do the women's roles as depicted in the Hebrew Bible compare with their roles in other times, places, or societies?

Notes

Chapter 1: Introduction

1. I use the terms Hebrew Bible and Old Testament somewhat interchangeably, even though they do not denote precisely the same Scriptures. The Hebrew Bible refers to the Jewish canon of Scripture, sometimes also called the Tanakh (a word comprised of three terms: Torah, the first five books; Nebi'im, the prophets; and Kethubim, the writings) or the first testament. The term Old Testament refers both to the Protestant first testament, which includes the same books as the Hebrew Bible, although in a different order, and to the Roman Catholic and Eastern Orthodox first testament, which includes additional books and additions to books in the Hebrew Bible and the Protestant Old Testament. Unfortunately there is no neutral term. The term Hebrew Bible is preferable to the term Old Testament because the latter suggests an antiquated text that is no longer viable, a suggestion that is strongly to be resisted.

2. Carolyn DeSwarte Gifford, "American Women and the Bible: The Nature of Woman as a Hermeneutical Issue," in Adela Yarbro Collins, ed., *Feminist Perspectives on Biblical Scholarship* (SBLBSNA 10, Chico, CA: Scholar Press, 1985), 15.

3. Dorothy Sterling, *Ahead of Her Time: Abby Kelley and the Politics of Anti-Slavery* (New York: W. W. Norton & Co., 1991), 117–18.

4. Barbara Brown Zikmund, "Feminist Consciousness in Historical Perspective," in Letty M. Russell, ed., *Feminist Interpretation of the Bible* (Philadelphia: Westminster Press, 1985), 22–23.

5. Ibid., 23.

6. Jarena Lee, "Life of Jarena Lee," in Dorothy Parker, ed., *Early Negro Writing: 1760–1837* (Boston: Beacon Press, 1971), 494–514. See also Marilyn Richardson, *Black Women and Religion: A Bibliography* (Boston: G. K. Hall & Co., 1980), xvi–xix; and David W. Wills and Richard Newman, eds., *Black Apostles at Home and Abroad: Afro-Americans and the Christian Movement from the Revolution to Reconstruction* (Boston: G. K. Hall & Co., 1982), 137–38.

7. Elizabeth Cady Stanton and the Revising Committee, *The Woman's Bible* (New York: European Publishing Co., 1898), cited in Zikmund, "Historical Perspective," 23–24, 166.

8. Zikmund, "Historical Perspective," 23–24.

9. See Donna A. Behnke, "The Female Exegetes" and "The Weight of Biblical Evidence," in *Religious Issues in Nineteenth Century Feminism* (Troy, NY: Whitson Publishing Co., 1982), 113–40, 221–44.

10. Zikmund, "Historical Perspective," 24.

11. Ibid.

12. Gifford, "American Women and the Bible," 31.

13. Katherine C. Bushnell, *God's Word to Women*, cited in Schüssler Fiorenza, *But She Said: Feminist Practices of Biblical Interpretation* (Boston: Beacon, 1992), 20.

14. Gifford, "American Women and the Bible," 31.

15. Ibid., 31–32.

16. Ibid., 32–33.

17. Letty M. Russell, ed., *The Liberating Word: A Guide to Nonsexist Interpretation of the Bible* (Philadelphia: Westminster Press, 1976).

18. See Doreen Kimura, "Sex Differences in the Brain," *Scientific American,* September 1992, 119–25, and the literature cited there. See also Sue V. Rosser, *Biology and Feminism: A Dynamic Interaction* (New York: Twayne Publishers, 1992), 91–92, 97, and the literature cited there.

19. However, "difference feminism," the view that women are inherently different, is intellectually fashionable. For a different view, see the critique of Nancy Chodorow's *The Reproduction of Mothering* (Berkeley and Los Angeles: University of California Press, 1978), Carol Gilligan's *In a Different Voice: Psychological Theory and Women's Development* (Cambridge: Harvard University Press, 1982); and Deborah Tannen's *You Just Don't Understand: Women and Men in Conversation* (New York: Morrow, 1990); in Pollitt, "Are Women Morally Superior to Men?" *The Nation,* December 28, 1992, 799–807.

20. For a more theoretical discussion of the issues involved, see Jonathan D. Culler, "Reading as a Woman," in *On Deconstruction: Theory and Criticism after Structuralism* (Ithaca, NY: Cornell University Press, 1983), 43–63.

21. Carol P. Christ and Judith Plaskow, eds., *Womanspirit Rising: New Patterns in Feminist Spirituality* (San Francisco: Harper & Row, 1989), 13–14, cited in Mary Ann Tolbert, "Defining the Problem: The Bible and Feminist Hermeneutics," in *The Bible and Feminist Hermeneutics, Semeia* 28 (1983), 115.

22. Tolbert, "Defining the Problem," 116.

23. Fontaine, "The Abusive Bible: On the Use of Feminist Method in Pastoral Contexts," in Athalya Brenner and Carole Fontaine, eds., *A Feminist Companion to Reading the Bible: Approaches, Methods, and Strategies* (Sheffield, UK: Sheffield Academic Press, 1997), 112.

24. Tania Modleski, *Feminism without Women: Culture and Criticism in a "Postfeminist" Age* (New York: Routledge, 1991).

25. Cheryl J. Sanders, "Christian Ethics and Theology in Womanist Perspective," *JFSR* 5, no. 2 (1989): 83.

26. M. Shawn Copeland, "Response to Cheryl Sanders' 'Christian Ethics and Theology in Womanist Perspective," *JFSR* 5, no. 2 (1989): 99–100.

27. Michelle Wallace, "A Black Feminist's Search for Sisterhood," in Gloria T. Hull, Patricia Bell Scott, and Barbara Smith, eds., *All the Women Are White, All the Blacks Are Men, But Some of Us Are Brave* (Old Westbury, NY: Feminist Press, 1981), 49, cited in Copeland, "Response to Sanders' 'Christian Ethics,'" 102.

28. Gilkes, "Response to Sanders' 'Christian Ethics,'" *JFSR* 5, no. 2 (1989): 105.

29. Sanders, "Christian Ethics," 86.

30. Emilie M. Townes, "Response to Sanders' 'Christian Ethics,'" *JFSR* 5, no. 2 (1989): 95.

31. Sanders, "Christian Ethics," 84.

32. Ibid.

33. Ibid., 83.

34. Collins, "What's in a Name? Womanism, Black Feminism, and Beyond." *The Black Scholar* (San Francisco) 26:1 (Winter/Spring 1996): 9ff.

35. Ibid.

36. Madipoane Masenya, "A *Bosadi* (Womanhood) Reading of Proverbs 31:10–31," in Musa W. Dube, ed., *Other Ways of Reading: African Women and the Bible* (Atlanta: SBL Press; Geneva: WCC Publications, 2001), 148–49.

37. See, e.g., Elisabeth Schüssler Fiorenza, "The Ethics of Interpretation: De-Centering Biblical Scholarship," *JBL* 107 (1988): 3–17; and Walter Brueggemann, "At the Mercy of Babylon: A Subversive Rereading of the Empire," *JBL* 110 (1991): 3–22. For a womanist understanding of this issue, see Renita Weems, "Reading Her Way through the Struggle: African American Women and the Bible," in Cain Hope Felder, ed., *Stony the Road We Trod: African American Biblical Interpretation* (Minneapolis: Fortress Press, 1991), 57–80.

38. See Katie Geneva Cannon, "Slave Ideology and Biblical Interpretation," in Katie Geneva Cannon and Elisabeth Schüssler Fiorenza, *Interpretation for Liberation, Semeia* 47 (1989): 9–24.

39. See Kathleen Farmer's discussion of the difference between descriptive texts and prescriptive ones in *Who Knows What Is Good? A Commentary on the Books of Proverbs and Ecclesiastes* (Grand Rapids: Wm. B. Eerdmans Publishing Co., 1991), 10. She refers specifically to the slavery that is described in Sarah's and Hagar's stories. She writes: "Most of us realize . . . that we ought not to assume that the way things *were* in ancient times is necessarily the way things *ought to be* or the way *God wants* them to be in our time. We realize that those whom God chose to become instruments of blessing in the world lived in socially and historically limited settings" (emphasis hers).

40. I am indebted to Cheryl Sanders who pointed out to me that African American preacher Suzan Johnson read this story the same way I did, in a sermon, "God's Woman" (in Ella Pearson Mitchell, ed., *Those Preachin' Women: More Sermons by Black Women Preachers* [Valley Forge, PA: Judson Press, 1985], 121).

41. Heather McKay, "On the Future of Feminist Biblical Criticism" in Brenner and Fontaine, eds., *A Feminist Companion to Reading the Bible,* 62–63.

42. Alicia Ostriker, "A Triple Hermeneutic: Scripture and Revisionist Women's Poetry," in Brenner and Fontaine, eds., *A Feminist Companion to Reading the Bible,* 164–65.

43. Farmer, *Who Knows What Is Good?* 5–6. Another feminist interpreter who emphasizes the heterogeneity of biblical texts is Pardes, *Countertraditions.*

44. For an overview of the different epistemological approaches of feminists, see Janice Capel Anderson, "Mapping Feminist Biblical Criticism," in Eldon Jay Epp, ed., *Critical Review of Books in Religion, 1991* (Atlanta: Scholars Press, 1991), 24–26, and the literature cited there.

45. See Weems, "Reading Her Way through the Struggle," 67–68.

46. Phyllis Trible, *God and the Rhetoric of Sexuality* (Philadelphia: Fortress Press, 1978), 7.

47. Weems, "Reading Her Way through the Struggle," 73.

48. Tolbert, "Defining the Problem," 120.

49. Elsa Tamez, "Women's Rereading of the Bible," in Virginia Fabella and Mercy A. Oduyoye, eds., *With Passion and Compassion: Third World Women Doing Theology* (Maryknoll, NY: Orbis Books, 1988), 173–80. See also Ada Maria Isasi-Díaz, "The Bible and Mujerista Theology," in Susan Brooks Thistlethwaite and Potter Engel, eds., *Lift Every Voice: Constructing Christian Theologies from the Underside* (San Francisco: Harper & Row, 1990), 268, cited in Schüssler Fiorenza, *But She Said,* 155.

50. Kwok Pui-lan, "Discovering the Bible in the Non-Biblical World," *Semeia* 47 (1989): 25–42, cited in Schüssler Fiorenza, *But She Said,* 155.

51. Chung Hyun Kyung, *Struggle to Be the Sun Again: Introducing Asian Women's Theology* (Maryknoll, NY: Orbis Books, 1990), 111, cited in Schüssler Fiorenza, *But She Said,* 155.

52. Katharine Doob Sakenfeld, "Old Testament Perspectives: Methodological Issues," *JSOT* 22 (1982): 13–20.

53. See Phyllis Bird, "Images of Women in the Old Testament," in Rosemary Radford Ruether, ed., *Religion and Sexism: Images of Woman in the Jewish and Christian Traditions* (New York: Simon & Schuster, 1974), 77n1; Frymer-Kensky, *In the Wake of the Goddesses: Women, Culture, and the Biblical Transformation of Pagan Myth* (New York: Free Press, 1992), 120; and Meyers, *Discovering Eve: Ancient Israelite Women in Context* (New York: Oxford University Press, 1988), 24–46.

54. Trible, "Depatriarchalizing in Biblical Interpretation," *JAAR* 41 (1973): 31.

55. Schüssler Fiorenza, *But She Said.* Other helpful discussions of this issue are found in Deborah F. Middleton, "Feminist Interpretation," in R. J. Coggins and J. L. Houlden, eds., *A Dictionary of Biblical Interpretation* (Philadelphia: Trinity Press International, 1990), 231–34; Carolyn Osiek, RSCJ, "The Feminist in the Bible," in Adela Yarbro Collins, ed., *Feminist Perspectives on Biblical*

Scholarship (Chico, CA: Scholars Press, 1985), 93–105; and Tolbert, "Defining the Problem," 113–26.

56. Schüssler Fiorenza, *But She Said*, 145–46, 245n28.

57. Letty Russell, *Feminist Interpretation of the Bible* (Philadelphia: Westminster Press, 1985), cited by Schüssler Fiorenza, *But She Said*, 147.

58. Schüssler Fiorenza, *But She Said*, 146–49.

59. Ibid., 144–56.

60. Schüssler Fiorenza, "Feminist Hermeneutics," in *ABD*, 2:790. For a similar approach from a Hebrew Bible scholar, see Ilana Pardes, *Countertraditions: A Feminist Approach* (Cambridge: Harvard University Press, 1992).

61. Schüssler Fiorenza, "Feminist Hermeneutics," 790.

62. Ibid.

63. Ibid. For an example of this moment, see Miriam Therese Winter, *Woman Wisdom: A Feminist Lectionary and Psalter: Women of the Hebrew Scriptures, Part One* and *Woman Witness: A Feminist Lectionary and Psalter: Women of the Hebrew Scriptures, Part Two* (New York: Crossroad Publishing Co., 1991–92).

64. See Caroline Vander Stichele and Todd Penner, "Mastering the Tools or Retooling the Masters? The Legacy of Historical-Critical Discourse," in *Her Master's Tools? Feminist and Postcolonial Engagements of Historical-Critical Discourse* (Atlanta: SBL Press, 2005), 1–29.

65. Sakenfeld, "Feminist Bible Interpretation," 154–68.

66. Ibid., 161.

67. For a brief introduction to some of the concepts involved, see Danna Nolan Fewell, ed., *Reading between Texts: Intertextuality and the Hebrew Bible* (Louisville, KY: Westminster/John Knox Press, 1992).

68. Sakenfeld, "Feminist Biblical Interpretation," 161–62.

69. See especially Gail Yee, *Poor Banished Children of Eve: Women as Evil in the Hebrew Bible* (Louisville, KY: Westminster John Knox Press, 2003).

70. Sakenfeld,"Feminist Biblical Interpretation," 162.

71. Schüssler Fiorenza is concerned in chap. 6 of *But She Said* about the split between the supposedly objective historical/literary study of the Bible and subjective theological/ethical evaluation and application of it.

72. The following summary is taken from Bird, "Images of Women in the Old Testament," 48–57. See also Trible, "Women in the Old Testament," 961–66; and Frymer-Kensky, "Women," in *Harper's Bible Dictionary* (New York: Harper & Row, 1985), 1138–41.

73. See Meyers, "Recovering Objects, Re-Visioning Subjects: Archaeology and Feminist Biblical Study," in Athalya Brenner and Carole Fontaine, eds., *A Feminist Companion to Reading the Bible: Approaches, Methods and Strategies* (Sheffield, UK: Sheffield Academic Press, 1997), 283–84.

74. Bird, "Images of Women in the Old Testament," 56–57.

75. Meyers, *Discovering Eve*.

76. Naomi Steinberg, "The Deuteronomic Law Code and the Politics of State Centralization," in David Jobling, ed., *The Bible and the Politics of Exegesis* (Cleveland: Pilgrim, 1991), 161–70.

77. In an e-mail message, dated 6–29-06, Carol Meyers wrote, "[T]he dynamics of daily life relate to the agrarian (rather than urban) setting that I believe was the norm for most people throughout the biblical period. The only true city was Jerusalem, after the 8th century; other sites called 'cities' in the HB were really walled agricultural towns."

78. Meyers, "Women, Israelite," in Judith Baskin, ed., *Cambridge Dictionary of Jewish History, Religion, and Culture* (Cambridge: Cambridge University Press, forthcoming).

79. Meyers, "Marriage and Family, Israelite," in Baskin, *Cambridge Dictionary of Jewish History.*

80. Tamara C. Eskenazi, "Out from the Shadows: Biblical Women in the Postexilic Era," *JSOT* 54 (1992): 31.

81. Ibid., 35.

82. Ibid., 36–41.

83. Cain Hope Felder, *Troubling Biblical Waters: Races, Class, and Family* (Maryknoll, NY: Orbis Books, 1989).

84. Cain Hope Felder, ed., *Stony the Road We Trod: African American Biblical Interpretation* (Minneapolis: Fortress Press, 1991).

85. Renita J. Weems, *Just a Sister Away: A Womanist Vision of Women's Relationships in the Bible* (San Diego: LuraMedia, 1988).

86. Felder, *Troubling Biblical Waters*, 37–38; idem, "Race, Racism, and the Biblical Narratives," in *Stony the Road*, 127–45; and Weems, *Just a Sister Away*, 1.

87. Marvin H. Pope, *Song of Songs*, Anchor Bible (New York: Doubleday, 1977), 307–18.

88. Randall C. Bailey, "Beyond Identification: The Use of Africans in Old Testament Poetry and Narratives," in Felder, ed., *Stony the Road*, 165–86.

89. Charles B. Copher, "The Black Presence in the Old Testament," in Felder, ed., *Stony the Road*, 155.

90. For a full discussion, see ibid., 146–64, and the literature cited there. The term "Afri-" in Afri-Asiatic is used, rather than the more common "Afro-," because the continent to which the term refers is Africa, not Afroca. Afro- is used after the analogy of Euro-.

91. The Hebrew for harlot or prostitute is *zonâ*. For a discussion of the meaning of this noun and the related verb *znh*, see Bird, "'To Play the Harlot,'" in Peggy L. Day, ed., *Gender and Difference in Ancient Israel* (Minneapolis: Fortress Press, 1989), 75–94.

92. Harold Bloom, *The Book of J* (New York: G. Weidenfeld, 1990).

93. Bledstein, "A Feminist Response to the Book of J," in *Lilith*, Summer 1991, 28. For another insightful feminist evaluation of Bloom's *Book of J*, see Pardes, *Countertraditions*, 33–37.

94. Adrien Bledstein, "A Feminist Response to the Book of J," 28. See also her "Woman's Humor in the Bible?" *Humanist Judaism* 19:3 (Summer 1991): 10, and idem, "So J Was a Woman?" *Sh'ma, A Journal of Jewish Responsibility* 21/407 (February 8, 1991): 49–52.

95. Athalya Brenner and Fokkelien van Dijk-Hemmes, *On Gendering Texts: Female and Male Voices in the Hebrew Bible* (Leiden/New York/Cologne: E. J. Brill, 1993).

Chapter 2: The Story of Eve

1. The P source is thought to have been brought into final form after the return from Babylonian exile, that is, sometime after 538 BCE. See Bernhard W. Anderson, *Understanding the Old Testament*, 4th ed. (Englewood Cliffs, NJ: Prentice-Hall, 1986), 451–52.

2. The Hebrew of key words is included for the benefit of scholars. Knowledge of Hebrew is not necessary in order to follow the ideas that are presented. š = sh; ḥ = ch as in Bach; ṣ = ts as in cats; ' and ' are not pronounced in English. The transliteration system is the one recommended by the 1992 *SBL Membership Directory and Handbook* (Decatur, GA: SBL, 1992), 212.

3. See Phyllis Bird, "'Male and Female He Created Them,' Gen 1:27b in the Context of the Priestly Account of Creation," *HTR* 74 (1981): 129–59.

4. It is believed by many scholars that the J source was written down during the early part of the monarchical period, beginning around 950 BCE. See Anderson, *Understanding the Old Testament*, 453.

5. See Deut. 26:4–11; Jer. 2:2–7; 31:32; Ezek. 29:5–6; Amos 9:7; Hos. 2:14–15; 11:1; 13:4; Mic. 6:4; Pss. 66:6; 78:7–55; 81:8–10; 136:10–11.

6. Sirach 25:24. See Carol Meyers, *Discovering Eve: Ancient Israelite Women in Context* (New York: Oxford University Press, 1988), 75.

7. Ibid.

8. Ibid.

9. Ibid., 75–76.

10. Ibid., 76–77.

11. Phyllis Trible, *God and the Rhetoric of Sexuality* (Philadelphia: Fortress Press, 1978), 73.

12. Ibid., 72–143. For an earlier, much shorter study of the same material, see Trible, "Depatriarchalizing in Biblical Interpretation," 35–42.

13. Trible, *God and the Rhetoric of Sexuality*, 80. Trible is not unique in her reading. Origen and John of Damascus also interpreted Adam in this fashion.

14. Ibid., 88–90.

15. David J. A. Clines, "What Does Eve Do to Help? And Other Irredeemably Androcentric Orientations in Genesis 1–3," in *What Does Eve Do to Help? And Other Readerly Questions to the Old Testament* (Sheffield, UK: JSOT Press, 1990), 29–48.

16. Trible, *God and the Rhetoric of Sexuality*, 94–99.

17. Ibid., 99–105.

18. Ibid., 105–8.

19. Jean M. Higgins analyzes Gen. 3:6b in "The Myth of Eve: The Temptress," *JAAR* 44 (1976): 639–47. She looks both at the ways commentators have interpreted this passage, reading in the temptress image, and at what the words of the text actually say. She notes that the statement "the eyes of them both were opened," which suggests that they ate at the same time, is in tension with the narrative as we have it, with Eve eating first and then offering the fruit to Adam. Genesis 3:6b reads literally, "and-she-gave also-to-her husband with-her." There are two ways of dealing with the Hebrew *'immah*, "with her." The first is to take it as modifying Adam. This is consistent with Trible's interpretation. But Higgins is unsure that this can be right. She writes: "There is something comical in the image of the man standing there and never entering into the conversation at all, never intervening to stop the temptation, leaving the woman to do the talking, thinking, deciding, acting, and only at the end reaching out his hand to accept and eat what his wife put into his hand. Such an interpretation certainly turns the tables on all claims for the natural inferiority of the woman. But it is hard to take seriously" (pp. 646–47n58).

It may be hard for Higgins to take this seriously. Perhaps she is so accustomed to male domination that it is hard for her to imagine another world. Perhaps it is hard for her to imagine the biblical authors, who are often very androcentric, producing such a meaning. We are on dangerous ground, however, if we reject a possibility on this basis. We must be careful not to read our assumptions into the text.

The word *'immah* can also be taken as adverbial. The idea here would be that she took and ate and along with herself gave some to her husband. When taken in this sense, *'immah* would not be translated into English. Indeed, the RSV and the NEB have left the phrase untranslated, as also did Jerome in the Vulgate.

When forced to choose between grammatical renderings, Higgins says there is no way to be certain and suggests that we have "incoherence resulting from the compilation of earlier stories" (p. 646). I disagree. What we have here is two choices. The first makes better sense out of the story. See my discussion of Carol Meyers's reading of this story as a wisdom tale in which the woman figures prominently because of the mythological associations of wisdom and women, pp. 49–53.

See also Esther Fuchs, "Who Is Hiding the Truth? Deceptive Women and Biblical Androcentrism" in Adela Yarbro Collins, ed., *Feminist Perspectives on Biblical Scholarship* (Chico, CA: Scholars Press, 1985), 137–44. Fuchs sees Eve's role in giving the fruit to Adam as deceptive. In addition, see Ilana Pardes's critique of Fuchs in *Countertraditions in the Bible: A Feminist Approach* (Cambridge: Howard University Press, 1992), 25–26.

20. Trible, *God and the Rhetoric of Sexuality*, 115–17.

21. Ibid., 119.

22. Ibid., 119–20.

23. Ibid., 123–32.

24. Ibid., 126–28.

25. Ibid., 133–34.

26. Ibid., 134.

27. Ibid., 137. See also Trible, "Not a Jot, Not a Tittle: Genesis 2–3 after Twenty Years," in Linda S. Schearing, Valarie H. Ziegler, Kristen E. Kvam, eds., *Eve & Adam: Jewish, Christian, and Muslim Readings on Genesis and Gender* (Bloomington: Indiana University Press, 1999), 439–44.

28. Mieke Bal, "Sexuality, Sin, and Sorrow: The Emergence of the Female Character," in *Lethal Love: Feminist Literary Readings of Biblical Love Stories* (Bloomington: Indiana University Press, 1987), 104–30.

29. See Pardes's critique of Bal in *Countertraditions*, 26–33.

30. Bal, "Sexuality, Sin, and Sorrow," 113.

31. Ibid., 112–29.

32. Ibid., 117.

33. Ibid., 124–25.

34. Ibid., 125.

35. Jarich Oosten and David Moyer, "De mythische omkering: een analyse van de sociale code van de scheppingsmythen van Genesis 2–11," *Anthropologische verkenningen* I, 1 (1982): 83, cited in Bal, *Lethal Love*, 126–27.

36. Susan Lanser, "(Feminist) Criticism in the Garden: Inferring Genesis 2–3," *Semeia* 41 (1988): 67–84. See also Milne, "The Patriarchal Stamp of Scripture: The Implication of Structural Analyses for Feminist Hermeneutics," *JFSR* 5, no. 1 (1989): 17–34; and Pardes, "Preliminary Excavations" and "Creation according to Eve," in *Countertraditions*, 2–3, 20–25; and see also Pamela J. Milne, "Eve and Adam: Is a Feminist Reading Possible?" *Bible Review* 4, no. 3 (1988): 12–29, 39.

37. Lanser, "Criticism in the Garden," 67.

38. Ibid., 67–71.

39. Ibid., 72.

40. Ibid., 73.

41. Ibid., 75.

42. Ibid., 75–76.

43. Ibid., 79.

44. Mary Phil Korsak, "Genesis: A New Look," in Athalya Brenner, ed., *A Feminist Companion to Genesis* (Sheffield, UK: Sheffield Academic Press, 1993, rep. 1997), 39–52.

45. R. David Freedman, "Woman, A Power Equal to Man: Translation of Woman as a 'Fit Helpmate' for Man Is Questioned," *BARev* 9, no. 1 (January/February 1983): 56–58.

46. Ibid., 56.

47. Ibid., 56, 58n3. See, e.g., Ps. 70:5 (Heb 70:6):

> I am completely destitute;
> O God, hurry to my rescue ('*ezrî*).
> You are my deliverer.
> O Lord, do not delay. (Freedman's translation)

The parallelism between "rescue" and "deliverer" suggests this meaning. The other occurrences of 'ezer in the meaning of "rescue" or "save" are Exod. 18:4; Hos. 13:9; Pss. 20:2; 121:1, 2; 124:8; 146:5.

48. Ibid., 56–57, 58n4. See, e.g., Deut. 33:26:

> There is none like God, O Jeshurun,
> The Ruler of the Sky in your strength (be'ezreka),
> in the heavens in your majesty. (Freedman's translation)

Other occurrences are Deut. 33:7, 29; Pss. 28:7; 33:20; 68:34; 93:1; 115:9, 10, 11; Ezek. 12:14; Isa. 30:5; Dan. 11:34.

49. Ibid., 57. For a different view of 'ezer kenegdô, see David Clines, "What Does Eve Do to Help?" in What Does Eve Do to Help? And Other Readerly Questions in the Old Testament, JSOTSup 94 (Sheffield, UK: Sheffield Academic Press, 1990, 29–48.

50. Freedman, "Woman, A Power Equal to Man," 57–58.

51. Mary Callaway, Sing, O Barren One: A Study in Comparative Midrash, (Atlanta: Scholars Press, 1986), 74.

52. Many scholars are suspicious of a popular theory that before patriarchy there was matriarchy. See especially Tikva Frymer-Kensky, In the Wake of the Goddesses: Women, Culture, and the Biblical Transformation of Pagan Myth (New York: Free Press, 1992); see also Pardes, Countertraditions, 94–95, and Phyllis Bird, "Women—O.T.," in ABD, 6:951–57. Although there is no evidence that matriarchy ever existed, it is clear that ancient Near Eastern mythology included some powerful goddesses who were eliminated in biblical monotheism.

53. Adrien Janis Bledstein, "The Genesis of Humans: The Garden of Eden Revisited," Judaism 26, no. 2 (1977): 200.

54. Ibid.

55. Lyn Bechtel, "Rethinking the Interpretation of Genesis 2.4b–3.24," in Athalya Brenner, ed., A Feminist Companion to Genesis (Sheffield, UK: Sheffield Academic Press, 1993).

56. Bechtel is not unique in this approach. Van Wolde notes in A Semiotic Analysis of Genesis 2–3, 218, that S. R. Driver (The Book of Genesis: With Introduction and Notes [London, 1904]); H. Gunkel (Genesis: Übersetzt und erklärt [Göttingen, 1971]); and U. Cassuto (From Adam to Noah, 1: Gen 1:1–6:8 [Jerusalem, 1961]) each recognized in Gen. 2–3 the growth toward maturity.

57. Ellen J. Van Wolde, A Semiotic Analysis of Genesis 2–3: A Semiotic Theory and Method of Analysis Applied to the Story of the Garden of Eden (Maastricht, The Netherlands: Van Gorcum/Assen, 1989), 217.

58. Meyers, Discovering Eve, 95–121.

59. Ibid., 86–87.

60. Ibid., 87.

61. Ibid., 88.

62. Ibid., 91.

63. Ibid., 99–101.

64. Ibid., 101–3.

65. Ibid., 103–5.

66. Ibid., 105.

67. Ibid., 105–9.

68. Ibid., 109–13. Bledstein suggests in "Are Women Cursed in Genesis 3.16?" in Athalya Brenner, ed., A Feminist Companion to Genesis (Sheffield, UK: Sheffield Academic Press, 1993, rep. 1997), 142–45, that the word normally translated "desire" is the equivalent of an Akkadian word that means "sexual allure." This has the effect of reversing the meaning of the line. She translates, "You are powerfully attractive to your husband." She then reads the last part of the verse, "but he can rule over you." She explains. "Woman's 'desire' does not throw her at the feet of a man as we

have been led to believe the text reads by previous translations and commentaries; instead, woman is cautioned about life outside of Eden, that her attractiveness may threaten the man, a fear documented in myths and legends from the ancient world." This is an attractive reading from a feminist perspective, but whether there is enough evidence to support the translation is questionable.

69. Meyers, *Discovering Eve*, 117.

70. Ibid., 113–17.

71. Bledstein, "Was Eve Cursed or Did a Woman Write Genesis?" *Bible Review* (February 1993), 42–43.

72. Gale Yee, *Poor Banished Children of Eve: Woman as Evil in the Hebrew Bible* (Minneapolis: Fortress, 2003), 59–80.

73. Ibid., 72–74.

74. See Phyllis Bird, *Missing Persons and Mistaken Identities: Women and Gender in Ancient Israel* (Minneapolis: Fortress Press, 1997), 174–93.

75. For this view, see Trible, *God and the Rhetoric of Sexuality*, 123, 126–28.

Chapter 3: The Women in Genesis

1. Sharon Pace Jeansonne, *The Women in Genesis: From Sarah to Potiphar's Wife* (Minneapolis: Fortress Press, 1990).

2. Mary Callaway, *Sing, O Barren One: A Study in Comparative Midrash* (Atlanta: Scholars Press, 1986), 13–14.

3. See Deut. 25:5–10.

4. See, e.g., Johanna W. H. Bos, "Out of the Shadows: Genesis 38; Judges 4:17–22; Ruth 3," in J. Cheryl Exum and Johanna W. H. Bos, eds., *Reasoning with the Foxes: Female Wit in a World of Male Power, Semeia* 42(1985): 37–67, in which she studies what she describes as "'counter-type-scenes' to the betrothal type scene." Bos writes: "By 'counter' I refer to a reversal which takes place in the turn of events, as well as in the arrangement of the central characters. Like the betrothal type-scene, it looks as if the counter-type-scene is about a male in pursuit of success/fortune. But soon loss of life threatens the male and his group, and events take a downward turn. A woman then moves to the center of the narrative to change the course of events toward success/increase of life" (p. 39). See also Athalya Brenner, "Female Social Behaviour: Two Descriptive Patterns within the 'Birth of the Hero' Paradigm," *VT* 36 (1986): 257–73; Nelly Furman, "His Story versus Her Story: Male Genealogy and Female Strategy in the Jacob Cycle," in Adela Yarbro Collins, ed., *Feminist Perspectives on Biblical Literature* (Chico, CA: Scholars Press, 1985): 107–16; Esther Fuchs, "The Literary Characterization of Mothers and Sexual Politics in the Hebrew Bible," in Adela Yarbro Collins, ed., *Feminist Perspectives on the Bible* (Chico, CA: Scholars Press, 1985), 117–36; and idem, "Structure and Patriarchal Functions in the Biblical Betrothal Type-Scene: Some Preliminary Notes," *JFSR* 3 (1987): 7–13.

5. See Phyllis Bird, "The Harlot as Heroine: Narrative Art and Social Presupposition in Three Old Testament Texts," *Semeia* 46 (1989): 119–39; Susan Niditch, "The Wronged Woman Righted: An Analysis of Genesis 38," *HTR* 72 (1979): 143–49; and Naomi Steinberg, "Gender Roles in the Rebekah Cycle," *USQR* 39 (1984): 175–88.

6. Esther Fuchs, "The Literary Characterization of Mothers and Sexual Politics in the Hebrew Bible," in Adela Yarbro Collins, ed., *Feminist Perspectives on Biblical Scholarship*, SBLBSNA 10 (Chico, CA: Scholars Press, 1985), 136.

7. See Cheryl Exum, "'Mother in Israel: A Familiar Figure Reconsidered," in Letty M. Russell, ed., *Feminist Interpretation of the Bible* (Philadelphia: Westminster Press, 1985), 73–85; and Athalya Brenner, *The Israelite Woman: Social Role and Literary Type in Biblical Narrative* (Sheffield, UK: JSOT Press, 1985), 92–105.

8. Potiphar's wife is not clearly a mother. Indeed, her husband's title can mean "eunuch." See Jeansonne, *The Women of Genesis*, 109. However, Joseph marries Asenath, daughter of Potiphara (Gen. 41:45, 50; 46:20). Some have asked whether Potiphar and Potiphara may be the same person. See Jeansonne, *The Women of Genesis*, 109.

9. On the varieties of harlots in ancient Israel, see Bird, "To Play the Harlot,"in Peggy L. Day, ed. *Gender and Difference in Ancient Israel* (Minneapolis: Fortress Press, 1989), 75–84.

10. See Fuchs, "Who Is Hiding the Truth? Deceptive Women and Biblical Androcentrism," in Adela Yarbro Collins, ed., *Feminist Perspectives on Biblical Scholarship* (Chico, CA: Scholars Press, 1985), 137–44; J. Cheryl Exum and Johanna W. H. Bos, *Reasoning with the Foxes: Female Wit in a World of Male Power, Semeia* 42 (1988); and Susan Niditch, *Underdogs and Tricksters: A Prelude to Biblical Folklore* (San Francisco: Harper & Row, 1987).

11. Niditch, "Genesis," *WBC,* 18.

12. The sisters Rachel and Leah are equal in their sisterhood, but because Leah is the first wife, this gives her greater status. Jacob's love of Rachel counterbalances Leah's status, however.

13. Sarah has the power of ownership or at least being the "employer," which outweighs Hagar's power of fertility.

14. On the use and development of this motif, see Callaway, *Sing, O Barren One.*

15. See Jeansonne, *The Women of Genesis*, 20–21.

16. Fuchs, "The Literary Characterization of Mothers," 120–21.

17. Tammi Schneider, *Sarah: Mother of Nations* (London: Continuum, 2004), 70–74.

18. Pamela Tamarkin Reis, "Hagar Requited," *JSOT* 87 (2000): 77–80.

19. Aviva Zornberg, *The Beginning of Desire* (New York: Doubleday, 1995), 51–54, cited in Reis, "Hagar Requited," 83.

20. Reis, "Hagar Requited," 83–87.

21. Ibid., 88.

22. This is Teubal's representation of womanist theologian Delores Williams found in Teubal, *Hagar the Egyptian: The Lost Tradition of the Matriarchs* (San Francisco: Harper & Row, 1990), 194, 201n7.

23. Fuchs, "The Literary Characterization of Mothers," 131–32.

24. Reis, "Hagar Requited," 94–96a.

25. Weems, "A Mistress, a Maid, and No Mercy (Sarah and Hagar)," in *Just A Sister Away: A Womanist Vision of Women's Relationships in the Bible* (San Diego: Luva Media, 1988), 1. See also Randall C. Bailey, "Beyond Identification: The Use of Africans in Old Testament Poetry and Narratives," in Cain Hope Felder, ed., *Stony the Road We Trod: African American Biblical Interpretation* (Minneapolis: Fortress Press, 1991), 165–84.

26. Weems, "A Mistress, a Maid, and No Mercy," 2.

27. Phyllis Trible, "Hagar: The Desolation of Rejection," in *Texts of Terror: Literary-Feminist Readings of Biblical Narratives* (Philadelphia: Fortress Press, 1984), 27.

28. John W. Waters, "Who Was Hagar?" in Felder, ed., *Stony the Road,* 190, 192.

29. Hagar names God *'el ro'i,* "God of seeing, " in Gen. 16:13.

30. Trible, "Hagar: The Desolation of Rejection," 28.

31. Elsa Tamez, "The Woman Who Complicated the History of Salvation," in John S. Pobee and Bärbel von Wartenburg-Potter, eds., *New Eyes for Reading: Biblical and Theology Reflections by Women from the Third World* (Oak Park, IL: Meyer Stone Books, 1987), 14.

32. Delores Williams, "Hagar in African American Biblical Appropriation," in Phyllis Trible and Letty M. Russell, eds., *Hagar, Sarah, and Their Children: Jewish, Christian, and Muslim Perspectives* (Louisville: Westminster John Knox Press, 2006), 171–84.

33. Niditch, "Genesis," 18.

34. Trible, *Texts of Terror,* 28–29.

35. Weems, "A Mistress, a Maid, and No Mercy," 18–19.

36. See Jeansonne, *The Women of Genesis*, 31–42.

37. See Gerda Lerner, *The Creation of Patriarchy, Women and History* (New York and Oxford: Oxford University Press, 1986), 172–75, cited in Jeansonne, *The Women of Genesis*, 36.

38. See Jeansonne, *The Women of Genesis*, 35–37, who quotes Bruce Vawter and John Skinner. Vawter writes in *On Genesis: A New Reading* (Garden City, NY: Doubleday, 1977): "Certainly to our tastes he [Lot] proves himself to be more sensitive to the duties of hospitality than those of fatherhood. . . . The spectacle of a father offering his virgin daughters to the will and pleasure of a mob that was seeking to despoil his household would not have seemed as shocking to the ancient sense of proprieties as it may seem to us. . . . Really, there is no need to make excuses for him, as far as the biblical perspective is concerned. In all the stories about him the soundness of Lot's judgment is never the point at issue. . . . He is a good and not a bad man, but neither is he a hero in any way" (235–36). Skinner says in *A Critical and Exegetical Commentary on Genesis*, International Critical Commentary, 2nd ed. (Edinburgh: T. & T. Clark, 1930): "Lot's readiness to sacrifice the honour of his daughters, though abhorrent to Hebrew morality, . . . shows him as a courageous champion of the obligations of hospitality in a situation of extreme embarrassment, and is recorded to his credit" (1:307).

39. For a different reading, see Weems, *Just a Sister Away*, 129–42. See also Rebecca Goldstein, "Looking Back at Lot's Wife," in Celina Spiegel and Christina Buchmann, eds., *Out of the Garden: Women Writers on the Bible* (New York: Fawcett Columbine, 1994), 37–41.

40. Gail Corrington Streete, *The Strange Woman: Power and Sex in the Bible* (Louisville: Westminster John Knox Press, 1997), 28.

41. Janice Nunnally-Cox, *Foremothers: Women of the Bible* (San Francisco: Harper & Row, 1981), 11–12.

42. Melissa Jackson, "Lot's Daughters and Tamar as Tricksters and the Patriarchal Narratives as Feminist Theology," *JSOT* 98 (2002): 46.

43. See Callaway, *Sing, O Barren One*, 30–32.

44. Alice Laffey, *An Introduction to the Old Testament: A Feminist Perspective* (Philadelphia: Fortress Press, 1988), 32.

45. Adrien Janis Bledstein, "Binder, Trickster, Heel and Hairy-man: Rereading Genesis 27 as a Trickster Tale Told by a Woman," in Athalya Brenner, ed., *A Feminist Companion to Genesis* (Sheffield, UK: Sheffield Academic Press, 1993), 282–95.

46. Christine Garside Allen, "Who Was Rebekah? 'On Me Be the Curse My Son,'" in Rita M. Gross, ed., *Beyond Androcentrism: New Essays on Women and Religion* (Missoula, MT: Scholars Press, 1977), 183–216.

47. Ibid., 208.

48. Bledstein, "Binder, Trickster, Heel and Hairy-man."

49. Allen asks in "Who Was Rebekah?" whether "the most serious error that Rebekah committed in the mind of most male interpreters was to deceive her husband" (193).

50. Ibid., 211.

51. The students were Rodney Aist, Leander Coles, Gloria Nurse, Linda Patterson, Joan Scott, and Andrés Thomas Conteris.

52. See Callaway, *Sing, O Barren One*, 23–29.

53. Gale Yee, "Leah," *Anchor Bible Dictionary*, 4:265.

54. Cohen, "Sibling Rivalry in Genesis," *Judaism* 32 (1983): 331–42, cited in Yee, "Leah," 268.

55. Jeansonne, *The Women of Genesis*, 81.

56. Rtziah Spanier, "Rachel's Theft of the Teraphim: Her Struggle for Family Primacy," *VT* 42 (1992): 404–12.

57. Ilana Pardes, "Rachel's Dream of Grandeur," in Celina Spiegel and Christina Buchmann, eds., *Out of the Garden: Women Writers on the Bible* (New York: Fawcett Columbine, 1994), 70.

58. J. Cheryl Exum, "The (M)other's Place," in *Fragmented Women: Feminist (Sub)versions of Biblical Narratives* (Valley Forge, PA: Trinity Press International, 1993), 128.

59. Jacqueline E. Lapsley, "The Voice of Rachel: Resistance and Polyphony in Genesis 31:14–35," in Brenner, ed., *Genesis,* 232–48. See also Jeansonne, *The Women of Genesis,* 83, and Frymer-Kensky, *In the Wake of the Goddesses: Women, Culture and the Transformation of Pagan Myth* (New York: Free Press, 1992), 261n114. For a different view, see Fuchs, "For I Have the Way of Women: Deception, Gender, and Ideology in Biblical Narrative," in Exum and Bos, eds., *Reasoning with the Foxes,* 68–83. Frymer-Kensky believes that Fuchs's evaluation is based on her "negative apperception of deception, and her belief that the Bible presented tales of women's deceitfulness in order to dishonor them" (*In the Wake of the Goddesses,* 261).

60. Pardes, "Rachel's Dream," 77.

61. Danna Nolan Fewell and David M. Gunn, "Tipping the Balance: Sternberg's Reader and the Rape of Dinah," *JBL* 110 (1991): 196. See also Meir Sternberg's persuasive rebuttal in "Biblical Poetics and Sexual Politics: From Reading to Counter-Reading," *JBL* 111 (1992): 476–79. For a critique of Sternberg's work in general, see Burke O. Long, "The New Biblical Poetics of Alter and Sternberg," *JSOT* 51 (1991): 71–84.

62. Ita Sheres, *Dinah's Rebellion: A Biblical Parable for Our Time* (New York: Crossroad, 1990).

63. Fewell and Gunn, "Tipping the Balance," 193–211.

64. Ibid., 195–210.

65. Ibid., 211.

66. Ibid.

67. Meir Sternberg, "Biblical Poetics and Sexual Politics," 463–88.

68. Ibid., 476–79.

69. Ibid., 478.

70. Lyn Bechtel, "What If Dinah Is Not Raped? (Genesis 34)," *JSOT* 62 (1994): 19–36.

71. Ibid.

72. Ibid. See also Ellen Van Wolde, "Does 'innâ Denote Rape? A Semantic Analysis of a Controversial Word," *VT* 52:4 (2002): 528–44.

73. Anita Diamant, *The Red Tent* (New York: Picador, 1997).

74. Actually, the word used in Hebrew is *qedešâ,* meaning "holy woman," but with an overtone of sexuality. Bird writes in "The Harlot as Heroine," 126: "Here the issue of opprobrium surfaces. Judah, a man of standing, who has surrendered his insignia to a prostitute in a moment of weakness, does not go back in person to retrieve his goods, but sends a friend, a man of the region, to inquire discreetly of the local inhabitants. Hirah knows how to handle the situation; he uses a euphemism—comparable to our substitution of the term 'courtesan' for the cruder expression 'whore'—(a substitution of court language in the latter instance, cult language in the former). . . . And a *qedešâ,* I would argue, is not a prostitute, though she may share important characteristics with her sister of the streets and highways, including sexual intercourse with strangers."

75. Bos, "Out of the Shadows," 48–49.

76. Ibid., 48.

77. Jackson, "Lot's Daughters and Tamar as Tricksters," 77.

78. Bal, "One Woman, Many Men, and the Dialectic of Chronology," in *Lethal Love: Feminist Literary Readings of Biblical Love Stories* (Bloomington: Indiana University Press, 1987), 89–103.

79. Brenner, *The Israelite Woman* (see n. 7 above), 121.

80. Susan Tower Hollis, "The Woman in Ancient Examples of the Potiphar's Wife Motif, K2111," in Peggy L. Day, ed., *Gender and Difference in Ancient Israel* (Minneapolis: Fortress Press, 1989), 28–42.

81. Heather McKay, "Confronting Redundancy as Middle Manager and Wife: The Feisty Woman of Genesis 39," *Semeia* 87 (1999): 215–31. For a cultural-historical analysis of the text and

its interpretive history in art and literature, see Athalya Brenner and J. W. Van Henten, "Madame Potiphar through a Culture Trip or, Which Side Are You On?" In J. Cheryl Exum and Stephen D. Moore, eds., *Biblical Studies/Cultural Studies: The Third Sheffield Colloquium* (Sheffield, UK: Sheffield Academic Press, 1998), 203–19.

Chapter 4: The Women in Exodus and Numbers

1. Whether the adult Miriam is really Moses' sister is questioned by some. Rita Burns believes Miriam is called Moses' sister to establish her leadership alongside Moses, but she is skeptical of the historicity of this kinship tie. See Rita Burns, *Has the Lord Indeed Spoken Only through Moses? A Study of the Biblical Portrait of Miriam* (Atlanta: Scholars Press, 1987), 1–2n2, 8, 81–100, 121.

2. J. Cheryl Exum, "'You Shall Let Every Daughter Live': A Study of Exodus 1:8–2:10," *Semeia* 28 (1983): 63–82.

3. Ibid., 67.

4. Ibid., 68–70.

5. Ibid., 70.

6. Ibid., 72.

7. See Renita Weems, "The Hebrew Women Are Not Like the Egyptian Women: The Ideology of Race, Gender, and Sexual Reproduction in Exodus 1," in David Jobling and Tina Pippin, eds., *Ideological Criticism of Biblical Texts, Semeia* 59 (1992): 25–34.

8. Ibid., 75.

9. Phyllis Trible, "Bringing Miriam out of the Shadows," *Bible Review* (February 1989), 16.

10. Exum, "'You Shall Let Every Daughter Live,'" 78.

11. Ibid., 79.

12. Ibid., 79–81.

13. Ibid., 81–82.

14. Exum, "Second Thought about Secondary Characters: Women in Exodus 1.8–2.10," in *A Feminist Companion to Exodus to Deuteronomy* (Sheffield, UK: Sheffield Academic Press, 1994), 77.

15. Ibid., 82.

16. Trible, "Bringing Miriam out of the Shadows," 18.

17. Exactly what the designation of prophet means here is unclear. Miriam does not behave in the ways that later prophets do. Burns believes it is applied to her anachronistically. See *Has the Lord Indeed Spoken Only through Moses?* 41–79.

18. Trible, "Bringing Miriam out of the Shadows," 18.

19. Ibid., 19–20. The scholarly consensus described by Trible has been challenged by J. Gerald Janzen in "Song of Moses, Song of Miriam: Who Is Seconding Whom?" (*CBQ* 54 [1992]: 211–20). What is challenged is not the bottom line, which is Miriam's authorship of the song, but the view that Scripture has diminished Miriam's role.

20. Fokkelien van Dijk-Hemmes, "Some Recent Views on the Presentation of the Song of Miriam," in Athalya Brenner, ed., *A Feminist Companion to Exodus to Deuteronomy,* 205–6.

21. Janzen, "Song of Moses, Song of Miriam?" 187–99.

22. Trible, "Bringing Miriam out of the Shadows," 20.

23. Burns, *Has the Lord Indeed Spoken Only through Moses?* 124.

24. Susan Ackerman, "Why Is Miriam Also among the Prophets? (And Is Zipporah among the Priests?)" *JBL* 121/1 (2002): 47–80.

25. Cain Hope Felder argues, in *Troubling Biblical Waters: Race, Class, and Family* (Maryknoll, NY: Orbis Books, 1989), 12, that Cush designates a broad area: "There was not just one land of Cush but two. The first was south of Egypt; the second, across the Red Sea, included the Arabian peninsula and extended toward the Mesopotamian (Tigris and Euphrates) basin." John Waters

suggests in "Who Was Hagar?" in Felder, ed., *Stony the Road We Trod: African American Biblical Interpretation* (Minneapolis: Fortress Press, 1991), 204, that "Cush, Nubia, Put (Phut), and Egypt were not always distinct geographical entities. It was during the twelfth dynasty that Cush was conquered and annexed by Egypt (ca. 1991–1786 BCE). Thus, during the early patriarchal period in the life of Israel, Cush was a geographical part of Egypt."

26. Burns writes in *Has the Lord Indeed Spoken Only to Moses?* (68–69) that it is quite possible that the designations of Moses' wife as Cushite (Num. 12:1), Midianite (Num. 10:29; Exod. 2:15–21; 3:1), and Kenite (Judg. 1:16; 4:11) represent different versions of the community's memory that Moses had a foreign wife.

27. Weems, "In-Law, In Love (Miriam and Her Cushite Sister-in-Law)," in *Just a Sister Away: A Womanist Vision of Women's Relationships in the Bible* (San Diego: LuraMedia, 1988), 71–84.

28. Burns, *Has the Lord Indeed Spoken Only to Moses?* 69–70.

29. See Frank Moore Cross Jr., *Canaanite Myth and Hebrew Epic: Essays on the History of Israel* (Cambridge: Harvard University Press, 1973), 204; and Felder, *Troubling Biblical Waters*, 42. See also Randall C. Bailey, "Beyond Identification: The Use of Africans in Old Testament Poetry and Narratives," in Felder, ed., *Stony the Road*, 179–80. Bailey sees the conflict as a racial one but one in which Miriam objects to Moses' marriage to a Cushite woman because it gives him additional status.

30. *Interpreter's Dictionary of the Bible* (Nashville: Abingdon Press, 1962), 3:402.

31. Burns, *Has the Lord Indeed Spoken Only to Moses?* 125.

32. I argued this position in "Miriam and Moses' Cushite Wife: The Intersection of Race and Gender in Numbers 12:1, 10," which I presented at the Mid-Atlantic Regional meeting of the SBL in Washington, D.C., in February 1992. Other suggestions are that the Cushite wife was Moses' second wife and the objection was to bigamy; that the objection was just a pretext for the real issue, which was prophetic authority; and that the source of conflict was a cultic or purity issue. Only the last suggestion comes from a feminist interpreter. See Trible, "Bringing Miriam out of the Shadows," 21.

33. Irmtraud Fischer, "The Authority of Miriam: A Feminist Rereading of Numbers 12 Prompted by Jewish Interpretation," in Brenner, ed., *Exodus to Deuteronomy* (Sheffield, UK: Sheffield Academic Press, 2000), 159–73.

34. Ibid.

35. Ibid, 172–73.

36. See Ilana Pardes's treatment of this verse in *Countertraditions in the Bible: A Feminist Approach* (Cambridge: Harvard University Press, 1992), 6–12.

37. Frank Moore Cross identifies the Cushite wife of Num. 12:1 with Zipporah, whom he calls a Midianite priestess in *Canaanite Myth and Hebrew Epic*, 204.

38. Alice Laffey, *An Introduction to the Old Testament: A Feminist Perspective* (Philadelphia: Fortress Press, 1988), 49.

39. Drorah Setel, "Exodus," in *WBC* 31.

40. Pardes (*Countertraditions*, 79–97) sees this story as a modified version of the Egyptian myth of Isis and Osiris, in which Isis, the Egyptian savior goddess, resurrects her husband-brother Osiris, who had been dismembered by his jealous brother Seth. Isis collected the parts of Osiris's body and brought him back to life by magic formulas and by waving her wings, thus filling him with breath. The focus of the procedure is on revivifying Osiris's penis and impregnating Isis. Pardes notes the common themes: a violent persecutor, a savior wife, a penis undergoing treatment, and wings (Zipporah means bird).

Pardes believes that the opposition between history and mythology is not clear. She writes: "Mythologies (particularly Greek and Roman ones) rely in part on historical events, and monotheistic history is not innocent of mythical tendencies (as in its cyclical patterning of given historical phenomena). The difference in emphasis is nevertheless significant" (95). Of the historical Zipporah, Pardes says that it would take some of Zipporah's magical powers to "deliver fully a history that has been so severely curtailed" (97).

41. Ackerman, "Why Is Miriam among the Prophets?" 71–75.

42. Gene Rice, "Africans and the Origins of the Worship of Yahweh," *JRT* 50 (1993–94): 27–34.

43. Trible, "Bringing Miriam out of the Shadows," 21.

44. Ackerman, "Why Is Miriam among the Prophets?" 78–80.

45. Trible, "Bringing Miriam out of the Shadows," 25.

46. Ibid.

47. Katharine Doob Sakenfeld, "Feminist Biblical Interpretation," *Theology Today* 46 (1989): 154–68.

48. Ibid., 157.

49. Ibid., 157–58.

50. Ibid., 158–59.

51. Ibid., 159.

52. Ibid.

53. Ibid., 158–60.

54. Sakenfeld, "Numbers," in *WBC* 50.

Chapter 5: The Women in Joshua and Judges

1. Phyllis A. Bird, "The Harlot as Heroine: Narrative Art and Social Presupposition in Three Old Testament Texts," *Semeia* 46 (1989): 119–39.

2. Ibid., 120–21.

3. Ibid., 121.

4. The evidence for the existence of sacred prostitution among ancient Israel's neighbors is not nearly so strong as once thought. See Robert A. Oden Jr., "Religious Identity and the Sacred Prostitution Accusation," in *The Bible without Theology: The Theological Tradition and Alternatives to It* (San Francisco: Harper & Row, 1987), 131–53.

5. Ibid., 127.

6. Ibid., 128.

7. Danna Nolan Fewell, "Joshua," in *WBC*, 69.

8. Norman Gottwald, *The Tribes of Yahweh: A Sociology of the Religion of Liberated Israel 1250–1050 B.C.E.* (Maryknoll, NY: Orbis Books, 1979).

9. Bird, "The Harlot as Heroine," 129.

10. Ibid., 131.

11. Naomi Franklin, *The Stranger within Their Gates (How the Israelite Portrayed the Non-Israelite in Biblical Literature)* (Conway, AR: UCA Press, 1991), 112–13.

12. Judith E. McKinlay, "Reading Rahab and Ruth," in *Reframing Her: Biblical Women in Postcolonial Focus* (Sheffield, UK: Sheffield Phoenix Press, 2004), 37–56.

13. Musa W. Dube, *Postcolonial Feminist Interpretation of the Bible* (St. Louis: Chalice, 2000), 201.

14. Lori L. Rowlett, "Disney's Pocahontas and Joshua's Rahab in Post-colonial Perspective," in George Aichele, ed., *Culture, Entertainment and the Bible* (Sheffield, UK: Sheffield Academic Press, 2000), 75.

15. Mieke Bal, *Death and Dissymmetry: The Politics of Coherence in the Book of Judges* (Chicago: University of Chicago Press, 1988), 208–9.

16. See Rachel C. Rasmussen, "Deborah the Woman Warrior" in Mieke Bal, ed., *Anti-Covenant: Counterreading Women's Lives in the Hebrew Bible*, Bible and Literature Series 99 (Sheffield, UK: Almond Press, 1989), 79–93. See also Susan Ackerman, *Warrior, Dancer, Seductress, Queen: Women in Judges and Biblical Israel* (New York: Doubleday, 1998), 27–88.

17. Denise Lardner Carmody, *Biblical Woman: Contemporary Reflections on Scriptural Texts* (New York: Crossroad, 1988), 29.

18. Bal, *Death and Dissymmetry*, 209.

19. Jo Ann Hackett, "In the Days of Jael: Reclaiming the History of Women in Ancient Israel," in Clarissa W. Atkinson, Constance H. Buchanan, and Margaret R. Miles, eds., *Immaculate and Powerful: The Female in Sacred Image and Social Reality* (Boston: Beacon Press, 1985), 27–28.

20. Ibid., 22–28.

21. Ackerman, *Warrior, Dancer, Seductress, Queen*, 27–88.

22. Ackerman, "Digging Up Deborah: Recent Hebrew Bible Scholarship on Gender and the Contribution of Archaeology," *Near Eastern Archaeology* 66:4 (2003): 172–84 [177].

23. Julia Esquivel, "Liberation, Theology, and Women," in John S. Pobee and Bärbel von Wartenberg-Potter, eds., *New Eyes for Reading: Biblical and Theological Reflections by Women from the Third World* (Oak Park, IL: Meyer-Stone Books, 1987), 99.

24. Lillian Sigal, "Models of Love and Hate," *Daughters of Sarah* 16, no. 2 (March/April 1990), 8.

25. Danna Nolan Fewell and David M. Gunn, "Controlling Perspectives: Women, Men, and the Authority of Violence in Judges 40–5," *JAAR* 58 (1991): 397.

26. Ibid., 409.

27. Yee, "By the Hand of a Woman," 100.

28. Ibid., 110–14.

29. Ibid., 114–17.

30. Ibid., 117–21.

31. Ackerman, *Warrior, Dancer, Seductress, Queen*, 89–127.

32. Yee, "By the Hand of a Woman: The Metaphor of the Woman Warrior in Judges 4," in Claudia V. Camp and Carole R. Fontaine, eds., *Women, War, and Metaphor: Language and Society in the Study of the Hebrew Bible, Semeia* 61 (1993): 116.

33. Cited in Yee, "By the Hand of a Woman," 122.

34. Elizabeth Cady Stanton, *The Woman's Bible* (New York: European Publishing Co., 1895–98), 20, cited in Yee, "By the Hand of a Woman," 123.

35. For an exposition of the way various disciplines, such as historical criticism, theology, anthropology, and literary criticism, and transdisciplinary matters, such as theme and gender, operate in the two versions of Sisera's death, see Bal, *Murder and Difference: Gender, Genre, and Scholarship on Sisera's Death* (Bloomington: Indiana University Press, 1988).

36. Johanna W. H. van Wijk-Bos, *Reformed and Feminist: A Challenge to the Church* (Louisville: Westminster John Knox Press, 1991), 73–74.

37. Fewell, "Judges," 75. For a similar reading, see Fewell and Gunn, "Controlling Perspectives," 395–96.

38. Susan Ackerman, "Most Blessed of Women," in *Warrior, Dancer, Seductress, Queen: Women in Judges and Biblical Israel* (New York: Doubleday, 1998), 102.

39. Katharine Doob Sakenfeld, "Deborah, Jael, and Sisera's Mother: Reading the Scriptures in Cross-Cultural Context," in Jane Dempsey Douglass and James F. Kay, eds., *Women, Gender, and Christian Community* (Louisville: Westminster John Knox Press, 1997), 22.

40. Adele Reinhartz argues in "Samson's Mother: An Unnamed Protagonist" *JSOT* 55 (1992) that in this case the protagonist's anonymity is not symbolic of her lesser status.

41. J. Cheryl Exum, "Promise and Fulfillment: Narrative Art in Judges 13," *JBL* 99 (1980): 59.

42. Exum, *Fragmented Women: Feminist (Sub)Versions of Biblical Narratives* (Valley Forge, PA: Trinity Press International, 1993), 61–93.

43. Ackerman, "Most Blessed of Women," 116.

44. See Bal, *Death and Dissymmetry*, 224; and Mary Cartledge-Hayes, *To Love Delilah: Claiming Women of the Bible* (San Diego: Lura Media, 1990), 36–45.

45. Betsy Merideth, "Desire and Danger: The Drama of Betrayal," in Mieke Bal, ed., *Anti-Covenant: Counter-Reading Women's Lives in the Hebrew Bible* (Sheffield, UK: Almond Press, 1989), 72–73.

46. Frymer-Kensky suggests that this assumption is not necessarily true. She argues in *In the Wake of the Goddesses: Women, Culture, and the Biblical Transformation of Pagan Myth* (New York: Free Press, 1992), 260n105, that "the text never tells us that Delilah was a foreigner. The valley of Sorek is only thirteen miles west-southwest of Jerusalem, guarded by Beth Shemesh. This was Danite territory, and was still occupied by Israelites. It was a border area that may not even have been under Philistine control. Even if it had been, the population had not been displaced or deported. Since the text does not mention that Delilah was a Philistine, there is no reason to assume it."

47. Lillian R. Klein, "The Book of Judges: Paradigm and Deviation in Images of Women," in Athalya, Brenner, ed., *A Feminist Companion to Judges* (Sheffield, UK: Sheffield Academic Press, 1999), 66.

48. Cartledge-Hayes, *To Love Delilah*, 43.

49. Danna Nolan Fewell, "Judges," 73.

50. Carol Smith, "Delilah: A Suitable Case for (Feminist) Treatment?" in Athalya Brenner, *Judges* (Sheffield, UK: Sheffield Academic Press, 1999), 109.

51. J. Cheryl Exum, "Samson's Women," in *Fragmented Women: Feminist (Sub) Versions of Biblical Narratives* (Valley Forge, PA: Trinity Press International, 1993), 61–93.

52. Smith, "Samson and Delilah: A Parable of Power?" *JSOT* 76 (1997): 45–57, [49].

53. See Bal, *Death and Dissymmetry*. See also Anne Michelle Tapp, "An Ideology of Expendability: Virgin Daughter Sacrifice," 157–74; Beth Gerstein, "A Ritual Processed," 175–94; Cynthia Baker, "Pseudo-Philo and the Transformation of Jephthah's Daughter," 195–210; and Bal, "Between Altar and Wandering Rock," 211–32—all in Bal, ed., *Anti-Covenant*. See also Peggy L. Day, "From the Child Is Born the Woman: The Story of Jephthah's Daughter," in *Gender and Difference in Ancient Israel* (Minneapolis: Fortress Press, 1989), 58–74; J. Cheryl Exum, "Murder They Wrote: Ideology and the Manipulation of Female Presence in Biblical Narrative," in Alice Bach, ed., *Ad Feminam, USQR* 43 (1989): 19–39; Esther Fuchs, "Marginalization, Ambiguity, Silencing: The Story of Jephthah's Daughter," *JFSR* 5, no. 1 (1989): 35–45; Laffey, *An Introduction to the Old Testament*, 97–98; Phyllis Trible, "The Daughter of Jephthah: An Inhuman Sacrifice," in *Texts of Terror: Literary-Feminist Readings of Biblical Narratives* (Philadelphia: Fortress Press, 1984), 93–118; Renita J. Weems, "A Crying Shame (Jephthah's Daughter and the Mourning Women)," in *Just a Sister Away: A Womanist Vision of Women's Relationships in the Bible* (San Diego: Lura Media, 1988), 53–70; and Fewell, "Judges," 70–72.

54. Bal argues in *Death and Dissymmetry* that Jephthah's mother was not a prostitute but rather a patrilocal wife, i.e., a wife who continued living in her father's house rather than moving into her husband's house: "Jephthah is also a patrilocal son. His mother is referred to as an *'ishah zonah*, widely translated as 'a harlot.' We have seen that the 'unfaithfulness' implied in the root *zanah* can be related to the leaving behind of the father in favor of 'any man,' or the other way around, and the case of Jephthah further confirms this possibility. The noun *zonah* hardly fits our view of prostitution; how would it account for the acceptance of the son in a father-house? A prostitute as the term is commonly understood is by definition promiscuous, hence, unable to identify the father of her child. In fact, the only way to provide her child with a father would be to remain patrilocal and thereby to attribute fatherhood to the mother's father. This is one of the ways prostitution and patrilocy may eventually—through the ideological imposition of virilocy—have become conflated. If this woman is a patrilocal wife, the noun *zonah* could indicate that her temporary 'unfaithfulness' from her father's house or her relinquishing of her son, indirectly implied by the fact that Jephthah seems to have grown up in the virilocal house, turns her into a 'woman of

unfaithfulness' in the eyes of the patrilocal ideology, while her residence in her father's house turns her into a 'prostitute' from the virilocal perspective. The term becomes pejorative in both cases, but not in the same sense. The motive the other sons allege for their expulsion of Jephthah is indeed that he is the 'son of another woman'" (177–78).

55. Exum, "Murder They Wrote," 32.

56. Fuchs, "Marginalization, Ambiguity, Silencing," 35–45.

57. Day, "From the Child Is Born the Woman," 58–74.

58. Weems, "A Crying Shame," 53–54.

59. Ibid., 67.

60. Trible, "The Daughter of Jephthah," 105.

61. Ibid., 107.

62. Ibid., 108.

63. Laffey, An Introduction to the Old Testament, 99.

64. Fewell, "Judges," 71.

65. Note, however, that Exum suggests that the vow could plausibly be understood to be made under the influence of God's Spirit (Tragedy and Biblical Narrative: Arrows of the Almighty [Cambridge: Cambridge University Press, 1992]).

66. Bal, "Between Altar and Wandering Rock," 228.

67. Weems, "A Crying Shame," 61.

68. Fewell, "Judges," 71.

69. Valerie C. Cooper, "Some Place to Cry: Jephthah's Daughter and the Double Dilemma of Black Women in America," in Cheryl A. Kirk-Duggan, ed., Pregnant Passion: Gender, Sex, and Violence in the Bible (Atlanta: SBL Press, 2003), 87.

70. Exum points out in "Raped by the Pen," in Fragmented Women, 178, that the text does not promote the idea that the woman was sexually promiscuous. If this were the case, why would she go to her father's house and why would the Levite try to get her back? Exum also cites Bal (Death and Dissymmetry, 86), who suggests that the verb referred to a woman's breach of patrilocal marriage (residence with the father) in favor of living with her husband. In addition, Exum cites Yair Zakovitch ("The Woman's Rights in the Biblical Law of Divorce," The Jewish Law Annual 4 [1981]: 28–46), who suggests that perhaps the term zanâ was applied to women who left their husbands without the possibility of going back to their father's house and therefore became prostitutes to survive.

71. Bal, Death and Dissymmetry, 80–93. See also n. 54 above. In addition, see Fewell, "Judges," 75.

72. Exum, "Raped by the Pen," 177. See also Susan Ackerman, Warrior, Dancer, Seductress, Queen, 220.

73. Trible, "An Unnamed Woman: The Extravagance of Violence," in Texts of Terror, 65–92.

74. Ibid., 82–87.

75. Ibid., 82–84.

76. Ibid., 84.

77. Ibid.

78. Ibid., 84–85.

79. Ibid., 85–86.

80. Ibid., 86.

81. Ibid., 87.

82. Stuart Lasine, "Guest and Host in Judges 19: Lot's Hospitality in an Inverted World," JSOT 29 (1984): 37.

83. Koala Jones-Warsaw, "Toward a Womanist Hermeneutic: A Reading of Judges 19–21," in Brenner, ed., A Feminist Companion to Judges, 181.

84. Jacqueline Lapsley, *Whispering the Word: Hearing Women's Stories in the Old Testament* (Louisville: Westminster John Knox Press, 2005), 64–65.

Chapter 6: The Women in 1 and 2 Samuel

1. For the development of the barren woman motif in Hannah's story, see Mary Callaway, *Sing, O Barren One: A Study in Comparative Midrash*, SBLDS 91 (Atlanta: Scholars Press, 1986), 35–58.

2. Lillian R. Klein, "Hannah: Marginalized Victim and Social Redeemer," in *From Deborah to Esther: Sexual Politics in the Hebrew Bible* (Minneapolis: Fortress Press, 2003), 46.

3. For various interpretations of his questions, see Yairah Amit, "'Am I Not More Devoted to You Than Ten Sons?' (1 Samuel 1.8): Male and Female Interpretations," in Athalya Brenner, ed., *A Feminist Companion to Samuel and Kings* (Sheffield, UK: Sheffield Academic Press, 1994), 58–76.

4. On the significance of her vow, see Carol Meyers, "Hannah and Her Sacrifice: Reclaiming Female Agency," in Athalya Brenner, ed., *A Feminist Companion to Samuel and Kings* (Sheffield, UK: Sheffield Academic Press, 1994), 93–104.

5. Janice Nunnally-Cox, *Foremothers: Women of the Bible* (San Francisco: Harper & Row, 1981), 65.

6. Edith Deen, *All of the Women of the Bible* (San Francisco: Harper & Row, 1955), 106–7, cited in Nunnally-Cox, *Foremothers*, 65–66.

7. Nunnally-Cox, *Foremothers*, 66.

8. See Jo Ann Hackett, "1 and 2 Samuel," in *WBC* 91, for an enumeration of possibilities.

9. J. Cheryl Exum, "Murder They Wrote: Ideology and Manipulation of Female Presence in Biblical Narrative," in Alice Bach, ed., *Ad Feminam, USQR* 43 (1989): 19–39.

10. David J. A. Clines, "Michal Observed: An Introduction to Reading Her Story," in David J. A. Clines and Tamara C. Eskenazi, eds., *Telling Queen Michal's Story: An Experiment in Comparative Interpretation* (Sheffield, UK: Sheffield Academic Press, 1991), 60.

11. Katharine Doob Sakenfeld, "Michal, Abigail, and Bathsheba: In the Eye of the Beholder," in *Just Wives: Stories of Power and Survival in the Old Testament and Today* (Louisville: Westminster John Knox Press, 2003), 69–90.

12. Shoshanna Gershenzon, "Michal Bat Shaul," in Clines and Eskenazi, *Telling Queen Michal's Story*, 199–200.

13. For different views, see Sakenfeld, "Michal, Abigail, and Bathsheba," 69–90.

14. Alice Bach, "The Pleasure of Her Text," in *Ad Feminam, USQR* 43 (1989): 42.

15. Ibid., 49.

16. For a different view see Klein, "Bathsheba Revealed," in Brenner, ed., *A Feminist Companion to Samuel and Kings*, 47–64. See also Sakenfeld, "Michal, Abigail, and Bathsheba," 69–90.

17. On the many ambiguous aspects of this narrative, see Gale Yee, "Fraught with Background: Literary Ambiguity in II Samuel 11," *Interpretation* 42 (1988): 240–53.

18. Regina M. Schwartz, "Adultery in the House of David: The Metanarrative of Biblical Scholarship and the Narratives of the Bible," *Semeia* 54 (1991): 47.

19. Alice Laffey, *An Introduction to the Old Testament: A Feminist Perspective* (Philadelphia: Fortress Press, 1988), 121.

20. Bal, "The Emergence of the Lethal Woman, or the Use of the Hermeneutic Model," in *Lethal Love: Feminist Literary Readings of Biblical Love Stories* (Bloomington: Indiana University Press, 1987), 26.

21. Ibid., 34.

22. Ibid., 34–35.

23. Bach, "The Pleasure of Her Text," 45.

24. Adele Berlin, "Characterization in Biblical Narrative: David's Wives," *JSOT* 23 (1982): 69–85.

25. Ibid., 79.

26. Phyllis Trible, "Tamar: The Royal Rape of Wisdom," in *Texts of Terror: Literary-Feminist Readings of Biblical Narrative* (Philadelphia: Fortress Press, 1984), 37–63.

27. Ibid., 55–56.

28. Ibid., 57.

29. Denise Lardner Carmody, *Biblical Woman: Contemporary Reflections on Scriptural Texts* (New York: Crossroad, 1988), 45–46.

30. Ibid., 47–48.

31. Laffey, *An Introduction to the Old Testament*, 125–26.

32. Ibid., 126.

33. Patricia K. Willey, "The Importunate Woman of Tekoa and How She Got Her Way," in Danna Nolan Fewell, ed., *Reading Between Texts: Intertextuality and the Hebrew Bible* (Louisville: Westminster John Knox Press, 1992), 116.

34. Ibid., 125–26.

35. Ibid., 128.

36. Claudia V. Camp, "2 Sam 20:14–22: Wise Woman of Abel of Beth-maacah," in *WIS*, 267.

Chapter 7: The Women in 1 and 2 Kings

1. Adele Berlin, "Characterization in Biblical Narrative: David's Wives," *JSOT* 23 (1982): 74–76.

2. Ibid., 76.

3. Renita J. Weems, *Just a Sister Away: A Womanist Vision of Women's Relationships in the Bible* (San Diego: Lura Media, 1988), 1.

4. Randall C. Bailey, "Beyond Identification: The Use of Africans in Old Testament Poetry and Narratives," in *Stony the Road We Trod: African American Biblical Interpretation*, ed. Cain Hope Felder (Minneapolis: Fortress Press, 1991), 180–81.

5. Esther Fuchs, "The Literary Characterization of Mothers and Sexual Politics in the Hebrew Bible," in Adela Yarbro Collins, ed., *Feminist Perspectives on Biblical Scholarship* (Chico, CA: Scholars Press, 1985), 131–32.

6. Claudia V. Camp, "1 and 2 Kings," in *WBC*, 100.

7. Ibid., 102.

8. Cain Hope Felder, *Troubling Biblical Waters: Race, Class, and Family* (Maryknoll, NY: Orbis Books, 1989), 23–27.

9. Ibid., 31–33.

10. Ibid., 25–28.

11. Ibid., 22–36.

12. Tina Pippin, "Jezebel Re-Vamped," in Athalya Brenner, ed., *A Feminist Companion to Samuel and Kings* (Sheffield, UK: Sheffield Academic Press, 1994), 196.

13. Camp, "1 and 2 Kings," 103.

14. Judith E. McKinlay, *Reframing Her: Biblical Women in Postcolonial Focus* (Sheffield, UK: Sheffield Academic Press, 2004), 77.

15. Camp, "1 and 2 Kings," 103–4.

16. Eleanor Ferris Beach, *The Jezebel Letters: Religion and Politics in Ninth Century Israel* (Minneapolis: Fortress Press, 2005). See also her "The Samaria Ivories, *Marzeaḥ* and Biblical Texts," *BA* 56 (1992): 130–39.

17. Denise Lardner Carmody, *Biblical Woman: Contemporary Reflections on Scriptural Texts* (New York: Crossroad, 1988), 50.

18. Camp, "1 and 2 Kings," 104.

19. Ibid., 108. See also Stuart Lasine, "Jehoram and the Cannibal Mothers (2 Kings 6:24–33): Solomon's Judgment in an Inverted World," *JSOT* 50 (1991): 27–53.

20. Laurel Lanner, "Cannibal Mothers and Me: A Mother's Reading of 2 Kings 6:24–7:20," in Athalya Brenner, ed., *Samuel and Kings* (Sheffield, UK: Sheffield Academic Press, 2000), 136.

21. Paula S. Hiebert, "'Whence Shall Help Come to Me?' The Biblical Widow," in Peggy L. Day, ed., *Gender and Difference in Ancient Israel* (Minneapolis: Fortress, 1989), 125–41.

22. Ibid., 127–30.

23. Jopie Siebert-Hommes, "The Widow of Zarephath and the Great Woman of Shunem: A Comparative Analysis of Two Stories," in Bob Becking and Meindert Dijkstra, eds., *On Reading Prophetic Texts: Gender Specific and Related Studies in Memory of Fokkelien van Dijk-Hemmes* (Leiden: E. J. Brill, 1996), 104.

24. Johanna W. H. van Wijk-Bos, *Reformed and Feminist: A Challenge to the Church* (Louisville: Westminster/John Knox Press, 1991), 77.

25. Ibid., 79.

26. Ibid., 79–80.

27. Ibid., 80.

28. Ibid., 81.

29. Note also Siebert-Hommes's comparison of the stories of the healing of the sons of the widow of Zarephath and the Shunammite woman and the way the women are instrumental in revealing the differences between the prophets Elijah and Elisha ("The Widow of Zarephath and the Great Woman of Shunem: A Comparative Analysis of Two Stories," 98–114).

30. Fokkelien van Dijk-Hemmes, "The Great Woman of Shunem and the Man of God: A Dual Interpretation of 2 Kings 4:8–37," in Brenner, ed., *A Feminist Companion to Samuel and Kings*, 218–30.

31. Mary Shields, "Subverting a Man of God, Elevating a Woman: Role and Power Reversals in 2 Kings 4," in Brenner, ed., *Samuel and Kings*, 115–24.

32. Diana Edelman, "Huldah the Prophet—Of Yahweh or Asherah," in Brenner, ed., *A Feminist Companion to Samuel and Kings*, 231–50.

Chapter 8: The Women in the Prophets

1. Cf. Jer. 7:18; 44:15–19.

2. Ella Pearson Mitchell and Henry H. Mitchell, "Women: A Historical Perspective," in Ella Pearson Mitchell, ed., *Women: To Preach or Not to Preach: Twenty-One Outstanding Black Preachers Say Yes!* (Valley Forge, PA: Judson Press, 1991), 7.

3. For feminist interpretations of this imagery, see Susan Ackerman, "Isaiah"; Kathleen O'Connor, "Jeremiah"; Katheryn Phisterer Darr, "Ezekiel"; and Gale Yee, "Hosea"; and the literature cited in these articles, in *WBC*, 169–77, 178–86, 192–200, 207–15. See also the various articles in Pornoprophetic sections of the Feminist Companion to the Bible volumes listed in the bibliography.

4. Gale Yee in *Composition and Tradition in the Book of Hosea: A Redaction Critical Investigation* (Atlanta: Scholars Press, 1987) believes that before compilers and redactors brought the book of Hosea into its final form, the original work began in Hosea 2 as a legal complaint lodged against "your mother," who is understood to be Rachel, the mother of the northern tribes. According to Yee, Hosea viewed as "harlotrous" the northern kingdom's ever-changing political alliances with foreign powers and the intrigue that surrounded them. Yee believes that the person(s) responsible for collecting the Hosean material added Hosea 1, thus reinterpreting the imagery in more personal terms. She believes that the final redactor added Hosea 3, as well as other additions, to provide a tripartite structure for the book: chaps. 1–3 focus on the wife/Israel motif; chaps. 4–11 use the imagery of Israel as a youth; and chaps. 12–14 return to the original motif.

5. Phyllis A. Bird, "'To Play the Harlot': An Inquiry into an Old Testament Metaphor," in Peggy L. Day, ed., *Gender and Difference in Ancient Israel* (Minneapolis: Fortress Press, 1989), 80.

6. See Tikva Frymer-Kensky, *In the Wake of the Goddesses: Women, Culture, and the Biblical Transformation of Pagan Myth* (New York: Free Press, 1992), 199–202, and Alice A. Keefe, "The Female Body, the Body Politic and the Land: A Sociopolitical Reading of Hosea 1–2," in Athalya Brenner, ed., *A Feminist Companion to the Prophets and Daniel* (Sheffield, UK: Sheffield Academic Press, 2001), 76–89.

7. T. Drorah Setel, "Prophets and Pornography: Female Sexual Imagery in Hosea," in Letty M. Russell, ed., *Feminist Interpretation of the Bible* (Philadelphia: Westminster Press, 1985), 86–95, 157–59.

8. Ibid., 87.

9. Ibid.

10. Ibid., 88–89.

11. Ibid., 89.

12. Ibid., 89–90.

13. Ibid., 92.

14. Ibid.

15. Ibid.

16. Ibid.

17. Ibid., 93.

18. See Robert P. Carroll's critique of articles by Fokkelien van Dijk-Hemmes and Athalya Brenner, which in turn take Setel's definition of pornography (based on the work of Andrea Dworkin) as their point of departure: "Desire under the Terebinths: On Pornographic Representations in the Prophets—a Response," in Athalya Brenner, ed., *A Feminist Companion to the Latter Prophets* (Sheffield, UK: Sheffield Academic Press, 1995; London/New York: T. & T. Clark, 2004), 275–307.

19. Setel, "Prophets and Pornography," 95.

20. Renita J. Weems, "Gomer: Victim of Violence or Victim of Metaphor?" in Katie Geneva Cannon and Elisabeth Schüssler Fiorenza, eds., *Interpretation for Liberation, Semeia* 47 (1989): 87–104.

21. Ibid., 87.

22. Ibid., 98.

23. Ibid.

24. Ibid., 100.

25. Ibid.

26. Ibid., 101.

27. Ibid.

28. Gale Yee, "Faithless Israel in Hosea," in *Poor Banished Children of Eve: Woman as Evil in the Hebrew Bible* (Minneapolis: Fortress Press, 2003), 108–9.

29. Ibid., 109. For a similar view, see Keefe, "The Female Body, The Body Politic and the Land," 70–100.

30. Helen Schüngel-Straumann, "God as Mother in Hosea 11," in Brenner, ed., *The Feminist Companion to the Latter Prophets,* 194–218.

31. Commentators debate to what degree the book of Jeremiah can be trusted as a source of information about the person Jeremiah. Robert P. Carroll (*The Book of Jeremiah, A Commentary*, Old Testament Library [Philadelphia: Westminster Press, 1986]) is especially pessimistic. William Holladay (*Jeremiah 1: A Commentary on the Book of the Prophet Jeremiah Chapters 1–25* and *Jeremiah 2: A Commentary on the Book of the Prophet Jeremiah Chapters 26–52*, Hermeneia [Minneapolis: Fortress Press, 1989]) is much more optimistic.

32. Sandra L. Gravett, "Oholah, Woman Samaria," in *WIS*, 536.

33. Susan Ackerman, "'And the Women Knead Dough': The Worship of the Queen of Heaven in Sixth Century Judah" in Day, ed., *Gender and Difference in Ancient Israel*, 109–24.

34. Ibid., 110–17.

35. Ibid., 116–18.

36. Ibid., 117.

37. Ibid., 118.

38. Judith M. Hadley, "The Queen of Heaven—Who Is She?" in Brenner, ed., *The Prophets and Daniel*, 51.

39. See Phyllis Trible, "Gift of a Poem: A Rhetorical Study of Jeremiah 31:15–22," *Andover Newton Quarterly* 17 (1977): 271–80. For bovine divine imagery, see also Eleanor Ferris Beach, "The Samaria Ivories, *Marzeaḥ* and Biblical Texts," *BA* 56 (1992): 130–39.

40. Mary Callaway, *Sing, O Barren One: A Study in Comparative Midrash* (Atlanta: Scholars Press, 1986), 58–62.

41. Ibid., 64.

42. On the personification of Jerusalem as a woman, see Aloysius Fitzgerald, "The Mythological Background for the Presentation of Jerusalem as a Queen and False Worship in the O.T.," *CBQ* 34 (1972): 403–16.

43. Callaway, *Sing, O Barren One*, 65–67.

44. Ibid., 68–69.

45. Ibid., 69.

46. See Gerlinde Baumann, "Prophetic Objections to YHWH as the Violent Husband of Israel: Reinterpretations of the Prophetic Marriage Metaphor in Second Isaiah (Isaiah 40–55)," in Brenner, ed., *The Prophets and Daniel*, 88–120, and Margo C. A. Korpel, "The Female Servant of the Lord in Isaiah 54," in Bob Becking and Meindert Dijkstra, eds., *On Reading Prophetic Texts: Gender Specific and Related Studies in Memory of Fokkelien van Dijk-Hemmes* (Leiden: E. J. Brill, 1996), 153–68.

47. Callaway, *Sing, O Barren One*, 79.

48. Ibid., 80. For a broader discussion of "Zion, the Beloved Woman," see Frymer-Kensky, *In the Wake of the Goddesses*, 168–78. See also Mary Donovan Turner, "Daughter Zion: Giving Birth to Redemption," in Cheryl Kirk-Duggan, ed., *Pregnant Passion: Gender, Sex, and Violence in the Bible* (Atlanta: SBL Press, 2003), 193–204.

Chapter 9: The Women in the Wisdom Literature and the Song of Songs

1. Carol A. Newsom, "Job," in *WBC*, 138–44.

2. Ellen van Wolde, "The Development of Job: Mrs Job as Catalyst," in Athalya Brenner, ed., *A Feminist Companion to Wisdom Literature* (Sheffield, UK: Sheffield Academic Press, 1995), 201–4.

3. See Christi Maier and Silvia Schroer, "What About Job? Questioning the Book of 'The Righteous Sufferer,'" in Athalya Brenner and Carole Fontaine, eds., *Wisdom and Psalms* (Sheffield, UK: Sheffield Academic Press, 1998), 194.

4. Van Wolde, "The Development of Job: Mrs Job as Catalyst," 204–5.

5. Newsom, "Job," 139–40.

6. Ibid. See also van Wolde's five phases of Joban development in response to Mrs. Job's speech in "The Development of Job," 201–21.

7. Ilana Pardes, *Countertraditions in the Bible: A Feminist Approach* (Cambridge: Harvard University Press, 1992), 153.

8. Ibid.

9. Ibid., 154.

10. Carol A. Newsom, "Woman and the Discourse of Patriarchal Wisdom: A Study of Proverbs 1–9," in Day, ed., *Gender and Difference,* 142.

11. Athalya Brenner, "Proverbs 1–9: An F Voice?" in Athalya Brenner and Fokkelien van Dijk-Hemmes, eds., *On Gendering Texts: Female and Male Voices in the Hebrew Bible* (Leiden: E. J. Brill, 1993), 117–19.

12. Newsom, "Woman and the Discourse of Patriarchal Wisdom," 143–44.

13. Ibid., 148–49.

14. Brenner, "Proverbs 1–9: An F Voice?" 121–25.

15. Gale Yee, "The Other Woman in Proverbs," in *Poor Banished Children of Eve: Woman as Evil in the Hebrew Bible* (Minneapolis: Fortress Press, 2003), 135–58. See also Harold C. Washington, "The Strange Woman (אשה זרה/נכריה) of Proverbs 1–9 and Post-Exilic Judaean Society," in Brenner, ed., *A Feminist Companion to Wisdom Literature,* 157–84.

16. Newsom, "Woman and the Discourse of Patriarchal Wisdom," 148–49.

17. Gerlinde Baumann, "A Figure with Many Facets: The Literary and Technological Functions of Personified Wisdom in Proverbs 1–9," in Athalya Brenner and Carole Fontaine, eds., *Wisdom and Psalms* (Sheffield, UK: Sheffield Academic Press, 1998), 44–78.

18. Ibid., 72.

19. Ibid., 75.

20. Toril Moi, *Sexual/Textual Politics: Feminist Literary Theory* (London: Methuen, 1985), 167, cited in Newsom, "Woman and the Discourse of Patriarchal Wisdom," 157.

21. Newsom, "Woman and the Discourse of Patriarchal Wisdom," 157–59.

22. Yee, "'I Have Perfumed My Bed with Myrrh': The Foreign Woman" (*'iššâ zārâ*) in Proverbs 1–9," *JSOT* 43 (1989): 66–67.

23. Tikva Frymer-Kensky, "Wisdom, the Lover of Man," in *In the Wake of the Goddesses: Women, Culture, and the Biblical Transformation of Pagan Myth* (New York: Free Press, 1992), 183.

24. Denise Lardner Carmody, *Biblical Woman: Contemporary Reflections on Subscriptural Texts* (New York: Crossroad, 1988), 73.

25. Ibid., 76.

26. Ella Pearson Mitchell and Henry H. Mitchell, "Women: A Historical Perspective," in Ella Pearson Mitchell, ed., *Women: To Preach or Not to Preach: Twenty-one Outstanding Black Preachers Say Yes!* (Valley Forge, PA: Judson Press, 1991), 7.

27. Kathleen O'Connor, *The Wisdom Literature* (Wilmington, DE: Michael Glazier, 1988), 77. O'Connor is drawing on the work of Thomas P. McCreesh, "Wisdom as Wife: Proverbs 31:10–3l," *RB* 92:1 (1985): 25–46.

28. Carol R. Fontaine, "Proverbs," in *WBC* 154.

29. Camp, *Wisdom and the Feminine in the Book of Proverbs* (Sheffield, UK: Sheffield Almond Press, 1985), 283.

30. See Robert Wilkins, ed., *Aspects of Wisdom in Judaism and Christianity* (Notre Dame, IN: University of Notre Dame Press, 1975).

31. See Susan Cady, Marian Ronan, and Hal Taussig, *Wisdom's Feast: Sophia in Study and Celebration* (San Francisco: Harper & Row, 1989); Elizabeth A. Johnson, *She Who Is: The Mystery of God in Feminist Theological Discourse* (New York: Crossroad, 1992); and Elisabeth Schüssler Fiorenza, *In Memory of Her: A Feminist Theological Reconstruction of Christian Origins* (San Francisco: Harper & Row, 1989), 130–51.

32. Marcia Falk, *The Song of Songs: A New Translation and Interpretation* (San Francisco: Harper & Row, 1990), 113.

33. Phyllis Trible, "A Human Comedy," in *God and the Rhetoric of Sexuality* (Philadelphia: Fortress Press, 1978), 161–62.

34. Danna Nolan Fewell, "Feminist Reading of the Hebrew Bible: Affirmation, Resistance, and Transformation," *JSOT* 39 (1987): 80. See also Ilana Pardes's critique of Trible's approach in "'I Am a Wall, and My Breasts like Towers,'" in *Countertraditions,* 118–19.

35. J. Cheryl Exum, "Ten Things That Every Feminist Should Know about the Song of Songs," in Athalya Brenner and Carole R. Fontaine, eds., *The Song of Songs* (Sheffield, UK: Sheffield Academic Press, 2000), 25.

36. Ibid., 27.

37. Ibid.

38. Ibid., 28.

39. Ibid., 30.

40. Ibid.

41. Ibid., 32.

42. Ibid.

43. Ibid., 33.

44. Ibid., 34.

45. Ibid., 35.

46. Carol Meyers, "Gender Imagery in the Song of Songs," in Reuben Ahroni, ed., *Biblical and Other Studies: Tenth Anniversary Volume, Hebrew Annual Review* 10 (1986): 221.

47. O'Connor, *The Wisdom Literature,* 81.

48. Ibid., 82.

49. Pardes, "'I Am a Wall, and My Breasts Like Towers,'" 127.

50. Ibid., 142–43.

51. See Renita J. Weems, *Just a Sister Away: A Womanist Vision of Women's Relationships in the Bible* (San Diego: Lura Media, 1988), 1; Randall C. Bailey, "Beyond Identification: The Use of Africans in Old Testament Poetry and Narratives," in *Stony the Road We Trod: African American Biblical Interpretation,* ed. Cain Hope Felder (Minneapolis: Fortress Press, 1991), 165–86.

52. See, however, Weems, "Song of Songs," in *WBC,* 160, and Carole R. Fontaine, "The Voice of the Turtle: Now It's *My* Song of Songs," in Brenner and Fontaine, eds., *Songs of Songs,* 179–80.

Chapter 10: Subversive Women in Subversive Books: Ruth, Esther, Susanna, and Judith

1. Phyllis Trible, "A Human Comedy," in *God and the Rhetoric of Sexuality* (Philadelphia: Fortress Press, 1978), 166–99. See Danna Nolan Fewell's critique of Trible's position in "Feminist Reading of the Hebrew Bible: Affirmation, Resistance and Transformation," *JSOT* 39 (1987): 77–87. See also Peter W. Coxon, "Was Naomi a Scold? A Response to Fewell and Gunn," *JSOT* 45 (1989): 25–37. This article is a response to Fewell and Gunn, "'A Son Is Born to Naomi!': Literary Allusions and Interpretation in the Book of Ruth," *JSOT* 40 (1988): 99–108. Coxon argues against Fewell and Gunn's interpretation in favor of a position very similar to Trible's. In their response to Coxon, "Is Coxon a Scold?" 39–43, Fewell and Gunn say, "There is . . . no 'true' understanding of the character of Naomi, though some reconstructions will resonate more with some readers, seem 'truer' to the text, than others." Thus, here they suggest the multivalence of the book of Ruth. See also Ilana Pardes, "The Book of Ruth: Idyllic Revisionism" in *Countertraditions in the Bible: A Feminist Approach* (Cambridge: Harvard University Press, 1992), 2–3, for another more general critique of Trible.

2. See Esther Fuchs, "The History of Women in Ancient Israel: Theory, Method, and the Book of Ruth," in Caroline Vander Stichele and Todd Penner, eds., *Her Master's Tools: Feminist and Postcolonial Engagements of Historical-Critical Discourse* (Atlanta: SBL Press, 2005), 211–32. See also her "The Literary Characterization of Mothers and Sexual Politics in the Hebrew Bible," in Adela

Yarbro Collins, ed., *Feminist Perspectives on Biblical Scholarship* (Chico, CA: Scholars Press, 1985), 161, and "Who Is Hiding the Truth? Deceptive Women and Biblical Androcentrism" in Collins, ed., *Feminist Perspectives on Biblical Scholarship*, 118, 142. See Fewell, "Feminist Reading of the Hebrew Bible," for a critique of Fuchs. See also Pardes, "The Book of Ruth," 2–3.

3. André LaCocque, *The Feminine Unconventional: Four Subversive Figures in Israel's Tradition* (Minneapolis: Fortress Press, 1990), 89. See also Pardes, "The Book of Ruth," who writes: "For many commentators the idyllic aspects of the Book of Ruth have served as proof of the apolitical character of the text. Thus, B. M. Vellas criticizes the suggestion that the Book of Ruth is a polemic against the strict prohibition to marry foreign women in the period of Ezra and Nehemiah: 'A book which was written in those troubled times of Ezra and Nehemiah as a protest against those men could not possess that beautiful atmosphere and those idyllic surroundings which, so skillfully, the author of Ruth creates, nor could it be possible to possess an unforced, serene and calm tone of style' ("The Book of Ruth and Its Purpose," *Theologia* [Athens] 25 [1954]: 7). Whether or not this text was written in 'those troubled times,' its harmonious character does not preclude a polemical angle. Despite, or perhaps by means of, its beautiful idyllic facade, the Book of Ruth manages to challenge the biblical tendency to exclude the other (there is no need to limit oneself to Ezra and Nehemiah in this respect). Such tolerance toward the stranger, however, is inextricably bound up with a more respectful approach to femininity. Ruth is, after all, doubly other—both a foreigner and a woman. As such, her honorable incorporation within the house of Israel calls for a different perception of this house and a greater recognition of its female 'builders'" (pp. 98–99). For a more recent similar view see Irmtraud Fischer, "The Book of Ruth: A 'Feminist' Commentary to the Torah?" in Athalya Brenner, ed., *Ruth and Esther* (Sheffield, UK: Sheffield Academic Press, 1999), 24–49.

4. Ibid., 84–116.

5. Ibid., 91.

6. Ibid., 85–86.

7. Ibid., 86.

8. Ibid., 86–87.

9. Ibid., 95.

10. Ibid., 99–100.

11. Mieke Bal, "Heroism and Proper Names or the Fruits of Analogy," in *Lethal Love: Feminist Literary Readings of Biblical Love Stories* (Bloomington: Indiana University Press, 1987), 68–103. See Pardes's critique of Bal's interpretation of Ruth's story in "The Book of Ruth," 5–6.

12. Bal, "Heroism and Proper Names," 69–73.

13. See also Pardes, "The Book of Ruth," 98–117, for another feminist understanding of the way the book of Ruth rereads the story of Rachel and Leah.

14. Bal, "Heroism and Proper Names," 85.

15. Ibid., 86.

16. Danna Nolan Fewell and David M. Gunn read Ruth 4:5 differently in *Compromising Redemption: Relating Characters in the Book of Ruth* (Louisville: Westminster/John Knox Press, 1990) than most other translators: "Then Boaz said, 'the day you acquire the field from the hand of Naomi, I am also acquiring Ruth the Moabitess, the widow of the dead, in order to establish the name of the dead over his inheritance.'" They explain: "The problem arises in the second instance of the verb 'acquire.' . . . The consonantal text (the *kethib*, what is written in the Hebrew Masoretic text), supposedly the more ancient witness, has a first person singular form. Later scribes, presumably uncertain of what was going on in this scene, recommended an altered reading and expressed this reading in the vocalizing of the text (the *qere*, what is *read*): 'you are acquiring' instead of 'I am acquiring'" (90). Adrien Janis Bledstein also reads the *kethib* in "Female Companionships: If the Book of Ruth Were Written by a Woman," in Athalya Brenner, ed., *A Feminist Companion to Ruth*

(Sheffield, UK: Sheffield Academic Press, 1993). Her interpretation of this incident is similar to Fewell and Gunn's.

17. Fewell and Gunn, *Compromising Redemption*, 87–93.

18. Ibid., 91.

19. Ibid., 93.

20. Ibid., 105.

21. See the debate in *JSOT* over the interpretation of Ruth. The first article is Fewell and Gunn, "'A Son Is Born to Naomi!' Literary Allusions and Interpretation in the Book of Ruth," *JSOT* 40 (1988): 99–108. Coxon responds with "Was Naomi a Scold?: A Response to Fewell and Gunn," *JSOT* 45 (1989): 25–37. Fewell and Gunn respond in turn with "Is Coxon a Scold? On Responding to the Book of Ruth," *JSOT* 45 (1989): 39–43.

22. See Athalya Brenner and Fokkelien van Dijk-Hemmes, *On Gendering Texts: Female and Male Voices in the Hebrew Bible* (Leiden/New York/Cologne: E. J. Brill, 1993); Brenner, "Naomi and Ruth: Further Reflections," in *A Feminist Companion to Ruth* (Sheffield, UK: Sheffield Academic Press, 1993), 140–45; Van Dijk-Hemmes, "Ruth: A Product of Women's Culture," in Brenner, ed., *A Feminist Companion to Ruth* (Sheffield, UK: Sheffield Academic Press, 1993), 134–39. See also Bledstein, "Female Companionships: If the Book of Ruth were Written by a Woman," 116–33; Irmtraud Fischer, "The Book of Ruth: A 'Feminist' Commentary to the Torah?" in Athalya Brenner, ed., *Ruth and Esther* (Sheffield: Sheffield Academic Press, 1999), 24–49; and Carol Meyers, "Returning Home: Ruth 1.8 and the Gendering of the Book of Ruth," in Brenner, ed., *A Feminist Companion to Ruth*, 85–114, and "'Women of the Neighborhood' (Ruth 4.17): Informal Female Networks in Ancient Israel," in Brenner, ed., *Ruth and Esther*, 110–27.

23. Athalya Brenner, "Ruth as a Foreign Worker and the Politics of Exogamy," in *Ruth and Esther*, 162.

24. Judith E. McKinlay, "A Son Is Born to Naomi: A Harvest for Israel," in Brenner, ed., *Ruth and Esther*, 157. See also her "Reading Rehab and Ruth," in *Reframing Her: Biblical Women in Postcolonial Focus*, 37–56.

25. Laura E. Donaldson, "The Sign of Orpah: Reading Ruth through Native Eyes," in Brenner, ed., *Ruth and Esther*, 144.

26. Musa W. Dube, "The Unpublished Letters of Orpah to Ruth," in Brenner, ed., *Ruth and Esther*, 150.

27. Katharine Doob Sakenfeld, "Ruth and Naomi: Economic Survival and Family Values," in *Just Wives: Stories of Power and Survival in the Old Testament and Today* (Louisville: Westminster John Knox Press, 2003), 28.

28. Sarojini Nadar, "A South African Indian Womanist Reading of the Character of Ruth," in Musa W. Dube, ed., *Other Ways of Reading: African Women and the Bible* (Atlanta: SBL Press; Geneva: WCC Publications, 2001), 159–75.

29. Renita J. Weems, "A Crown of Thorns (Vashti and Esther)," in *Just A Sister Away: A Womanist Vision of Women's Relationships in the Bible* (San Diego: Lura Media, 1989), 99–110.

30. Ibid., 103.

31. Ibid., 105–6.

32. Ibid., 108.

33. Susan Niditch, "Esther: Folklore, Wisdom, Feminism, and Authority," in Athalya Brenner, ed., *A Feminist Companion to Esther, Judith, and Susanna* (Sheffield, UK: Sheffield Academic Press, 1995), 33–34.

34. Sidnie Ann White, "Esther: A Feminine Model for Jewish Diaspora," in Peggy L. Day, ed., *Gender and Difference in Ancient Israel* (Minneapolis: Fortress Press, 1989), 161–77.

35. Carey A. Moore, *Esther*, Anchor Bible 7B (Garden City, NY: Doubleday & Co., 1971), lii.

36. White, "Esther," 167.

37. Ibid., 168.

38. Ibid., 169.

39. Ibid.

40. Ibid., 170–72.

41. Ibid., 173.

42. LaCocque, *The Feminine Unconventional*, 71.

43. Ibid., 51.

44. Ibid., 54–55.

45. Danna Nolan Fewell, "Introduction: Reading, Writing, and Relating," in *Reading Between Texts: Intertextuality and the Hebrew Bible* (Louisville: Westminster/John Knox Press, 1992), 14.

46. Bal, "Lots of Writing," *Semeia* 54 (1991): 92–93.

47. Ibid., 96.

48. Klara Butting, "Esther: A New Interpretation of the Joseph Story in the Fight Against Anti-Semiticism and Sexism," in Brenner, ed., *Ruth and Esther*, 243.

49. Madipoane (Ngwana' Mphahlele) Masenya, "Esther and Northern Sotho Stories: An African–South African Woman's Commentary," in Dube, ed., *Other Ways of Reading*, 27–49.

50. The Roman Catholic canon of the Old Testament is based on the Greek translation known as the Septuagint, which was used by both the Hellenistic Jewish and the Christian communities. It was translated before the Jewish community had determined what books would be in their canon. A number of books that are in the Septuagint did not ultimately make it into the Hebrew canon. Since the early Christian community was using the Greek translation, it was natural that this should become authoritative. At the time of the Reformation, however, the Protestants decided to go with the Hebrew canon (although the King James Version includes the Apocrypha in a separate section). That is why the Catholics have more books in their Old Testament than do the Protestants. These "extra" books are called apocryphal by Protestants, although of course not by Catholics.

51. LaCocque, *The Feminine Unconventional*, 24.

52. Ibid., 22–23.

53. Ibid., 29–30.

54. Toni Craven, "Daniel and Its Additions," in *WBC*, 193.

55. Ibid., 194.

56. Amy-Jill Levine, "'Hemmed in on Every Side': Jews and Women in the Book of Susanna," in Fernando F. Segovia and Mary Ann Tolbert, eds., *Reading from This Place*, vol. 1: *Social Location and Biblical Interpretation in the United States* (Minneapolis: Fortress Press, 1995), 322–23.

57. Toni Craven, "Tradition and Convention in the Book of Judith," in Mary Ann Tolbert, ed., *The Bible and Feminist Hermeneutics, Semeia* 28 (1983): 60–61.

58. LaCocque, *The Feminine Unconventional*, 35.

59. Ibid.

60. Ibid., 39.

61. Patricia Montley, "Judith in the Fine Arts: The Appeal of the Archetypal Androgyne," *Anima* 4 (1978): 40, cited in LaCocque, *The Feminine Unconventional*, 38.

62. LaCocque, *The Feminine Unconventional*, 38.

63. Ibid., 48.

64. Eileen H. Schuller, "The Apocrypha," in *WBC*, 243.

65. Amy-Jill Levine, "Sacrifice and Salvation: Otherness and Domestication in the Book of Judith," in Brenner, ed., *A Feminist Companion to Esther, Judith, and Susanna*, 222–23.

Chapter 11: Summary and Conclusions

1. Elisabeth Schüssler Fiorenza, "Feminist Hermeneutics," *ABD*, 2:786.

2. Ilana Pardes, *Countertraditions in the Bible: A Feminist Approach* (Cambridge: Harvard University Press, 1992), 155.

3. Ibid., 2.

4. Feminists are not the only interpreters who raise questions about whether the "fall from grace" interpretation is the original meaning. Many nonfeminists are raising similar questions.

5. In a similar way, Pardes (*Countertraditions*, 6) notes the complexity of the relationship between ideology and reading strategies.

Bibliography

CHAPTER 1: INTRODUCTION

The History of Feminist Religious Studies

Bass, Dorothy C. "Women's Studies and Biblical Studies: An Historical Perspective." *JSOT* 22 (1982): 6–12.

Behnke, Donna A. *Religious Issues in Nineteenth Century Feminism*. Troy, NY: Whitston Publishing Co., 1982.

Gifford, Carolyn De Swarte. "American Women and the Bible: The Nature of Woman as a Hermeneutical Issue." In Adela Yarbro Collins, ed., *Feminist Perspectives on Biblical Scholarship*, 11–33. SBLB-SNA 10. Chico, CA: Scholars Press, 1985.

Kern, Kathi. *Mrs. Stanton's Bible*. Ithaca, NY: Cornell University Press, 2001.

Lee, Jarena. "Life of Jarena Lee." In Dorothy Parker, ed., *Early Negro Writing: 1760–1837*, 494–514. Boston: Beacon Press, 1971.

Milne, Pamela J. "Feminist Interpretations of the Bible: Then and Now." *Bible Review*, October 1992, 38–43, 52–54.

Richardson, Marilyn. *Black Women and Religion: A Bibliography*. Boston: G. K. Hall & Co., 1980.

Selvidge, Marla J. *Notorious Voices: Feminist Biblical Interpretation, 1550–1920*. New York: Continuum, 1996.

Sibel, John J. *Elizabeth Cady Stanton's Philosophy of Woman's Rights: Sources and Synthesis*. Rome: Pontificia Studiorum Universitas a S. Thoma Aquinate in Urbe, 1982.

Spretnak, Charlene, ed. *The Politics of Women's Spirituality: Essays on the Rise of Spiritual Power within the Feminist Movement*. Garden City, NY: Doubleday & Co., 1982.

Stanton, Elizabeth Cady. *The Original Feminist Attack on the Bible: The Woman's Bible*. Facsimile ed. New York: Arno Press, 1972.

Trible, Phyllis. "If the Bible's So Patriarchal, How Come I Love It?" *Bible Review* (October 1992): 44–47, 55.

Zikmund, Barbara Brown. "Feminist Consciousness in Historical Perspective." In Letty M. Russell, ed., *Feminist Interpretation of the Bible*, 21–29, 152. Philadelphia: Westminster Press, 1985.

Women on Women in the Bible: Popular or Early Works

Adams, Queenie M. *Neither Male nor Female: A Study of the Scriptures*. Ilfracombe: Stockwell, 1973.

Aguilar, Grace. *The Women of Israel, or, Characters and Sketches from the Holy Scriptures and Jewish History*. 2nd ed. New York: Appleton, 1853.

Ashton, Sophia Goodrich. *The Mothers of the Bible*. Boston: J. P. Jewett & Co.; New York: Sheldon, Lamport & Blakeman, 1855.

Batten, J. Rowena. *Women Alive: Twenty-Five Talks on Women of the Bible*. Grand Rapids: Zondervan, 1965.

Bibliography on Biblical Feminism. Minneapolis: Evangelical Women's Caucus, 1975.

Briscoe, Jill. *Prime Rib and Apple*. Grand Rapids: Zondervan, 1976.

Buchanan, Isabelia Reid. *Women of the Bible.* Minneapolis: Colwell, 1924.

Bushnell, Katherine C. *God's Word to Women: One Hundred Bible Studies on Women's Place in the Divine Economy.* Probably privately published by the author in 1921; reissued by Minneapolis: Christians for Biblical Equality, 2003.

Clapp, Marie W. *The Old Testament as It Concerns Women.* New York: Methodist Book Concern, 1934.

Crook, Margaret Brackenbury. *Women and Religion.* Boston: Beacon Press, 1964.

Crotwell, Helen, ed. *Women and the Word: Sermons.* Philadelphia: Fortress, 1977.

Culver, Elsie Thomas. *Women in the World of Religion.* Garden City, NY: Doubleday & Co., 1967.

Davis, Elizabeth Gould. *The First Sex.* New York: Putnam, 1971.

Deen, Edith. *All of the Women of the Bible.* San Francisco: Harper & Brothers, 1955.

———. *The Bible's Legacy for Womanhood.* Garden City, NY: Doubleday, 1969.

———. *Wisdom from Women in the Bible.* San Francisco: Harper & Row, 1978.

Demers, Patricia. *Women as Interpreters of the Bible.* Mahwah, NJ: Paulist Press, 1992.

Eider, Dorothy. *Women of the Bible Speak to Women of Today.* Marina del Rey, CA: De Vorss, 1986.

Emswiler, Sharon Neufer. *The Ongoing Journey: Women and the Bible.* New York: Women's Division, Board of Global Ministries, United Methodist Church, 1977.

Evans, Mary T. *Woman in the Bible.* Downers Grove, IL: InterVarsity Press, 1983.

Fischer, Clare Benedicks, Betsy Brenneman, and Anne McBraw Bennett, eds. *Women in a Strange Land: Search for a New Image.* Philadelphia: Fortress Press, 1975.

Foh, Susan T. *Women and the Word of God.* Grand Rapids: Baker Book House, 1979.

Fraine, Jean de. *Women of the Old Testament.* Translated by Forrest L. Ingram. De Pere, WI: St. Norbert Abbey Press, 1968.

Gilliland, Dolores Scott. *Selected Women of the Scriptures of Stamina and Courage.* Illustrated by Gael Scott. Spearfish, SD: Honor Books, 1978.

Hallet, Mary Thomas. *Their Names Remain: Seventeen Women of Old Testament Days.* New York: Abingdon Press, 1938.

Harrison, Eveleen. *Little-Known Women of the Bible.* New York: Round Table Press, 1936.

Hartsoe, Colleen Ivey. *Dear Daughter: Letters from Eve and Other Women of the Bible.* Wilton, CT: Morehouse-Barlow, 1981.

Herr, Ethel L. *Chosen Women of the Bible.* Chicago: Moody, 1976.

Hess, Margaret. *Esther: Courage in Crisis.* Wheaton, IL: Victor Books, 1980.

Honeywell, Betty. *Living Portraits.* Chicago: Moody, 1965.

Hunt, Gladys. *Women of the Old Testament.* Lifeguide Bible Studies. Downers Grove, IL: InterVarsity Press, 1990.

Jensen, Mary E. *Bible Women Speak to Us Today.* Minneapolis: Augsburg, 1983.

Keay, Kathy. *Men, Women, and God.* Basingstoke: Marshall Pickering, 1987.

Kirk, Martha Ann. *Celebrations of Biblical Women's Stories: Tears, Milk and Honey.* Kansas City, MO: Sheed & Ward, 1987.

Kulow, Nelle Wahler. *Even as You and I: Sketches of Human Women from the Divine Book.* Columbus, OH: Wartburg Press, 1955.

Lachs, Rosalyn. *Women and Judaism.* Garden City, NY: Doubleday, 1980.

Lewis, Ethel Clark. *Portraits of Bible Women.* New York: Vantage, 1956.

Lofts, Norah. *Women in the Old Testament: Twenty Psychological Portraits.* London: Religious Book Club, 1950.

McAllister, Grace Edna. *God Portrays Women.* Chicago: Moody, 1954.

———. *God Portrays More Women.* Chicago: Moody, 1956.

Marble, Annie Russell. *Women of the Bible.* New York and London: Century, 1923.

Marshall, Zona Bays. *Certain Women.* New York: Exposition Press, 1960.

Martyn, Sarah Towne. *Women of the Bible.* New York: American Tract Society, 1868.

Mason, Maggie. *Women Like Us: Learn More about Yourself through Studies of Biblical Women.* Waco, TX: Word Books, 1978.

Mollenkott, Virginia. *Women, Men, and the Bible.* Nashville: Abingdon, 1977.

Mulliken, Frances Hartman, and Margaret Salts. *Women of Destiny in the Bible.* Independence, MO: Herald Publishing House, 1978.

Musgrave, Peggy. *Who's Who among Bible Women*. Springfield, MO: Gospel Publishing House, 1981.

Neal, Hazel G. *Bible Women of Faith*. Anderson, IN: Warner Press, 1955.

Notable Women of Olden Times. Philadelphia: American Sunday School Union, 1852.

Nunnally-Cox, Janice. *Foremothers: Women of the Bible*. San Francisco: Harper & Row, 1981.

Pease, Alice Campbell. *Significant Women of the Bible*. Grand Rapids: Zondervan, 1941.

Price, Eugenia. *The Unique World of Women, in Bible Times and Now*. Grand Rapids: Zondervan, 1969.

Richards, Alberta Rae. *Women of the Bible*. Gastonia, NC: Geographical Publications Co., 1962.

Roddy, Lee. *Women in the Bible*. Chappaqua, NY: Christian Herald Books, 1980.

Rusche, Helga. *They Lived by Faith: Women of the Bible*. Trans. Elizabeth Williams. New York: Helicon, 1963.

Sangster, Margaret Elizabeth. *The Women of the Bible: A Portrait Gallery*. New York: Christian Herald, 1911.

Scanzoni, Letha. *All We're Meant to Be: A Biblical Approach to Women's Liberation*. Waco, TX: Word Books, 1974.

Smith, Joyce Marie. *A Woman's Priorities*. Wheaton, IL: Tyndale House, 1976.

Smith, Judith Florence. *In Our Lady's Library: Character Studies of the Women of the Old Testament*. London: Longmans, Green, & Co., 1923.

Stanton, Elizabeth Cady. *The Woman's Bible*. New York: European Publishing Co., 1895–98.

Starr, Lee Anna. *The Bible Status of Woman*. New York: Fleming H. Revell, 1926.

Staton, Julia. *What the Bible Says about Women*. Joplin, MO: College, 1980.

Steele, Eliza R. *Heroines of Sacred History*. 2nd ed. New York: J. S. Taylor Co., 1842.

Stowe, Harriet Elizabeth Beecher. *Woman in Sacred History*. New York: J. B. Ford, 1873.

Sudlow, Elizabeth W. *Career Women of the Bible*. New York: Pageant Press, 1951.

Thomas, Metta Newman. *Women of the Bible: A Study of Life and Character*. Nashville: Twentieth Century Christian, 1956.

Thompson, Lucy Gertsch. *Women of the Bible: A Book Telling the Life Stories of Twenty Prominent Women of the Old and New Testaments*. Salt Lake City: Deseret Book Co., 1957.

Tinney, Ethel. *Women of the Bible, in Verse*. New York: Pageant Press, 1953.

Tischler, Nancy Marie Patterson. *Legacy of Eve*. Atlanta: John Knox Press, 1977.

Turnbull, Agnes Sligh. *Far above Rubies*. New York: Fleming H. Revell Co., 1926.

Vander Velde, Frances. *She Shall Be Called Woman*. Grand Rapids: International Publications, 1957.

Wilson, Elizabeth. *A Scriptural View of Women's Rights and Duties*. Philadelphia: W. S. Young, 1849.

Men on Women of the Bible

Adams, Charles. *Women of the Bible*. New York: Land & Scott, 1851.

Angel, Leonard. *The Book of Miriam*. Buffalo, NY: Mosaic, 1997.

Bakan, David. *And They Took Themselves Wives*. New York: Harper & Row, 1979.

Baldwin, George Colfax. *Representative Women: From Eve . . . to Mary*. New York: Sheldon & Co.; Boston: Gould & Lincoln, 1855.

Barnard, David. *Biblical Women*. Cincinnati: Hart & Co., 1863.

Berquist, Jon L. *Reclaiming Her Story: The Witness of Women in the Old Testament*. St. Louis: Chalice Press, 1992.

Bilezikian, Gilbert. *Beyond Sex Roles: A Biblical Study of Female Roles*. Grand Rapids: Zondervan, 1985.

Bloom, Harold. *The Book of J*. New York: G. Weidenfeld, 1990.

Brooke, George J, ed. *Women in the Biblical Tradition*. Lewiston, NY: Edwin Mellen Press, 1992.

Burchard, Samuel. *The Daughters of Zion*. New York: J. S. Taylor, 1853.

Burgess, E. T. *Other Women of the Bible*. Little Rock, AR: Baptist Publications, 1964.

Carlisle, Thomas John. *Eve and After: Old Testament Women in Portrait*. Grand Rapids: Wm. B. Eerdmans Publishing Co., 1984.

Carmichael, Calum M. *Women, Law, and the Genesis Traditions*. Edinburgh, Scotland: Edinburgh University Press, 1979.

Chappell, Clovis Gilham. *Feminine Faces.* New York and Nashville: Abingdon-Cokesbury, 1942.

Collins, Stanley. *Courage and Submission: A Study of Ruth and Esther.* Glendale, CA: Regal, 1975.

Cottrell, Jack. *Gender Roles and the Bible: Creation, the Fall, and Redemption: A Critique of Feminist Biblical Interpretation.* Joplin, MO: College Press Publishing Co., 1994.

Cox, Francis August. *Female Scripture Biography.* 2 vols. Boston: Lincoln & Edmands, 1831.

Danker, Albert. *Heroines of Olden Time.* New York: Chapple & Tozer, 1875.

Dennis, Trevor. *Sarah Laughed: Women's Voice in the Old Testament.* Nashville: Abingdon Press, 1994.

Detrick, R. Blaine. *Favorite Women of the Bible.* Lima, OH: CSS, 1988.

Diesel, P. M. L. *Adam and Eve and the Universe.* New York: Exposition Press, 1971.

Drimmer, Frederick. *Daughters of Eve.* Illustrated by Hal Frenck. Norwalk, CT: C. R. Gibson, 1975.

Faulhaber, Michael von. *The Women of the Bible.* Westminster, MD: Newman Press, 1955.

Faulkner, James. *Romances and Intrigues of the Women of the Bible.* New York: Vantage, 1975.

Grelot, Pierre. *Man and Wife in Scripture.* New York: Herder & Herder, 1964.

Griffith, K.A. *Come and Meet Adam and Eve: The Story of Gen. 1–4.* Grand Rapids: Zondervan, 1977.

Headley, Phineas Camp. *Historical and Descriptive Sketches of the Women of the Bible, from Eve of the Old Testament to the Marys of the New Testament.* Auburn: Derby Miller & Co., 1850.

Hurley, James B. *Man and Woman in Biblical Perspective.* Grand Rapids: Zondervan, 1981.

Ide, Arthur Frederick. *Woman in Ancient Israel.* Mesquite, TX: Ide House, 1982.

Janzen, Waldemar. *Still in the Image: Essays in Biblical Theology and Anthropology.* Newton, KS: Faith and Life Press; Winnipeg: CMBC Publications, 1982.

Jay, William. *Lectures on Female Scripture Characters.* New York: Carter & Bros., 1854.

Kubler, Franz. *Her Children Call Her Blessed.* New York: Stephen Daye Press, 1955.

Kuyperk, Abraham. *Women of the Old Testament; Fifty Meditations.* Grand Rapids: Zondervan, 1936.

Jewett, Paul King. *Man as Male and Female: A Study in Sexual Relationships from a Theological Point of View.* Grand Rapids: Wm. B. Eerdmans Publishing Co., 1975.

Lockyer, Herbert. *The Women of the Bible.* Grand Rapids: Zondervan, 1971.

Lundholm, Algot Theodore. *Women of the Bible.* 2 vols. Rock Island, IL: Augustana Book Concern, 1923–26.

Maertens, Thierry. *The Advancing Dignity of Woman in the Bible.* De Pere, WI: St. Norbert Abbey Press, 1969.

Matheson, George. *The Representative Women of the Bible.* New York: A. C. Armstrong & Son, 1907; London: Hodder & Stoughton. 1907.

McKenzie, J. J. *I Will Love Unloved: A Linguistic Analysis of Women's Biblical Importance.* Lanham, MD: University Press of America, 1993.

Morton, Henry Vollam. *Women of the Bible.* New York: Dodd, Mead & Co., 1941; Nashville: Abingdon Press, 1977.

Murphy, Cullen. *The Word according to Eve: Women and the Bible in Ancient Times and Our Own.* Boston: Houghton Mifflin, 1998.

Nichol, Charles Ready. *God's Woman.* Clifton, TX: Mrs. C. R. Nichol, 1938.

O'Reilly, Bernard. *Heroic Women of the Bible and the Church.* New York: J. B. Ford & Co., 1878.

Ockenga, Harold J. *Women in the Bible.* Grand Rapids: Zondervan, 1962.

———. *Women Who Made Bible History.* Grand Rapids: Zondervan, 1972.

Otwell, John H. *And Sarah Laughed.* Philadelphia: Westminster Press, 1977.

Phillips, John A. *Eve, the History of an Idea.* San Francisco: Harper & Row, 1985.

Phipps, William E. *Assertive Biblical Women.* Contributions in Women's Studies 128. Westport, CT: Greenwood Press, 1992.

———. *Genesis and Gender: Biblical Myths of Sexuality and Their Cultural Impact.* New York: Praeger, 1989.

Reik, Theodor. *The Creation of Woman.* New York: Braziller, 1960.

Rutledge, David. *Reading Marginally: Feminism, Deconstruction, and the Bible.* Leiden and New York: E. J. Brill, 1996.

Scheppes, David. *Remarkable Women of Scripture.* Philadelphia: Dorrance & Co., 1976.

Sell, Henry Thorne. *Studies of Famous Bible Women.* New York: Fleming H. Revell, 1925.

Sprague, William Buell, ed. *Women of the Old and New Testament: A Series of Portraits.* 2nd ed. New York: D. Appleton & Co.; Philadephia: G. S. Appleton, 1851.

Stendahl, Krister. *The Bible and the Role of Women: A Case Study in Hermeneutics.* Philadelphia: Fortress Press, 1966.

Swartley, Willard M. *Slavery, Sabbath, War, and Women: Case Issues in Biblical Interpretation.* Scottdale, PA: Herald Press, 1983.

Swidler, Leonard. *Biblical Affirmations of Woman.* Philadelphia: Westminster Press, 1979.

Terrien, Samuel. *Till the Heart Sings: A Biblical Theology of Manhood and Womanhood.* Philadelphia: Fortress Press, 1985.

Thompson, Henry Adams. *Women of the Bible.* Dayton, OH: U. B. Publishing House, 1914.

Vos, Clarence J. *Women in Old Testament Worship.* Delft: Judel & Brinkman, 1968.

Weld, Horatio H. *The Women of the Old and New Testaments.* Philadelphia: Lindsay & Blakiston, 1848.

Williams, James G. *Women Recounted: Narrative Thinking and the God of Israel.* Bible and Literature Series 6. Sheffield, UK: Almond, 1982.

Feminist Perspectives on Biblical Women

Ackerman, Susan. "The Queen Mother and the Cult in Ancient Israel." In Alice Bach, ed., *Women in the Hebrew Bible: A Reader,* 179–94. New York and London: Routledge, 1999.

Ackerman, Susan. *Warrior, Dancer, Seductress, Queen: Women in Judges and Biblical Israel.* Anchor Bible Series. New York: Doubleday, 1998.

Anderson, Cheryl. *Women, Ideology and Violence: Critical Theory and the Construction of Gender in the Book of the Covenant and the Deuteronomic Law.* New York: Continuum, 2005.

Antonelli, Judith S. *In the Image of God: A Feminist Commentary on the Torah.* Northvale, NJ: Jason Aronson, 1997.

Aschkenasy, Nehama. *Woman at the Window: Biblical Tales of Oppression and Escape.* Detroit: Wayne State University Press, 1998.

Atkins, Anne. *Split Image: Male and Female after God's Likeness.* Grand Rapids: W. B. Eerdmans Publishing Co., 1987.

Bach, Alice. *Reading the Women of the Bible: A New Interpretation of Their Stories.* New York: Schocken Books, 2002.

———, ed. *The Pleasure of Her Text: Feminist Readings of Biblical and Historical Texts.* Philadelphia: Trinity Press International, 1990.

———. *Women in the Hebrew Bible: A Reader.* New York: Routledge, 1999.

———. *Women, Seduction, and Betrayal in Biblical Narrative.* Cambridge, UK, and New York: Cambridge University Press, 1997.

Bach, Alice, and J. Cheryl Exum. *Miriam's Well.* New York: Delacorte Press, 1991.

Bal, Mieke. *Anti-Covenant: Counter-Reading Women's Lives in the Hebrew Bible.* Sheffield, UK: Almond, 1989.

———. *Lethal Love: Feminist Literary Readings of Biblical Love Stories.* Bloomington: Indiana University Press, 1987.

Baskin, Judith. *Midrashic Women: Formations of the Feminine in Rabbinic Literature.* Brandeis Series on Jewish Women. Hanover, NH: Brandeis University Press, 2002.

Beach, Eleanor Ferris. *The Jezebel Letters: Religion and Politics in Ninth-Century Israel.* Minneapolis: Fortress Press, 2005.

Berlin, Adele. *Poetics and Interpretation of Biblical Narrative.* Sheffield, UK: Almond Press, 1983. Rep., Winona Lake, IN: Eisenbrauns, 1994.

Biale, Rachel. *Women and Jewish Law: The Essential Texts, Their History, and Their Relevance for Today.* New York: Schocken Books, 1995.

Bird, Phyllis A. "Images of Women in the Old Testament." In Rosemary Radford Ruether, ed., *Religion and Sexism: Images of Woman in the Jewish and Christian Traditions,* 41–88. New York: Simon & Schuster, 1974.

———. "Israelite Religion and the Faith of Israel's Daughters: Reflections on Gender and Religious Definition." In David Jobling, Peggy L. Day, and Gerald T. Sheppard, eds., *The Bible and the Politics of Exegesis: Essays in Honor of Norman K. Gottwald on His Sixty-fifth Birthday*, 97–108. Cleveland: Pilgrim Press, 1991.

———. *Missing Persons and Mistaken Identities: Women and Gender in Ancient Israel*. Minneapolis: Fortress Press, 1997.

———. "The Place of Women in the Israelite Cultus." In Patrick D. Miller Jr., Paul D. Hanson, and S. Dean McBride, eds., *Ancient Israelite Religion: Essays in Honor of Frank Moore Cross*, 397–419. Philadelphia: Fortress Press, 1987. And in Alice Bach, ed., *Women in the Hebrew Bible: A Reader*, 3–20. New York and London: Routledge, 1999.

———. "Women–O. T." In *ABD*, 6:951–57. New York: Doubleday & Co., 1991.

———. "Women's Religion in Ancient Israel." In Barbara S. Lesko, ed., *Women's Earliest Records from Ancient Egypt and Western Asia*, 294–98. Brown Judaic Studies 166. Atlanta: Scholars Press, 1990.

Brakeman, Lyn. *Spiritual Lemons: Biblical Women, Irreverent Laughter, and Righteous Rage*. Philadelphia: Innisfree Press, 1997.

Brenner, Athalya, ed. *A Feminist Companion to the Bible*. First series, 10 volumes. Sheffield, UK: Sheffield Academic Press, 1993–96.

———. *I Am . . . Biblical Women Tell Their Own Stories*. Minneapolis: Fortress Press, 2005.

———. *The Intercourse of Knowledge: On Gendered Sex and Desire in the Hebrew Bible*. Kinderhook, NY: E. J. Brill, 1997.

———. *The Israelite Woman: Social Role and Literary Type in Biblical Narrative*. Sheffield, UK: JSOT Press, 1985.

Brenner, Athalya, and Carole Fontaine, eds. *A Feminist Companion to the Bible*. 2nd series, 9 volumes. Sheffield, UK: Sheffield Academic Press, 1997–2001.

Brenner, Athalya, and Fokkelien van Dijk-Hemmes. *On Gendering Texts: Female and Male Voices in the Hebrew Bible*. Biblical Interpretation Series 1. Leiden/New York/Cologne: E. J. Brill, 1993.

———. *Reflections on Theology and Gender*. Kampen: Kok Pharos, 1994.

Bronner, Leila Leah. *From Eve to Esther: Rabbinic Reconstructions of Biblical Women*. Gender and the Biblical Tradition. Louisville, KY: Westminster John Knox Press, 1994.

Brown, Cheryl Anne. *No Longer Be Silent: First Century Jewish Portraits of Biblical Women*. Louisville, KY: Westminster/John Knox Press, 1992.

Buchmann, Christina, and Celina Spiegel. *Out of the Garden: Women Writers on the Bible*. New York: Fawcett Columbine, 1994.

Camp, Claudia V., and Carol R. Fontaine, eds. *Women, War, and Metaphor: Language and Society in the Study of the Hebrew Bible*. Semeia 61. Atlanta: Scholars Press, 1993.

Craven, Toni. "Women Who Lied for the Faith." In Douglas A. Knight and Peter J. Paris, eds., *Justice and the Holy: Essays in Honor of Walter Harrelson*, 35–49. Homage Series. Atlanta: Scholars, 1989.

Darr, Katheryn Pfisterer. *Far More Precious Than Jewels: Perspectives on Biblical Women*. Gender and the Biblical Tradition 1. Louisville, KY: Westminster/John Knox Press, 1991.

Dijkstra, Meindert, and Bob Becking, eds. *On Reading Prophetic Texts: Gender Specific and Related Studies in Memory of Fokkelien van Dijk-Hemmes*. Leiden: E. J. Brill, 1996.

Douglas, Mary. "Responding to Ezra: The Priests and the Foreign Wives." *BibInt* 10 (2002): 1–23.

Dube, Musa W., Nadar Sarojini, and Velma Love, eds. *Kimba Vita African Women's Bible Commentary*. Louisville, KY: Westminster John Knox Press, forthcoming.

Emmerson, Grace I. "Women in Ancient Israel." In R. E. Clements, ed., *The World of Ancient Israel: Sociological, Anthropological and Political Perspectives*, 371–94. Cambridge: Cambridge University Press, 1989.

Engar, Ann W. "Old Testament Women as Tricksters." In Vincent L. Tollers and John Maier, eds., *Mappings of the Biblical Terrain*, 143–57. Lewisburg, PA: Bucknell University Press, 1990.

Eskenazi, Tamara C. "Out from the Shadows: Biblical Women in the Postexilic Era." *JSOT* 54 (1992): 25–43.

Eskenazi, Tamara C., and Eleanore P. Judd. "Marriage to a Stranger in Ezra 9–10." In Tamara C. Eskenazi and Kent H. Richards, eds., *Second Temple Studies*, vol. 2: *Temple and Community in the Persian Period*, 266–95. JSOT Supplement Series 175. Sheffield, UK: Sheffield Academic Press, 1994.

Exum, J. Cheryl. "The Ethics of Biblical Volence against Women." In John W. Rogerson, Margaret Davies, and M. Daniel Carroll, eds., *The Bible in Ethics: The Second Sheffield Colloquium*, 248–71. JSOT Supplement Series 207. Sheffield, UK: Sheffield Academic Press, 1995.

————. *Fragmented Women: Feminist (Sub)Versions of Biblical Narratives.* Valley Forge, PA: Trinity Press International, 1993.

————. *Plotted, Shot, and Painted: Cultural Representations of Biblical Women.* Sheffield, UK: Sheffield Academic Press, 1996.

————. *Tragedy and Biblical Narrative: Arrows of the Almighty.* Cambridge, UK: Cambridge University Press, 1992.

Exum, J. Cheryl, and Johanna van Wijk Bos, eds. *Reasoning with the Foxes: Female Wit in a World of Male Power. Semeia* 42 (1988).

Fischer, Irmtraud. *Women Who Wrestled with God: Biblical Stories of Israel's Beginnings.* Trans. Linda Maloney. Collegeville, MN: Liturgical Press, 2005.

Fontaine, Carole R. "A Heifer from Thy Stable: On Goddesses and the Status of Women in the Ancient Near East." In Alice Bach, ed., *Women in the Hebrew Bible: A Reader,* 159–78. New York and London: Routledge, 1999.

Frankel, Ellen. *The Five Books of Miriam: A Woman's Commentary on the Torah.* New York: Putnam, 1996.

Frymer-Kensky, Tikva. *In the Wake of the Goddesses: Women, Culture, and the Biblical Transformation of Pagan Myth.* New York: Free Press, 1992.

————. "Pollution, Purification, and Purgation in Biblical Israel." In Carol L. Meyers and M. O'Connor, eds., *The Word of the Lord Shall Go Forth: Essays in Honor of David Noel Freedman,* 399–414. Winona Lake, IN: Eisenbrauns, 1983.

————. *Reading the Women of the Bible: A New Interpretation of Their Stories.* New York: Schocken Books, 2002.

————. "Women." In *Harper's Bible Dictionary,* 1138–41. New York: Harper & Row, 1985.

Fuchs, Esther. "The Literary Characterization of Mothers and Sexual Politics in the Hebrew Bible." In Alice Bach, ed., *Women in the Hebrew Bible: A Reader,* 127–40. New York and London: Routledge, 1999.

————. *Sexual Politics in the Biblical Narrative: Reading the Hebrew Bible as a Woman.* JSOT Supplement Series 310. Sheffield, UK: Sheffield Academic Press, 2000.

————. "Status and Role of Female Heroines in the Biblical Narrative." In Alice Bach, ed., *Women in the Hebrew Bible: A Reader,* 77–84. New York and London: Routledge, 1999.

Gallares, Judette A. *Images of Faith: Spirituality of Women in the Old Testament.* Maryknoll, NY: Orbis Books, 1992.

Goldstein, Elyse. *ReVisions: Seeing Torah through a Feminist Lens.* Woodstock, VT: Jewish Lights, 1998.

————. *The Women's Torah Commentary: New Insights from Women Rabbis on the 54 Weekly Torah Portions.* Woodstock, VT: Jewish Lights, 2000.

Handelman, Susan, and Ora Wiskind Elper, eds. *Torah of the Mothers: Contemporary Jewish Women Read Classical Jewish Texts.* New York: Urim Pub, 2000.

Hauptman, Judith. *Rereading the Rabbis: A Woman's Voice.* Boulder, CO: Westview Press, 1998, 1999.

Headen, Susan, and Jeffery L. Sheler, eds. *Women of the Bible: Provocative New Insights. U.S. News and World Report* Special Collector's Edition, 2005.

Hollyday, Joyce. *Clothed with the Sun: Biblical Women, Social Justice and Us.* Louisville, KY: Westminster John Knox Press, 1994.

Hyman, Naomi Mara. *Biblical Women in the Midrash: A Sourcebook.* Northvale, NJ, and London: Jason Aronson, 1997.

Kirk-Duggan, Cheryl A. *Pregnant Passion: Gender, Sex, and Violence in the Bible.* Semeia Studies 44. Atlanta: SBL Press, 2003.

Klein, Lillian R. *From Deborah to Esther: Sexual Politics in the Hebrew Bible.* Minneapolis: Fortress Press, 2003.

Kornbluth, Doron, and Sarah Tikvah Kornbluth, eds. *Jewish Women Speak about Jewish Matters.* Southfield, MI: Targum Press, 2000.

Kraemer, Ross Shepard. *Her Share of the Blessings: Women's Religions among Pagans, Jews, and Christians in the Greco-Roman World.* New York: Oxford University Press, 1992.

————. "Jewish Women in the Diaspora World of Late Antiquity." In *Jewish Women in Historical Perspective,* ed. Judith R. Baskin, 2nd ed., 46–72. Detroit: Wayne State University, 1998.

Lapsley, Jacqueline E. *Whispering the Word: Hearing Women's Stories in the Old Testament.* Louisville, KY: Westminster John Knox Press, 2005.

Levine, Amy-Jill. *Women Like This: New Perspectives on Jewish Women in the Greco-Roman World.*
    Atlanta: Scholars Press, 1991.
Levitt, Laura. *Jews and Feminism: The Ambivalent Search for Home.* New York: Routledge, 1997.
Manning, Christel. *God Gave Us the Right: Conservative Catholic, Evangelical Protestant, and Orthodox
    Jewish Women Grapple with Feminism.* New Brunswick, NJ: Rutgers University Press, 1999.
Matthews, Victor H., Bernard M. Levinson, and Tikva Frymer-Kensky, eds. *Gender and Biblical Law.*
    JSOT Supplement Series 262. Sheffield, UK: Sheffield Academic Press, 1998.
McKinlay, Judith E. *Reframing Her: Biblical Women in Postcolonial Focus.* The Bible in the Modern
    World I. Sheffield, UK: Sheffield Phoenix Press, 2004.
McNutt, Paula M. *Reconstructing the Society of Ancient Israel.* Library of Ancient Israel. Louisville, KY:
    Westminster John Knox Press, 1999.
Meyers, Carol L. *Discovering Eve: Ancient Israelite Women in Context.* New York: Oxford University
    Press, 1988.
———. "Guilds and Gatherings: Women's Groups in Ancient Israel." In Prescott H. Williams Jr. and
    Theodore Hiebert, eds., *Realia Dei: Essays in Archaeology and Biblical Interpretation in Honor of
    Edward F. Campbell, Jr., at His Retirement,* 154–84. Atlanta: Scholars Press, 1999.
———. *Households and Holiness: The Religious Culture of Israelite Women.* Minneapolis: Augsburg
    Fortress Press, 2005.
———. "Marriage and Family, Israelite." In Judith Baskin, ed., *Cambridge Dictionary of Jewish History,
    Religion, and Culture.* Cambridge: Cambridge University Press, forthcoming.
———. "Of Drums and Damsels: Women's Performance in Ancient Israel." *BA* (1991): 16–27.
———. "Procreation, Production, and Protection: Male-Female Balance in Early Israel." *JAAR* 5
    (1983): 569–93.
———. "The Roots of Restriction: Women in Early Israel." *BA* 41 (1978): 91–103.
———. "Tribes and Tribulations: Retheorizing Earliest 'Israel.'" In R. Boer, ed., *Tracking the Tribes of
    Yahweh: On the Trail of a Classic,* 35–45. London: Sheffield Academic Press, 2002.
———. "Women and the Domestic Economy of Early Israel." In Alice Bach, ed., *Women in the Hebrew
    Bible: A Reader,* 33–44. New York and London: Routledge, 1999.
———, ed. *Women in Scripture: A Dictionary of Named and Unnamed Women in the Hebrew Bible, the
    Apocryphal/Deuterocanonical Books, and the New Testament.* Grand Rapids: Wm. B. Eerdmans Pub-
    lishing Co., 2001.
———. "Women, Israelite." In Judith Baskin, ed., *Cambridge Dictionary of Jewish History, Religion, and
    Culture.* Cambridge: Cambridge University Press, forthcoming.
Newsom, Carol A., and Sharon H. Ringe, eds. *The Women's Bible Commentary: Expanded Edition with
    Apocrypha.* London: SPCK; Louisville, KY: Westminster/John Knox Press, 1992.
Niditch, Susan. *Underdogs and Tricksters: A Prelude in Biblical Folklore.* San Francisco: Harper & Row,
    1987.
Nowell, Irene. *Women in the Old Testament.* Collegeville, MN: Liturgical Press, 1997.
Orenstein, Debra, and Jane Rachel Litman, eds. *Lifecycles,* vol. 2: *Jewish Women on Biblical Themes in
    Contemporary Life.* Woodstock, VT: Jewish Lights, 1997.
Ostriker, Alicia Suskin. *The Nakedness of the Fathers: Biblical Vision and Revisions.* New Brunswick, NJ:
    Rutgers University Press, 1994.
Parales, Heidi Bright. *Hidden Voices: Biblical Women and Our Christian Heritage.* Smyth & Helwys,
    1998.
Pardes, Ilana. *Countertraditions in the Bible: A Feminist Approach.* Cambridge: Harvard University Press,
    1992.
Pressler, Carolyn. *The View of Women Found in Deuteronomic Family Law.* BZAW. Berlin: Walter de
    Gruyter, 1993.
Rabichev, Renata. "The Mediterranean Concepts of Honour and Shame As Seen in the Depiction of
    Biblical Women." *Religion and Theology* 3 (1996): 51–63.
Raver, Miki. *Listen to Her Voice: Women of the Hebrew Bible.* San Francisco: Chronicle Books, 1998.
Reinhartz, Adele. *Why Ask My Name? Anonymity and Identity in Biblical Narrative.* Oxford: Oxford Uni-
    versity Press, 1998.
Ronson, Barbara Thaw. *The Women of the Torah: Commentaries from the Talmud, Midrash, and Kab-
    balah.* Northvale, NJ: Jason Aronson, 1999.

Rosen, Norma. *Biblical Women Unbound: Counter-Tales.* Philadelphia: Jewish Publication Society, 1996.

Ruether, Rosemary Radford. *Religion and Sexism: Images of Woman in the Jewish and Christian Traditions.* New York: Simon & Schuster, 1974.

Russell, H. Diane, with Bernadine Barnes. *Eve/Ave: Women in Renaissance and Baroque Prints.* Washington, DC: National Gallery of Art; New York: The Feminist Press at the City University, 1990.

Sakenfeld, Katharine Doob. *Just Wives? Stories of Power and Survival in the Old Testament and Today.* Louisville, KY: Westminster John Knox Press, 2003.

Sawyer, Deborah F. *God, Gender and the Bible.* Biblical Limits. New York: Routledge, 2002.

Schaberg, Jane, Alice Bach, and Esther Fuchs, eds. *On the Cutting Edge: The Study of Women in Biblical Worlds.* New York: Continuum, 2003.

Schottroff, Luise, Silvia Schroer, and Marie-Theres Wacker. *Feminist Interpretation: The Bible in Women's Perspective.* Trans. Martin and Barbara Rumscheidt. Minneapolis: Fortress Press, 1998.

Schroer, Silvia, Linda M. Maloney, and William McDonough. *Wisdom Has Built Her House: Studies on the Figure of Sophia in the Bible.* Collegeville, MN: Liturgical Press, 2000.

Schroer, Silvia, and Sophia Bietenhard, eds. *Feminist Interpretation of the Bible and the Hermeneutics of Liberation.* JSOTSup 374. London: Sheffield Academic Press, 2003.

Schüssler Fiorenza, Elisabeth, with S. Matthews and A. Brock. *Searching the Scriptures.* 2 vols. London: SCM, 1993.

Selvidge, Marla J. *Woman, Violence, and the Bible.* Lewiston, NY: Edwin Mellen Press, 1996.

Smith, Elizabeth J. *Bearing Fruit in Due Season: Feminist Hermeneutics and the Bible in Worship.* Collegeville, MN: Liturgical Press, 1999.

Sölle, Dorothée, et al. *Great Women of the Bible in Art and Literature.* Trans. Joe H. Kirchberger. Macon, GA: Mercer University Press, 1994.

Thistlethwaite, Susan Brooks. "'You May Enjoy the Spoil of Your Enemies': Rape as a Biblical Metaphor for War." *Semeia* 61 (1993): 59–75.

Trible, Phyllis. *God and the Rhetoric of Sexuality.* Overtures to Biblical Theology. Philadelphia: Fortress Press, 1978.

———. *Texts of Terror: Literary-Feminist Readings of Biblical Narratives.* Overtures to Biblical Theology. Philadelphia: Fortress Press, 1984.

———. "Women in the Old Testament." In *Interpreter's Dictionary of the Bible, Supplementary Volume,* 961–66. Nashville: Abingdon Press, 1976.

Wenkart, Henny, ed. *Sarah's Daughters Sing: A Sampler of Poems by Jewish Women.* Hoboken, NJ: KTAV, 1990.

Wiskind-Elper, Ora, and Susan Handelman, eds. *Torah of the Mothers: Contemporary Jewish Women Read Classical Jewish Texts.* New York: Urim, 2000.

Yee, Gale. *Poor Banished Children of Eve: Woman as Evil in the Hebrew Bible.* Louisville, KY: Westminster John Knox Press, 2003.

Zlotnick, Helena. *Dinah's Daughters: Gender and Judaism from the Hebrew Bible to Late Antiquity.* Philadelphia: University of Pennsylvania Press, 2002.

Zones, Jane Sprague, ed. *Taking the Fruit: Modern Women's Tales of the Bible.* San Diego, CA: Women's Institute for Continuing Jewish Education, 1989.

Feminist Thought on Biblical Interpretation

Anderson, Janice Capel. "Mapping Feminist Biblical Criticism: The American Scene, 1983–1990." In Eldon Jay Epp, ed., *Critical Review of Books in Religion: 1991,* 21–44. Atlanta: Scholars Press, 1991.

Bach, Alice. "Introduction: Man's World, Women's Place: Sexual Politics in the Hebrew Bible." In Alice Bach, ed., *Women in the Hebrew Bible: A Reader,* xiii–xiv. New York and London: Routledge, 1999.

———. "Reading Allowed: Feminist Biblical Criticism Approaching the Millennium." *Currents in Research: Biblical Studies* 1 (1993): 191–215.

Bellis, Alice Ogden. "Feminist Biblical Scholarship." In *WIS,* 24–32.

Bird, Phyllis A. "What Makes a Feminist Reading Feminist? A Qualified Answer." In Harold C. Washington, S. L. Graham, Pamela L. Thimmes, eds., *Escaping Eden: New Feminist Perspectives on the Bible*, 124–31. New York: New York University Press, 1998.

Brenner, Athalya, and Carole Fontaine. *A Feminist Companion to Reading the Bible: Approaches, Methods, and Strategies*. Sheffield, UK: Sheffield Academic Press, 1997.

Camp, Claudia V. "Female Voice, Written Word: Women and Authority in Hebrew Scripture." In P. M. Cooey, S. A. Farmer, and M. E. Ross, eds., *Embodied Love: Sensuality and Relationship as Feminist Values*, 97–113. San Francisco: Harper & Row, 1987.

———. "Metaphor in Feminist Biblical Interpretation: Theoretical Perspectives." *Semeia* 61 (1993): 3–36.

Cheney, Emily. *She Can Read: Feminist Reading Strategies for Biblical Narrative*. Valley Forge, PA: Trinity Press International, 1996.

Choi Hee An and Katheryn Pfisterer Darr, eds. *Engaging the Bible: Critical Readings from Contemporary Women*. Minneapolis: Fortress Press, 2006.

Chung, Hyun Kyung. *Struggle to Be the Sun Again: Introducing Asian Women's Theology*. Maryknoll, NY: Orbis Books, 1990.

Collins, Adela Yarbro, ed. *Feminist Perspectives on Biblical Scholarship*. SBLBSNA 10. Chico, CA: Scholars Press, 1985.

Davies, Eryl W. *The Dissenting Reader: Feminist Approaches to the Hebrew Bible*. Burlington, VT: Ashgate Publishing Co., 2003.

Demers, Patricia. *Women as Interpreters of the Bible*. New York: Paulist Press, 1992.

Fewell, Danna Nolan. "Feminist Hermeneutics." In W. Watson, ed., *Mercer Dictionary of the Bible*. Macon, GA: Mercer University Press, 1990.

———. "Feminist Reading of the Hebrew Bible: Affirmation, Resistance and Transformation." *JSOT* 39 (1987): 77–87.

———. "Reading the Bible Ideologically: Feminist Criticism." In Steven L. McKenzie and Stephen R. Haynes, eds., *To Each Its Own Meaning: An Introduction to Biblical Criticisms and Their Applications*, 237–51. Louisville, KY: Westminster/John Knox Press, 1993.

Fewell, Danna Nolan, and Gary A. Phillips. "Ethics, Bible, Reading as If." *Semeia* 77 (1997): 1–21.

Gafney, Wilda. "Translation Matters: A Fem/Womanist Exploration of Translation Theory and Practice for Proclamation in Worship." SBL Forum, April 5–May 3, 2006. http://www.sbl-site.org/Article.aspx?ArticleId=509.

Hackett, Jo Ann. "Women's Studies and the Hebrew Bible." In Richard Eliot Friedman and Hugh G. M. Williamson, eds., *The Future of Biblical Studies: The Hebrew Scriptures*, 143–64. Semeia Studies. Atlanta: Scholars Press, 1987.

Hayter, Mary. "Biblical Criticism, Christian Woman and the Church." In *The New Eve in Christ: The Use and Abuse of the Bible in the Debate about Women in Church*, 146–71. Grand Rapids: Wm. B. Eerdmans Publishing Co., 1987.

Heister, Maria-Sybilla. *Frauen in der biblischen Glaubensgeschichte*. Göttingen: Vandenhoeck und Ruprecht, 1984.

Isasi-Díaz, Ada Maria. "The Bible and Mujerista Theology." In Susan Brooks Thistlethwaite and Potter Engel, eds., *Lift Every Voice: Constructing Christian Theologies from the Underside*. San Francisco: Harper & Row, 1990.

Kellenbach, Katharina von. *Anti-Judaism in Feminist Religious Writings*. AAR Cultural Criticism Series 1. Atlanta: Scholars Press, 1994.

Kim, Hyun Chul Paul. "Gender Complementarity in the Hebrew Bible." In Wonil Kim et al., eds., *Reading the Hebrew Bible for a New Millenium*, 1:253–91. Harrisburg, PA: Trinity Press International, 2000.

Kwok, Pui-Lan. "Discovering the Bible in the Non-Biblical World." *Semeia* 47 (1989): 25–42.

———. *Discovering the Bible in the Non-Biblical World*. Maryknoll, NY: Orbis, 1995.

Lancaster, Sarah Heaner. *Women and the Authority of Scripture: A Narrative Approach*. Harrisburg, PA: Trinity Press International, 2002.

McKinlay, Judith E. "Dead Spots of Living Texts? A Matter of Biblical Reading." *Pacifica* 5 (1992): 1–16.

Middleton, Deborah F. "Feminist Interpretation." In R. J. Coggins and J. L. Houlden, eds., *A Dictionary of Biblical Interpretation*, 231–34. Philadelphia: Trinity Press International, 1990.

Minh-ha, Trinh T. *Woman, Native, Other: Writing Postcoloniality and Feminism*. Bloomington: Indiana University Press, 1989.

Mollenkott, Virginia Ramey. *Women, Men, and the Bible*. Nashville: Abingdon Press, 1977.

Osiek, Carolyn, RSCJ. "The Feminist in the Bible." In Adela Yarbro Collins, ed., *Feminist Perspectives on Biblical Scholarship*, 93–105. SBLBSNA 10. Chico, CA: Scholars Press, 1985.

Pardes, Ilana. *Countertraditions in the Bible: A Feminist Approach*. Cambridge: Harvard University Press, 1992.

Perkins, Pheme. "Women in the Bible and Its World." *Interpretation* 42 (1988): 33–44.

Ringe, Sharon H. "When Women Interpret the Bible." In *WBC*, 1–9.

Ruether, Rosemary Radford. "Feminism and Patriarchal Religion: Principles of Ideological Critique of the Bible." *JSOT* 22 (1982): 54–66.

Russell, Letty M. "Feminist Critique: Opportunity for Cooperation." *JSOT* 22 (1982): 67–71.

———, ed. *Feminist Interpretation of the Bible*. Philadelphia: Westminster Press, 1985.

———, ed. *The Liberating Word: A Guide to Nonsexist Interpretation of the Bible*. Philadelphia: Westminster Press, 1976.

Sakenfeld, Katharine Doob. "The Bible and Women: Bane or Blessing?" *Theology Today* 32 (1975): 222–33.

———. "Feminist Biblical Interpretation." *Theology Today* 46 (1989): 154–68.

———. "Old Testament Perspectives: Methodological Issues." *JSOT* 22 (1982): 13–20.

Sawyer, Deborah F. *God, Gender, and the Bible*. Biblical Limits. New York: Routledge, 2002.

Schroer, Silvia, and Sophia Bietenhard, eds. *Feminist Interpretation of the Bible and the Hermeneutics of Liberation*. JSOTSup 374. London: Sheffield Academic Press, 2003.

Schüssler Fiorenza, Elisabeth. *Bread Not Stone: The Challenge of Feminist Biblical Interpretation*. Boston: Beacon, 1984. Rev. ed., 1995.

———. *But She Said: Feminist Practices of Biblical Interpretation*. Boston: Beacon, 1992.

———. "The Ethics of Interpretation: De-Centering Biblical Scholarship." *JBL* 107 (1988): 3–17.

———. "Feminist Hermeneutics." In *ABD*, 2:783–91.

———. *In Memory of Her: A Feminist Theological Reconstruction of Christian Origins*. New York: Crossroad, 1985.

———. *Rhetoric and Ethic: The Politics of Biblical Studies*. Minneapolis: Fortress Press, 1999.

———. "Toward a Feminist Biblical Hermeneutics: Biblical Interpretation and Liberation Theology." In Brian Mahan and L. Dale Richesin, eds., *The Challenge of Liberation Theology: A First World Response*, 91–112. Maryknoll, NY: Orbis Books, 1981.

———. *Wisdom Ways: Introducing Feminist Biblical Interpretation*. Maryknoll, NY: Orbis Books, 2001.

Tamez, Elsa. "Women's Rereading of the Bible." In Virginia Fabella and Mercy A. Oduyoye, eds., *With Passion and Compassion: Third World Women Doing Theology*. Maryknoll, NY: Orbis Books, 1988.

Tolbert, Mary Ann, ed. *The Bible and Feminist Hermeneutics. Semeia* 28 (1983).

———. "Defining the Problem: The Bible and Feminist Hermeneutics." In *The Bible and Feminist Hermeneutics. Semeia* 28 (1983): 113–26.

———. "Protestant Feminists and the Bible: On the Horns of a Dilemma." In Alice Bach, ed., *Ad Feminam. USQR* 43 (1989): 1–17. Also in Alice Bach, ed., *The Pleasure of Her Text: Feminist Readings of Biblical and Historical Texts*, 5–24. Philadelphia: Trinity Press International, 1990.

Trible, Phyllis. "Depatriarchalizing in Biblical Interpretation." *JAAR* 41 (1973): 30–48.

———. "The Effects of Women's Studies on Biblical Studies: An Introduction." *JSOT* 22 (1984): 3–6.

———. "Feminist Hermeneutics and Biblical Studies." *Christian Century* 99, no. 4 (February 3–10, 1982): 116–18.

———. "Five Loaves and Two Fishes: Feminist Hermeneutics and Biblical Theology." *TS* 50 (1989): 279–95.

———. "Good Tidings of Great Joy: Biblical Faith without Sexism." *Christianity and Crisis* 34, no. 1 (February 4, 1974): 12–16.

———. "The Pilgrim Bible on a Feminist Journey." *Daughters of Sarah* 15, no. 3 (May/June 1989): 4–7.

Wakeman, Mary K. "Biblical Prophecy and Modern Feminism." In Rita M. Gross, ed., *Beyond Andro-centrism: New Essays on Women and Religion*, 67–88. Aids for the Study of Religion 6. Missoula, MT: Scholars Press, 1977.

Washington, Harold C., Susan Lochrie Graham, and Pamela Thimmes, eds. *Escaping Eden: New Femi-nist Perspectives on the Bible*. New York: New York University Press, 1998.

Feminist Theology and Spirituality

Adler, Rachel. *Engendering Judaism: An Inclusive Theology and Ethics*. Philadelphia: Jewish Publication Society, 1998.

———.*On Being a Jewish Feminist*. New York: Schocken Books, 1995.

Aldred, Joe, ed. *Sisters with Power*. New York: Continuum, 2000.

Allen, Paula Gunn. *The Sacred Hoop: Recovering the Feminine in American Indian Traditions*. Boston: Beacon Press, 1986.

Anderson, Sherry R., and Patricia Hopkins. *The Feminine Face of God*. New York: Bantam, 1991.

Aquino, Maria Pilar. *Our Cry for Life: Feminist Theology from Latin America*. Maryknoll, NY: Orbis Books, 1993.

Armour, Ellen T. *Deconstruction, Feminist Theology, and the Problem of Difference: Subverting the Race/Gender Divide*. Chicago: University of Chicago Press, 1999.

Cady, Susan, Marian Ronan, and Hal Taussig. *Wisdom's Feast: Sophia in Study and Celebration*. San Fran-cisco: Harper & Row, 1989.

Cahill, Susan. *Wise Women: Over Two Thousand Years of Spiritual Writing by Women*. New York: W. W. Norton & Co., 1996.

Case-Winters, Anna. *God's Power: Traditional Understandings and Contemporary Challenges*. Louisville, KY: Westminster/John Knox Press, 1990.

Chopp, Rebecca S. *The Power to Speak: Feminism, Language, God*. New York: Crossroad, 1989.

Chopp, Rebecca S., and S. Greeve Davaney, eds. *Horizons in Feminist Theology: Identity, Tradition and Norms*. Minneapolis: Fortress, 1997.

Christ, Carol. "The New Feminist Theology: A Review of the Literature. " *RelSRev* 3 (1977): 203–7.

Christ, Carol P., and Judith Plaskow. *Weaving the Visions: New Patterns in Feminist Spirituality*. San Fran-cisco: Harper & Row, 1989.

———. *Womanspirit Rising: A Feminist Reader in Religion*. San Francisco: Harper & Row, 1992.

Chung, Hyun Kyung. *Struggle to Be the Sun Again: Introducing Asian Women's Theology*. Maryknoll, NY: Orbis Books, 1990.

Clanton, Jann Aldredge. *In Whose Image? God and Gender*. New York: Crossroad Publishing Co., 1990.

Clifford, Anne M. *Introducing Feminist Theology*. Maryknoll, NY: Orbis Books, 1999.

Daly, Mary. *Beyond God the Father: Toward a Philosophy of Women's Liberation*. Boston: Beacon Press, 1973, 1985.

———. *The Church and the Second Sex*. New York: Harper & Row, 1968, 1975, 1985.

———. *Gyn/Ecology: The Metaethics of Radical Feminism*. Boston: Beacon Press, 1978.

———. *Pure Lust: Elemental Feminist Philosophy*. Boston: Beacon Press, 1984.

Damico, Linda H. *The Anarchist Dimension of Liberation Theology*. New York: Peter Lang, 1987.

Davidman, Lynn, and Shelly Tenenbaum, eds. *Feminist Perspectives on Jewish Studies*. New Haven, CT: Yale University Press, 1995.

Dunfee, Susan Nelson. *Beyond Servanthood: Christianity and the Liberation of Women*. Lanham, MD: University Press of America, 1988.

Elwes, Teresa, ed. *Women's Voices: Essays in Contemporary Feminist Theology*. San Francisco: Harper, 1992.

Eriksson, Ann Louise. *The Meaning of Gender in Theology. Problems and Possibilities*. Acta Universitatis Upsaliensis (AUU). Uppsala, Sweden: University of Uppsala, 1995.

Esser, Annette, and Luise Schottroff, eds. *Feminist Theology in a European Context*. Kampen, The Netherlands: Kok/Pharos, 1993.

Fabella, Virginia, and Mercy A. Oduyoye, eds. *With Passion and Compassion: Third World Women Doing Theology*. Maryknoll, NY: Orbis Books, 1988.

Fabella, Virginia, and Sun Ai Lee Park. *We Dare to Dream: Doing Theology as Asian Women*. Kowloon, Hong Kong: Asian Women's Resource Center, 1989.

Farley, Wendy. *Tragic Vision and Divine Compassion: A Contemporary Theodicy*. Louisville, KY: Westminster/John Knox Press, 1990.

Fisher, Kathleen. *Women at the Well: Feminist Perspectives on Spiritual Direction*. New York: Paulist Press, 1988.

Fishman, Sylvia Barack. *A Breath of Life: Feminism in the American Jewish Community*. Brandeis Series in American Jewish History, Culture, and Life. New York: Free Press, 1993; Hanover, NH: Brandeis University Press, by University Press of New England, 1995.

Frankiel, Tamar. *The Voice of Sarah: Feminine Spirituality and Traditional Judaism*. New York: HarperCollins, 1992; Biblio Press, 1997.

Fulkerson, Mary McClintock. *Changing the Subject: Women's Discourses and Feminist Theology*. Minneapolis: Fortress Press, 1994.

Gottlieb, Lynn. *She Who Dwells Within: A Feminist Vision of a Renewed Judaism*. San Francisco: Harper & Row, 1995.

Graff, Ann O'Hara, ed. *In the Embrace of God: Feminist Approaches to Theological Anthropology*. Maryknoll, NY: Orbis Books, 1995.

Gross, Rita M., and Rosemary Radford Ruether. *Religious Feminism and the Future of the Planet: A Buddhist-Christian Conversation*. New York: Continuum, 2001.

Gundry, Patricia. *Neither Slave nor Free: Helping Women Answer the Call to Church Leadership*. San Francisco: Harper & Row, 1987.

Hampson, Daphne. *Theology and Feminism*. Oxford: Blackwell, 1990.

Heine, Susanne. *Christianity and the Goddess: Systematic Criticism of a Feminist Theology*. Philadelphia: Trinity Press International, 1988.

———. *Matriarchs, Goddesses, and Images of God: A Critique of Feminist Theology*. Trans. John Bowden. Minneapolis: Augsburg Publishing House, 1989.

Heschel, Susannah. *On Being a Jewish Feminist*. New York: Schocken Books, 1983, 1995.

Heywood, Carter. *Speaking of Christ: A Lesbian Feminist Voice*. New York: Pilgrim Press, 1989.

Hogan, Linda. *From Women's Experience to Feminist Theology*. Sheffield, UK: Sheffield Academic Press, 1996.

Hunt, Mary. *Fierce Tenderness: A Feminist Theology of Friendship*. New York: Crossroad, 1992.

Imboden, Roberta. *From the Cross to the Kingdom: Sartrean Dialectics and Liberation Theology*. San Francisco: Harper & Row, 1987.

Isasi-Díaz, Ada Maria, and F. F. Segovia, eds. *Hispanic/Latino Theology: Challenge and Promise*. Minneapolis: Fortress Press, 1996.

Isasi-Díaz, Ada Maria, and Yolanda Tarango, eds. *Hispanic Women, Prophetic Voice in the Church: Toward a Hispanic Women's Liberation Theology*. San Francisco: Harper & Row, 1988.

Isherwood, Lisa, and Dorothea McEwan. *Introducing Feminist Theology*. Sheffield, UK: Sheffield Academic Press, 1993.

———. *Themes in Christian Feminist Theology*. Sheffield, UK: Sheffield Academic Press, 1996.

Isherwood, Lisa, and Elizabeth Stuart. *Introducing Body Theology*. Introductions in Feminist Theology. Sheffield, UK: Sheffield Academic Press, 1998.

Jones, Serene. *Feminist Theory and Christian Theology*. Minneapolis: Fortress Press, 2000.

Kalven, Janet, and Mary I. Buckley, eds. *Women's Spirit Bonding*. New York: Pilgrim Press, 1984.

King, Ursula. *Feminist Theology from the Third World*. Maryknoll, NY: Orbis Books, 1994.

———. *Religion and Gender*. Oxford: Blackwell, 1995; Sheffield, UK: Sheffield Academic Press, 2000.

Kwok, Pui-lan. *Introducing Asian Feminist Theology*. Cleveland: Pilgrim Press, 2000.

LaCugna, Catherine Mowry, ed. *Freeing Theology: The Essentials of Theology in a Feminist Perspective*. New York: HarperCollins, 1993.

Loades, Ann, ed. *Feminist Theology: A Reader*. London: SPCK, 1990.

MacKinnon, Mary Heather, and Moni McIntyre, eds. *Readings in Ecology and Feminist Theology*. Kansas City, MO: Sheed & Ward, 1995.

McEwan, Dorothea, and Lisa Isherwood. *Introducing Feminist Theology.* Sheffield, UK: Sheffield Academic Press, 1993.

McFague, Sallie. *The Body of God: An Ecological Theology.* Minneapolis: Fortress Press, 1993.

———. *Metaphorical Theology: Models of God in Religious Language.* Minneapolis: Fortress Press, 1982.

———. *Models of God: Theology for an Ecological, Nuclear Age.* Philadelphia: Fortress Press, 1987.

Meyer-Wilmes, Hedwig. *Rebellion on the Borders: Feminist Theology between Theory and Praxis.* Kampen, the Netherlands: Kok Pharos, 1995.

Mickelsen, Alvera, ed. *Women, Authority, and the Bible.* Downers Grove, IL: InterVarsity Press, 1986.

Miller-McLemore, Bonnie J., and Brita Gill-Austern. *Feminist and Womanist Pastoral Theology.* Nashville: Abingdon Press, 1999.

Mollenkott, Virginia Ramey. *Men, Women, and the Bible.* New York: Crossroad, 1992.

———. *Sensuous Spirituality: Cut from Fundamentalism.* New York: Crossroad, 1992.

———. *Women of Faith in Dialogue.* New York: Crossroad, 1987.

Neal, Marie Augusta. *The Just Demands of the Poor: Essays in Socio-Theology.* New York: Paulist Press, 1987.

Oduyoye, Mercy Amba. *Daughters of Anowa: African Women and Patriarchy.* Maryknoll, NY: Orbis Books, 1995.

———. *Introducing African Women's Theology.* Cleveland: Pilgrim Press, 2001.

Osiek, Carolyn, RSCJ. "The New Handmaid: The Bible and the Social Sciences." *TS* 50 (1989): 260–78.

Parsons, Susan Frank. *The Cambridge Companion to Feminist Theology.* Cambridge: Cambridge University Press, 2002.

Plaskow, Judith. *Standing Again at Sinai: Judaism from a Feminist Perspective.* San Francisco: Harper & Row, 1991.

Plaskow, Judith, and Carol Christ. *Weaving the Visions.* San Francisco: Harper & Row, 1989.

———. *Womanspirit Rising.* San Francisco: Harper & Row, 1992.

Pobee, John S., and Bärbel von Wartenberg-Potter, eds. *New Eyes for Reading: Biblical and Theological Reflections by Women from the Third World.* Oak Park, IL: Meyer-Stone Books, 1987.

Pollitt, Katha. "Are Women Morally Superior to Men?" *The Nation,* December 28, 1992, 799–807.

Raphael, Melissa. *Introducing Thealogy: Discourse on the Goddess.* Introductions in Feminist Theology. Sheffield, UK: Sheffield Academic Press, 1998.

Ross, Susan A. *Extravagant Affections: A Feminist Sacramental Theology.* New York: Continuum, 2001.

Rudavsky, T. M., ed. *Gender and Judaism: The Transformation of Tradition.* New York: New York University Press, 1995.

Ruether, Rosemary Radford. *Introducing Redemption in Christian Feminism.* Introductions in Feminist Theology. Sheffield, UK: Sheffield Academic Press, 1998.

———. *Liberation Theology: Human Hope Confronts Christian History and American Power.* New York: Paulist Press, 1972.

———. *Mary—The Feminine Face of the Church.* Philadelphia: Westminster Press, 1977.

———. *New Woman/New Earth: Sexist Ideologies and Human Liberation.* San Francisco: Harper & Row, 1975.

———, ed. *Religion and Sexism: Images of Woman in the Jewish and Christian Traditions.* New York: Simon & Schuster, 1974.

———. *Sexism and God-Talk: Toward a Feminist Theology.* Boston: Beacon Press, 1983.

———. *To Change the World: Christology and Cultural Criticism.* New York: Crossroad, 1982.

———. *Womanguides: Readings toward a Feminist Theology.* Boston: Beacon Press, 1985.

———. *Women-Church: Theology and Practice of Feminist Liturgical Communities.* San Francisco: Harper & Row, 1985.

Russell, Letty M. *Household of Freedom: Authority in Feminist Theology.* Philadelphia: Westminster Press, 1987.

———. *Human Liberation in a Feminist Perspective—A Theology.* Philadelphia: Westminster Press, 1974.

Russell, Letty M., Kwok Pui-lan, Ada Maria Isasi-Díaz, and Katie Geneva Cannon, eds. *Inheriting Our Mothers' Gardens: Feminist Theology in Third World Perspective.* Philadelphia: Westminster Press, 1988.

Russell, Letty M., and J. Shannon Clarkson, eds. *Dictionary of Feminist Theologies.* Louisville, KY: Westminster John Knox Press, 1996.

Sands, Kathleen M. *Escape from Paradise: Evil and Tragedy in Feminist Theology.* Minneapolis: Fortress Press, 1993.

Sawyer, Deborah, and Diane Collier, eds. *Is There a Future for Feminist Theology?* Studies in Theology and Sexuality 4. Sheffield, UK: Sheffield Academic Press, 1999.

Schneider, Laurel C. *Re-Imagining the Divine: Confronting the Backlash against Feminist Theology.* New York: Pilgrim Press, 1998.

Schottroff, Luise. *Lydia's Impatient Sisters.* Louisville, KY: Westminster John Knox Press, 1995.

Schottroff, Luise, and Annette Esser, eds. *Feminist Theology in a European Context.* Kampen: Kok Pharos, 1993.

Schüssler Fiorenza, Elisabeth. *The Power of Naming: A Concilium Reader in Feminist Liberation Theology.* Maryknoll, NY: Orbis Books, 1996.

Sharma, Arvind, ed. *Feminism and World Religions.* Albany: State University of New York Press, 1998.

————. *Women in World Religions.* Albany: State University of New York Press, 1987.

Sölle, Dorothée. *The Window of Vulnerability: A Political Spirituality.* Minneapolis: Fortress Press, 1990.

Spretnak, Charlene, ed. *The Politics of Women's Spirituality: Essays on the Rise of Spiritual Power within the Feminist Movement.* Garden City, NY: Doubleday & Co., 1982.

Tamez, Elsa. *Bible of the Oppressed.* Maryknoll, NY: Orbis Books, 1982.

Tanner, Kathryn. *God and Creation in Creation Theology: Tyranny or Empowerment?* New York: Basil Blackwell, 1988.

Umansky, Ellen, and Dianne Ashton, eds. *Four Centuries of Jewish Women's Spirituality.* Boston: Beacon Press, 1992.

Thistlethwaite, Susan Brooks, and Toinette Eugene. "A Survey of Contemporary Global Feminist, Womanist, and Mujerista Theologies." In Eldon Jay Epp, ed., *Critical Review of Books in Religion: 1991,* 1–20. Atlanta: Scholars Press, 1991.

Webb, Val. *Why We're Equal: Introducing Feminist Theology.* St. Louis: Chalice Press, 1999.

Williams, Delores. *Black Theology in a New Key/Feminist Theology in a Different Voice.* Maryknoll, NY: Orbis Books, 1996.

————. *Sisters in the Wilderness: The Challenge of Womanist God-Talk.* Maryknoll, NY: Orbis Books, 1993.

Winter, Miriam Therese. Illustrated by Meinrad Craighead. *Womanwisdom: A Feminist Lectionary and Psalter: Women of the Hebrew Scriptures, Part One* and *Woman Witness: A Feminist Lectionary and Psalter: Women of the Hebrew Scriptures, Part Two.* New York: Crossroad Publishing Co., 1991–92.

Wong, Angela Wai-Ching. *The Poor Woman: A Critical Analysis of Asian Theology and Contemporary Chinese Fiction by Women.* New York: Lang, 2002.

Young, Pamela Dickey. *Feminist Theology/Christian Theology: In Search of Method.* Minneapolis: Fortress Press, 1990.

Goddesses

Ackerman, Susan. "'And the Women Knead Dough': The Worship of the Queen of Heaven in Sixth-Century Judah." In Peggy L. Day, ed., *Gender and Difference in Ancient Israel,* 109–24. Minneapolis: Fortress Press, 1989. And in Alice Bach, ed. *Women in the Hebrew Bible: A Reader,* 21–32. New York and London: Routledge, 1999.

————. "Asherah/Ahserim" and "Astarte." In *WIS,* 508–11, 512–13.

Ann, Martha, and Dorothy Myers Imel. *Goddesses in World Mythology.* New York: Oxford University Press, 1993.

Beach, Eleanor Ferris. "Transforming Goddess Iconography in Hebrew Narrative." In Karen L. King, ed., *Women and Goddess Traditions in Antiquity and Today,* 239–63. Studies in Antiquity and Christianity. Minneapolis: Fortress Press, 1997.

Binger, Tilde. *Ashera: Goddesses in Ugarit, Israel and the Old Testament.* Sheffield, UK: Sheffield Academic Press, 1997.

Eisler, Riane T. *The Chalice and the Blade: Our History, Our Future.* New York: Harper & Row, 1987.

Emmerson, Grace I. "A Fertility Goddess in Hosea IV 17–19." *VT* 4 (1974): 492–96.

Fontaine, Carole R. "A Heifer from Thy Stable: On Goddesses and the Status of Women in the Ancient Near East." In Alice Bach, ed., *The Pleasure of Her Text: Feminist Readings of Biblical and Historical Texts,* 69–116. Philadelphia: Trinity Press International, 1990.

Frymer-Kensky, Tikva. *In the Wake of the Goddesses: Women, Culture, and the Biblical Transformation of Pagan Myth.* New York: Free Press, 1992.

Hadley, Judith M. *The Cult of Asherah in Ancient Israel and Judah: Evidence for a Hebrew Goddess.* Cambridge: Cambridge University Press, 2000.

Hayter, Mary. "God and Goddess." In *The New Eve in Christ: The Use and Abuse of the Bible in the Debate about Women in the Church,* 7–20. Grand Rapids: Wm. B. Eerdmans Publishing Co., 1987.

Heine, Susanne. *Christianity and the Goddesses.* London: SCM Press, 1988.

———. "Eros of the Goddesses." In *Matriarchs, Goddesses, and Images of God: A Critique of Feminist Theology,* 41–73. Trans. John Bowden. Minneapolis: Augsburg Publishing House, 1989.

Keel, Othmar, and Christoph Uehlinger. *Goddesses, and Images of God in Ancient Israel.* Trans. Thomas H. Trapp. Minneapolis: Fortress Press, 1998.

Larocca-Pitts, Elizabeth C. "Anath." In *WIS,* 507.

Olyan, Saul. *Asherah and the Cult of Yahweh in Israel.* SBL Monograph Series 34. Atlanta: Scholars Press, 1988.

Patai, Raphael. *The Hebrew Goddess.* 3rd ed. Detroit: Wayne State University Press, 1990.

Smith, Mark S. *The Early History of God: Yahweh and the Other Deities in Ancient Israel.* 2nd ed. Grand Rapids: Wm. B. Eerdmans Publishing Co., 2002.

Stone, Merlin. *When God Was a Woman.* New York: Dial Press, 1976.

Feminine Imagery of the Divine

Anderson, Sherry Ruth, and Hopkins, Patricia. *The Feminine Face of God: The Unfolding of the Sacred in Women.* New York: Bantam Books, 1991.

Atkinson, Clarissa W., Constance H. Buchanan, and Margaret R. Miles, eds. *Immaculate and Powerful: The Female in Sacred Image and Social Reality.* Harvard Women's Studies in Religion. Boston: Beacon Press, 1985.

Borreson, K. E. *The Images of God: Gender Models in the Judeo-Christian Tradition.* Minneapolis: Fortress Press, 1995.

Bruns, J. Edgar. *God as Woman, Woman as God.* New York: Paulist Press, 1973.

Clanton, Jann Aldredge. *In Whose Image: God and Gender.* Revised and expanded ed. New York: Crossroad, 2001.

Englesman, Joan. *The Feminine Dimension of the Divine.* Philadelphia: Westminster Press, 1979.

Gerstenberger, Erhard S. *Yahweh—The Patriarch: Ancient Images of God and Feminist Theology.* Philadelphia: Fortress Press, 1996.

Gruber, Mayer I. *The Motherhood of God and Other Studies.* Atlanta: Scholars Press, 1992.

Hayter, Mary. "Feminine and Masculine Theological Vocabulary." In *The New Eve in Christ: The Use and Abuse of the Bible in the Debate about Women in the Church,* 21–44. Grand Rapids: Wm. B. Eerdmans Publishing Co., 1987.

Heine, Susanne. "God the Father, God the Mother." In *Matriarchs, Goddesses, and Images of God: A Critique of Feminist Theology,* 10–40. Trans. John Bowden. Minneapolis: Augsburg Publishing House, 1989.

Meyers, Carol. "Female Images of God in the Hebrew Bible." In *WIS,* 525–28.

Mollenkott, Virginia Ramey. *The Divine Feminine: The Biblical Imagery of God as Female.* New York: Crossroad, 1983.

Ramshaw, Gail. *God beyond Gender: Feminist Christian God-Language.* Minneapolis: Augsburg Fortress Publishers, 1995.

Saussy, Carroll. *God Images and Self Esteem: Empowering Women in a Patriarchal Society.* Louisville, KY: Westminster/John Knox Press, 1991.

Feminist and Postfeminist Theory

Alcoff, Linda, and Elizabeth Potter, eds. *Feminist Epistemologies*. New York: Routledge, 1993.
Anderson, Pamela. *A Feminist Philosophy of Religion: The Rationality and Myths of Religious Beliefs.* Malden, CT: Blackwell Publishers, 1997.
Barrett, Michelle. *Women's Oppression Today: The Marxist/Feminist Encounter.* London: Verso, 1988.
Baumgardner, Jennifer, and Amy Richards. *Manifesta: Young Women, Feminism, and the Future.* New York: Farrar, Straus & Giroux, 2000.
Benhabib, Seyla, et al., eds. *Feminist Contentions: A Philosophical Exchange.* New York: Routledge, 1995.
Benstock, Shari. *Feminist Issues in Literary Scholarship.* Bloomington: Indiana University Press, 1987.
Butler, Judith. *Gender Trouble: Feminism and the Subversion of Identity.* New York: Routledge, 1990.
Butler, Judith, and Joan W. Scott, eds. *Feminists Theorize the Political.* New York: Routledge 1992.
Chodorow, Nancy. *The Reproduction of Mothering: Psychoanalysis and the Sociology of Gender.* Berkeley and Los Angeles: University of California Press, 1978.
Cleage, Pearl. *Deals with the Devil and Other Reasons to Riot.* New York: Ballantine Books, 1993.
Collins, Patricia Hill. *Black Feminist Thought: Knowledge, Consciousness, and the Politics of Empowerment.* New York: Routledge, Chapman & Hall, 1990.
———. "What's in a Name? Womanism, Black Feminism, and Beyond." *The Black Scholar* (San Francisco) 26:1 (Winter/Spring 1996): 9ff. http://www.gse.buffalo.edu/FAS/Bromley/classes/theory/Collins.htm
Cooke, Miriam, and A. Woollacott. *Gendering War-Talk.* Princeton, NJ: Princeton University Press, 1993.
De Beauvoir, Simone. *The Second Sex.* Trans. and ed. H. M. Parshley. New York: Alfred A. Knopf, 1953.
de Lauretis, Teresa. *Alice Doesn't: Feminism, Semiotics, Cinema.* Bloomington: Indiana University Press, 1984.
Denfeld, Rene. *The New Victorians: A Young Woman's Challenge to the Old Feminist Order.* New York: Warner Books, 1995.
di Leonardo, M., ed. *Gender at the Crossroads of Knowledge: Feminist Anthropology in the Postmodern Era.* Berkeley and Los Angeles: University of California Press, 1991.
Diamond, Irene, and Lee Quinby, eds. *Feminism and Foucault: Reflections on Resistance.* Boston: Northeastern University Press, 1988.
Donovan, Josephine. *Feminist Theory: The Intellectual Traditions of American Feminism.* New York: Frederick Ungar Publishing Co., 1985.
Eisenstein, Hester. *Contemporary Feminist Thought.* London: Allen & Unwin, 1984.
Flynn, Elizabeth A., and Patrocinio Schweickart. *Gender and Reading: Essays on Readers, Texts and Contexts.* Baltimore: Johns Hopkins University Press, 1986.
French, Marilyn. *Beyond Power: On Women, Men, and Morals.* New York: Summit Books, 1985.
Friedan, Betty. *The Feminine Mystique.* New York: Dell Publishing Co., 1963.
Gallop, Jane. *The Daughter's Seduction: Feminism and Psychoanalysis.* Ithaca, NY: Cornell University Press, 1982.
Gates, Henry Louis, ed. *Reading Black, Reading Feminist: A Critical Anthology.* New York: Meridian, 1990.
Gillis, Stacy, Gillian Howie, and Rebecca Munford, eds. *Third Wave Feminism: A Critical Exploration.* Houndmills, Basingstoke, Hampshire; New York: Palgrave MacMillan, 2004.
Harding, Sandra, ed. *Feminism and Methodology.* Bloomington: Indiana University Press, 1987.
Henry, Astrid. *Not My Mother's Sister: Generational Conflict and Third-Wave Feminism.* Bloomington: Indiana University Press 2004.
Heywood, Leslie, and Jennifer Drake, eds. *Third Wave Agenda: Being Feminist, Doing Feminism.* Minneapolis: University of Minnesota Press, 1997.
Hirsch, Marianne, and Evelyn Fox Keller, eds. *Conflicts in Feminism.* New York: Routledge & Kegan Paul, 1990.
Hohne, Karen, and Helen Wussow, eds. *A Dialogue of Voices: Feminist Literary Theory and Bakhtin.* Minneapolis: University of Minnesota Press, 1994.
Horney, Karen. *Feminine Psychology.* New York: W. W. Norton & Co., 1967.
Hoy, Pat C., Esther Schor, and Robert DiYanni. *Women's Voices: Visions and Perspectives.* New York: McGraw-Hill Book Co., 1990.

Irigaray, Luce. *Elemental Passions.* Trans. J. Collie and J. Still. London: Athlone, 1992.
———. *Speculum of the Other Woman.* Trans. G. Gill. Ithaca, NY: Cornell University Press, 1985.
———. *This Sex Which Is Not One.* Trans. C. Porter and C. Burke. Ithaca, NY: Cornell University Press, 1993.
Jacobus, Mary. *Reading Women: Essays in Feminist Criticism.* New York: Columbia University Press, 1986.
James, Stanlie, and Abena Busia, eds. *Theorizing Black Feminisms.* New York: Routledge, 1994.
Jones, Amelia. "Postfeminism, Feminist Pleasures, and Embodied Theories of Art." In Joana Frueh, Cassandra L. Langer, and Arlene Raven, eds., *New Feminist Criticism: Art, Identity, Action,* 16–41. New York: HarperCollins, 1994.
Keohane, N.O., et al., eds. *Feminist Theory: A Critique of Ideology.* Chicago: University of Chicago Press, 1982.
Kristeva, Julia. *Strangers to Ourselves.* Trans. L. S. Roudiez. New York: Columbia University Press, 1991.
———. *Tales of Love.* Trans. L. S. Roudiez. New York: Columbia University Press, 1987.
Lerner, Gerda. *The Creation of Patriarchy.* Women and History. Oxford: Oxford University Press, 1986.
Malson, M. R., J. F. O'Barr, Sarah Westphal-Wihl, and Mary Wyer, eds. *Feminist Theory in Practice and Process.* Chicago: University of Chicago Press, 1989.
Meese, Elizabeth. *Crossing the Double-Cross: The Practice of Feminist Criticism.* Chapel Hill: University of North Carolina Press, 1986.
Millett, Kate. *Sexual Politics.* Garden City, NY: Doubleday & Co., 1970.
Modleski, Tania. *Feminism without Women: Culture and Criticism in a "Postfeminist" Age.* New York: Routledge, 1991.
Moi, Toril. *"Whatz Is a Woman?" and Other Essays.* New York: Oxford University Press, 1999.
Nicholson, Linda J., ed. *Feminism/Postmodernism.* New York: Routledge, 1990.
———. *Gender and History: The Limits of Social Theory in the Age of the Family.* New York: Columbia University Press, 1986.
Ortner, Sherry, and Harriet Whitehead, eds. *Sexual Meanings: The Cultural Construction of Gender and Sexuality.* Cambridge: Cambridge University Press, 1981.
Paglia, Camille. *Sex, Art and American Culture: Essays.* New York: Vintage, 1992.
Rich, Adrienne. *Of Woman Born: Motherhood as Experience and Institution.* New York: W. W. Norton & Co., 1976.
Rosaldo, Michelle, and Louise Lamphere, eds. *Women, Culture and Society.* Stanford, CA: Stanford University Press, 1974.
Rosen, Ruth. *The World Split Open: How the Modern Women's Movement Changed America.* New York: Viking, 2000.
Scott, Joan W. *Gender and the Politics of History.* New York: Columbia University Press, 1988.
———. *Only Paradoxes to Offer: French Feminists and the Rights of Man.* Cambridge: Harvard University Press, 1996.
Showalter, Elaine. *The New Feminist Criticism: Essays on Women, Literature, and Theory.* New York: Pantheon Books, 1985.
Suleiman, Susan Rubin, ed. "(Re)Writing the Body: The Politics and Poetics of Female Eroticism." In *The Female Body in Western Culture: Contemporary Perspectives,* 7–29. Cambridge: Harvard University Press, 1986.
Thornham, Sue. *Feminist Theory and Cultural Studies: Stories of Unsettled Relations.* London: Arnold; New York: Oxford University Press, 2000.
Woolf, Virginia. *A Room of One's Own.* New York: Harcourt Brace & Co., 1929.

African, African American (Womanist and Black Feminist), Latin American, Asian Feminist Thought

Bird, Phyllis, ed. *Reading the Bible as Women: Perspectives from Africa, Asia, and Latin America.* Semeia 78. Atlanta: Scholars Press, 1997.

Briggs, Sheila. "Buried with Christ: The Politics of Identity and the Poverty of Interpretation." In Regina Schwartz, ed., *The Book and the Text: The Bible and Literary Theory,* 276–303. New York: Blackwell, 1990.

Brown, Kelly Delaine. "God Is as Christ Does: Toward a Womanist Theology." *JRT* 46, no. 1 (1989): 7–16.

Cannon, Katie Geneva. *Black Womanist Ethics.* Atlanta: Scholars Press, 1988.

————. "Response to Cheryl Sanders' "Christian Ethics and Theology in Womanist Perspective." *JFSR* 5, no. 2 (1989): 92–94.

Cannon, Katie Geneva, and Elisabeth Schüssler Fiorenza, eds. *Interpretation for Liberation. Semeia* 47 (1989).

Chung, Hyun Kyung. *Struggle to Be the Sun Again: Introducing Asian Women's Theology.* Maryknoll, NY: Orbis Books, 1990.

Cleage, Pearl. *Deals with the Devil and Other Reasons to Riot.* New York: Ballantine Books, 1993.

Collins, Patricia Hill. *Black Feminist Thought: Knowledge, Consciousness, and the Politics of Empowerment.* New York: Routledge, 1991.

————. "What's in a Name? Womanism, Black Feminism, and Beyond." *The Black Scholar* (San Francisco) 26:1 (Winter/Spring 1996): 9ff. http://www.gse.buffalo.edu/FAS/Bromley/classes/theory/Collins.htm

Cooper, Valerie C. "Some Place to Cry: Jephthah's Daughter and the Double Dilemma of Black Women in America." In Cheryl A. Kirk-Duggan, ed., *Pregnant Passion: Gender, Sex, and Violence in the Bible,* 181–92. Semeia Studies 44. Atlanta: SBL Press, 2003.

Copeland, M. Shawn. "Response to Cheryl Sanders' 'Christian Ethics and Theology in Womanist Perspective.'" *JFSR* 5, no. 2 (1989): 97–102.

Douglas, Kelly Brown. *The Black Christ.* Maryknoll, NY: Orbis Books, 1994.

Dube (Shomanah), Musa W. "Jumping the Fire with Judith: Postcolonial Feminist Hermeneutics of Liberation." In Silvia Schroer and Sophia Bietenhard, eds., *Feminist Interpretation of the Bible and the Hermeneutics of Liberation,* 60–76. JSOTSup 374. Sheffield, UK: Sheffield Academic Press, 2003.

————, ed. *Other Ways of Reading: African Women and the Bible.* Global Perspectives on Biblical Scholarship 2. Atlanta: SBL Press; Geneva: WCC Publications, 2001.

————. *Postcolonial Feminist Interpretation of the Bible.* St. Louis: Chalice Press, 2000.

Gates, Henry Louis, ed. *Reading Black, Reading Feminist: A Critical Anthology.* New York: Meridian, 1990.

Grant, Jacquelyn. *White Women's Christ and Black Women's Jesus: Feminist Christology and Womanist Response.* Atlanta: Scholars Press, 1989.

Hayes, Diana L. "And When We Speak: To Be Black, Catholic, and Womanist." In Diana L. Hayes and Cyprian Davis, eds., *Taking Down Our Harps,* 102–19. Maryknoll, NY: Orbis Books, 1989.

————. *Hagar's Daughters: Womanist Ways of Being in the World.* Mahwah, NJ: Paulist Press, 1995.

hooks, bell. *Feminist Theory from Margin to Center.* Boston: South End Press, 1984.

————. "Response to Cheryl Sanders' 'Christian Ethics and Theology in Womanist Perspective.'" *JFSR* 5, no. 2 (1989): 102–4.

————. *Talking Back: Thinking Feminist, Thinking Black.* Boston: South End Press, 1989.

————. *Yearning: Race, Gender, and Cultural Politics.* Boston: South End Press, 1990.

Hull, Gloria T., Patricia Bell Scott, and Barbara Smith, eds. *All the Women Are White, All the Blacks Are Men, But Some of Us Are Brave.* Old Westbury, NY: Feminist Press, 1981.

Isasi-Díaz, Ada Maria. "The Bible and Mujerista Theology." In Susan Brooks Thistlethwaite and Potter Engel, eds., *Lift Every Voice: Constructing Christian Theologies from the Underside.* San Francisco: Harper & Row, 1990.

Isasi-Díaz, Ada Maria, and F. F. Segovia, eds. *Hispanic/Latino Theology: Challenge and Promise.* Minneapolis: Fortress Press, 1996.

James, Stanlie M., and Abena P. A. Busia, eds. *Theorizing Black Feminisms: The Visionary Pragmatism of Black Women.* London: Routledge, 1993.

Kim, Hyun Chul Paul. "Gender Complementarity in the Hebrew Bible." In Wonil Kim et al., eds., *Reading the Hebrew Bible for a New Millennium,* 1:253–91. Harrisburg, PA: Trinity Press International, 2000.

Kwok, Pui-Lan. "Discovering the Bible in the Non-Biblical World." *Semeia* 47 (1989): 25–42.

——. *Discovering the Bible in the Non-Biblical World*. Maryknoll, NY: Orbis, 1995.

Lee, Oo Chung, et al., eds. *Women of Courage: Asian Women Reading the Bible*. Seoul, Korea: Asian Women's Resource Centre for Culture and Theology, 1992.

Lorde, Audre. "The Master's Tools Will Never Dismantle the Master's House: Comments at 'The Personal and the Political' Panel (Second Sex Conference, October 29, 1979)." In C. Moraga and G. Anzaldúa, eds., *This Bridge Called My Back: Writings by Radical Women of Color*, 2nd ed., 98–101. New York: Kitchen Table, 1983.

——. *Sister Outsider: Essays and Speeches*. Freedom, CA: Crossing Press, 1984.

Masenye, Madipoane (ngwana' Mphahlele). "A *Bosadi* (Womanhood) Reading of Proverbs 31:10–31." In Musa W. Dube, ed., *Other Ways of Reading: African Women and the Bible*, 145–57.

——. *Making the Context of African–South African Women a Hermeneutical Focus in Theological Education*. A National Initiative for the Contextualisation of Theological Education Publication 21. Johannesburg, South Africa: NICTE, 2000.

——. "Rereading the Bible the Bosadi (Womanhood) Way." *Bulletin of Contextual Theology in South Africa* 4 (1997): 15–16.

Minh-ha, Trinh T. *Women, Native, Other: Writing Postcoloniality and Feminism*. Bloomington: Indiana University Press, 1989.

Moraga, Cherrie, and Gloria Anzaidúa, eds. *This Bridge Called My Back: Writings by Radical Women of Color*. Watertown, MA: Persephone Press, 1984.

Mwaura, Philomean Njeri. "Feminist Biblical Interpretation and the Hermeneutics of Liberation: An African Woman's Perspective." In Silvia Schroer and Sophia Bietenhard, eds., *Feminist Interpretation of the Bible and the Hermeneutics of Liberation*, 77–85. JSOTSup 374. Sheffield, UK: Sheffield Academic Press, 2003.

Pereira, Nancy Cardoso. "Changing Seasons: About the Bible and Other Sacred Texts in Latin America." In Silvia Schroer and Sophia Bietenhard, eds., *Feminist Interpretation of the Bible and the Hermeneutics of Liberation*, 48–58. JSOTSup 374. Sheffield, UK: Sheffield Academic Press, 2003.

Saldívar-Hull, Sonia. *Feminism on the Border: Chicana Gender Politics and Literature*. Berkeley and Los Angeles: University of California Press, 2000.

Sanders, Cheryl J. "Christian Ethics and Theology in Womanist Perspective" and "A Final Rejoinder." *JFSR* 5, no. 2 (1989): 83–91, 109–12.

——. "Womanist Theology/Feminist Theology: A Dialogue." *Daughters of Sarah* 15, no. 2 (March/April 1989): 6–7.

Smith, Barbara, ed. *Home Girls: A Black Feminist Anthology*. New York: Kitchen Table–Women of Color Press, 1983.

Tan, Yak-Hwee. "The Question of Social Location and Postcolonial Feminist Hermeneutics of Liberation." In Silvia Schroer and Sophia Bietenhard, eds., *Feminist Interpretation of the Bible and the Hermeneutics of Liberation*, 171–78. JSOTSup 374. Sheffield, UK: Sheffield Academic Press, 2003.

Townes, Emilie M. "Response to Cheryl Sanders' 'Christian Ethics and Theology in Womanist Perspective.'" *JFSR* 5, no. 2 (1989): 94–97.

Walker, Alice. *The Color Purple*. New York: Harcourt Brace Jovanovich, 1982.

——. *In Search of Our Mothers' Gardens: Womanist Prose*. San Diego: Harcourt Brace Jovanovich, 1983.

Weems, Renita J. *Just a Sister Away: A Womanist Vision of Women's Relationships in the Bible*. San Diego: LuraMedia, 1988.

——. "Reading Her Way through the Struggle: African American Women and the Bible." In Cain Hope Felder, ed., *Stony the Road We Trod: African American Biblical Interpretation*. Minneapolis: Fortress Press, 1991.

——. "Rereading for Liberation: African American Women and the Bible." In Silvia Schroer and Sophia Bietenhard, eds., *Feminist Interpretation of the Bible and the Hermeneutics of Liberation*, 19–32. JSOTSup 374. Sheffield, UK: Sheffield Academic Press, 2003.

Williams, Delores. "Breaking and Bonding." *Daughters of Sarah* 15, no. 3 (May/June 1989): 20–21.

——. "The Color of Feminism: Or Speaking the Black Woman's Tongue." *JRT* 43, no. 1 (1986): 42–58.

——. *Sisters in the Wilderness: The Challenge of Womanist God-Talk*. Maryknoll, NY: Orbis Books, 1993.

African and African American Issues in Classical and Biblical Literature

Bernal, Martin. *Black Athena: The Afroasiatic Roots of Classical Civilization.* New Brunswick, NJ: Rutgers University Press, 1987.

Dube, Musa W., Nadar Sarojini, and Velma Love, eds. *Kimba Vita African Women's Bible Commentary.* Louisville, KY: Westminster John Knox Press, forthcoming.

Felder, Cain Hope. ed. *Stony the Road We Trod: African American Biblical Interpretation.* Minneapolis: Fortress Press, 1991.

———. *Troubling Biblical Waters: Race, Class, and Family.* Maryknoll, NY: Orbis Books, 1989.

Gier, Nicholas F. "The Color of Sin/The Color of Skin: Ancient Color Blindness and the Philosophical Origins of Modern Racism." *JRT* 46, no. 1 (1989): 42–52.

Holter, Kurt. *Yahweh in Africa: Essays on Africa and the Old Testament.* Bible and Theology in Africa 1. New York: Lang, 2000.

James, George G. M. *Stolen Legacy: The Greeks Were Not the Authors of Greek Philosophy, But the People of North Africa, Commonly Called the Egyptians.* London: African Publication Society, 1972.

Mosala, Itumelung. *Biblical Hermeneutics and Black Theology in South Africa.* Grand Rapids: Wm. B. Eerdmans Publishing Co., 1989.

Snowden, Frank M., Jr. *Before Color Prejudice: The Ancient View of Blacks.* Cambridge: Harvard University Press, 1983.

———. *Blacks in Antiquity: Ethiopians in the Greco-Roman Experience.* Cambridge: Harvard University Press, 1970.

Van Sertima, Ivan, ed. *Black Women in Antiquity.* New Brunswick, NJ: Transaction Books, 1984.

West, Gerald O. *Biblical Hermeneutics of Liberation: Modes of Reading the Bible in the South African Context.* 2nd edition. Maryknoll, NY: Orbis Books, 1995.

West, Gerald O., and Musa W. Dube, eds. *The Bible in Africa: Transaction, Trajectories and Trends.* Leiden: E. J. Brill, 2001.

Wimbush, Vincent L., ed. *African Americans and the Bible.* New York: Continuum, 2001.

Global, Postcolonial, and Postmodern Thought

Beverly, J., M. Aronna, and J. Oviedo. *The Postmodernism Debate in Latin America.* Durham: Duke University Press, 1995.

The Bible and Culture Collective. *The Postmodern Bible.* New Haven, CT: Yale University Press, 1995.

Donaldson, Laura E., ed. *Postcolonialism and Scriptural Reading. Semeia* 75. Atlanta: SBL Press, 1996.

Dube (Shomanah), Musa W. "Postcolonial Feminist Interpretation of the Bible." In Phyllis A. Bird, Katharine Doob Sakenfeld, and Sharon H. Ringe, eds., *Reading the Bible as Women: Perspectives from Latin America, Africa, and Asia. Semeia* 78 (1997): 11–26.

———. *Postcolonial Feminist Interpretation of the Bible.* St. Louis: Chalice, 2000.

Ferro, Marc. *Colonization: A Global History.* London: Routledge, 1997.

Gandhi, Leela. *Postcolonial Theory: A Critical Introduction.* New York: Columbia University Press, 1998.

Harvey, David. *The Condition of Postmodernity: An Enquiry into the Origins of Cultural Change.* Oxford: Blackwell, 1990.

Hopkins, D. N., E. Mendieta, and D. Batstone, eds. *Religions/Globalizations: Theories and Cases.* Durham: Duke University Press, 2001.

Jameson, Fredric, and Masao Miyoshi, eds. *The Cultures of Globalization.* Durham: Duke University Press, 1998.

Jenkins, Keith. *The Postmodern History Reader.* New York: Routledge, 1997.

Jobling, David, Tina Pippin, and Ronald Schleifer, eds. *The Postmodern Bible Reader.* Oxford: Blackwell, 2001.

López, Alfred J. *Posts and Pasts: A Theory of Postcolonialism.* Explorations in Postcolonial Studies. Albany: State University of New York Press, 2001.

Loomba, Ania. *Colonialism/Postcolonialism.* The New Critical Idiom. London: Routledge, 1998.

McKinlay, Judith E. *Reframing Her: Biblical Women in Postcolonial Focus.* Sheffield, UK: Sheffield Phoenix Press, 2004.

Moore, Stephen, and Fernando F. Segovia, eds. *Postcolonial Biblical Interpretation: Interdisciplinary Intersections.* Bible and Postcolonialism. London: T. & T. Clark, 2005.

Nicholson, Linda, ed. *Feminism/Postmodernism.* New York: Routledge, 1990.

Patte, Daniel. *Global Bible Commentary.* Nashville: Abingdon, 2004.

Pui-lan, Kwok. *Discovering the Bible in the Non-Biblical World.* Bible and Liberation Series. Maryknoll, NY: Orbis Books, 1995.

Segovia, F. F. *Decolonizing Biblical Studies: A View from the Margins.* Maryknoll, NY: Orbis Books, 2000.

———. *Interpreting beyond Borders.* Bible and Postcolonialism 3. Sheffield, UK: Sheffield Academic Press, 2000.

Segovia, F. F., and Mary Ann Tolbert, eds. *Social Location and Biblical Interpretation in Global Perspective,* vol. 2 of *Reading from This Place.* Minneapolis: Fortress Press, 1995.

———. *Social Location and Biblical Interpretation in the United States,* vol. 1 of *Reading from This Place.* Minneapolis: Fortress Press, 1995.

Sugirtharajah, Rasiah S. *Asian Biblical Hermeneutics and Postcolonialism: Contesting the Interpretations.* Biblical Seminar 64. Sheffield, UK: Sheffield Academic Press, 1998.

———. *The Bible and the Third World: Precolonial, Colonial and Postcolonial Encounters.* Cambridge: Cambridge University Press, 2001.

———. ed. *The Postcolonial Bible.* Bible and Postcolonialism 1. Sheffield, UK: Sheffield Academic Press, 1998.

———. *Postcolonial Criticism and Biblical Interpretation.* Oxford: Oxford University Press, 2002.

———. *Postcolonial Reconfigurations: An Alternative Way of Reading the Bible and Doing Theology.* London: SCM, 2003.

———. *Voices from the Margin: Interpreting the Bible in the Third World.* Maryknoll, NY: Orbis Books, 1994.

Tan, Yak-Hwee. "The Question of Social Location and Postcolonial Feminist Hermeneutics of Liberation." In Silvia Schroer and Sophia Bietenhard, eds., *Feminist Interpretation of the Bible and the Hermeneutics of Liberation,* 171–78. JSOTSup 374. Sheffield, UK: Sheffield Academic Press, 2003.

Vander Stichele, Caroline, and Todd Penner, eds. *Her Master's Tools? Feminist and Postcolonial Engagements of Historical-Critical Discourse.* Global Perspectives on Biblical Scholarship 9. Atlanta: SBL Press, 2005.

Williams, P., and L. Chrisman, eds. *Colonial Discourse and Postcolonial Theory: A Reader.* New York: Harvester Wheatsheaf, 1993.

CHAPTER 2: THE STORY OF EVE

Bal, Mieke. "Sexuality, Sin, and Sorrow: The Emergence of the Female Character." In *Lethal Love: Feminist Literary Readings of Biblical Love Stories,* 104–30. Indiana Studies in Biblical Literature. Bloomington: Indiana University Press, 1987.

Bechtel, Lyn M. "Genesis 2:4b-3:24: A Myth about Human Maturation." *JSOT* 67 (1995): 3–26.

———. "Rethinking the Interpretation of Genesis 2.4b–3.24." In Athalya Brenner, ed., *A Feminist Companion to Genesis,* 17–117. FCB 1/2. Sheffield, UK: Sheffield Academic Press, 1993.

Bellis, Alice Ogden. "Eve in the Apocryphal/Deuterocanonical Books." In *WIS,* 82–83.

Bird, Phyllis A. "Genesis 1–3." Part III of *Missing Persons and Mistaken Identities: Women and Gender in Ancient Israel,* 123–93. Overtures to Biblical Theology. Minneapolis: Fortress, 1997.

———. "'Male and Female He Created Them': Gen 1:27b in the Context of the Priestly Account of Creation." *HTR* 74 (1981): 129–59.

Bledstein, Adrien Janis. "Are Women Cursed in Genesis 3.16?" In Athalya Brenner, ed., *A Feminist Companion to Genesis,* 142–45. FCB 1/2. Sheffield, UK: Sheffield Academic Press, 1993, rep., 1997.

———. "The Genesis of Humans: The Garden of Eden Revisited." *Judaism* 26, no. 2 (1977): 187–200.

———. "Was Eve Cursed or Did a Woman Write Genesis?" *Bible Review,* February 1993, 42–45.

Bronner, Leila Leah. "Eve's Estate: Temptation, Modesty, and the Valorization of Matrimony." In *From Eve to Esther: Rabbinic Reconstructions of Biblical Women*, 22–41. Louisville, KY: Westminster John Knox, 1994.

Brueggemann, Walter. "Of the Same Flesh and Bone (GN 2, 23a)." *CBQ* 32 (1970): 532–42.

Cainion, Ivory J. "An Analogy of the Song of Songs and Genesis Chapters Two and Three." *SJOT* 14:2 (2000): 219–59.

Callaway, Mary. *Sing, O Barren One: A Study in Comparative Midrash*. SBLDS 91. Atlanta: Scholars Press, 1986.

Cary, Phillip. "Seeing through Adam's Excuse." *Daughters of Sarah* 14, no. 4 (July/August 1988): 7–11.

Clines, David J. A. "What Does Eve Do to Help? And Other Irredeemably Androcentric Orientations in Genesis 1–3." In *What Does Eve Do to Help? And Other Readerly Questions to the Old Testament*, 29–48. JSOTSup 94. Sheffield, UK: JSOT Press, 1990.

Davies, Philip R. "Women, Men, Gods, Sex and Power: The Birth of a Biblical Myth." In Athalya Brenner, ed., *A Feminist Companion to Genesis*, 194–201. FCB 1/2. Sheffield, UK: Sheffield Academic Press, 1993, rep., 1997.

Freedman, R. David. "Woman, A Power Equal to Man: Translation of Woman as a 'Fit Helpmate' for Man Is Questioned." *BARev* 9, no. 1 (January/February 1983): 56–58.

Frymer-Kensky, Tikva. "The Atrahasis Epic and Its Significance for Our Understanding of Genesis 1–9." *BA* 40 (1977): 147–55.

Fuchs, Esther. "Who Is Hiding the Truth? Deceptive Women and Biblical Androcentrism." In Adela Yarbro Collins, ed., *Feminist Perspectives on Biblical Scholarship*, 137–44. SBLBSNA 10. Chico, CA: Scholars Press, 1985.

Gardner, Anne E. "Genesis 2:4b–3: A Mythological Paradigm of Sexual Equality or of the Religious History of Pre-Exilic Israel?" *Scottish Journal of Theology* 43 (1990): 1–18.

Goldstein, Rebecca. "Looking Back at Lot's Wife." In Celina Spiegel and Christina Buchmann, eds., *Out of the Garden: Women Writers on the Bible*, 37–41. New York: Fawcett Columbine, 1994.

Haag, Herbert, Dorothee Sölle, Katharina Elliger, and Marianne Grohmann. Trans. Brian McNeil. *Great Couples of the Bible*. Minneapolis: Fortress Press, 2006.

Hayter, Mary. "Man and Woman in Creation and Fall." In *The New Eve in Christ: The Use and Abuse of the Bible in the Debate about Women in the Church*, 95–117. Grand Rapids: Wm. B. Eerdmans Publishing Co., 1987.

Higgins, Jean M. "The Myth of Eve: The Temptress." *JAAR* 44 (1976): 639–47.

Horowitz, Maryanne Cline. "The Image of God in Man—Is Woman Included?" *HTR* 72 (1979): 175–206.

Hyman, Naomi Mara. "Lilith and Eve." In *Biblical Women in the Midrash: A Sourcebook*, 1–14. Northvale, NJ, and London: Jason Aronson, 1997.

Jobling, David. "Myth and Its Limits in Genesis 2:4b–3:24." In Lowell K. Handy, ed., *The Sense of Biblical Narrative: Structural Analyses in the Hebrew Bible*, 2:470–92. Leiden: E. J. Brill, 1986.

Kimelman, Reuven. "The Seduction of Eve and the Exegetical Politics of Gender." In Alice Bach, ed., *Women in the Hebrew Bible: A Reader*, 241–70. New York and London: Routledge, 1999.

Korsak, Mary Phil. ". . . et GENETRIX." In Athalya Brenner, ed., *Genesis*, 22–31. FCB 2/1. Sheffield, UK: Sheffield Academic Press, 1998.

———. "Genesis: A New Look." In Athalya Brenner, ed., *A Feminist Companion to Genesis*, 39–52. FCB 1/2. Sheffield, UK: Sheffield Academic Press, 1993, rep., 1997.

Kvam, Kristen E., Linda S. Schearing, and Valarie H. Ziegler, eds. *Eve and Adam: Jewish, Christian, and Muslim Readings on Genesis and Gender*. Bloomington: Indiana University Press, 1999.

Lanser, Susan S. "(Feminist) Criticism in the Garden: Inferring Genesis 2–3." *Semeia* 41 (1988): 67–84.

Layton, Scott C. "Remarks on the Canaanite Origin of Eve." *CBQ* 59 (1997): 22–32.

Levison, Jack. "Is Eve to Blame? A Contextual Analysis of Sirach 25:24." *CBQ* 47 (1985): 617–23.

Meyers, Carol. *Discovering Eve: Ancient Israelite Women in Context*. New York: Oxford University Press, 1988.

———. "Eve." In *WIS*, 79–81.

Mikaelsson, Lisbeth. "Sexual Polarity: An Aspect of the Ideological Structure in the Paradise Narrative, Gen 2,4–3,24." *Temenos* 16 (1980): 84–91.

Millett, Craig Ballard. "The Wife." In *Archetypes of Women in Scripture: In God's Image*, 73–90. San Diego: LuraMedia, 1989.

Milne, Pamela J. "Eve and Adam: Is a Feminist Reading Possible?" *Bible Review* 4, no. 3 (1988): 12–21, 39.

———. "The Patriarchal Stamp of Scripture: The Implication of Structural Analyses for Feminist Hermeneutics." *JFSR* 5, no. 1 (1989): 17–34. And in Athalya Brenner, ed., *A Feminist Companion to Genesis*, 146–72. FCB 1/2. Sheffield, UK: Sheffield Academic Press, 1993, rep. 1997.

Morris, Paul, and Deborah Sawyer, eds. *A Walk in the Garden: Biblical, Iconographical, and Literary Images of Eden*. Sheffield, UK: Sheffield Academic Press, 1992.

Niditch, Susan. "Genesis." In *WBC*, 13–29.

Nowell, Irene. "Woman, Image of God: Eve, Wisdom/Sophia." In *Women in the Old Testament*, 131–52. Collegeville, MN: Liturgical Press, 1997.

Pagels, Elaine. *Adam, Eve, and the Serpent*. New York: Random House, 1988.

Pardes, Ilana. "Beyond Genesis 3: The Politics of Maternal Naming." In *Countertraditions in the Bible: A Feminist Approach*, 39–59. Cambridge: Harvard University Press, 1992. And in Athalya Brenner, ed., *A Feminist Companion to Genesis*, 173–93. FCB 1/2, Sheffield, UK: Sheffield Academic Press, 1993, rep., 1997.

———. "Creation according to Eve." In *Countertraditions in the Bible: A Feminist Approach*, 13–38. Cambridge: Harvard University Press, 1992.

Phillips, John A. *Eve: The History of an Idea*. San Francisco: Harper & Row, 1984.

Phipps, William E. *Genesis and Gender: Biblical Myths of Sexuality and Their Cultural Impact*. New York: Praeger Publishers, 1989.

Piskorowski, Anna. "In Search of Her Father: A Lacanian Approach to Genesis 2–3." In P. Morris and Deborah Sawyer, eds., *A Walk in the Garden: Biblical, Iconographic, and Literary Images of Eden*, 310–18. Sheffield, UK: Sheffield Academic Press, 1992.

Rashkow, Ilona R. "Daughters and Fathers in Genesis . . . Or, What is Wrong with this Picture?" In Athalya Brenner, ed., *A Feminist Companion to Exodus and Deuteronomy*, 22–36. FCB 1/6. Sheffield, UK: Sheffield Academic Press, 1994.

Rosenblatt, Naomi Harris. "The First Rebel." In Susan Headen and Jeffery L. Sheler, eds., *Women of the Bible: Provocative New Insights*, 10–17. *U.S. News and World Report* Special Collector's Edition, 2005.

Ross, Ellen M. "Human Persons as Images of the Divine." In Alice Bach, ed., *The Pleasure of Her Text: Feminist Readings of Biblical and Historical Texts*, 97–116. Philadelphia: Trinity Press International, 1990.

Russell, H. Diane. "Eve." In H. Diane Russell, ed., with Bernadine Barnes, *Eve/Ave: Women in Renaissance and Baroque Prints*, 113–30. Washington, DC: National Gallery of Art; New York: The Feminist Press at the City University, 1990.

Sawyer, Deborah F. "Resurrecting Eve? Feminist Critique of the Garden of Eden." In P. Morris and Deborah Sawyer, eds., *A Walk in the Garden: Biblical, Iconographic, and Literary Images of Eden*, 273–89. Sheffield, UK: Sheffield Academic Press, 1992.

Schottroff, Luise. "The Creation Narrative: Genesis 1.1—2.4a." In Athalya Brenner, ed., *A Feminist Companion to Genesis*, 24–38. FCB 1/2. Sheffield, UK: Sheffield Academic Press, 1993, rep., 1997.

Schüngel-Straumann, Helen. "On the Creation of Man and Woman in Genesis 1–3: The History and Reception of the Texts Reconsidered." In Athalya Brenner, ed., *A Feminist Companion to Genesis*, 53–76. FCB 1/2. Sheffield, UK: Sheffield Academic Press, 1993, rep. 1997.

Sharon, Diane M. "The Doom of Paradise: Literary Patterns in Accounts of Paradise and Mortality in the Hebrew Bible and the Ancient Near East." In Athalya Brenner, ed., *Genesis*, 53–80. FCB 2/1. Sheffield, UK: Sheffield Academic Press, 1998.

Shemesh, Yael. "Rape Is Rape Is Rape: The Story of Dinah and Shechem (Genesis 34)." *ZAW*, forthcoming.

Simkins, Ronald A. "Gender Construction in the Yahwist Creation Myth." In Athalya Brenner, ed., *Genesis*, 32–52. FCB 2/1. Sheffield, UK: Sheffield Academic Press, 1998.

Sölle, Dorothée, et al. "Eve and Lilith." In *Great Women of the Bible in Art and Literature*, 10–31. Trans. Joe H. Kirchberger. Macon, GA: Mercer University Press, 1994.

Spanier, Ktziah. "Rachel's Theft of the Teraphim: Her Struggle for Family Primacy." *VT* 42 (1992): 404–12.

Stratton, Beverly J. *Out of Eden: Reading, Rhetoric, and Ideology in Genesis 2–3.* JSOTSup 208. Sheffield, UK: JSOT Press, 1995.

Streete, Gail Corrington. *The Strange Woman: Power and Sex in the Bible.* Louisville, KY: Westminster John Knox Press, 1997.

Trenchard, Warren C. *Ben Sira's Analysis of Women: A Literary Analysis.* Chico, CA: Scholars Press, 1982.

Trible, Phyllis. "Depatriarchalizing in Biblical Interpretation." *JAAR* 41 (1973): 35–42.

———. "Eve and Adam: Genesis 2–3 Reread." *Andover Newton Quarterly* 13 (1973): 251–58.

———. "Eve and Miriam: From the Margins to the Center." In Hershel Shanks, ed., *Feminist Approaches to the Bible,* 5–26. Washington, DC: Biblical Archaeology Society, 1995.

———. *God and the Rhetoric of Sexuality.* Overtures to Biblical Theology. Philadelphia: Fortress Press, 1978.

———. "Not a Jot, Not a Tittle: Genesis 2–3 after Twenty Years." In Linda S. Schearing, Valarie H. Ziegler, Kristen E. Kvam, eds., *Eve and Adam: Jewish, Christian, and Muslim Readings on Genesis and Gender.* Bloomington: Indiana University Press, 1999.

Trible, Phyllis, and Letty M. Russell. *Hagar, Sarah, and Their Children: Jewish, Christian, and Muslim Perspectives.* Louisville, KY: Westminster John Knox Press, 2006.

van der Horst, Pieter W. "Eve in the New Testament." In *WIS,* 84.

Van Wolde, Ellen J. *A Semiotic Analysis of Genesis 2–3: A Semiotic Theory and Method of Analysis Applied to the Story of the Garden of Eden.* Studia semitica neerlandica. Maastricht, The Netherlands: Van Gorcum/Assen, 1989.

Yee, Gale. "Eve in Genesis: The Mother of All Living and We Her Children." In *Poor Banished Children of Eve: Woman as Evil in the Hebrew Bible,* 59–80. Minneapolis: Fortress Press, 2003.

———. "Gender, Class, and the Social-Scientific Study of Genesis 2–3." *Semeia* 87 (1999): 177–92.

CHAPTER 3: THE WOMEN IN GENESIS

Allen, Christine Garside. "Who Was Rebekah? 'On Me Be the Curse, My Son.'" In Rita M. Gross, ed., *Beyond Androcentrism: New Essays on Women and Religion,* 183–216. Missoula, MT: Scholars Press, 1977.

Amit, Yairah. "Implicit Reduction and Latent Polemic in the Story of the Rape of Dinah." In Michael V. Fox et al., eds., *Texts, Temples and Tradition: A Tribute to Menahem Haran,* 11–28. Winona Lake, IN: Eisenbrauns, 1996.

Armstrong, Karen. *In the Beginning: A New Interpretation of Genesis.* New York: Knopf, 1996.

Bach, Alice. *Reading the Women of the Bible: A New Interpretation of Their Stories.* New York: Schocken Books, 2002.

———. *Women, Seduction, and Betrayal in Biblical Narrative.* Cambridge: Cambridge University Press, 1997.

Bailey, Clinton. "How Desert Culture Helps Us Understand the Bible: Bedouin Law Explains Reaction to Rape of Dinah." *Bible Review* 7 (1991): 14–21, 38.

Bailey, Wilma Ann. "Black and Jewish Women Consider Hagar." *Encounter* 63:1–2 (2002): 37–44.

———. "Hagar: A Model for an Anabaptist Feminist?" *Mennonite Quarterly Review* 68:2 (1994): 219–28.

Bal, Mieke. "One Woman, Many Men, and the Dialectic of Chronology." In *Lethal Love: Feminist Literary Readings of Biblical Love Stories,* 89–103. Bloomington: Indiana University Press, 1987.

Bechtel, Lyn M. "Dinah." In *WIS,* 69–71.

———. "A Feminist Reading of Genesis 19:1–11." In Athalya Brenner, ed., *Genesis,* 108–29. FCB 2/1. Sheffield, UK: Sheffield Academic Press, 1998.

———. "What If Dinah Is Not Raped? (Genesis 34)." *JSOT* 62 (1994): 19–36.

Bellis, Alice Ogden. "A Sister Is a Forever Friend." *JRT* 55:2/56:1 (1999): 109–116.

Benvenuto, Christine. "In the Wilderness with Hagar." *Tikkun* 14 (1999): 62–63.

Bird, Phyllis A. "The Harlot as Heroine: Narrative Art and Social Presupposition in Three Old Testament Texts." *Semeia* 46 (1989): 119–39. And in Alice Bach, ed., *Women in the Hebrew Bible: A Reader,* 99–118. New York and London: Routledge, 1999.

———. "To Play the Harlot." In Peggy L. Day, ed., *Gender and Difference in Ancient Israel*, 75–94. Minneapolis: Fortress Press, 1989.

Bledstein, Adrien Janis. "Binder, Trickster, Heel and Hairy-man: Rereading Genesis 27 as a Trickster Tale Told by a Woman." In Athalya Brenner, ed., *A Feminist Companion to Genesis*, 282–95. FCB 1/2. Sheffield, UK: Sheffield Academic Press, 1993.

———. "The Trials of Sarah." *Judaism* 30 (1981): 411–17.

Bos, Johanna W. H. "An Eye Opener at the Gate: George Coats and Genesis 38." *Lexington Theological Quarterly* 27 (1992): 119–23.

———. "Out of the Shadows: Genesis 38; Judges 4:17–22; Ruth 3." In J. Cheryl Exum and Johanna W. H. Bos, eds., *Reasoning with the Foxes: Female Wit in a World of Male Power. Semeia* 42 (1988): 37–67.

Brenner, Athalya. "Female Social Behaviour: Two Descriptive Patterns within the 'Birth of the Hero' Paradigm." *VT* 36 (1986): 257–73.

———, ed. *A Feminist Companion to Genesis*. FCB 1/2. Sheffield, UK: Sheffield Academic Press, 1993.

———. ed. *Genesis*. FCB 2/1. Sheffield, UK: Sheffield Academic Press, 1998.

———. "War, Culture, Wives—Mothers from A to Z: We Are Adah and Zillah," "I Am the Twelfth Sheep: Dinah," "Lust Is My Middle Name, I Have No Other: Potiphar's Wife," and "A Double Date: We Are Tamar and Tamar." In *I Am . . . Biblical Women Tell Their Own Stories*, 9–24, 25–49, 50–57, 133–46. Minneapolis: Fortress Press, 2005.

Brenner, Athalya, and J. W. van Henten. "Madame Potiphar through a Culture Trip, or, Which Side Are You On?" In J. Cheryl Exum and Stephen D. Moore, eds., *Biblical Studies/Cultural Studies: The Third Sheffield Colloquium*, 203–19. JSOTSup 266. Sheffield, UK: Sheffield Academic Press, 1998.

Callaway, Mary. *Sing, O Barren One: A Study in Comparative Midrash*. SBLDS 91. Atlanta: Scholars Press, 1986.

Cannon, Katie Geneva. "On Remembering Who We Are." In Ella Pearson Mitchell, ed., *Those Preachin' Women: Sermons by Black Women Preachers*, 43–50. Valley Forge, PA: Judson Press, 1985.

Cartledge-Hayes, Mary. "Sarah. Laughing." *Daughters of Sarah* 13, no. 1 (January/February 1987): 8–9.

Castelli, Elizabeth A. "Allegories of Hagar Reading Galatians 4:21–31 with Postmodern Feminist Eyes." In Edgar V. McKnight and Elizabeth Struthers Malbon, eds., *The New Literary Criticism and the New Testament*, 228–50. Sheffield, UK: Sheffield Academic Press, 1994.

Chittister, Joan. *The Friendship of Women: The Hidden Tradition of the Bible*. Erie, PA: Bluebridge Benetvision, 2006.

Cook, Joan E. "Four Marginalized Foils—Tamar, Judah, Joseph and Potiphar's Wife: A Literary Study of Genesis 38–39." *Proceedings—Great Lakes and Midwest Biblical Societies* 21 (2001): 115–28.

Darr, Katheryn Pfisterer. *Far More Precious Than Jewels: Perspectives on Biblical Women*. Louisville, KY: Westminster/John Knox Press, 1991.

———. "More Than the Stars of the Heavens: Critical Rabbinical, and Feminist Perspectives on Sarah" and "More Than a Possession: Critical Rabbinical, and Feminist Perspectives on Hagar." In *Far More Precious Than Jewels: Perspectives on Biblical Women*, 55–84, 132–63. Gender and the Biblical Tradition 1. Louisville, KY: Westminster/John Knox Press, 1991.

Davidson, Jo Ann. "Genesis Matriarchs Engage Feminism." *Andrews University Seminary Studies* 40:2 (2002): 159–78.

Delaney, Carol. "Abraham and the Seeds of Patriarchy." In Athalya Brenner, ed., *Genesis*, 129–49. FCB 2/1. Sheffield, UK: Sheffield Academic Press, 1998.

Diamant, Anita. *The Red Tent*. New York: Picador, 1997.

Engar, Ann W. "Old Testament Women as Tricksters." In Vincent L. Tollers and John R. Maier, eds., *Mappings of the Biblical Terrain: The Bible as Text*, 143–57. Lewisburg, PA: Bucknell University Press, 1990.

Enright, Louisa. "Let's Stop Using the Bible to Buttress Misogynist Views." *Daughters of Sarah* 19, no. 1 (January/February 1993): 36–38.

Exum, J. Cheryl. "Desire Distorted and Exhibited: Lot and His Daughters in Psychoanalysis, Painting, and Film." In Saul M. Olyan and Robert C. Culley, eds., *"A Wise and Discerning Mind": Essays in Honor of Burke O. Long*, 83–108. Brown Judaic Studies 325. Atlanta: SBL Press, 2000.

——. "'Mother in Israel': A Familiar Figure Reconsidered." In Letty M. Russell, ed., *Feminist Interpretation of the Bible*, 73–85. Philadelphia: Westminster Press, 1985.

——. "The Mothers of Israel: The Patriarchal Narratives from a Feminist Perspective." *Bible Review* 2, no. 1 (1986): 60–67.

——. "The (M)other's Place" and "Who's Afraid of 'The Endangered Ancestress'?" In *Fragmented Women: Feminist (Sub)Versions of Biblical Narratives*, 94–147, 148–69. Valley Forge, PA: Trinity Press International, 1993.

——. "Who's Afraid of 'The Endangered Ancestress'?" In J. Cheryl Exum and David J. A. Clines, ed., *The New Literary Criticism and the Hebrew Bible*, 91–113. Sheffield, UK: JSOT Press, 1993. And in Alice Bach, ed., *Women in the Hebrew Bible: A Reader*, 141–56. New York and London: Routledge, 1999.

Fewell, Danna Nolan. "Changing the Subject: Retelling the Story of Hagar the Egyptian." In Athalya Brenner, ed., *Genesis*, 182–94. FCB 2/1. Sheffield, UK: Sheffield Academic Press, 1998.

——. "Drawn to Excess, or Reading beyond Betrothal." *Semeia* 77 (1997): 23–58.

Fewell, Danna Nolan, and David M. Gunn. "Tipping the Balance: Sternberg's Reader and the Rape of Dinah." *JBL* 110 (1991): 193–211.

Fischer, Irmtraud. "'Go and Suffer Oppression!' Said God's Messenger to Hagar: Repression of Women in Biblical Texts." In Elisabeth Schüssler Fiorenza and M. Shawn Copeland, eds., *Violence against Women*, 75–82. Maryknoll, NY: Orbis, 1994.

Frankel, Ellen. *The Five Books of Miriam: A Woman's Commentary on the Torah*. San Francisco: HarperSanFrancisco, 1998.

Freedman, David Noel. "Dinah and Shechem, Tamar and Amnon." *Austin Seminary Bulletin: Faculty Edition* 105 (1990): 51–63.

Frymer-Kensky, Tikva. "Hagar," "Leah," "Rachel," "Sarah," "Tamar 1" In *WIS*, 86–87, 108–9, 138–40, 150–51, 161–62.

——. "Sarah and Hagar." In *Talking about Genesis: A Resource Guide*, 94–97. New York: Main Street Books, Doubleday, 1996.

Fuchs, Esther. "For I Have the Way of Women: Deception, Gender, and Ideology in Biblical Narrative." In J. Cheryl Exum and Johanna W. H. Bos, eds., *Reasoning with the Foxes: Female Wit in a World of Male Power. Semeia* 42 (1988): 68–83.

——. "The Literary Characterization of Mothers and Sexual Politics in the Hebrew Bible." In Adela Yarbro Collins, ed., *Feminist Perspectives on Biblical Scholarship*, 117–36. SBLBSNA 10. Chico, CA: Scholars Press, 1985.

——. "Structure and Patriarchal Functions in the Biblical Betrothal Type-Scene: Some Preliminary Notes." *JFSR* 3 (1987): 7–13. And in Alice Bach, ed., *Women in the Hebrew Bible: A Reader*, 45–52. New York and London: Routledge, 1999.

——. "Who Is Hiding the Truth? Deceptive Women and Biblical Androcentrism." In Adela Yarbro Collins, ed., *Feminist Perspectives on Biblical Scholarship*, 137–44. SBLBSNA 10. Chico, CA: Scholars Press, 1985.

Furman, Nelly. "His Story versus Her Story: Male Genealogy and Female Strategy in the Jacob Cycle." In Adela Yarbro Collins, ed., *Feminist Perspectives on Biblical Scholarship*, 107–16. SBLBSNA 10. Chico, CA: Scholars Press, 1985. And in Alice Bach, ed., *Women in the Hebrew Bible: A Reader*, 119–26. New York and London: Routledge, 1999.

Gillmayr-Bucher, Susanne. "The Woman of Their Dreams: The Image of Rebekah in Genesis 24." In Philip R. Davies and David J. A. Clines, eds., *The World of Genesis: Persons, Places, Perspectives*, 90–101. Sheffield, UK: Sheffield Academic Press, 1998.

Goldstein, Rebecca. "Looking Back at Lot's Wife." In Celina Spiegel and Christina Buchmann, eds., *Out of the Garden: Women Writers on the Bible*, 37–41. New York: Fawcett Columbine, 1994.

Gruber, Mayer I. "Genesis 21.12: A New Reading of an Ambiguous Text." In Athalya Brenner, ed., *Genesis*, 172–79. FCB 2/1. Sheffield, UK: Sheffield Academic Press, 1998.

——. "A Re-examination of the Charges against Shechem Son of Hamor." *Beit Mikra Quarterly* 44: 157 (1999): 119–27.

Haag, Herbert, Dorothee Sölle, Katharina Elliger, and Marianne Grohmann. *Great Couples of the Bible*. Minneapolis: Fortress, 2006.

Hens-Piazza, Gina. "Why Did Sarah Laugh?" In Holly E. Hearon, ed., *Distant Voices Drawing Near: Essays in Honor of Antoinette Clark Wire*, 57–67. Collegeville, MN: Liturgical Press, 2004.

Herron-Palmore, Yolande. "And Sarah Laughed: The Humor of God." In Ella Pearson Mitchell, ed., *Those Preaching Women: More Sermons by Black Women Preachers*, 40–47. Valley Forge, PA: Judson Press, 1988.

Hollis, Susan Tower. *The Ancient Egyptian "Tale of Two Brothers": The Oldest Fairy Tale in the World*. Norman: University of Oklahoma Press, 1990.

———. "The Wife of Potiphar." In *WIS*, 184.

———. "The Woman in Ancient Examples of the Potiphar's Wife Motif, K2111." In Peggy L. Day, ed., *Gender and Difference in Ancient Israel*, 28–42. Minneapolis: Fortress Press, 1989.

Hyman, Naomi Mara. "Sarah and Hagar," "Lot's Wife and Daughters," "Rebekah," "Leah and Rachel," "Dinah," "Tamar," and "Leah's Blessing." In *Biblical Women in the Midrash: A Sourcebook*, 15–30, 31–38, 39–52, 53–64, 65–72, 73–86, 173–82. Northvale, NJ, and London: Jason Aronson, 1997.

Jackson, Melissa. "Lot's Daughters and Tamar as Tricksters and the Patriarchal Narratives as Feminist Theology." *JSOT* 28:4 (2004): 402–29.

Jacobs, Mignon R. "Love, Honor, and Violence: Socioconceptual Matrix in Genesis 34." In Cheryl A. Kirk-Duggan, ed., *Pregnant Passion: Gender, Sex, and Violence in the Bible*, 11–36. Semeia Studies 44. Atlanta: SBL, 2003.

Jay, Elisabeth. "Why 'Remember Lot's Wife'? Religious Identity and the Literary Canon." In Erik Borgman, Bart Philipsen, and Lea Verstricht, eds., *Literary Canons and Religious Identity*, 33–50. Burlington, VT: Ashgate, 2004.

Jeansonne, Sharon Pace. *The Women of Genesis: From Sarah to Potiphar's Wife*. Minneapolis: Fortress Press, 1990.

Jones, Monica C. "The Spirit of Hagar: Living in an Unfriendly House." *Journal of the Interdenominational Theological Center* 31:1–2 (2003–04): 61–83.

Keefe, Alice A. "Rapes of Women/Wars of Men." *Semeia* 63 (1993): 79–97.

Klagsburn, Francine. "Ruth and Naomi, Rachel and Leah: Sisters under the Skin." In Judith A. Kates and Gail Twersky Reimer, eds., *Reading Ruth: Contemporary Women Reclaim a Sacred Story*. New York: Ballantine Books, 1994.

Klein, Julia M. "Dueling Mothers." In Susan Headen and Jeffery L. Sheler, eds., *Women of the Bible: Provocative New Insights*, 18–21. *U.S. News and World Report* Special Collector's Edition, 2005.

Kraemer, Ross Shepard. "Asenath as Wisdom." In Athalya Brenner and Carole Fontaine, eds., *Wisdom and Psalms*, 218–39. FCB 2/2. Sheffield, UK: Sheffield Academic Press, 1998.

———. *When Asenath Met Joseph: A Late Antique Tale of the Biblical Patriarch and His Egyptian Wife*. New York: Oxford University Press, 1998.

Kramer, Phyllis Silverman. "Biblical Women That Come in Pairs: The Use of Female Pairs as a Literary Device in the Hebrew Bible." In Athalya Brenner, ed., *Genesis*, 217–31. FCB 2/1. Sheffield, UK: Sheffield Academic Press, 1998.

———. "The Dismissal of Hagar in Five Art Works of the Sixteenth and Seventeenth Centuries." In Athalya Brenner, ed., *Genesis*, 195–217. FCB 2/1. Sheffield, UK: Sheffield Academic Press, 1998.

Laffey, Alice L. *An Introduction to the Old Testament: A Feminist Perspective*. Philadelphia: Fortress Press, 1988.

Lapsley, Jacqueline E. "Hearing Whispers: Attending to Women's Words in the Voice of Rachel." In *Whispering the Word: Hearing Women's Stories in the Old Testament*, 21–34. Louisville, KY: Westminster John Knox Press, 2005.

———. "The Voice of Rachel: Resistance and Polyphony in Genesis 31.14–35." In Athalya Brenner, ed., *Genesis*, 232–48. FCB 2/1. Sheffield, UK: Sheffield Academic Press, 1998.

Maddox, Randy L. "Damned If You Do and Damned If You Don't: Tamar—A Feminist Foremother: Genesis 38:6–26." *Daughters of Sarah* 13, no. 4 (July/August 1987): 14–17.

Mazor, Yair. "'Cherchez la femme,' or Sex, Lies and the Bible: Exposing the Anti-Feminist Face of the Biblical Text." *SJOT* 18:1 (2004): 23–59.

Mbuwayesango, Dora R. "Childlessness and Woman-to-Woman Relationships in Genesis and in African Patriarc[h]al Society: Sarah and Hagar from a Zimbabwean Woman's Perspective (Gen 16:1–16; 21:8–21)." *Semeia* 78 (1997): 27–36.

McKay, Heather A. "Confronting Redundancy as Middle Manager and Wife: The Feisty Woman of Genesis 39." *Semeia* 87 (1999): 215–31.
———. "Eve's Sisters Re-Cycled: The Literary Nachleben of Old Testament Women." In Athalya Brenner and Jan W. van Henten, eds., *Recycling Biblical Figures*, 169–91. Leiden: Deo, 1999.
McKinlay, Judith E. "Reading with Choices and Controls: Genesis 12." *Feminist Theology* 17 (1998): 75–87.
———. "Sarah and Hagar: What Have I to Do with Them?" In Caroline Vander Stichele and Todd Penner, eds., *Her Master's Tools? Feminist and Postcolonial Engagements of Historical-Critical Discourse*, 150–78. Global Perspectives on Biblical Scholarship 9. Atlanta: SBL Press, 2005.
Meyers, Carol. "Rebekah." In *WIS*, 143–44.
Millett, Craig Ballard. "The Mother." In *Archetypes of Women in Scripture: In God's Image*, 91–108. San Diego: LuraMedia, 1989.
Niditch, Susan. "Genesis." In *WBC*, 13–29.
———. *Underdogs and Tricksters: A Prelude to Biblical Folklore*. San Francisco: Harper & Row, 1987.
———. "The Wronged Woman Righted: An Analysis of Genesis 38." *HTR* 72 (1979): 143–49.
Niehoff, Maren. "Mother and Maiden, Sister and Spouse: Sarah in Philonic Midrash." *HTR* 97:4 (2004): 23–59.
Nobuko, Morimura. "The Story of Tamar: A Feminist Interpretation of Genesis 38." *Japan Christian Review* 59 (1993): 55–67.
Nowell, Irene. "Women of Israel's Beginnings: Sarah and Hagar" and "More Women of Israel's Beginnings: Rebekah, Leah and Rachel, the Maids, Dinah, Tamar." In *Women in the Old Testament*, 3–46. Collegeville, MN: Liturgical Press, 1997.
Nunnally-Cox, Janice. *Foremothers: Women of the Bible*. San Francisco: Harper & Row, 1981.
Ochs, Vanessa L. *Sarah Laughed: Modern Lessons from the Wisdom and Stories of Biblical Women*. New York: McGraw-Hill, 2005.
Oh Soo Hae. "The Story of Two Women." In Oo Chung Lee et al., eds., *Women of Courage: Asian Women Reading the Bible*. Seoul: Asian Women's Resource Center for Culture and Theology, 1992.
Ostriker, Alicia. *The Nakedness of the Fathers: Biblical Visions and Revisions*. New Brunswick, NJ: Rutgers University Press, 1994.
Pardes, Ilana. "Rachel's Dream of Grandeur." In Celina Spiegel and Christina Buchmann, eds., *Out of the Garden: Women Writers on the Bible*, 336–37. New York: Fawcett Columbine, 1994.
———. "Rachel's Dream: The Female Subplot." In *Countertraditions in the Bible: A Feminist Approach*. Cambridge: Harvard University Press, 1992.
Parry, Robin. "Feminist Hermeneutics and Evangelical Concerns: The Rape of Dinah as a Case Study." *Tyndale Bulletin* 53:1 (2002): 1–28.
———. "Source Criticism and Genesis 34." *Tyndate Bulletin* 51:1 (2000): 121–38.
Pitt-Rivers, Julian. *The Fate of Shechem in the Politics of Sex: Essays in the Anthropology of the Mediterranean*. Cambridge: Cambridge University Press, 1977.
Polaski, Sandra Hack. *Inside the Red Tent*. St. Louis: Chalice Press, 2006.
Ramras-Rauch, Gila. "Fathers and Daughters: Two Biblical Narratives." In Vincent L. Tollers and John R. Maier, eds., *Mappings of the Biblical Terrain: The Bible as Text*, 158–69. Lewisburg, PA: Bucknell University Press, 1990.
Rashkow, Ilona N. "Daddy Dearest and the 'Invisible Spirit of Wine.'" In Athalya Brenner, ed., *Genesis*, 82–107. FCB 2/1. Sheffield, UK: Sheffield Academic Press, 1998.
———. "The Rape(s) of Dinah (Gen 34): False Religion and Excess in Revenge." In J. Harold Ellens, ed., *Destructive Power of Religion*, vol. 3: *Models and Cases of Violence in Religion*, 53–80. Westport and London: Praeger, 2004.
Reimer, Gail Twersky, and Judith A. Kates, eds. *Beginning Anew: A Woman's Companion to the High Holy Days*. New York: Simon & Schuster, 1997.
Reis, Pamela Tamarkin. "Hagar Requited." *JSOT* 87 (2000): 75–109.
———. *Reading the Lines: A Fresh Look at the Hebrew Bible*. Peabody, MA: Hendrickson, 2002.
Rosen, Norma. *Biblical Women Unbound: Counter-Tales*. Philadelphia: Jewish Publication Society, 1996.
———. "Rebekah and Isaac: A Marriage Made in Heaven." In Celina Spiegel and Christina Buchmann, eds., *Out of the Garden: Women Writers on the Bible*, 13–26. New York: Fawcett Columbine, 1994.

Ross-Burstall, Joan. "Leah and Rachel: A Tale of Two Sisters [Gen 29:31–30:24]." *Word & World* 14 (1994): 162–70.

Rulon-Miller, Nina. "Hagar: A Woman with an Attitude." In Philip R. Davies and David J. A. Clines, eds., *The World of Genesis: Persons, Places, Perspectives,* 60–89. Sheffield, UK: Sheffield Academic Press, 1998.

Sakenfeld, Katharine Doob. "Sarah and Hagar: Power and Privileges." In *Just Wives? Stories of Power and Survival in the Old Testament and Today,* 7–26. Louisville, KY: Westminster John Knox Press, 2003.

Schkop, Esther M. "Rivka: The Enigma behind the Veil." *Tradition* 36:3 (2002): 46–59.

Schneider, Tammi J. *Sarah: Mother of Nations.* London: Continuum, 2004.

Scholz, Susanne. *Rape Plots: A Feminist Cultural Study of Genesis 34.* Studies in Biblical Literature 13. New York: Lang, 2000.

———. "Through Whose Eyes? A 'Right' Reading of Genesis 34." In Athalya Brenner, ed., *Genesis,* 150–71. FCB 2/1. Sheffield, UK: Sheffield Academic Press, 1998.

———. "Was It Really Rape in Genesis 34? Biblical Scholarship as a Reflection of Cultural Assumptions." In Harold C. Washington, Susan Lochrie Graham, and Pamela Thimmes, eds., *Escaping Eden: New Feminist Perspectives on the Bible,* 182–98. Sheffield, UK: Sheffield Academic Press, 1998.

Sheres, Ita. *Dinah's Rebellion: A Biblical Parable for Our Time.* New York: Crossroad, 1990.

Shishanya, Constance. "A Reflection on the Hagar Narratives in Genesis through the Eyes of a Kenyan Woman." In Mary N. Getui, Knut Holter, and Victor Zinkuratire, eds., *Interpreting the Old Testament in Africa: Papers from the International Symposium on Africa and the Old Testament in Nairobi, October 1999,* 147–52. Oxford: Lang, 2001.

Smith, Carol. "The Story of Tamar: A Power-Filled Challenge to the Structures of Power." In George J. Brooke, ed., *Women in the Biblical Tradition,* 16–28. Studies in Women and Religion 31. Lewiston, NY: Edwin Mellen Press, 1992.

Sölle, Dorothée, et al. "Sarah and Hagar," "Lot's Wife and Daughters," "Rebekah, Daughter of Bethuel," "Rachel and Leah," "Tamar, Cunning Versus Power," "Potiphar's Wife." In *Great Women of the Bible in Art and Literature,* 32–47, 48–57, 58–73, 74–87, 88–93, 94–103. Trans. Joe H. Kirchberger. Macon, GA: Mercer University Press, 1994.

Spanier, Ktziah. "Rachel's Theft of the Teraphim: Her Struggle for Family Primacy." *VT* 42 (1992): 404–12.

Steinberg, Naomi. "Alliance or Descent: The Function of Marriage." *JSOT* 51 (1991): 45–55.

———. "Gender Roles in the Rebekah Cycle." *USQR* 39 (1984): 175–88.

———. *Kinship and Marriage in Genesis: A Household Economics Perspective.* Minneapolis: Fortress Press, 1993.

Streete, Gail Corrington. *The Strange Woman: Power and Sex in the Bible.* Louisville, KY: Westminster John Knox Press, 1997.

Stone, Ken. "Lot's Daughters." In *WIS,* 179.

Tamez, Elsa. "The Woman Who Complicated the History of Salvation. " In John S. Pobee and Bärbel von Wartenberg-Potter, eds., *New Eyes for Reading: Biblical and Theological Reflections by Women from the Third World,* 5–17. Oak Park, IL: Meyer-Stone Books, 1987.

Tarlin, Jan William. "Tamar's Veil: Ideology at the Entrance to Enaim." In George Aichele, ed., *Culture, Entertainment and the Bible.* JSOTSup 309. Sheffield, UK: Sheffield Academic Press, 2000.

Taylor, Katy. "From Lavender to Purple: A Feminist Reading of Hagar and Celie in the Light of Womanism." *Theology* 97 (1994): 352–62.

Teubal, Savina J. *Hagar the Egyptian: The Lost Tradition of the Matriarchs.* San Francisco: Harper & Row, 1990.

———. *Sarah the Priestess: The First Matriarch of Genesis.* Athens, OH: Swallow Press, 1984.

Teugels, Lieve. "Gap Filling and Linkage in the Midrash on the Rebekah Cycle." In A. Wénin, ed., *Studies in the Book of Genesis: Literature, Redaction and History,* 585–98. BETL 155. Louvain: University Press and Peeters, 2001.

———. "'A Strong Woman Who Can Find?' A Study of Characterization in Genesis 24 with Some Perspectives on the General Presentation of Isaac and Rebekah in the Genesis Narrative." *JSOT* 63 (1994): 89–104.

Thistlethwaite, Susan Brooks. "'You May Enjoy the Spoil of Your Enemies': Rape as a Biblical Metaphor for War." In Claudia V. Camp and Carole R. Fontaine, eds., *Woman War, and Metaphor: Language and Society in the Study of the Hebrew Bible. Semeia* 61 (1993): 59–75.

Trible, Phyllis. "Genesis 22: The Sacrifice of Sarah." In Jason P. Rosenblatt and Joseph C. Sitterson Jr., eds., *"Not in Heaven": Coherence and Complexity in Biblical Narrative*, 170–91. Indiana Studies in Biblical Literature. Bloomington and Indianapolis: Indiana University Press, 1991. And in Alice Bach, ed., *Women in the Hebrew Bible*, 271–92. New York: Routledge, 1999.

———. "Hagar: The Desolation of Rejection." In *Texts of Terror: Literary-Feminist Readings of Biblical Narratives*, 9–36. Overtures to Biblical Theology. Philadelphia: Fortress Press, 1984.

Trible, Phyllis, and Letty M. Russell, eds. *Hagar, Sarah, and Their Children: Jewish, Christian, and Muslim Perspectives*. Louisville, KY: Westminster John Knox Press, 2006.

Van Wolde, Ellen J. "Does *'innā* Denote Rape? A Semantic Analysis of a Controversial Word." *VT* 52:4 (2002): 528–44.

———. "Love and Hatred in a Multiracial Society: The Dinah and Shechem Story in Genesis 34 in Context of Genesis 28–35." In J. Cheryl Exum and H. G. M. Williamson, eds., *Reading from Right to Left: Essays on the Hebrew Bible in Honour of David J. A. Clines*. JSOTSup 373. Sheffield, UK: Sheffield Academic Press, 2003.

———. "Texts in Dialogue with Texts: Intertextuality in the Ruth and Tamar Narratives." *BibInt* 5.1 (1997): 1–28.

———. *Words Became Worlds: Semantic Studies of Genesis 1–11*. BibInt Series 6. Leiden: E. J. Brill, 1994.

Vennum, Eileen. "Sarah as a Hero of Faith." *Daughters of Sarah* 13, no. 1 (January/February 1987): 4–7.

Weems, Renita J. "A Mistress, a Maid, and No Mercy." In *Just a Sister Away: A Womanist Vision of Women's Relationships in the Bible*. San Diego: LuraMedia, 1988.

Weisberg, Dvora E. "The Widow of Our Discontent: Levirate Marriage in the Bible and Ancient Israel." *JSOT* 28:4 (2004): 403–29.

Weiss, Richard D. "Stained Glass Window, Kaleidoscope or Catalyst: The Implications of Difference in Readings of the Hagar and Sarah Stories." In David McLain Carr and Richard D. Weiss, eds., *A Gift of God in Due Season: Essays on Scripture and Community in Honor of James A Sanders*, 253–73. Sheffield, UK: Sheffield Academic Press, 1996.

Westbrook, Deeanne. "Paradise and Paradox." In Vincent L. Tollers and John R. Maier, eds., *Mappings of the Biblical Terrain: The Bible as Text*, 121–33. Lewisburg, PA: Bucknell University Press, 1990.

Westenholz, Joan Goodnick, "Tamar, *Qedeśâ, Qadištu*, and Sacred Prostitution in Mesopotamia." *HTR* 82 (1989): 245–65.

Williams, Delores. "Breaking and Bonding." *Daughters of Sarah* 15, no. 3 (May/June 1989): 20–21.

———. *Sisters in the Wilderness: The Challenge of Womanist God-talk*. Maryknoll, NY: Orbis Books, 1993.

Yaron, Shlomith. "Sperm Stealing: A Moral Crime by Three of David's Ancestresses." Illustrated by Marc Chagall. *Bible Review* 17:1 (2001): 34–38.

Zornberg, Aviva. *The Beginning of Desire*. New York: Doubleday, 1995.

CHAPTER 4: THE WOMEN IN EXODUS AND NUMBERS

Ackerman, Susan. "Why Is Miriam Also among the Prophets? (and Is Zipporah among the Priests?)" *JBL* 121 (2002): 47–80.

Anderson, Cheryl. *Women, Ideology and Violence: Critical Theory and the Construction of Gender in the Book of the Covenant and the Deuteronomic Law*. New York: Continuum, 2005.

Bach, Alice. "Detoxifying Miriam." In Saul M. Olyan and Robert C. Culley, eds., *"A Wise and Discerning Mind": Essays in Honor of Burke O. Long*, 1–10. Atlanta: SBL Press, 2000.

———. "Dreaming of Miriam's Well." In Athalya Brenner, ed., *Exodus to Deuteronomy*, 151–58. FCB 2/5. Sheffield, UK: Sheffield Academic Press, 2000.

————. *Reading the Women of the Bible: A New Interpretation of Their Stories.* New York: Schocken Books, 2002.

————. "With a Song in Her Heart. Listening to Scholars Listening for Miriam." In *Women in the Hebrew Bible: A Reader,* 419–28. New York and London: Routledge, 1999.

————. "With a Song in Her Heart: Listening to Scholars Listening for Miriam." In Athalya Brenner, ed., *A Feminist Companion to Exodus to Deuteronomy,* 243–54. FCB 1/6. Sheffield, UK: Sheffield Academic Press, 1994.

Barton, Mukti. "The Skin of Miriam Became as White as Snow: the Bible, Western Feminism and Colour Politics." *Feminist Theology* 27 (2001): 68–80.

Bellis, Alice Ogden. "Cushite Woman, Wife of Moses." In *WIS,* 219.

Berlin, Adele. "Numinous *Nomos*: On the Relationship between Narrative and Law." In Saul M. Olyan and Robert C. Culley, eds., *"A Wise and Discerning Mind": Essays in Honor of Burke O. Long,* 25–32. Brown Judaic Studies 325. Atlanta: SBL Press, 2000.

Brenner, Athalya. "An Afterword: The Decalogue—Am I an Addressee?" In Athalya Brenner, ed., *A Feminist Companion to Exodus to Deuteronomy,* 255–58. FCB 1/6. Sheffield, UK: Sheffield Academic Press, 1994.

————. "I Am the Bird Woman: Zipporah." In. *I Am . . . Biblical Women Tell Their Own Stories,* 58–81. Minneapolis: Fortress Press, 2005.

Bronner, Leila Leah. "Serah and the Exodus: A Midrashic Miracle." In *Exodus to Deuteronomy,* 187–98. FCB 2/5. Sheffield, UK: Sheffield Academic Press, 2000.

————. "Serah bat Asher: The Transformative Power of Aggadic Invention." In *From Eve to Esther: Rabbinic Reconstructions of Biblical Women,* 42–60. Gender and the Biblical Tradition. Louisville, KY: Westminster John Knox Press, 1994.

Brophy, Beth. "The Woman Who Stood Up to God." In Susan Headen and Jeffery L. Sheler, eds., *Women of the Bible: Provocative New Insight,* 22–25. *U.S. News and World Report* Special Collector's Edition, 2005.

Burns, Rita J. *Has the Lord Indeed Spoken Only through Moses? A Study of the Biblical Portrait of Miriam.* SBLDS 84. Atlanta: Scholars Press, 1987.

Exum, J. Cheryl. "The Hand That Rocks the Cradle." In *Plotted, Shot, and Painted: Cultural Representations of Biblical Women,* 80–100. Sheffield, UK: Sheffield Academic Press, 1996.

————. "Second Thoughts about Secondary Characters: Women in Exodus 1.8–2.10." In Athalya Brenner, ed., *A Feminist Companion to Exodus to Deuteronomy,* 75–87. FCB 1/6. Sheffield, UK: Sheffield Academic Press, 1994.

————. "'You Shall Let Every Daughter Live': A Study of Exodus 1:8–2:10." *Semeia* 28 (1983): 63–82. And in Athalya Brenner, ed., *A Feminist Companion to Exodus to Deuteronomy,* 37–61. FCB 1/6. Sheffield, UK: Sheffield Academic Press, 1994.

Fischer, Irmtraud. "The Authority of Miriam: A Feminist Rereading of Numbers 12 Prompted by Jewish Interpretation." In Athalya Brenner, ed., *Exodus to Deuteronomy,* 159–73. FCB 2/5. Sheffield, UK: Sheffield Academic Press, 2000.

Frankel, Ellen. *The Five Books of Miriam: A Woman's Commentary on the Torah.* San Francisco: HarperSanFrancisco, 1998.

Fuchs, Esther. "A Jewish-Feminist Reading of Exodus 1–2." In Alice Ogden Bellis and Joel Kaminsky, eds., *Jews, Christians, and the Theology of Hebrew Scriptures,* 307–26. SBL Symposium Series 8. Atlanta: SBL Press, 2000.

Frymer-Kensky, Tikva. "Zipporah." In *WIS,* 170–71.

Gafney, Wilda. "Miriam's Snow in the Desert: A Portrait of a Partial Punishment among Prophets." *AME Zion Quarterly Review* 111 (July 1999): 10–17.

Graetz, Naomi. "Did Miriam Talk Too Much?" In Athalya Brenner, ed., *A Feminist Companion to Exodus to Deuteronomy,* 231–42. FCB 1/6. Sheffield, UK: Sheffield Academic Press, 1994.

Gruber, Mayer I. "Puah," "Shifrah,"and "Hebrew Women in Egypt." In *WIS,* 137–38, 156, 185–86.

Hyman, Naomi Mara. "Miriam" and "The Daughters of Zelophehad." In *Biblical Women in the Midrash: A Sourcebook,* 87–94, 95–100. Northvale, NJ, and London: Jason Aronson, 1997.

Ilan, Tal. "The Daughters of Zelophehad and Women's Inheritance: The Biblical Injunction and Its Outcome." In Athalya Brenner, ed., *Exodus to Deuteronomy,* 176–86. FCB 2/5. Sheffield, UK: Sheffield Academic Press, 2000.

Janzen, J. Gerald. "Song of Moses, Song of Miriam: Who Is Seconding Whom?" In Athalya Brenner, ed., *A Feminist Companion to Exodus to Deuteronomy*, 187–99. FCB 1/6. Sheffield, UK: Sheffield Academic Press, 1994.

John, Cresy, et al. "An Asian Feminist Perspective: The Exodus Story (Exodus 1.8–22, 2.1–10)." In R. S. Sugirtharajah, ed., *Voices from the Margin: Interpreting the Bible in the Third World*, 267–79. Maryknoll, NY: Orbis Books, 1991.

Kirk-Duggan, Cheryl. "Divine Puppeteer: Yahweh of Exodus." In Athalya Brenner, ed., *Exodus to Deuteronomy*, 75–102. FCB 2/5. Sheffield, UK: Sheffield Academic Press, 2000.

Kramer, Phyllis Silverman. "Miriam." In Athalya Brenner, ed., *Exodus to Deuteronomy*, 104–33. FCB 2/5. Sheffield, UK: Sheffield Academic Press, 2000.

Laffey, Alice. *An Introduction to the Old Testament: A Feminist Perspective*. Philadelphia: Fortress Press, 1988.

Lapsley, Jacqueline E. "Saving Women: Transgressive Values of Deliverance in Exodus 1–4." In *Whispering the Word: Hearing Women's Stories in the Old Testament*, 69–88. Louisville, KY: Westminster John Knox Press, 2005.

Leneman, Helen. "Miriam Re-Imagined, and Imaginary Women of Exodus in Musical Settings." In Athalya Brenner, ed., *Exodus to Deuteronomy*, 134–50. FCB 2/5. Sheffield, UK: Sheffield Academic Press, 2000.

Masenye, Madipoane (ngwana' Mphahlele). "'. . . But You Shall Let Every Girl Live': Reading Exodus 1:2–2:10 the Bosadi (Womanhood) Way." *Old Testament Essays* 15 (2002): 99–112.

Meyers, Carol. "Jochebed." In *WIS*, 103.

Niditch, Susan. "War, Women, and Defilement in Numbers 31." *Semeia* 61 (1993): 39–57.

Nowell, Irene. "Women of Israel's Passover: The Midwives, Moses' Mother, Pharaoh's Daughter, Miriam, Zipporah." In *Women in the Old Testament*, 47–58. Collegeville, MN: Liturgical Press, 1997.

Pardes, Ilana. "Miriam and Her Brothers" and "Zipporah and the Struggle for Deliverance." In *Countertraditions in the Bible: A Feminist Approach*, 6–12, 79–97. Cambridge: Harvard University Press, 1992.

Phillips, Elaine A. "The Singular Prophet and Ideals of Torah: Miriam, Aaron, and Moses in Early Rabbinic Texts." In Craig A. Evans and James A. Sanders, eds., *Function of Scripture in Early Jewish and Christian Tradition*, 78–88. Sheffield, UK: Sheffield Academic Press, 1998.

Rashkow, Ilona. "Oedipus Wrecks: Moses and God's Rod." In Athalya Brenner, ed., *Exodus to Deuteronomy*, 59–78. FCB 2/5. Sheffield, UK: Sheffield Academic Press, 2000.

Russaw, Kimberly D. "Zipporah and Circumcision as a Form of Preparation: Cutting Away at the Comfort Zone." *Journal of the Interdenominational Theological Center* 31:1–2 (2003–4): 103–12.

Sakenfeld, Katharine Doob. "Daughters of Zelophehad." In *WIS*, 220.

———. "Feminist Biblical Interpretation." *Theology Today* 46 (1989): 154–68.

———. "Numbers." In *WBC*, 49–56.

Scholz, Susanne, "The Complexities of 'His' Liberation Talk: A Literary Feminist Reading of the Book of Exodus." In Athalya Brenner, ed., *Exodus to Deuteronomy*, 20–40. FCB 2/5. Sheffield, UK: Sheffield Academic Press, 2000.

Schroer, Silvia. "'Under the shadow of your Wings': The Metaphor of God's Wings in the Psalms, Exodus 19.4, Deuteronomy 32.11 and Malachi 3.20, as Seen through the Perspectives of Feminism and the History of Religion." In Athalya Brenner and Carole Fontaine, eds., *Wisdom and Psalms*. 264–82. FCB 2/2. Sheffield, UK: Sheffield Academic Press, 1998.

Setel, Drorah O'Donnell. "Exodus." In *WBC*, 30–39.

Siebert-Hommes, Jopie. "But If She Be a Daughter . . . She May Live! 'Daughters' and 'Sons' in Exodus 1–2." In Athalya Brenner, ed., *A Feminist Companion to Exodus to Deuteronomy*, 62–74. FCB 1/6. Sheffield, UK: Sheffield Academic Press, 1994.

Sivan, Helena Z. "The Rape of Cozbi (Numbers XXV)." *VT* 51 (2001): 69–80.

Sölle, Dorothée, et al. "Potiphar's Wife." In *Great Women of the Bible in Art and Literature*, 94–103. Trans. Joe H. Kirchberger. Macon, GA: Mercer University Press, 1994.

Sterring, Ankie. "The Will of the Daughters." In Athalya Brenner, ed., *A Feminist Companion to Exodus to Deuteronomy*, 88–99. FCB 1/6. Sheffield, UK: Sheffield Academic Press, 1994.

Trible, Phyllis. "Bringing Miriam out of the Shadows." *Bible Review* (February 1989): 14–25, 34. And in Athalya Brenner, ed., *A Feminist Companion to Exodus to Deuteronomy*, 166–86. FCB 1/6. Sheffield, UK: Sheffield Academic Press, 1994.

————. "Eve and Miriam: From the Margins to the Center." In Hershel Shanks, ed., *Feminist Approaches to the Bible*. Washington, DC: Biblical Archaeology Society, 1995.

————. "Miriam 1." In *WIS*, 127–29.

van Dijk-Hemmes, Fokkelien. "Some Recent Views on the Presentation of the Song of Miriam." In Athalya Brenner, ed., *A Feminist Companion to Exodus to Deuteronomy*, 200–206. FCB 1/6. Sheffield, UK: Sheffield Academic Press, 1994.

Washington, Harold C. "Signifying on Exodus: Reading Race and Culture in Zora Neale Hurston's *Moses, Man of the Mountain*." In Athalya Brenner, ed., *Exodus to Deuteronomy*, 41–58. FCB 2/5. Sheffield, UK: Sheffield Academic Press, 2000.

Weems, Renita J. "The Hebrew Women Are Not Like the Egyptian Women: The Ideology of Race, Gender and Sexual Reproduction in Exodus 1. " In David Jobling and Tina Pippin, eds., *Ideological Criticism of Biblical Texts. Semeia* 59 (1992): 25–34.

————. "In-Law, In Love (Miriam and Her Cushite Sister-in-Law)." In *Just a Sister Away: A Womanist Vision of Women's Relationships in the Bible*, 71–84. San Diego: LuraMedia, 1988.

Winslow, Karen Strand. "Jewish Memories of Moses' Wives in Rewritten Bibles of the Greek Period." *Proceedings—Eastern Great Lakes and Midwest Biblical Societies* 24 (2004): 61–74.

CHAPTER 5: THE WOMEN IN JOSHUA AND JUDGES

Ackerman, Susan. "Digging Up Deborah: Recent Hebrew Bible Scholarship on Gender and the Contribution of Archaeology." *Near Eastern Archaeology* 66:4 (2003): 172–84.

————. *Warrior, Dancer, Seductress, Queen: Women in Judges and Biblical Israel*. Anchor Bible Reference Library. New York: Doubleday, 1998.

————. "What If Judges Had Been Written by a Woman?" *BibInt* 8:1–2 (2000): 33–41.

Amit, Yairah. *The Book of Judges. The Art of Editing*. Trans. Jonathan Chipman. Biblical Interpretation Series 38. Leiden: E. J. Brill, 1999.

————. "Judges 4: Its Content and Form." *JSOT* 39 (1987): 89–111.

————. "'Manoah Promptly Followed His Wife' (Judges 13.11): On the Place of the Woman in Birth Narratives." In Athalya Brenner, ed., *A Feminist Companion to Judges*, 146–56. FCB 1/4. Sheffield, UK: Sheffield Academic Press, 1993.

Bach, Alice. *Reading the Women of the Bible: A New Interpretation of Their Stories*. New York: Schocken Books, 2002.

————. "Rereading the Body Politic: Women and Violence in Judges 21." *BibInt* 6 (1998): 1–19. And in Athalya Brenner, ed., *Judges*, 143–59. FCB 2/4. Sheffield, UK: Sheffield Academic Press, 1999. And in Alice Bach, ed., *Women in the Hebrew Bible: A Reader*, 389–402. New York and London: Routledge, 1999.

Baker, Cynthia. "Pseudo-Philo and the Transformation of Jephthah's Daughter." In Mieke Bal, ed., *Anti-Covenant: Counter-Reading Women's Lives in the Hebrew Bible*, 195–210. JSOTSup 81. Bible and Literature Series 22. Sheffield, UK: Almond Press, 1989.

Bal, Mieke. "Between Altar and Wandering Rock: Toward a Feminist Philology." In Mieke Bal, ed., *Anti-Covenant: Counter-Reading Women's Lives in the Hebrew Bible*, 211–32. JSOTSup 81. Bible and Literature Series 22. Sheffield, UK: Almond Press, 1989.

————. "A Body of Writing: Judges 19." In Athalya Brenner, ed., *A Feminist Companion to Judges*, 208–30. FCB 1/4. Sheffield, UK: Sheffield Academic Press, 1993.

————. "Dealing/With/Women: Daughters in the Book of Judges." In Alice Bach, ed., *Women in the Hebrew Bible: A Reader*, 317–34. New York and London: Routledge, 1999.

————. *Death and Dissymmetry: The Politics of Coherence in the Book of Judges*. Chicago: University of Chicago Press, 1988.

————. "Delilah Decomposed: Samson's Talking Cure and the Rhetoric of Subjectivity." In *Lethal Love: Feminist Literary Readings of Biblical Love Stories*, 37–67. Indiana Studies in Biblical Literature. Bloomington: Indiana University Press, 1987.

————. *Murder and Difference: Gender, Genre, and Scholarship on Sisera's Death*. Trans. Matthew Gumpert. Indiana Studies in Biblical Literature. Bloomington: Indiana University Press, 1988.

Barnes, Bernadine. "Heroines and Worthy Women." In H. Diane Russell with Bernadine Barnes, *Eve/Ave: Women in Renaissance and Baroque Prints*, 29–74. Washington, DC: National Gallery of Art; New York: The Feminist Press at the City University, 1990.

Bellis, Alice Ogden. "The Jael Enigma." *Daughters of Sarah* 21 (1995): 19–20.

Bird, Phyllis A. "Harlot and Hierodule." Part IV in *Missing Persons and Mistaken Identities: Women and Gender in Ancient Israel*, 197–236. Overtures to Biblical Theology. Minneapolis: Fortress, 1997.

———. "The Harlot as Heroine: Narrative Art and Social Presupposition in Three Old Testament Texts." *Semeia* 46 (1989): 119–39. And in Alice Bach, ed., *Women in the Hebrew Bible: A Reader*, 99–118. New York and London: Routledge, 1999.

Bledstein, Adrien Janis. "Is Judges a Woman's Satire on Men Who Play God?" In Athalya Brenner, ed., *A Feminist Companion to Judges*, 34–54. FCB 1/4. Sheffield, UK: Sheffield Academic Press, 1993.

Bohmbach, Karla. "Conventions/Contraventions: The Meanings of Public and Private for the Judges 19 Concubine." *JSOT* 83 (1999): 83–98.

———. "Daughter of Jephthah." In *WIS*, 243–44.

Bos, Johanna W. H. "Out of the Shadows: Genesis 38; Judges 4:17–22; Ruth 3." In J. Cheryl Exum and Johanna W. H. Bos, eds., *Reasoning with the Foxes: Female Wit in a World of Male Power. Semeia* 42 (1988): 37–67.

Brenner, Athalya. "I Am Rahab, the Broad." In *I Am . . . Biblical Women Tell Their Own Stories*, 82–98. Minneapolis: Fortress Press, 2005.

———, ed. *Judges*. FCB 2/4. Sheffield, UK: Sheffield Academic Press, 1999.

———. "A Triangle and a Rhombus in Narrative Structure: A Proposed Integrative Reading of Judges IV and V." *VT* 40 (1990): 129–38. In *A Feminist Companion to Judges*, 98–109. FCB 1/4. Sheffield, UK: Sheffield Academic Press, 1993.

Bronner, Leila Leah. "'Deborah, Say Your Song': Female Prophecy in Talmudic Tradition." In *From Eve to Esther: Rabbinic Reconstructions of Biblical Women*, 163–84. Gender and the Biblical Tradition. Louisville, KY: Westminster John Knox Press, 1994.

———. "Valorized or Vilified? The Women of Judges in Midrashic Sources." In Athalya Brenner, ed., *A Feminist Companion to Judges*, 72–95. FCB 1/4. Sheffield, UK: Sheffield Academic Press, 1993.

Burnett-Bletsch, Rhonda. "At the Hands of a Woman: Rewriting Jael in Pseudo-Philo." *Journal for the Study of the Pseudepigrapha* 17 (1998): 53–64.

Carmody, Denise Lardner. *Biblical Woman: Contemporary Reflections on Scriptural Texts*. New York: Crossroad, 1988.

Cartledge-Hayes, Mary. *To Love Delilah: Claiming the Women of the Bible*. San Diego: LuraMedia, 1990.

Chittister, Joan. *The Friendship of Women: The Hidden Tradition of the Bible*. Erie, PA: Bluebridge Benetvision, 2006.

Cooper, Valerie C. "Some Place to Cry: Jephthah's Daughter and the Double Dilemma of Black Women in America." In Cheryl A. Kirk-Duggan, ed., *Pregnant Passion: Gender, Sex, and Violence in the Bible*, 181–92. Semeia Studies 44. Atlanta: SBL Press, 2003.

Creighton, Linda L. "One Feisty Femme." In Susan Headen and Jeffery L. Sheler, eds., *Women of the Bible: Provocative New Insights*, 44–47. U.S. News and World Report Special Collector's Edition, 2005.

Curry, Andrew. "Facing Down '900 Chariots of Iron.'" In Susan Headen and Jeffery L. Sheler, eds., *Women of the Bible: Provocative New Insights*, 48–51. U.S. News and World Report Special Collector's Edition, 2005.

Day, Peggy L. "From the Child Is Born the Woman: The Story of Jephthah's Daughter." In *Gender and Difference in Ancient Israel*, 58–74. Minneapolis: Fortress Press, 1989.

Dube, Musa W. *Postcolonial Feminist Interpretation of the Bible*. St. Louis: Chalice, 2000.

Duran, Nicole. *Having Men for Dinner: Biblical Women's Deadly Banquets*. Cleveland: Pilgrim Press, 2006.

Engar, Ann W. "Old Testament Women as Tricksters." In Vincent L. Tollers and John R. Maier, eds., *Mappings of the Biblical Terrain: The Bible as Text*, 143–57. Lewisburg, PA: Bucknell University Press, 1990.

Esquivel, Julia. "Liberation, Theology, and Women." In John S. Pobee and Bärbel von Wartenberg-Potter, eds., *New Eyes for Reading: Biblical and Theological Reflections by Women from the Third World*, 21–24. Oak Park, IL: Meyer-Stone Books, 1987.

Exum, J. Cheryl. "Concubine (Secondary Wife) of a Levite," "Delilah," "Mother of Samson," and "Wife of Samson." In *WIS*, 248–49, 68–69, 245–46, 246–47.

———. "Feminist Criticism: Whose Interests Are Being Served?" In Gale A. Yee, ed., *Judges and Method: New Approaches in Biblical Studies*, 65–90. Minneapolis: Fortress Press, 1995.

———. *Fragmented Women: Feminist (Sub)Versions of Biblical Narratives*. Valley Forge, PA: Trinity Press International, 1993.

———. "Lethal Woman. 2, Reflections on Delilah and Her Incarnation as Liz Hurley." In Martin O'Kane, ed., *Borders, Boundaries, and the Bible*, 254–73. JSOTSup 313. Sheffield, UK: Sheffield Academic Press, 2002.

———. "'Mother in Israel' A Familiar Figure Reconsidered." In Letty M. Russell, ed., *Feminist Interpretation of the Bible*, 82–84. Philadelphia: Westminster Press, 1985.

———. "Murder They Wrote: Ideology and the Manipulation of Female Presence in Biblical Narrative." In Alice Bach, ed., *Ad Feminam*. USQR 43 (1989): 19–39. And in Alice Bach, ed., *The Pleasure of Her Text: Feminist Readings of Biblical and Historical Texts*, 45–68. Philadelphia: Trinity Press International, 1990.

———. "On Judges 11." In Athalya Brenner, ed. *A Feminist Companion to Judges*, 131–44. FCB 1/4. Sheffield, UK: Sheffield Academic Press, 1993.

———. "Promise and Fulfillment: Narrative Art in Judges 13." *JBL* 99 (1980): 43–59.

———. "Samson's Women" and "Raped by the Pen." In *Fragmented Women: Feminist (Sub)Versions of Biblical Narratives*, 61–93, 170–201. Valley Forge, PA: Trinity Press International, 1993.

———. "The Theological Dimension of the Samson Saga." *VT* 33 (1983): 30–45.

———. *Tragedy and Biblical Narrative: Arrows of the Almighty*. Cambridge: Cambridge University Press, 1992.

———. "Why, Why Why, Delilah?" In *Plotted, Shot, and Painted: Cultural Representations of Biblical Women*, 175–237. Sheffield, UK: Sheffield Academic Press, 1996.

———. *Women, Seduction, and Betrayal in Biblical Narrative*. Cambridge: Cambridge University Press, 1997.

Fewell, Danna Nolan. "Deconstructive Criticism: Achsah and the (E)razed City of Writing." In Gale A. Yee, ed., *Judges and Method: New Approaches in Biblical Studies*, 119–45. Minneapolis: Fortress Press, 1995.

———. "Joshua" and "Judges." In *WBC*, 69–72, 73–83.

Fewell, Danna Nolan, and David Miller Gunn. "Controlling Perspectives: Women, Men, and the Authority of Violence in Judges 4 & 5." *JAAR* 58 (1991): 389–411.

Fienberg, Nona. "Jephthah's Daughter: The Parts Ophelia Plays." In Raymond-Jean Frontain and Jan Vojcik, eds., *Old Testament Women in Western Literature*, 128–43. Conway, AR: UCA Press, 1991.

Franklin, Naomi Patricia. "The Stranger within Their Gates (How the Israelite Portrayed the Non-Israelite in Biblical Literature)." Diss., Duke University, 1990.

Frymer-Kensky, Tikva. "Deborah 2," "Jael," "Rahab." In *WIS*, 66–67, 97–98, 140–41.

———. "Reading Rahab." In Mordechai Cogan, Barry Eichler, and Jeffrey Tigay, eds., *Tehillah Lemoshe: Biblical and Judaic Studies in Honor of Moshe Greenberg*, 57–72. Winona Lake, IN: Eisenbrauns, 1997.

Fuchs, Esther. "Marginalization, Ambiguity, Silencing: The Story of Jephthah's Daughter." *JFSR* 5, no. 1 (1989): 35–45. And in Athalya Brenner, ed., *A Feminist Companion to Judges*, 116–30. FCB 1/4. Sheffield, UK: Sheffield Academic Press, 1993.

———. *Sexual Politics of the Biblical Narrative: Reading the Hebrew Bible as a Woman*. Sheffield, UK: Sheffield Academic Press, 2000.

Gerstein, Beth. "A Ritual Processed." In Mieke Bal, ed., *Anti-Covenant: Counter-Reading Women's Lives in the Hebrew Bible*, 175–94. JSOTSup 81. Bible and Literature Series 22. Sheffield, UK: Almond Press, 1989.

Goldstein, Elyse. *ReVisions: Seeing Torah through a Feminist Lens*. Woodstock, VT: Jewish Lights, 1998.

Hackett, Jo Ann. "In the Days of Jael: Reclaiming the History of Women in Ancient Israel." In Clarissa W. Atkinson, Constance H. Buchanan, and Margaret R. Miles, eds., *Immaculate and Powerful: The Female in Sacred Image and Social Reality*, 15–38. Harvard Women's Studies in Religion Series. Boston: Beacon Press, 1985.

Hyman, Naomi Mara. "Deborah" and "Jephthah's Daughter." In *Biblical Women in the Midrash: A Sourcebook*, 101–12, 113–20. Northvale, NJ, and London: Jason Aronson, 1997.

Jay, Nancy. "Sacrifice as Remedy for Having Been Born of Woman." In Clarissa W. Atkinson, Constance H. Buchanan, and Margaret R. Miles, eds., *Immaculate and Powerful: The Female in Sacred Image and Social Reality*, 283–310. Harvard Women's Studies in Religion Series. Boston: Beacon Press, 1985.

Jones-Warsaw, Koala. "Toward a Womanist Hermeneutic: A Reading of Judges 19–21." In Athalya Brenner, ed., *A Feminist Companion to Judges*, 172–86. FCB 1/4. Sheffield, UK: Sheffield Academic Press, 1993.

Jost, Renate. "God of Love/God of Vengeance, or Samson's 'Prayer for Vengeance.'" In Athalya Brenner, ed., *Judges*, 117–25. FCB 2/4 Sheffield, UK: Sheffield Academic Press, 1999.

Kamuf, Peggy. "Author of a Crime." In Athalya Brenner, ed., *A Feminist Companion to Judges*, 187–206. FCB 1/4. Sheffield, UK: Sheffield Academic Press, 1993.

Keefe, Alice A. "Rapes of Women/Wars of Men." *Semeia* 63 (1993): 79–97.

Kellenbach, Katharina von. "Am I a Murderer? Judges 19–21 as a Parable of Meaningless Suffering." In Tod Linafelt, ed., *Strange Fire: Reading the Hebrew Bible after the Holocaust*, 176–91. New York: New York University Press, 2000.

Klein, Lillian R. "Achsah: What Price This Prize?" In Athalya Brenner, ed., *Judges*, 18–26. FCB 2/4. Sheffield, UK: Sheffield Academic Press, 1999.

———. "The Book of Judges: Paradigm and Deviation in Images of Women." In Athalya Brenner, ed., *A Feminist Companion to Judges*, 55–71. FCB 1/4. Sheffield, UK: Sheffield Academic Press, 1993.

———. "A Spectrum of Female Characters." In Athalya Brenner, ed., *A Feminist Companion to Judges*, 24–33. FCB 1/4. Sheffield, UK: Sheffield Academic Press, 1993.

———. *The Triumph of Irony in the Book of Judges*. JSOTSup 68. Sheffield, UK: Almond, 1988.

———. "Wives and Daughters in the Book of Judges" and "Deborah and Jael: Audacious Female Role Models." In *From Deborah to Esther: Sexual Politics in the Hebrew Bible*, 9–32, 33–40. Minneapolis: Fortress Press, 2003.

Koosed, Jennifer L., and Tod Linafelt. "How the West Was Not One: Delilah Deconstructs the Western." *Semeia* 74 (1996): 167–81.

Kramer, Phyllis Silverman. "Jephthah's Daughter: A Thematic Approach to the Narrative as Seen in Selected Rabbinic Exegesis and in Artwork." In Athalya Brenner, ed., *Judges*, 67–92. FCB 2/4. Sheffield, UK: Sheffield Academic Press, 1999.

———. "Rahab: From Peshat to Pedagogy, or: the Many Faces of a Heroine." In George Aichele, ed., *Culture, Entertainment and the Bible*, 156–72. JSOTSup 309. Sheffield, UK: Sheffield Academic Press, 2000.

Laffey, Alice L. *An Introduction to the Old Testament: A Feminist Perspective*. Philadelphia: Fortress Press, 1988.

Lapsley, Jacqueline. *Whispering the Word: Hearing Women's Stories in the Old Testament*. Louisville, KY: Westminster John Knox Press, 2005.

Lasine, Stuart. "Guest and Host in Judges 19: Lot's Hospitality in an Inverted World." *JSOT* 29 (1984): 37–59.

Leneman, Helen. "Portrayals of Power in the Stories of Delilah and Bathsheba: Seduction in Song." In George Aichele, ed., *Culture, Entertainment and the Bible*, 139–55. JSOTSup 309. Sheffield, UK: Sheffield Academic Press, 2000.

McKinlay, Judith E. "Rahab: A Hero/ine?" *BibInt* 7 (1999): 44–57.

———. "Reading Rahab and Ruth." In *Reframing Her: Biblical Women in Postcolonial Focus*, 37–56. The Bible in the Modern World 1. Sheffield, UK: Sheffield Phoenix Press, 2004.

Merideth, Betsy. "Desire and Danger: The Drama of Betrayal." In Mieke Bal, ed., *Anti-Covenant: Counter-Reading Women's Lives in the Hebrew Bible*, 61–78. JSOTSup 81. Bible and Literature Series 22. Sheffield, UK: Almond Press, 1989.

Miller, Barbara. *Tell It on the Mountain: The Daughter of Jephthah in Judges 11*. Interfaces. Collegeville, MN: Liturgical Press, 2005.

Millett, Craig Ballard. "The Sister." In *Archetypes of Women in Scripture: In God's Image*, 39–56. San Diego: LuraMedia, 1989.

Müllner, Ilse. "Lethal Differences: Sexual Violence as Violence against Others in Judges 19." In Athalya Brenner, ed., *Judges*, 126–42. FCB 2/4. Sheffield, UK: Sheffield Academic Press, 1999.

Niditch, Susan. "Eroticism and Death in the Tale of Jael." In Peggy L. Day, ed., *Gender and Difference in Ancient Israel*, 43–57. Minneapolis: Fortress Press, 1989. And in Alice Bach, ed., *Women in the Hebrew Bible: A Reader*, 305–16. New York and London: Routledge, 1999.

———. "The Sodomite Theme in Judges 19–20: Family, Community, and Social Disintegration." *CBQ* 44 (1982): 364–78.

———. *Underdogs and Tricksters: A Prelude to Biblical Folklore*. San Francisco: Harper & Row, 1987.

Nowell, Irene. "Women of Israel's Early Tribes: Rahab, Deborah and Jael, Jephthah's Daughter, Samson's Mother, Samson's Wife, Delilah." In *Women in the Old Testament*, 59–84. Collegeville, MN: Liturgical Press, 1997.

Ostriker, Alicia. "Jephthah's Daughter: A Lament." In Jane Schaberg, Alice Bach, and Esther Fuchs, eds., *On the Cutting Edge: The Study of Women in Biblical Worlds*, 230–49. New York: Continuum, 2003.

Rakel, Claudia. "'I Will Sing a New Song to My God': Some Remarks on the Intertextuality of Judith 16.1–17." In Athalya Brenner, ed., *Judges*, 27–47. FCB 2/4. Sheffield, UK: Sheffield Academic Press, 1999.

Ramras-Rauch, Gila. "Fathers and Daughters: Two Biblical Narratives." In Vincent L. Tollers and John R. Maier, eds., *Mappings of the Biblical Terrain: The Bible as Text*, 158–69. Lewisburg, PA: Bucknell University Press, 1990.

Rasmussen, Rachel C. "Deborah the Woman Warrior." In Mieke Bal, ed., *Anti-Covenant: Counter-Reading Women's Lives in the Hebrew Bible*, 79–93. JSOTSup 81. Bible and Literature Series 99. Sheffield, UK: Almond Press, 1989.

Reinhartz, Adele. "Samson's Mother: An Unnamed Protagonist." *JSOT* 55 (1992): 25–37. And in Athalya Brenner, ed., *A Feminist Companion to Judges*, 157–70. FCB 1/4. Sheffield, UK: Sheffield Academic Press, 1993.

Reis, Pamela Tamarkin. "Spoiled Child: A Fresh Look at Jephthah's Daughter." *Prooftexts* 17 (1997): 279–98.

———. "Uncovering Jael and Sisera: A New Reading." *SJOT* 19:1 (2005): 24–47.

Rowlett, Lori L. "Disney's Pocahontas and Joshua's Rahab in Postcolonial Perspective." In George Aichele, ed., *Culture, Entertainment and the Bible*, 66–75. JSOTSup 309. Sheffield, UK: Sheffield Academic Press, 2000.

Sakenfeld, Katharine Doob. "Deborah, Jael, and Sisera's Mother: Reading the Scriptures in Cross-Cultural Context." In Jane Dempsey Douglass and James F. Kay, eds., *Women, Gender, and Christian Community*, 13–22. Louisville, KY: Westminster John Knox Press, 1997.

———. "Feminist Biblical Interpretation." *Theology Today* 46 (1989): 154–68.

Schneider, Tammi J. *Judges*. Berit Olam: Studies in Hebrew Narrative and Poetry. Collegeville, MN: Liturgical Press, 2000.

Sheldon, Rose Mary. "Spy Tales." *Bible Review* 19:5 (2003): 12–19, 41–42.

Sigal, Lillian. "Models of Love and Hate." *Daughters of Sarah* 16, no. 2 (March/April 1990): 8–10.

Sjoberg, Mikael. *Wrestling with Textual Violence: The Jephthah Narrative in Antiquity and Modernity*. Sheffield, UK: Sheffield Phoenix, 2005.

Smith, Carol. "Delilah: A Suitable Case for (Feminist) Treatment?" In Athalya Brenner, ed., *Judges*, 93–116. FCB 2/4. Sheffield, UK: Sheffield Academic Press, 1999.

———. "Samson and Delilah: A Parable of Power?" *JSOT* 76 (1977): 45–57.

Sölle, Dorothée, et al. "Rahab the Harlot," "Deborah, Judge of Israel," "Jephthah's Daughter," "Delilah and Samson's Secret." In *Great Women of the Bible in Art and Literature*, 104–13, 114–21, 122–33, 134–47. Trans. Joe H. Kirchberger. Macon, GA: Mercer University Press, 1994.

Tapp, Anne Michelle. "An Ideology of Expendability: Virgin Daughter Sacrifice." In Mieke Bal, ed., *Anti-Covenant: Counter-Reading Women's Lives in the Hebrew Bible*, 157–74. JSOTSup 81. Bible and Literature Series 22. Sheffield, UK: Almond Press, 1989.

Trible, Phyllis. "An Unnamed Woman: The Extravagance of Violence" and "The Daughter of Jephthah: An Inhuman Sacrifice." In *Texts of Terror: Literary-Feminist Readings of Biblical Narratives*, 65–92, 93–118. Overtures to Biblical Theology. Philadelphia: Fortress Press, 1984.

Valler, Shulamit. "The Story of Jephthah's Daughter in the Midrash." In Athalya Brenner, ed., *Judges*, 48–66. FCB 2/4. Sheffield, UK: Sheffield Academic Press, 1999.

van Dijk-Hemmes, Fokkelien. "Mothers and a Mediator in the Song of Devorah." In Athalya Brenner, ed., *A Feminist Companion to Judges*, 110–14. FCB 1/4. Sheffield, UK: Sheffield Academic Press, 1993.

van Wijk-Bos, Johanna W. H. *Reformed and Feminist: A Challenge to the Church*. Louisville, KY: Westminster/John Knox Press, 1991.

van Wolde, Ellen. "Deborah and Ya'el in Judges 4." In Meindert Dijkstra and Bob Becking, eds., *On Reading Prophetic Texts: Gender Specific and Related Studies in Memory of Fokkelien van Dijk-Hemmes*, 283–95. Leiden: E. J. Brill, 1996.

———. "Ya'el in Judges 4." *ZAW* 107 (1995): 240–46.

Weems, Renita J. "A Crying Shame (Jephthah's Daughter and the Mourning Women)." In *Just a Sister Away: A Womanist Vision of Women's Relationships in the Bible*, 53–70. San Diego: LuraMedia, 1988.

Weldon, Fay. "Samson and His Women." In Celina Spiegel and Christina Buchmann, eds., *Out of the Garden: Women Writers on the Bible*, 72–81. New York: Fawcett Columbine, 1994.

Yee, Gale A. "By the Hand of a Woman: The Metaphor of the Woman Warrior in Judges 4." In Claudia V. Camp and Carole R. Fontaine, eds., *Women, War, and Metaphor: Language and Society in the Study of the Hebrew Bible*. *Semeia* 61 (1993): 99–132.

———. "Ideological Criticism: Judges 17–21 and the Dismembered Body." In *Judges and Method: New Approaches in Biblical Studies*, 146–70. Minneapolis: Fortress Press, 1995.

———, ed. *Judges and Method: New Approaches in Biblical Studies*. Minneapolis: Fortress Press, 1995.

Yoo, Yani. "*Han*-Laden Women: Korean 'Comfort Women' and Women in Judges 19–21." *Semeia* 78 (1997): 37–46.

CHAPTER 6: THE WOMEN IN 1 AND 2 SAMUEL

Amit, Yairah. "'Am I Not More Devoted to You Than Ten Sons?' (1 Samuel 1.8): Male and Female Interpretations." In Athalya Brenner, ed., *A Feminist Companion to Samuel and Kings*, 58–76. FCB 1/5. Sheffield, UK: Sheffield Academic Press, 1994.

Bach, Alice. "The Pleasure of Her Text." Article in *Ad Feminam*. *USQR* 43 (1989): 41–58. And chap. in *The Pleasure of Her Text: Feminist Readings of Biblical and Historical Texts*, 25–44. Philadelphia: Trinity Press International, 1990. Also in Athalya Brenner, ed., *A Feminist Companion to Samuel and Kings*, 106–28. FCB 1/5. Sheffield, UK: Sheffield Academic Press, 1994.

———. *Reading the Women of the Bible: A New Interpretation of Their Stories*. New York: Schocken Books, 2002.

———. *Women, Seduction, and Betrayal in Biblical Narrative*. Cambridge, UK: Cambridge University Press, 1997.

Bal, Mieke. "The Emergence of the Lethal Woman, or the Use of the Hermeneutic Model." In *Lethal Love: Feminist Literary Readings of Biblical Love Stories*. Indiana Studies in Biblical Literature. Bloomington: Indiana University Press, 1987.

Berlin, Adele. "Abigail 1" and "Bathsheba," In *WIS*, 43–42, 57–58.

———. "Characterization in Biblical Narrative: David's Wives." *JSOT* 23 (1982): 69–85.

Bledstein, Adrien Janis. "Tamar and the 'Coat of Many Colors.'" In Athalya Brenner, ed., *A Feminist Companion to Samuel and Kings*, 65–83. FCB 1/5. Sheffield, UK: Sheffield Academic Press, 1994.

Brenner, Athalya, ed. *A Feminist Companion to Samuel and Kings*. FCB 1/5. Sheffield, UK: Sheffield Academic Press, 1994.

———, ed. *Samuel and Kings*. FCB 2/7. Sheffield, UK: Sheffield Academic Press, 2000.

———. "Tamar 2." In *WIS*, 163–64.

Brueggemann, Walter. "1 Samuel 1: A Sense of a Beginning." In *Old Testament Theology: Essays on Structure Theme and Text*, 219–34. Minneapolis: Fortress Press, 1992.

Callaway, Mary. *Sing, O Barren One: A Study in Comparative Midrash*. SBLDS 91. Atlanta: Scholars Press, 1986.

Camp, Claudia V. "Wise Woman of Abel of Beth-maacah" and "Wise Woman of Tekoa." In *WIS*, 266–67, 263–66.

————. "The Wise Women of 2 Samuel: A Role Model for Women in Early Israel?" *CBQ* 43 (1981): 14–29. And in Alice Bach, ed., *Women in the Hebrew Bible: A Reader*, 195–207. New York and London: Routledge, 1999.

Carmody, Denise Lardner. *Biblical Woman: Contemporary Reflections on Scriptural Texts*. New York: Crossroad, 1988.

Clines, David J. A. "Michal Observed: An Introduction to Reading Her Story." In David J. A. Clines and Tamara C. Eskenazi, eds., *Telling Queen Michal's Story: An Experiment in Comparative Interpretation*, 24–63. JSOTSup 119. Sheffield, UK: Sheffield Academic Press, 1991.

Clines, David J. A., and Tamara C. Eskenazi, eds. *Telling Queen Michal's Story: An Experiment in Comparative Interpretation*. JSOTSup 119. Sheffield, UK: Sheffield Academic Press, 1991.

Cook, Joan E. "Hannah's Later Songs: A Study in Comparative Methods of Interpretation." In Craig A. Evans and James A. Sanders, eds., *The Function of Scripture in Early Jewish and Christian Tradition*, 241–61. JSOTSup 154. Studies in Scripture in Early Judaism and Christianity 6. Sheffield, UK: Sheffield Academic Press, 1998.

Cooper-White, Pamela. *The Cry of Tamar: Violence against Women and the Church's Response*. Minneapolis: Fortress Press, 1995.

Edelman, Diana Vikander. "Rizpah." In *WIS*, 145–46.

Exum, J. Cheryl. "Bathsheba Plotted, Shot, and Painted" and "Michal at the Window, Michal in the Movies." In *Plotted, Shot, and Painted: Cultural Representations of Biblical Women*, 19–53, 54–79. Sheffield, UK: Sheffield Academic Press, 1996.

————. "Michal." In *WIS*, 125–26.

————. "Michal at the Movies." In M. Daniel Carroll R., David J. A. Clines, and Philip R. Davies, eds., *The Bible in Human Society: Essays in Honour of John Rogerson*, 273–92. JSOTSup 200. Sheffield, UK: Sheffield Academic Press, 1995.

————. "Michal: The Whole Story" and "Raped by the Pen." In *Fragmented Women: Feminist (Sub)Versions of Biblical Narratives*, 42–60, 170–201. Valley Forge, PA: Trinity Press International, 1993.

————. "Murder They Wrote: Ideology and the Manipulation of Female Presence in Biblical Narrative." In Alice Bach, ed., *Ad Feminam. USQR* 43 (1989): 19–39. And in Alice Bach, ed., *The Pleasure of Her Text: Feminist Readings of Biblical and Historical Texts*, 45–68. Philadelphia: Trinity Press International, 1990. In slightly revised form in J. Cheryl Exum, *Fragmented Women: Feminist (Sub)Versions of Biblical Narratives*, 16–41. Valley Forge, PA: Trinity Press International, 1993.

————. "Rizpah." *Word & World* 17 (1997): 260–68.

————. *Tragedy and Biblical Narrative: Arrows of the Almighty*. Cambridge: Cambridge University Press, 1992.

Falk, Marcia. "Reflections on Hannah's Prayer." *Tikkun* 9 (1994): 61–64.

Feinstein, Jessica. "Wife, Mother, Queen, Object of Royal Lust." In Susan Headen and Jeffery L. Sheler, eds., *Women of the Bible: Provocative New Insights*, 26–29. *U.S. News and World Report* Special Collector's Edition, 2005.

Fontaine, Carole R. "The Bearing of Wisdom on the Shape of 2 Samuel 11–12 and 1 Kings 3." *JSOT* 34 (1986): 61–77. And in Athalya Brenner, ed., *A Feminist Companion to Samuel and Kings*, 143–60. FCB 1/5. Sheffield, UK: Sheffield Academic Press, 1994.

————. "A Response to 'The Bearing of Wisdom.'" In Athalya Brenner, ed., *A Feminist Companion to Samuel and Kings*, 161–68. FCB 1/5. Sheffield, UK: Sheffield Academic Press, 1994.

Gershenzon, Shoshanna. "Michal Bat Shaul." In David J. A. Clines and Tamara C. Eskenazi, eds., *Telling Queen Michal's Story: An Experiment in Comparative Interpretation*, 199–200. JSOTSup 119. Sheffield, UK: Sheffield Academic Press, 1991.

Gnadadason, Aruna. "We Dare to Be Pregnant and Give Birth to Our Dreams Again: Searching Our Faith and Rediscovering Our Power—and Our History of Resistance and of Struggle." *Church & Society* 86 (1996): 62–68.

Green, Barbara. "Enacting the Unthinkable: 1 Sam 25 and the Story of Saul." *BibInt* 11:1 (2003): 1–23.

Hackett, Jo Ann. "1 and 2 Samuel." In *WBC*, 91–101.

Hollyday, Joyce. "Voices out of the Silence: Recovering the Biblical Witness of Women." *Sojourners* 15 (1986): 20–23.

Hyman, Naomi Mara. "Hannah" and "Bathsheba." In *Biblical Women in the Midrash: A Sourcebook*, 121–128, 129–134. Northvale, NJ, and London: Jason Aronson, 1997.

Keefe, Alice A. "Rapes of Women/Wars of Men." *Semeia* 61 (1993): 79–97.

Kim, Hyun Chul Paul, and M. Fulgence Nyengele. "Murder S/He Wrote? A Cultural and Psychological Reading of 2 Samuel 11–12." In Cheryl A. Kirk-Duggan, ed., *Pregnant Passion: Gender, Sex, and Violence in the Bible*, 95–116. Semeia Studies 44. Atlanta: SBL Press, 2003.

Kirk-Duggan, Cheryl A. "Slingshots, Ships, and Personal Psychosis: Murder, Sexual Intrigue, and Power in the Lives of David and Otello." In Kirk-Duggan, ed., *Pregnant Passion: Gender, Sex, and Violence in the Bible*, 37–70. Semeia Studies 44. Atlanta: SBL Press, 2003.

Klein, Lillian R."Bathsheba Revealed," and "Michal, the Barren Wife." In Athalya Brenner, ed., *A Feminist Companion to Samuel and Kings*, 47–64, 37–46. FCB 1/5. Sheffield, UK: Sheffield Academic Press, 1994. And in *From Deborah to Esther: Sexual Politics in the Hebrew Bible*, 55–72, 85–94. Minneapolis: Fortress Press, 2003.

———. "Hannah." In *WIS*, 90–91.

———. "Hannah: Marginalized Victim and Social Redeemer." In Athalya Brenner, ed., *A Feminist Companion to Samuel and Kings*, 77–92. FCB 1/5. Sheffield, UK: Sheffield Academic Press, 1994. And in *From Deborah to Esther: Sexual Politics in the Hebrew Bible*, 41–54. Minneapolis: Fortress Press, 2003.

Laffey, Alice L. *An Introduction to the Old Testament: A Feminist Perspective*. Philadelphia: Fortress Press, 1988.

McKinlay, Judith E. "To Eat or Not to Eat: Where Is Wisdom in This Choice?" *Semeia* 86 (1999): 73–84.

Meyers, Carol. "Hannah and Her Sacrifice: Reclaiming Female Agency." In Athalya Brenner, ed., *A Feminist Companion to Samuel and Kings*, 93–104. FCB 1/5. Sheffield, UK: Sheffield Academic Press, 1994.

———. "The Hannah Narrative in Feminist Perspective." In Joseph Coleson and Victor Matthews, eds., *Go to the Land I Will Show You: Studies in Honor of Dwight W. Young*, 117–26. Winona Lake, IN: Eisenbrauns, 1996.

Muraoka, Takamitsu. "1 Sam 1,15 Again." *Bib* 77:1 (1996): 98–99.

Nowell, Irene. "More Women of Israel's Early Tribes: Ruth, Naomi, and Orpah, Hannah and Peninnah" and "Women of Israel's Monarchy: Michal, Bathsheba, Tamar, Queen of Sheba, Jezebel." In *Women in the Old Testament*, 85–130. Collegeville, MN: Liturgical Press, 1997.

Nunnally-Cox, Janice. *Foremothers: Women of the Bible*. San Francisco: Harper & Row, 1981.

Overholt, Thomas W. "Medium of Endor." In *WIS*, 258–59.

Reinhartz, Adele. "Anonymity and Character in the Books of Samuel." *Semeia* 63 (1993): 117–41.

———. "Anonymous Women and the Collapse of the Monarchy: A Study in Narrative Technique." In Athalya Brenner, ed., *A Feminist Companion to Samuel and Kings*, 43–65. FCB 1/5. Sheffield, UK: Sheffield Academic Press, 1994.

Reis, Pamela Tamarkin. "Cupidity and Stupidity: Woman's Agency and the 'Rape' of Tamar." *Journal of the Ancient Near Eastern Society* 25 (1997): 43–60.

Sakenfeld, Katharine Doob. "Michal, Abigail, and Bathsheba: In the Eye of the Beholder," In *Just Wives? Stories of Power and Survival in the Old Testament and Today*, 69–90. Louisville, KY: Westminster John Knox Press, 2003.

Schwartz, Regina M. "Adultery in the House of David: The Metanarrative of Biblical Scholarship and the Narratives of the Bible." *Semeia* 54 (1991): 35–56. And in Alice Bach, ed., *Women in the Hebrew Bible: A Reader*, 335–50. New York and London: Routledge, 1999.

———. "The Histories of David: Biblical Scholarship and Biblical Stories." In Jason P. Rosenblatt and Joseph C. Sitterson Jr., eds.,*"Not in Heaven": Coherence and Complexity in Biblical Narrative*, 192–210. Indiana Studies in Biblical Literature. Bloomington and Indianapolis: Indiana University Press, 1991.

Shargent, Karla G. "Living on the Edge: The Liminality of Daughters in Genesis to 2 Samuel." In Athalya Brenner, ed., *A Feminist Companion to Samuel and Kings*, 26–42. FCB 1/5. Sheffield, UK: Sheffield Academic Press, 1994.

Smith, Jenny. "The Discourse Structure of the Rape of Tamar (2 Samuel 13:1–22)." *Vox Evangelica* 20 (1990): 21–42.

Sölle, Dorothée, et al. "Hannah and Her Vow to the Lord," "Abigail," "The Witch of Endor," and "Bathsheba, Uriah's Beautiful Wife." In *Great Women of the Bible in Art and Literature*, 158–65, 166–75, 176–83, 184–93. Trans. Joe H. Kirchberger. Macon, GA: Mercer University Press, 1994.

Tamar [pseud.]. "Tamar and Amnon Revisited: Brother Violates Sister." *Daughters of Sarah* 13, no. 5 (September/October 1989): 11–13.

Trible, Phyllis. "Tamar: The Royal Rape of Wisdom." In *Texts of Terror: Literary-Feminist Readings of Biblical Narratives*. Overtures to Biblical Theology. Philadelphia: Fortress Press, 1984.

Valler, Shulamit. "King David and 'His' Women: Biblical Stories and Talmudic Discussions." In Athalya Brenner, ed., *A Feminist Companion to Samuel and Kings*, 129–42. FCB 1/5. Sheffield, UK: Sheffield Academic Press, 1994.

van Wolde, Ellen J. "A Leader Led by a Lady: David and Abigail in 1 Samuel 25." *ZAW* 114:3 (2002): 355–75.

Willey, Patricia K. "The Importunate Woman of Tekoa and How She Got Her Way." In Danna Nolan Fewell, ed., *Reading between Texts: Intertextuality and the Hebrew Bible*, 115–31. Literary Currents in Biblical Interpretation. Louisville, KY: Westminster/John Knox Press, 1992.

Winters, Alicia. "The Subversive Memory of a Woman: 2 Samuel 21:1–14." In Leif E. Vaage, ed. and trans., *Subversive Scriptures: Revolutionary Readings of the Christian Bible in Latin America*. Valley Forge, PA: Trinity Press International, 1997.

Yee, Gale A. "Fraught with Background: Literary Ambiguity in II Samuel 11." *Interpretation* 42 (1988): 240–53.

CHAPTER 7: THE WOMEN IN 1 AND 2 KINGS

Bach, Alice. *Reading the Women of the Bible: A New Interpretation of Their Stories*. New York: Schocken Books, 2002.

Beach, Eleanor Ferris. *The Jezebel Letters: Religion and Politics in Ninth Century Israel*. Minneapolis: Fortress Press, 2005.

———. "The Samaria Ivories, *Marzeah* and Biblical Texts." *BA* 56 (1992): 130–39.

Ben-Barak, Zafrira. "The Status and Right of the *gᵉbîrâ*." In Athalya Brenner, ed., *A Feminist Companion to Samuel and Kings*, 170–85. FCB 1/5. Sheffield, UK: Sheffield Academic Press, 1994.

Berlin, Adele. "Bathsheba." In *WIS*, 57–58.

———. "Characterization in Biblical Narrative: David's Wives." *JSOT* 23 (1982): 69–85.

Bird, Phyllis. "The Harlot as Heroine: Narrative Art and Social Presupposition in Three Old Testament Texts." *Semeia* 46 (1989): 119–39. And in Alice Bach, ed., *Women in the Hebrew Bible: A Reader*, 99–118. New York and London: Routledge, 1999.

Brenner, Athalya. "Athaliah," and "Jezebel 1." In *WIS*, 55, 100–102.

———, ed. *A Feminist Companion to Samuel and Kings*. FCB 1/5. Sheffield, UK: Sheffield Academic Press, 1994.

———. "I Am the Rat: Huldah the Prophet." In *I Am . . . Biblical Women Tell Their Own Stories*, 155–62. Minneapolis: Fortress Press, 2005.

———, ed. *Samuel and Kings*. FCB 2/7. Sheffield, UK: Sheffield Academic Press, 2000.

Camp, Claudia V. "Abishag," "Huldah," "Shunammite," and "Two Mothers Who Agree to Eat Their Sons." In *WIS*, 45–46, 96–97, 274–75, 275–76.

———. "Female Voice, Written Word: Women and Authority in Hebrew Scripture." In Paula M. Cooey, Sharon A. Farmer, and Mary Ellen Ross, eds., *Embodied Love: Sensuality and Relationship as Feminist Values*. San Francisco: Harper & Row, 1987.

———. "1 and 2 Kings." In *WBC*, 102–16.

Carmody, Denise Lardner. *Biblical Woman: Contemporary Reflections on Scriptural Texts*. New York: Crossroad, 1988.

Dutcher-Walls, Patricia. *Jezebel: Portraits of a Queen*. Interfaces. Collegeville, MN: Liturgical Press, 2004.

Edelman, Diana. "Huldah the Prophet—of Yahweh or Asherah?" In Athalya Brenner, ed., *A Feminist Companion to Samuel and Kings*, 231–50. FCB 1/5. Sheffield, UK: Sheffield Academic Press, 1994.

Exum, J. Cheryl. *Tragedy and Biblical Narrative: Arrows of the Almighty.* Cambridge: Cambridge University Press, 1997.

Fewell, Danna Nolan. "The Gift: World Alternation and Obligation in 2 Kings 4:8–37." In Saul M. Olyan and Robert C. Culley, eds., *"A Wise and Discerning Mind": Essays in Honor of Burke O. Long,* 109–24. Brown Judaic Studies 325. Atlanta: SBL Press, 2000.

Finger, Reta Halteman. "Huldah, the First Biblical Text Critic." *Other Side* 35:2 (1999): 51, 53.

Fontaine, Carole R. "Queen of Sheba." In *WIS,* 270–71.

Frick, Frank S. "Widow of Zarephath" and "Widow Whose Oil Is Multiplied." In *WIS,* 272–73, 274.

Fuchs, Esther. "The Literary Characterization of Mothers and Sexual Politics in the Hebrew Bible." In Adela Yarbro Collins, ed., *Feminist Perspectives on Biblical Scholarship,* 117–36. SBLBSNA 10. Chico, CA: Scholars Press, 1985.

Gaines, Janet Howe. "How Bad Was Jezebel?" *Bible Review* 16 (2000): 12–23.

——. *Music in the Old Bones: Jezebel through the Ages.* Carbondale and Edwardsville: Southern Illinois University Press, 1999.

Goodfriend, Elaine Adler. "Two Prostitutes as Mothers." In *WIS,* 268–69.

Hiebert, Paula S. "'Whence Shall Help Come to Me?' The Biblical Widow." In Peggy L. Day, ed., *Gender and Difference in Ancient Israel,* 125–41. Minneapolis: Fortress Press, 1989.

Holt, Else Kragelund. "'. . . Urged on by His Wife Jezebel': A Literary Reading of 1 Kgs 18 in Context." *SJOT* 9:1 (1995): 83–96.

Lanner, Laurel. "Cannibal Mothers and Me: A Mother's Reading of 2 Kings 6:24–7:20." In Athalya Brenner, ed., *Samuel and Kings,* 129–37. FCB 2/7. Sheffield, UK: Sheffield Academic Press, 2000.

Lasine, Stuart. "Jehoram and the Cannibal Mothers (2 Kings 6:24–33): Solomon's Judgment in an Inverted World." *JSOT* 50 (1991): 27–53.

Lassner, Jacob. *Demonizing the Queen of Sheba: Boundaries of Gender and Culture in Postbiblical Judaism and Medieval Islam.* Chicago: University of Chicago Press, 1993.

McGee, Paula L. "Divine Divas." *Journal for the Interdenominational Theological Center* 31:1–2 (2003–04): 207–14.

McKinlay, Judith E. "Negotiating the Frame for Viewing the Death of Jezebel." *BibInt* 10:3 (2002): 205–23.

——. "Reading Jezebel" and "Viewing the Death of Jezebel." In *Reframing Her: Biblical Women in Postcolonial Focus,* 57–78, 79–95. The Bible in the Modern World 1. Sheffield, UK: Phoenix Press, 2004.

Millett, Craig Ballard. "The Wise One." In *Archetypes of Women in Scripture: In God's Image,* 57–72. San Diego: LuraMedia, 1989.

Mitchell, Mozella. "Pro-vi-dence." In Ella Pearson Mitchell, ed., *Those Preaching Women: More Sermons by Black Women Preachers,* 48–54. Valley Forge, PA: Judson Press, 1988.

Nowell, Irene. "Women of Israel's Monarchy: Michal, Bathsheba, Tamar, Queen of Sheba, Jezebel." In *Women in the Old Testament,* 103–30. Collegeville, MN: Liturgical Press, 1997.

Nunnally-Cox, Janice. *Foremothers: Women of the Bible.* San Francisco: Harper & Row, 1981.

Pippin, Tina. "Jezebel Re-Vamped." In Athalya Brenner, ed., *A Feminist Companion to Samuel and Kings,* 196–206. FCB 1/5. Sheffield, UK: Sheffield Academic Press, 1994.

Satchell, Michael. "The Reigning Icon of Womanly Evil." In Susan Headen and Jeffery L. Sheler, eds., *Women of the Bible: Provocative New Insights,* 30–33. *U.S. News and World Report* Special Collector's Edition, 2005.

Schmidt, Uta. "Center or Fringe? Positioning the Wife of Jeroboam (1 Kings 14:1–18)." In Athalya Brenner, ed., *Samuel and Kings,* 86–97. FCB 2/7. Sheffield, UK: Sheffield Academic Press, 2000.

Shields, Mary. "Self-Response to 'Subverting a Man of God, Elevating a Woman: Role and Power Reversals in 2 Kings 4.'" In Athalya Brenner, ed., *Samuel and Kings,* 125–28. FCB 2/7. Sheffield, UK: Sheffield Academic Press, 2000.

——. "Subverting a Man of God, Elevating a Woman: Role and Power Reversal in 2 Kings 4." *JSOT* 58 (1993): 59–69. And in Athalya Brenner, ed., *Samuel and Kings,* 115–24. FCB 2/7. Sheffield, UK: Sheffield Academic Press, 2000.

Siebert-Hommes, Jopie. "The Widow of Zarephath and the Great Woman of Shunem: A Comparative Analysis of Two Stories." In Bob Becking and Meindert Dijkstra, eds., *On Reading Prophetic Texts:*

Gender-Specific and Related Studies in Memory of Fokkelien van Dijk-Hemmes, 231–50. Leiden: E. J. Brill, 1996. And in Athalya Brenner, ed., *Samuel and Kings*, 98–114. FCB 2/7. Sheffield, UK: Sheffield Academic Press, 2000.

Smith, Carol. "'Queenship' in Israel? The Cases of Bathsheba, Jezebel and Athaliah." In John Day, ed., *King and Messiah in Israel and the Ancient Near East*. JSOTSup 270. Sheffield, UK: Sheffield Academic Press, 1998.

Sölle, Dorothée, et al. "The Queen of Sheba." In *Great Women of the Bible in Art and Literature*, 194–205. Trans. Joe H. Kirchberger. Macon, GA: Mercer University Press, 1994.

Spanier, Ktziah. "The Queen Mother in the Judaean Royal Court: Maacah—A Case Study." In Athalya Brenner, ed., *A Feminist Companion to Samuel and Kings*, 186–95. FCB 1/5. Sheffield, UK: Sheffield Academic Press, 1994.

Tarlin, Jan. "Toward a 'Female' Reading of the Elijah Cycle: Ideology and Gender in the Interpretation of 1 Kings 17–19, 21 and 2 Kings 1–2, 18." In Athalya Brenner, ed., *A Feminist Companion to Samuel and Kings*, 208–17. FCB 1/5. Sheffield, UK: Sheffield Academic Press, 1994.

Trible, Phyllis. "Exegesis for Storytellers and Other Strangers." *JBL* 114 (1995): 3–19.

———. "The Odd Couple: Elijah and Jezebel." In Christina Buchmann and Celina Spiegel, eds., *Out of the Garden: Women Writers on the Bible*, 155–79. New York: Fawcett Columbine, 1994.

van Dijk-Hemmes, Fokkelien. "The Great Woman of Shunem and the Man of God: A Dual Interpretation of 2 Kings 4:8–37." In Athalya Brenner, ed., *A Feminist Companion to Samuel and Kings*, 218–30. FCB 1/5. Sheffield, UK: Sheffield Academic Press, 1994.

van Wijk-Bos, Johanna W. H. *Reformed and Feminist: A Challenge to the Church*. Louisville, KY: Westminster/John Knox Press, 1991.

———. "Who Speaks for God." *Perspectives* 9 (1994): 8–9.

van Wolde, Ellen. "Who Guides Whom? Embeddedness and Perspective in Biblical Hebrew and in 1 Kings 3:16–28." *JBL* 114 (1995): 623–42.

Weems, Renita J. "Hulda, the Prophet: Reading a (Deuteronomistic) Woman's Identity." In Brent A. Strawn and Nancy R. Bowen, eds., *A God So Near: Essays on Old Testament Theology in Honor of Patrick D. Miller*, 321–40. Winona Lake, IN: Eisenbrauns, 2003.

Zlotnick, Helena. "From Jezebel to Esther: Fashioning Images of Queenship in the Hebrew Bible." *Bib* 82 (2001): 477–95.

CHAPTER 8: THE WOMEN IN THE PROPHETS

Ackerman, Susan. "'And the Women Knead Dough': The Worship of the Queen of Heaven in Sixth-Century Judah." In Peggy L. Day, ed., *Gender and Difference in Ancient Israel*, 109–24. Minneapolis: Fortress Press, 1989. And in Alice Bach, ed., *Women in the Hebrew Bible: A Reader*, 21–32. New York and London: Routledge, 1999.

———. "Isaiah." In *WBC*, 169–77.

———. "Prophetess (Wife of Isaiah)," "Queen of Heaven," "Woman Jerusalem/Zion in Isaiah," and "Young Woman (Isa 7:14)." In *WIS*, 317, 538–39, 544–45, 317–18.

Bach, Alice. *Reading the Women of the Bible: A New Interpretation of Their Stories*. New York: Schocken Books, 2002.

Bauer, Angela. *Gender in the Book of Jeremiah: A Feminist Literary Reading*. New York: Peter Lang, 1999.

———. "Woman Encompassing a Man" and "Women in Imagery for Jerusalem, Judah, and Israel in Jeremiah." In *WIS*, 330–31, 555.

Baumann, Gerlinde. "Prophetic Objections to YHWH as the Violent Husband of Israel: Reinterpretations of the Prophetic Marriage Metaphor in Second Isaiah (Isaiah 40–55)." In Athalya Brenner, ed., *The Prophets and Daniel*, 88–120. FCB 2/8. Sheffield, UK: Sheffield Academic Press, 2001.

Beach, Eleanor Ferris. "The Samaria Ivories, *Marzeah* and Biblical Texts." *BA* 56 (1992): 130–39.

Bird, Phyllis A. "The Harlot as Heroine: Narrative Art and Social Presupposition in Three Old Testament Texts." *Semeia* 46 (1989): 119–39.

———. "'To Play the Harlot': An Inquiry into an Old Testament Metaphor." In Peggy L. Day, ed., *Gender and Difference in Ancient Israel*, 75–94. Minneapolis: Fortress Press, 1989.

Bohmbach, Karla G. "Daughter." In *WIS*, 517–19.

Bowen, Nancy R. "Can God Be Trusted? Confronting the Deceptive God." In Athalya Brenner, ed., *A Feminist Companion to the Latter Prophets*, 354–65. FCB 1/8. Sheffield, UK: Sheffield Academic Press, 1995; London and New York: T. & T. Clark, 2004.

———. "The Daughters of Your People: Female Prophets in Ezekiel 13:17–23." *JBL* 118 (1999): 417–33.

Brenner, Athalya, ed. *A Feminist Companion to the Latter Prophets*. FCB 8. Sheffield, UK: Sheffield Academic Press, 1995; London and New York: T. & T. Clark, 2004.

———. "On Prophetic Propaganda and the Politics of 'Love': The Case of Jeremiah." In *A Feminist Companion to the Latter Prophets*, 256–74. FCB 1/8. Sheffield, UK: Sheffield Academic Press, 1995; London and New York: T. & T. Clark, 2004.

———. "Pornoprophetics Revisited: Some Additional Reflections." *JSOT* 70 (1996): 63–86.

———. "Who's Afraid of Feminist Criticism? Who's Afraid of Biblical Humour? The Case of the Obtuse Foreign Ruler in the Hebrew Bible" and "Self-Response to 'Who's Afraid of Feminist Criticism?'" In *The Prophets and Daniel*, 228–44, 245–46. FCB 2/8. Sheffield, UK: Sheffield Academic Press, 2001.

Callaway, Mary. *Sing, O Barren One: A Study in Comparative Midrash*. SBLDS 91. Atlanta: Scholars Press, 1986.

Carroll, Robert P. "Desire under the Terebinths: On Pornographic Representation in the Prophets—A Response." In Athalya Brenner, ed., *A Feminist Companion to the Latter Prophets*, 275–307. FCB 1/8. Sheffield, UK: Sheffield Academic Press, 1995; London and New York: T. & T. Clark, 2004.

Darr, Katheryn Phisterer. "Ezekiel." In *WBC*, 192–200.

———. "Oholah, Woman of Samaria" and "Women Weeping for Tammuz." In *WIS*, 536–38, 335–36.

Day, Linda M. "Rhetoric and Domestic Violence in Ezekiel 16." *BibInt* 8 (2000): 205–30.

Day, Peggy L. "Adulterous Jerusalem's Imagined Demise: Death of a Metaphor in Ezekiel XVI." *VT* 50 (2000): 285–309.

———. "The Bitch Had It Coming to Her: Rhetoric and Interpretation in Ezekiel 16." *BibInt* 8 (2000): 231–54.

Dempsey, Carol J. "The 'Whore' of Ezekiel 15: The Impact and Ramifications of Gender-Specific Metaphors in Light of Biblical Law." In Victor H. Matthews, Bernard M. Levinson, and Tikva Frymer-Kensky, eds., *Gender and Law in the Hebrew Bible and the Ancient Near East*, 57–78. JSOTSup 262. Sheffield, UK: Sheffield Academic Press, 1998.

Diamond, A. R. Pete, and Kathleen M. O'Connor. "Unfaithful Passions: Coding Women Coding Men in Jeremiah 2–3 (4.2)" *BibInt* 4 (1996): 288–310.

Dijkstra, Meindert, and Bob Becking, eds. *On Reading Prophetic Texts: Gender-Specific and Related Studies in Memory of Fokkelien van Dijk-Hemmes*. Leiden: E. J. Brill, 1996.

Emmerson, Grace I. *Hosea: An Israelite Prophet in Judean Perspective*. JSOTSup 28. Sheffield, UK: JSOT Press, 1984.

Exum, J. Cheryl. "Prophetic Pornography." In *Plotted, Shot, and Painted: Cultural Representations of Biblical Women*, 101–28. Sheffield, UK: Sheffield Academic Press, 1996.

Fontaine, Carole R. "Hosea" and "A Response to 'Hosea.'" In Athalya Brenner, ed., *A Feminist Companion to the Latter Prophets*, 40–59, 60–69. FCB 1/8. Sheffield, UK: Sheffield Academic Press, 1995; London and New York: T. & T. Clark, 2004.

Frymer-Kensky, Tikva. "Asherah and Abundance," "The Wanton Wife of God," and "Zion, the Beloved Woman." In *In the Wake of the Goddesses: Women, Culture, and the Biblical Transformation of Pagan Myth*, 153–61, 144–52, 168–78. New York: Free Press, 1992.

Fuchs, Esther. "Prophecy and the Construction of Women: Inscription and Erasure." In Athalya Brenner, ed., *The Prophets and Daniel*, 54–69. FCB 2/8. Sheffield, UK: Sheffield Academic Press, 2001.

Galambush, Julie. *Jerusalem in the Book of Ezekiel: The City as Yahweh's Wife*. SBLDS 130. Atlanta: Scholars Press, 1992.

Glazier-McDonald, Beth. "Joel," "Obadiah," "Haggai," "Zechariah," and "Malachi." In *WBC*, 203–4, 210–11, 228–29, 230–31, 232–34.

Goldingay, John. "Hosea 1–3, Genesis 1–4 and Masculist Interpretation." In Athalya Brenner, ed., *A Feminist Companion to the Latter Prophets*, 161–68. FCB 1/8. Sheffield, UK: Sheffield Academic Press, 1995; London and New York: T. & T. Clark, 2004.

Gordon, Pamela, and Harold C. Washington. "Rape as a Military Metaphor in the Hebrew Bible." In
    Athalya Brenner, ed., *A Feminist Companion to the Latter Prophets*, 308–25. FCB 1/8. Sheffield, UK:
    Sheffield Academic Press, 1995; London and New York: T. & T. Clark, 2004.
Graetz, Naomi. "God Is to Israel as Husband Is to Wife: The Metaphoric Battering of Hosea's Wife." In
    Athalya Brenner, ed., *A Feminist Companion to the Latter Prophets*, 126–45. FCB 1/8. Sheffield, UK:
    Sheffield Academic Press, 1995; London and New York: T. & T. Clark, 2004.
Gravett, Sandra L. "Female Images for Nations in Ezekiel," "Oholah," and "Oholibah, Woman/Whore
    Jerusalem." In *WIS*, 523–24, 536–38, 538.
Gruber, Mayer I. "Marital Fidelity and Intimacy: A View from Hosea 4." In Athalya Brenner, ed., *A
    Feminist Companion to the Latter Prophets*, 169–79. FCB 1/8. Sheffield, UK: Sheffield Academic
    Press, 1995; London and New York: T. & T. Clark, 2004.
———. "Nineveh the Adulteress." In Athalya Brenner, ed., *The Prophets and Daniel*, 220–25. FCB 2/8.
    Sheffield, UK: Sheffield Academic Press, 2001.
Hadley, Judith M. "The Queen of Heaven—Who Is She?" In Athalya Brenner, ed., *The Prophets and
    Daniel*, 30–53. FCB 2/8. Sheffield, UK: Sheffield Academic Press, 2001.
Jost, Renate. "The Daughters of Your People Prophesy." In Athalya Brenner, ed., *The Prophets and
    Daniel*, 70–76. FCB 2/8. Sheffield, UK: Sheffield Academic Press, 2001.
Kamionkowski, S. Tamar. "Gender Reversal in Ezekiel 16." In Athalya Brenner, ed., *The Prophets and
    Daniel*, 170–85. FCB 2/8. Sheffield, UK: Sheffield Academic Press, 2001.
Keefe, Alice A. "The Female Body, The Body Politic and the Land: A Sociopolitical Reading of Hosea
    1–2." In Athalya Brenner, ed., *A Feminist Companion to the Latter Prophets*, 70–100. FCB 1/8.
    Sheffield, UK: Sheffield Academic Press, 1995; London and New York: T. & T. Clark, 2004.
Kessler, Rainer. "Miriam and the Prophecy of the Persian Period." In Athalya Brenner, ed., *The Prophets
    and Daniel*, 77–86. FCB 2/8. Sheffield, UK: Sheffield Academic Press, 2001.
Korpel, Marjo C. A. "The Female Servant of the Lord in Isaiah 54." In Bob Becking and Meindert Dijk-
    stra, eds., *On Reading Prophetic Texts: Gender-Specific and Related Studies in Memory of Fokkelien van
    Dijk-Hemmes*, 153–68. Leiden/New York/Cologne: E. J. Brill, 1996.
Landy, Francis. "Fantasy and the Displacement of Pleasure: Hosea 2.4–17." In Athalya Brenner, ed., *A
    Feminist Companion to the Latter Prophets*, 146–60. FCB 1/8. Sheffield, UK: Sheffield Academic
    Press, 1995; London/New York: T. & T. Clark, 2004.
Lee, Archie Chi Chung. "Mothers Bewailing: Reading Lamentations." In Caroline Vander Stichele and
    Todd Penner, eds., *Her Master's Tools? Feminist and Postcolonial Engagements of Historical-Critical Dis-
    course*, 195–210. Global Perspectives on Biblical Scholarship 9. Atlanta: SBL Press, 2005.
Leith, Mary Joan Winn. "Verse and Reverse: The Transformation of the Woman, Israel, in Hosea 1–3."
    In Peggy L. Day, ed., *Gender and Difference in Ancient Israel*, 95–108. Minneapolis: Fortress Press,
    1989.
Magdalene, F. Rachel. "Ancient Near Eastern Treaty-Curses and the Ultimate Texts of Terror: A Study
    of the Language of Divine Sexual Abuse in the Prophetic Corpus." In Athalya Brenner, ed., *A Femi-
    nist Companion to the Latter Prophets*, 326–52. FCB 1/8. Sheffield, UK: Sheffield Academic Press,
    1995; London and New York: T. & T. Clark, 2004.
Mitchell, Ella Pearson, ed. *Women: To Preach or Not to Preach: Twenty-one Outstanding Black Preachers
    Say Yes!* Valley Forge, PA: Judson Press, 1991.
Mitchell, Ella Pearson, and Henry H. Mitchell. "Women: A Historical Perspective." In Ella Pearson
    Mitchell, ed., *Women: To Preach or Not to Preach: Twenty-one Outstanding Black Preachers Say Yes!*
    1–17. Valley Forge, PA: Judson Press, 1991.
O'Brien, Julia M. "On Saying 'No' to a Prophet" and "In Retrospect . . . Self-Response to 'On Saying
    "No" to a Prophet.'" In Athalya Brenner, ed., *The Prophets and Daniel*, 206–17, 218–19. FCB 2/8.
    Sheffield, UK: Sheffield Academic Press, 2001.
O'Connor, Kathleen. "Jeremiah." In *WBC*, 178–86.
Odell, Margaret S. "I Will Destroy Your Mother: The Obliteration of a Cultic Role in Hosea 4.4–6." In
    Athalya Brenner, ed., *A Feminist Companion to the Latter Prophets*, 180–93. FCB 1/8. Sheffield, UK:
    Sheffield Academic Press, 1995; London and New York: T. & T. Clark, 2004.
Patton, Corrine. "'Should Our Sister Be Treated Like a Whore?' A Response to Feminist Critiques of
    Ezekiel 23." In Margaret S. Odell and John T. Strong, eds., *The Book of Ezekiel: Theological and
    Anthropological Perspectives*, 221–38. SBL Symposium Series 9. Atlanta: SBL Press, 2000.

Rallis, Irene Kerasote. "Nuptial Imagery in the Book of Hosea: Israel as the Bride of Yahweh." *St. Vladimir's Theological Quarterly* 34 (1990): 197–219.

Runions, Erin. "Violence and the Economy of Desire in Ezekiel 16.1–45." In Athalya Brenner, ed., *The Prophets and Daniel*, 156–69. FCB 2/8. Sheffield, UK: Sheffield Academic Press, 2001.

Sakenfeld, Katharine Doob. "Gomer: Who Betrayed Whom?" In *Just Wives? Stories of Power and Survival in the Old Testament and Today*, 91–116. Louisville, KY: Westminster John Knox Press, 2003.

Sampson, Emily. "Daniel, Belshazzar, and Julia: The Rediscovery and Vindication of the Translation of Julia E. Smith (1792–1886)." In Athalya Brenner, ed., *The Prophets and Daniel*, 262–82. FCB 2/8. Sheffield, UK: Sheffield Academic Press, 2001.

Sanderson, Judith. "Amos," "Micah," "Nahum," "Habakkuk," and "Zephaniah." In *WBC*, 218–23, 229–31, 237–39, 240–42.

Schroer, Silvia. "'Under the Shadow of Your Wings': The Metaphor of God's Wings in the Psalms, Exodus 19.4, Deuteronomy 32.11 and Malachi 3.20, as Seen through the Perspectives of Feminism and the History of Religion." In Athalya Brenner and Carole Fontaine, eds., *Wisdom and Psalms*, 264–82. FCB 2/2. Sheffield, UK: Sheffield Academic Press, 1998.

Schüngel-Straumann, Helen. "God as Mother in Hosea 11." In Athalya Brenner, ed., *The Feminist Companion to the Latter Prophets*, 194–218. FCB 1/8. Sheffield, UK: Sheffield Academic Press, 1995; London and New York: T. & T. Clark, 2004.

Setel, T. Drorah. "Prophets and Pornography: Female Sexual Imagery in Hosea." In Letty M. Russell, ed., *Feminist Interpretation of the Bible*, 86–95, 157–59. Philadelphia: Westminster Press, 1985. And in Athalya Brenner, ed., *A Feminist Companion to the Song of Songs*, 143–55. FCB 1/1. Sheffield, UK: Sheffield Academic Press, 1993.

Sherwood, Yvonne. "Boxing Gomer: Controlling the Deviant Woman in Hosea 1–3." In Athalya Brenner, ed., *A Feminist Companion to the Latter Prophets*, 101–25. FCB 1/8. Sheffield, UK: Sheffield Academic Press, 1995; London and New York: T. & T. Clark, 2004.

———. *The Prostitute and the Prophet: Hosea's Marriage in Literary-Theoretical Perspective*. JSOTSup 212. Gender, Culture, Theory 2. Sheffield, UK: Sheffield Academic Press, 1996.

Shields, Mary E. "An Abusive God? Identity and Power/Gender and Violence in Ezekiel 23." In A. K. M. Adam, ed., *Postmodern Interpretation of the Bible: A Reader*, 129–52. St. Louis: Chalice, 2001.

———. "Circumcision of the Prostitute: Gender, Sexuality, and the Call to Repentance to Jeremiah 3.1–4.4" and "Self-Response to 'Circumcision of the Prostitute.'" In Athalya Brenner, ed., *The Prophets and Daniel*, 121–33, 134–36. FCB 2/8. Sheffield, UK: Sheffield Academic Press, 2001.

———. "Circumcision of the Prostitute: Gender, Sexuality and the Call to Repentance in Jer 3.1–4.4." *BibInt* 3 (1995): 61–74.

———. *Circumscribing the Prostitute: The Rhetorics of Intertextuality, Metaphor and Gender in Jeremiah 3.1–4.4*. London: T. & T. Clark, 2004.

———. "Multiple Exposures: Body Rhetoric and Gender Characterization in Ezekiel 16." *JFSR* 14 (1998): 5–18.

———. "Self-Response to 'Multiple Exposures.'" In Athalya Brenner, ed., *The Prophets and Daniel*, 154–55. FCB 2/8. Sheffield, UK: Sheffield Academic Press, 2001.

Stiebert, Johanna. *The Construction of Shame in the Hebrew Bible: The Prophetic Contribution*. JSOTSup 346. London: Sheffield Academic Press, 2002.

———. *The Exile and the Prophet's Wife: Historic Events and Marginal Perspectives*. Interfaces. Collegeville, MN: Liturgical Press, 2005.

Trible, Phyllis. "Gift of a Poem: A Rhetorical Study of Jeremiah 31:15–22." *Andover Newton Quarterly* 17 (1977): 271–80.

Turner, Mary Donovan. "Daughter Zion: Giving Birth to Redemption." In Cheryl A. Kirk-Duggan, ed., *Pregnant Passion: Gender, Sex, and Violence in the Bible*, 193–204. Semeia Studies 44. Atlanta: SBL Press, 2003.

van Deventer, H. J. M. "Another Wise Queen (Mother)—Women's Wisdom in Daniel 5.10–12?" In Athalya Brenner, ed., *The Prophets and Daniel*, 247–61. FCB 2/8. Sheffield, UK: Sheffield Academic Press, 2001.

van Dijk-Hemmes, Fokkelien. "The Metaphorization of Woman in Prophetic Speech: An Analysis of Ezekiel 23." In Athalya Brenner, ed., *A Feminist Companion to the Latter Prophets*, 244–55. FCB 1/8. Sheffield, UK: Sheffield Academic Press, 1995; London and New York: T. & T. Clark, 2004.

Wacker, Marie-Theres. "Traces of the Goddess in the Book of Hosea." In Athalya Brenner, ed., *A Feminist Companion to the Latter Prophets*, 219–41. FCB 1/8. Sheffield, UK: Sheffield Academic Press, 1995; London and New York: T. & T. Clark, 2004.

Walfish, Barry Dov. *Esther in Medieval Garb: Jewish Interpretation of the Book of Esther in the Middle Ages.* Judaica: Hermeneutics, Mysticism, and Religion. Albany: State University of New York Press, 1993.

Weems, Renita J. *Battered Love: Marriage, Sex, and Violence in the Hebrew Prophets.* Minneapolis: Fortress Press, 1995.

———. "Gomer: Victim of Violence or Victim of Metaphor?" In Katie Geneva Cannon and Elisabeth Schüssler Fiorenza, eds., *Interpretation for Liberation. Semeia* 47 (1989): 87–104.

White, Marsha C. "Jonah." In *WBC*, 226–28.

Willey, Patricia Tull. *Remember the Former Things: The Recollection of Previous Texts in Second Isaiah.* SBLDS 161. Atlanta: Scholars Press, 1997.

Yee, Gale A. "The Book of Hosea: Introduction, Commentary, and Reflections." In *NIB* 7, 195–297. Nashville: Abingdon Press, 1996.

———. *Composition and Tradition in the Book of Hosea: A Redaction Critical Investigation.* SBLDS 102. Atlanta: Scholars Press, 1987.

———. "Faithless Israel in Hosea: She Is Not My Wife and I Am Not Her Husband" and "The Two Sisters in Ezekiel: They Played the Whore in Egypt." In *Poor Banished Children of Eve: Woman as Evil in the Hebrew Bible*, 81–110, 111–34. Minneapolis: Fortress Press, 2003.

———. "Gomer." In *WIS*, 84–86.

———. "Hosea." In *WBC*, 207–15.

———. "'She Is Not My Wife and I Am Not Her Husband': A Materialist Analysis of Hosea 1–2." *Bib-Int* 9 (2000): 145–83.

CHAPTER 9: THE WOMEN IN THE WISDOM LITERATURE AND THE SONG OF SONGS

Arbel, Daphna V. "'My Vineyard, My Very Own, Is for Myself.'" In Athalya Brenner and Carole R. Fontaine, eds., *The Song of Songs*, 90–101. FCB 2/6. Sheffield, UK: Sheffield Academic Press, 2000.

Barr, Jane. "Luis de León and the Song of Songs." In Athalya Brenner and Carole R. Fontaine, eds., *The Song of Songs*, 130–41. FCB 2/6. Sheffield, UK: Sheffield Academic Press, 2000.

Baumann, Gerlinde. "A Figure with Many Facets: The Literary and Theological Functions of Personified Wisdom in Proverbs 1–9." In Athalya Brenner and Carole Fontaine, eds., *Wisdom and Psalms*, 44–78. FCB 2/2. Sheffield, UK: Sheffield Academic Press, 1998.

Bechtel, Lyn M. "A Feminist Approach to the Book of Job." In Athalya Brenner, ed., *A Feminist Companion to Wisdom Literature*, 222–51. FCB 1/9. Sheffield, UK: Sheffield Academic Press, 1995.

Bekkenkamp, Jonneke. "Into Another Scene of Choices: The Theological Value of the Song of Songs." In Athalya Brenner and Carole R. Fontaine, eds., *The Song of Songs*, 55–89. FCB 2/6. Sheffield, UK: Sheffield Academic Press, 2000.

Bekkenkamp, Jonneke, and Fokkelien van Dijk. "The Canon of the Old Testament and Women's Cultural Traditions." In Athalya Brenner, ed., *A Feminist Companion to the Song of Songs*, 67–85. FCB 1/1. Sheffield, UK: Sheffield Academic Press, 1993.

Bellis, Alice Ogden. "The Gender and Motives of the Wisdom Teacher in Proverbs 7." In Athalya Brenner and Carole Fontaine, eds., *Wisdom and Psalms*, 79–91. FCB 2/2. Sheffield, UK: Sheffield Academic Press, 1998.

Black, Fiona C. "Unlikely Bedfellows: Allegorical and Feminist Readings of Song of Songs 7.1–8." In Athalya Brenner and Carole R. Fontaine, eds., *The Song of Songs*, 104–29. FCB 2/6. Sheffield, UK: Sheffield Academic Press, 2000.

Bloch, Ariel, and Chana Bloch. *The Song of Songs: A New Translation.* New York: Random House, 1995.

Bloch, Chana. "Woman/Lover/Shulammite." In *WIS*, 310–12.

Brenner, Athalya, ed. *A Feminist Companion to the Wisdom Literature.* FCB 1/9. Sheffield, UK: Sheffield Academic Press, 1996.

———. "God's Answer to Job." *VT* 31 (1981): 129–37.

———. *The Intercourse of Knowledge: On Gendering Desire and 'Sexuality' in the Hebrew Bible.* Leiden: E. J. Brill, 1997.

———. "Job the Pious? The Characterization of Job in the Narrative Framework of the Book." *JSOT* 43 (1989): 37–52.

———. "Love Me Tender, Love Me True . . . : I Am an Anonymous Woman from the Song of Songs." In *I Am . . . Biblical Women Tell Their Own Stories*, 163–90. Minneapolis: Fortress Press, 2005.

———. "'My' Song of Songs." In Athalya Brenner and Carole R. Fontaine, eds., *The Song of Songs*, 154–68. FCB 2/6. Sheffield, UK: Sheffield Academic Press, 2000.

———. "On Feminist Criticism of the Song of Songs," "Women Poets and Authors," "'Come Back, Come Back the Shulammite' (Song of Songs 7.1–10): A Parody of the *wasf* Genre," and "An Afterword." In *A Feminist Companion to the Song of Songs*, 28–37, 86–97, 234–57, 279–80. FCB 1/1. Sheffield, UK: Sheffield Academic Press, 1993.

———. "Proverbs 1–9: An F Voice?" In Athalya Brenner and Fokkelien van Dijk-Hemmes, eds., *On Gendering Texts: Female and Male Voices in the Hebrew Bible*, 117–19, 121–25. Leiden/New York/Cologne: E. J. Brill, 1993.

———. "Some Observations on the Figurations of Woman in Wisdom Literature." In Heather A. McKay and David J. A. Clines, eds., *Of Prophets' Visions and the Wisdom of Sages: Essays in Honour of R. Norman Whybray on His Seventieth Birthday*, 192–208. Sheffield, UK: JSOT Press, 1993. And in Athalya Brenner, ed., *A Feminist Companion to Wisdom Literature*, 50–66. FCB 1/9. Sheffield, UK: Sheffield Academic Press, 1995.

———. *The Song of Songs.* Old Testament Guides. Sheffield, UK: JSOT Press, 1989.

———, ed. *Song of Songs.* FCB 2/1. Sheffield, UK: Sheffield Academic Press, 1993.

———. "To See Is to Assume: Whose Love Is Celebrated in the Song of Songs?" *BibInt* 3 (1993): 1–20.

Brenner, Athalya, and Carole R. Fontaine, eds. *Wisdom and Psalms.* FCB 2/2. Sheffield, UK: Sheffield Academic Press, 1998.

Butting, Klara. "Go Your Way: Women Rewrite the Scriptures (Song of Songs 2.8–14)." In Athalya Brenner and Carole R. Fontaine, eds., *The Song of Songs*, 142–51. FCB 2/6. Sheffield, UK: Sheffield Academic Press, 2000.

Cady, Susan, Marian Ronan, and Hal Taussig. *Wisdom's Feast: Sophia in Study and Celebration.* San Francisco: Harper & Row, 1989.

Camp, Claudia V. "The Female Sage in Ancient Israel and in the Biblical Wisdom Literature." In J. G. Gammie and L. G. Perdue, eds., *The Sage in Israel and the Ancient Near East*, 185–204. Winona Lake, IN: Eisenbrauns, 1990.

———. "The Strange Woman of Proverbs: A Study in the Feminization and Divinization of Evil in Biblical Thought." In Karen L. King, ed., *Women and Goddess Traditions in Antiquity and Today*, 310–29. Studies in Antiquity and Christianity. Minneapolis: Fortress Press, 1997.

———. "What's So Strange about the Strange Woman?" In David Jobling, Peggy L. Day, and Gerald T. Sheppard, eds., *The Bible and the Politics of Exegesis: Essays in Honor of Norman K. Gottwald on His Sixty-fifth Birthday*, 17–31. Cleveland: Pilgrim Press, 1991.

———. *Wisdom and the Feminine in the Book of Proverbs.* Bible and Literature Series 11. Sheffield, UK: Almond Press, 1985.

———. "Wise and Strange: An Interpretation of the Female Imagery in Proverbs in Light of Trickster Mythology." In J. Cheryl Exum and Johanna W. H. Bos, eds., *Reasoning with the Foxes: Female Wit in a World of Male Power. Semeia* 42 (1988): 14–37. And in Athalya Brenner, ed., *A Feminist Companion to Wisdom Literature*, 131–56. FCB 1/9. Sheffield, UK: Sheffield Academic Press, 1995.

———. *Wise, Strange, and Holy: The Strange Woman and the Making of the Bible.* JSOTSup 320. Gender, Culture, and Theory 9. Sheffield, UK: Sheffield Academic Press, 2000.

———. "Woman Wisdom." In *WIS*, 548–550.

———. "Woman Wisdom as Root Metaphor: A Theological Consideration." In K. G. Hoglund et al., eds., *The Listening Heart: Essays in Wisdom and the Psalms Presented to Roland E. Murphy*, 56–76. JSOTSup 58. Sheffield, UK: JSOT Press, 1987.

Carmody, Denise Lardner. *Biblical Woman: Contemporary Reflections on Scriptural Texts.* New York: Crossroad, 1988.

Christianson, Eric S. "Qoheleth the 'Old Boy' and Qoheleth the 'New Man': Misogynism, the Womb, and a Paradox in Ecclesiastes." In Athalya Brenner and Carole Fontaine, eds., *Wisdom and Psalms*, 109–26. FCB 2/2. Sheffield, UK: Sheffield Academic Press, 1998.

Crawford, Sidnie White. "Lady Wisdom and Dame Folly at Qumran." In Athalya Brenner and Carole Fontaine, eds., *Wisdom and Psalms*, 205–17. FCB 2/2. Sheffield, UK: Sheffield Academic Press, 1998.

Deckers, M. "The Structure of the Song of Songs and the Centrality of *nepeš.*" In Athalya Brenner, ed., *A Feminist Companion to the Song of Songs*, 172–96. FCB 1/1. Sheffield, UK: Sheffield Academic Press, 1993.

Domeris, W. R. "Shame and Honour in Proverbs: Wise Women and Foolish Men." *Old Testament Essays* 8 (1995): 86–102.

Exum, J. Cheryl. "Developing Strategies of Feminist Criticism/Developing Strategies for Commentating the Song of Songs." In David J. A. Clines and Stephen D. Moore, eds., *Auguries: The Jubilee Volume of the Sheffield Department of Biblical Studies*, 206–49. JSOTSup 269. Gender, Culture, and Theory 7. Sheffield, UK: Sheffield Academic Press, 1998.

———. "How Does the Song of Songs Mean? On Reading the Poetry of Desire." *SEÅ* 64 (1999): 47–63.

———. "A Literary and Structural Analysis of the Song of Songs." *ZAW* 85 (1973): 47–79.

———. *Song of Songs*. Old Testament Library. Louisville, KY: Westminster John Knox Press, 2005.

———. "Ten Things Every Feminist Should Know about the Song of Songs." In Athalya Brenner and Carole R. Fontaine, eds., *The Song of Songs*, 24–35. FCB 2/6. Sheffield, UK: Sheffield Academic Press, 2000.

Falk, Marcia. *Love Lyrics from the Hebrew Bible: A Translation and Literary Study of the Song of Songs*. Sheffield, UK: Almond Press, 1982.

———. *The Song of Songs: A New Translation and Interpretation*. San Francisco: Harper & Row, 1990.

———. "The *wasf.*" In Athalya Brenner, ed., *A Feminist Companion to the Song of Songs*, 225–33. FCB 1/1. Sheffield, UK: Sheffield Academic Press, 1993.

Farmer, Kathleen A. *Who Knows What Is Good? A Commentary on the Books of Proverbs and Ecclesiastes*. International Theological Commentary. Grand Rapids: Wm. B. Eerdmans Publishing Co., 1991.

Fewell, Danna Nolan. "Feminist Reading of the Hebrew Bible: Affirmation, Resistance and Transformation." *JSOT* 39 (1987): 77–87.

Fontaine, Carole R. "'Many Devices' (Qoheleth 7.23–8.1): Qoheleth, Misogyny and the *Malleus Maleficarum.*" In Athalya Brenner and Carole Fontaine, eds., *Wisdom and Psalms*, 137–68. FCB 2/2. Sheffield, UK: Sheffield Academic Press, 1998.

———. "Proverbs." In *WBC*, 153–60.

———. "The Social Roles of Women in the World of Wisdom." In Athalya Brenner, ed., *A Feminist Companion to Wisdom Literature*, 24–49. FCB 1/9. Sheffield, UK: Sheffield Academic Press, 1995.

———. "The Voice of the Turtle: Now It's *MY* Song of Songs." In Athalya Brenner and Carole R. Fontaine, eds., *The Song of Songs*, 169–85. FCB 2/6. Sheffield, UK: Sheffield Academic Press, 2000.

———. "Woman Folly (Foolish Woman)." "Woman Stranger (Loose Woman/Adulteress)." In *WIS*, 543–44, 546–47.

Frymer-Kensky, Tikva. "Wisdom, the Lover of Man." In *In the Wake of the Goddesses: Women, Culture, and the Biblical Transformation of Pagan Myth*, 179–83. New York: Free Press, 1992.

Ginsburg, C. D. "The Importance of the Book." In Athalya Brenner, ed., *A Feminist Companion to the Song of Songs*, 47–54. FCB 1/1. Sheffield, UK: Sheffield Academic Press, 1993.

Goitein, S. D. "The Song of Songs: A Female Composition." In Athalya Brenner, ed., *A Feminist Companion to the Song of Songs*, 58–66. FCB 1/1. Sheffield, UK: Sheffield Academic Press, 1993.

Häusl, Maria, and Ursula Silber. "'You Are Beautiful, My Love'" The Song of Songs of Women." In Athalya Brenner and Carole R. Fontaine, eds., *The Song of Songs*, 186–95. FCB 2/6. Sheffield, UK: Sheffield Academic Press, 2000.

Heijerman, Mieke. "Who Would Blame Her? The 'Strange' Woman of Proverbs 7." In Fokkelien van Dijk-Hemmes and Athalya Brenner, eds., *Reflections on Theology and Gender*, 21–31. Kampen, The Netherlands: Kok Pharos, 1994. And in Athalya Brenner, ed., *A Feminist Companion to Wisdom Literature*, 100–109. FCB 1/9. Sheffield, UK: Sheffield Academic Press, 1995.

Johnson, Elizabeth A. *She Who Is: The Mystery of God in Feminist Theological Discourse.* New York: Crossroad, 1992.

Klein, Lillian R. "Job and the Womb." In *From Deborah to Esther: Sexual Politics in the Hebrew Bible*, 73–84. Minneapolis: Fortress Press, 2003.

———. "Job and the Womb: Text about Men, Subtext about Women." In Athalya Brenner, ed., *A Feminist Companion to Wisdom Literature*, 186–200. FCB 1/9. Sheffield, UK: Sheffield Academic Press, 1995.

LaCocque, André. *Romance She Wrote: Hermeneutical Essay on the Song of Songs.* Harrisburg, PA: Trinity Press International, 1998.

Landy, Francis. "Two Versions of Paradise" and "Mishneh Torah: A Response to Myself and Phyllis Trible." In Athalya Brenner, ed., *A Feminist Companion to the Song of Songs*, 129–42, 260–65. FCB 1/1. Sheffield, UK: Sheffield Academic Press, 1993.

Maier, Christl. "Conflicting Attractions: Parental Wisdom and the 'Strange Woman' in Proverbs 1–9." In Athalya Brenner and Carole Fontaine, eds., *Wisdom and Psalms*, 92–108. FCB 2/2. Sheffield, UK: Sheffield Academic Press, 1998.

Maier, Christl, and Silvia Schroer. "What about Job? Questioning the Book of 'The Righteous Sufferer.'" In Athalya Brenner and Carole Fontaine, eds., *Wisdom and Psalms*, 175–204. FCB 2/2. Sheffield, UK: Sheffield Academic Press, 1998.

Masenye, Madipoane (ngwana' Mphahlele). "A *Bosadi* (Womanhood) Reading of Proverbs 31:10–31." In Musa W. Dube, ed., *Other Ways of Reading: African Women and the Bible*, 145–57. Atlanta: SBL; Geneva: WCC Publications, 2001.

———. *How Worthy Is the Woman of Worth? Reading Proverbs 31:10–31 in African South Africa.* New York: Lang, 2004.

———. "Proverbs 31:10–31 in a South African Context: A Reading for the Liberation of African (Northern Sotho) Women." In Phyllis A. Bird, Katharine Doob Sakenfeld, and Sharon H. Ringe, eds., *Reading the Bible as Women: Perspectives from Latin America, Africa, and Asia. Semeia* 78 (1997): 55–68.

McKinlay, Judith E. *Gendering Wisdom the Host: Biblical Invitations to Eat and Drink.* JSOTSup 216. Gender, Culture, Theory 4. Sheffield, UK: Sheffield Academic Press, 1996.

Merkin, Daphne. "The Women in the Balcony: On Rereading the Song of Songs." In Christina Buchmann and Celina Spiegel, eds., *Out of the Garden: Women Writers on the Bible*, 238–51. New York: Fawcett Columbine, 1994.

Meyers, Carol. "Gender Imagery in the Song of Songs." In Reuben Ahroni, ed., *Biblical and Other Studies: Tenth Anniversary Volume. Hebrew Annual Review* 10 (1986): 209–22. And in Athalya Brenner, ed., *A Feminist Companion to the Song of Songs*, 197–212. FCB 1/1. Sheffield, UK: Sheffield Academic Press, 1993.

Mitchell, Ella Pearson, ed. *Women: To Preach or Not to Preach: Twenty-one Outstanding Black Preachers Say Yes!* Valley Forge, PA: Judson Press, 1991.

Newsom, Carol A. *The Book of Job: A Contest of Moral Imagination.* Oxford: Oxford University Press, 2003.

———. "Cultural Politics and the Reading of Job." *BibInt* 1 (1993): 119–38.

———. "Job." In *WBC*, 138–44.

———. "Woman and the Discourse of Patriarchal Wisdom: A Study of Proverbs 1–9." In Peggy L. Day, ed., *Gender and Difference in Ancient Israel*, 142–60. Minneapolis: Fortress Press, 1989. And in Alice Bach, ed., *Women in the Hebrew Bible: A Reader,*. 85–98. New York and London: Routledge, 1999.

Noonan, Brian B. "Wisdom Literature among the Witchmongers." In Athalya Brenner and Carole Fontaine, eds., *Wisdom and Psalms*, 169–74. FCB 2/2. Sheffield, UK: Sheffield Academic Press, 1998.

Nowell, Irene. "Woman, Image of God: Eve, Wisdom/Sophia." In *Women in the Old Testament*, 131–52. Collegeville, MN: Liturgical Press, 1997.

O'Connor, Kathleen M. *The Wisdom Literature.* Message of Biblical Spirituality. Wilmington, DE: Michael Glazier, 1988.

Ostriker, Alicia. "A Holy of Holies: The Song of Songs as Countertext." In Athalya Brenner and Carole R. Fontaine, eds., *The Song of Songs*, 36–54. FCB 2/6. Sheffield, UK: Sheffield Academic Press, 2000.

Pardes, Ilana. "Daughters of Job," "Mother of Job," and "Wife of Job." In *WIS*, 292–93.

———. "'I Am a Wall, and My Breasts like Towers': The Song of Songs and the Question of Canonization." In *Countertraditions in the Bible: A Feminist Approach*, 118–43. Cambridge: Harvard University Press, 1992.

Perkins, Pheme. "Sophia as Goddess in the Nag Hammadi Codices." In Karen King, ed., *Images of the Feminine in Gnosticism*, 96–112. Philadelphia: Fortress Press, 1988.

Pope, Marvin H. "The Song of Songs and Women's Liberation: An 'Outsider's' Critique." In Athalya Brenner, ed., *A Feminist Companion to the Song of Songs*, 121–28. FCB 1/1. Sheffield, UK: Sheffield Academic Press, 1993.

Sakenfeld, Katharine Doob. "The Good Wife: Who *Is* a Worthy Woman?" In *Just Wives? Stories of Power and Survival in the Old Testament and Today*, 117–134. Louisville, KY: Westminster John Knox Press, 2003.

Schroer, Sylvia. *Wisdom Has Built Her House: Studies in the Figure of Wisdom in the Bible*. Collegeville, MN: Liturgical Press, 2000.

———. "Wise and Counselling Women in Ancient Israel: Literary and Historical Ideals of the Personified *hokmâ*." In Athalya Brenner, ed., *A Feminist Companion to Wisdom Literature*, 67–84. FCB 1/9. Sheffield, UK: Sheffield Academic Press, 1995.

Schulmann, Grace. "The Song of Songs: Love Is Strong as Death." In David Rosenberg, ed., *Congregation: Contemporary Writers Read the Jewish Bible*, 346–60. New York: Harcourt Brace Javonovich, 1987.

Schüssler Fiorenza, Elisabeth. *In Memory of Her: A Feminist Theological Reconstruction of Christian Origins*. New York: Crossroad, 1985.

Soulen, Richard N. "The *wasfs* of the Song of Songs and Hermeneutic." In Athalya Brenner, ed., *A Feminist Companion to the Song of Songs*, 214–24. FCB 1/1. Sheffield, UK: Sheffield Academic Press, 1993.

Stanton, Elizabeth Cady. "The Women's Movement and the Bible" and "The Song of Solomon." In Athalya Brenner, ed., *A Feminist Companion to the Song of Songs*, 40–46, 55. FCB 1/1. Sheffield, UK: Sheffield Academic Press, 1993.

Streete, Gail Corrington. *The Strange Woman: Power and Sex in the Bible*. Louisville, KY: Westminster John Knox Press, 1997.

Trible, Phyllis. "A Human Comedy." In *God and the Rhetoric of Sexuality*, 166–99. Overtures to Biblical Theology. Philadelphia: Fortress Press, 1978.

———. "Love's Lyrics Redeemed." In Athalya Brenner, ed., *A Feminist Companion to the Song of Songs*, 100–120. FCB 1/1. Sheffield, UK: Sheffield Academic Press, 1993.

Valler, Shulamit. "Who is *ēšet ḥayil* in Rabbinic Literature?" In Athalya Brenner, ed., *A Feminist Companion to Wisdom Literature*, 85–97. FCB 1/9. Sheffield, UK: Sheffield Academic Press, 1995.

van Dijk-Hemmes, Fokkelien. "The Imagination of Power and the Power of Imagination." In Athalya Brenner, ed., *A Feminist Companion to the Song of Songs*, 156–70. FCB 1/1. Sheffield, UK: Sheffield Academic Press, 1993.

———. "Who Would Blame Her? The 'Strange' Woman of Proverbs 7." In Fokkelien van Dijk-Hemmes and Athalya Brenner, eds., *Reflections on Theology and Gender*, 21–32. Kampen, The Netherlands: Kok, 1994.

van Wolde, Ellen. "The Development of Job: Mrs Job as Catalyst." In Athalya Brenner, ed., *A Feminist Companion to Wisdom Literature*, 201–21. FCB 1/9. Sheffield, UK: Sheffield Academic Press, 1995.

Walsh, Carey Ellen. *Religion, The Erotic and The Song of Songs*. Minneapolis: Fortress Press, 2000.

Washington, Harold C. "The Strange Woman (אשה זרה/נכריה) of Proverbs 1–9 and Post-Exilic Judaean Society." In Athalya Brenner, ed., *A Feminist Companion to Wisdom Literature*, 157–84. FCB 1/9. Sheffield, UK: Sheffield Academic Press, 1995.

Webster, Jane S. "Sophia: Engendering Wisdom in Proverbs, Ben Sira and the Wisdom of Solomon," *JSOT* 78 (1998): 63–79.

Weems, Renita J. *Just a Sister Away: A Womanist Vision of Women's Relationships in the Bible*. San Diego: LuraMedia, 1988.

———. "Song of Songs." In *WBC*, 164–68.

————. "Song of Songs." In *NIB*, 363–434. Nashville: Abingdon Press, 1997.

Whedbee, J. William. "Paradox and Parody in the Song of Solomon: Towards a Comic Reading of the Most Sublime Song." In Athalya Brenner, ed., *A Feminist Companion to the Song of Songs*, 266–78. FCB 1/1. Sheffield, UK: Sheffield Academic Press, 1993.

Wilkins, Robert, ed. *Aspects of Wisdom in Judaism and Christianity*. Notre Dame, IN: University of Notre Dame Press, 1975.

Yee, Gale A. "'I Have Perfumed My Bed with Myrrh': The Foreign Woman ('*iššâ zarâ*) in Proverbs 1–9." *JSOT* 43 (1989): 53–68. And in Athalya Brenner, ed., *A Feminist Companion to Wisdom Literature*, 110–26. FCB 1/9. Sheffield: Sheffield Academic Press, 1995.

————. "The Other Woman in Proverbs: My Man's Not Home—He Took His Moneybag with Him." In *Poor Banished Children of Eve: Woman as Evil in the Hebrew Bible*, 135–158. Minneapolis: Fortress Press, 2003.

————. "The Socio-Literary Production of the 'Foreign Woman' in Proverbs." In Athalya Brenner, ed., *A Feminist Companion to Wisdom Literature*, 127–30. FCB 1/9. Sheffield, UK: Sheffield Academic Press, 1995.

Yoder, Christine Roy. *Wisdom as a Woman of Substance: A Socioeconomic Reading of Proverbs 1–9 and 31:10–31*. BZAW 304. Berlin: de Gruyter, 2001.

CHAPTER 10: SUBVERSIVE WOMEN IN SUBVERSIVE BOOKS: RUTH, ESTHER, SUSANNA, AND JUDITH

Bach, Alice. "Mirror, Mirror in the Text: Reflections on Reading and Rereading." In Athalya Brenner, ed., *A Feminist Companion to Esther, Judith, and Susanna*, 81–86. FCB 1/7. Sheffield, UK: Sheffield Academic Press, 1995; London and New York: T. & T. Clark, 2004.

————. *Reading the Women of the Bible: A New Interpretation of Their Stories*. New York: Schocken Books, 2002.

————. *Women, Seduction, and Betrayal in Biblical Narrative*. Cambridge: Cambridge University Press, 1997.

Bal, Mieke. "The Elders and Susanna." *BibInt* 1 (1993): 1–19.

————. "Head Hunting: 'Judith' on the Cutting Edge of Knowledge." In Athalya Brenner, ed., *A Feminist Companion to Esther, Judith, and Susanna*, 253–85. FCB 1/7. Sheffield, UK: Sheffield Academic Press, 1995; London and New York: T. & T. Clark, 2004.

————. "Heroism and Proper Names, or the Fruits of Analogy." In *Lethal Love: Feminist Literary Readings of Biblical Love Stories*, 68–103. Indiana Studies in Biblical Literature. Bloomington: Indiana University Press, 1987. And in Athalya Brenner, ed., *A Feminist Companion to the Book of Ruth*, 42–69. FCB 1/3. Sheffield, UK: Sheffield Academic Press, 1993.

————. "Lots of Writing." *Semeia* 54 (1991): 77–102. And in Athalya Brenner, ed., *Ruth and Esther*, 212–38. FCB 2/3. Sheffield, UK: Sheffield Academic Press, 1999.

Bankson, Marjory Zoet. *Braided Streams: Esther and a Woman's Way of Growing*. San Diego: LuraMedia, 1985.

————. *Seasons of Friendship: Naomi and Ruth as a Pattern*. San Diego: LuraMedia, 1987.

Barnes, Bernadine. "Heroines and Worthy Women." In H. Diane Russell with Bernadine Barnes, ed., *Eve/Ave: Women in Renaissance and Baroque Prints*, 29–74. Washington, DC: National Gallery of Art; New York: The Feminist Press at the City University, 1990.

Beal, Timothy K. "Tracing Esther's Beginnings." In Athalya Brenner, ed., *A Feminist Companion to Esther, Judith, and Susanna*, 87–110. FCB 1/7. Sheffield, UK: Sheffield Academic Press, 1995; London and New York: T. & T. Clark, 2004.

Berg, Sandra Beth. *The Book of Esther: Motifs, Themes and Structure*. SBLDS 44. Missoula, MT: Scholars Press, 1979.

Bledstein, Adrien Janis. "Female Companionships: If the Book of Ruth Were Written by a Woman . . ." In Athalya Brenner, ed., *A Feminist Companion to Ruth*, 116–33. FCB 1/3. Sheffield, UK: Sheffield Academic Press, 1993.

Boer, Roland. "Culture, Ethics and Identity in Reading Ruth: A Response to Donaldson, Dube, McKinlay and Brenner." In Athalya Brenner, ed., *Ruth and Esther*, 163–70. FCB 2/3. Sheffield, UK: Sheffield Academic Press, 1999.

Bos, Johanna W. H. "Out of the Shadows: Genesis 38; Judges 4:17–22; Ruth 3." In J. Cheryl Exum and Johanna W. H. Bos, eds., *Reasoning with the Foxes: Female Wit in a World of Male Power. Semeia* 42 (1988): 37–67.

Brenner, Athalya, ed. *A Feminist Companion to Esther, Judith, and Susanna.* FCB 1/7. Sheffield, UK: Sheffield Academic Press, 1995; London and New York: T. & T. Clark, 2004.

———, ed. *A Feminist Companion to Ruth.* FCB 1/3. Sheffield, UK: Sheffield Academic Press, 1993.

———. "Looking at Esther through the Looking Glass." In *A Feminist Companion to Esther, Judith, and Susanna*, 71–80. FCB 1/7. Sheffield, UK: Sheffield Academic Press, 1995; London and New York: T. & T. Clark, 2004.

———. "Naomi and Ruth" and "Naomi and Ruth: Further Reflections." In *A Feminist Companion to the Book of Ruth*, 70–84, 140–44. FCB 1/3. Sheffield, UK: Sheffield Academic Press, 1993.

———, ed. *Ruth and Esther.* FCB 2/3. Sheffield, UK: Sheffield Academic Press, 1999.

———. "Ruth as a Foreign Worker and the Politics of Exogamy." In *Ruth and Esther*, 158–62. FCB 2/3. Sheffield, UK: Sheffield Academic Press, 1999.

Bronner, Leila Leah. "Esther Revisited: An Aggadic Approach." In Athalya Brenner, ed., *A Feminist Companion to Esther, Judith, and Susanna*, 176–97. FCB 1/7. Sheffield, UK: Sheffield Academic Press, 1995; London and New York: T. & T. Clark, 2004.

———. "The Invisible Relationship Made Visible: Biblical Mothers and Daughters." In Athalya Brenner, ed., *Ruth and Esther*, 172–91. FCB 2/3. Sheffield, UK: Sheffield Academic Press, 1999.

———. "The Regime of Modesty: Ruth and the Rabbinic Construction of the Feminine Ideal." In *From Eve to Esther: Rabbinic Reconstructions of Biblical Women*, 61–86. Gender and the Biblical Tradition. Louisville, KY: Westminster John Knox Press, 1994.

———. "A Thematic Approach to Ruth in Rabbinic Literature." In Athalya Brenner, ed., *A Feminist Companion to the Book of Ruth*, 146–69. FCB 1/3. Sheffield, UK: Sheffield Academic Press, 1993.

Brophy, Beth. "A Clever Heroine." In Susan Headen and Jeffery L. Sheler, eds., *Women of the Bible: Provocative New Insights*, 34–37. *U.S. News and World Report.* Special Collector's Edition, 2005.

Butting, Klara. "Esther: A New Interpretation of the Joseph Story in the Fight against Anti-Semitism and Sexism." In Athalya Brenner, ed., *Ruth and Esther*, 239–48. FCB 2/3. Sheffield, UK: Sheffield Academic Press, 1999.

Carmody, Denise Lardner. *Biblical Woman: Contemporary Reflections on Scriptural Texts.* New York: Crossroad, 1988.

Chittister, Joan. *The Friendship of Women: The Hidden Tradition of the Bible.* Erie, PA: Bluebridge Benetvision, 2006.

———. *The Story of Ruth: Twelve Moments in Every Woman's Life.* Illustrated by John August Swanson. Grand Rapids: Wm. B. Eerdmans Publishing Co., 2000.

Clines, David J. A. *The Esther Scroll: The Story of the Story.* JSOTSup 30. Sheffield, UK: Sheffield Academic Press, 1984.

Craven, Toni. *Artistry and Faith in the Book of Judith.* SBLDS 70. Chico, CA: Scholars Press, 1983.

———. "The Greek Book of Daniel." In *WBC*, 311–15.

———. "Judith 2" and "Maid of Judith." In *WIS*, 104–6, 362.

———. "Tradition and Convention in the Book of Judith." In Mary Ann Tolbert, ed., *The Bible and Feminist Hermeneutics. Semeia* 28 (1983): 49–62.

Crawford, Sidnie Ann White. "Esther." In *WBC*, 131–37.

———. "Esther" and "Vashti." In *WIS*, 74–77, 166–67.

Darr, Katheryn Pfisterer. "'More Than Seven Sons': Critical, Rabbinical, and Feminist Perspectives on Ruth," and "More Than Just a Pretty Face: Critical, Rabbinical, and Feminist Perspectives on Esther." In *Far More Precious Than Jewels: Perspectives on Biblical Women*, 55–84, 164–202. Gender and the Biblical Tradition 1. Louisville, KY: Westminster/John Knox Press, 1991.

Day, Linda. *Esther.* Abingdon Old Testament Commentaries. Nashville: Abingdon Press, 2005.

De Troyer, Kristin. "An Oriental Beauty Parlour: An Analysis of Esther 2.8–18 in the Hebrew, the Septuagint and the Second Greek Text." In Athalya Brenner, ed., *A Feminist Companion to Esther, Judith, and Susanna*, 47–70. FCB 1/7. Sheffield, UK: Sheffield Academic Press, 1995; London and New York: T. & T. Clark, 2004.

Donaldson, Laura E. "The Sign of Orpah: Reading Ruth through Native Eyes." In Athalya Brenner, ed., *Ruth and Esther*, 130–44. FCB 2/3. Sheffield, UK: Sheffield Academic Press, 1999.

Dube, Musa W. "Divining Ruth for International Relations." In *Other Ways of Reading: African Women and the Bible*. Atlanta: SBL; Geneva: WCC Publications, 2001.

———. "Jumping the Fire with Judith: Postcolonial Feminist Hermeneutics of Liberation." In Silvia Schroer and Sophia Bietenhard, eds., *Feminist Interpretation of the Bible and the Hermeneutics of Liberation*, 60–76. JSOTSup 374. Sheffield, UK: Sheffield Academic Press, 2003.

———. "The Unpublished Letters of Orpah to Ruth." In Athalya Brenner, ed., *Ruth and Esther*, 145–51. FCB 2/3. Sheffield, UK: Sheffield Academic Press, 1999.

Duran, Nicole. *Having Men for Dinner: Biblical Women's Deadly Banquets*. Cleveland: Pilgrim Press, 2006.

———. "Who Wants to Marry a Persian King? Gender Games and Wars and the Book of Esther." In Cheryl A. Kirk-Duggan, ed., *Pregnant Passion: Gender, Sex, and Violence in the Bible*, 71–84. Semeia Studies 44. Atlanta: SBL Press, 2003.

Exum, J. Cheryl. "Is This Naomi?" In *Plotted, Shot, and Painted: Cultural Representations of Biblical Women*, 129–74. Sheffield, UK: Sheffield Academic Press, 1996.

Fewell, Danna Nolan. "Feminist Reading of the Hebrew Bible: Affirmation, Resistance and Transformation." *JSOT* 39 (1987): 77–87.

———. "Introduction: Reading, Writing, and Relating." In *Reading between Texts: Intertextuality and the Hebrew Bible*, 11–20. Literary Currents in Biblical Interpretation. Louisville, KY: Westminster/John Knox Press, 1992.

Fewell, Danna Nolan, and David Miller Gunn. "Boaz, Pillar of Society: Measures of Worth in the Book of Ruth." *JSOT* 45 (1989): 45–59.

———. *Compromising Redemption: Relating Characters in the Book of Ruth*. Literary Currents in Biblical Interpretation. Louisville, KY: Westminster/John Knox Press, 1990.

———. "Is Coxon a Scold? On Responding to the Book of Ruth." *JSOT* 45 (1989): 39–43.

———. "'A Son Is Born to Naomi!': Literary Allusions and Interpretation in the Book of Ruth." *JSOT* 40 (1988): 99–108. And in Alice Bach, ed., *Women in the Hebrew Bible: A Reader*, 233–40. New York and London: Routledge, 1999.

Fischer, Irmtraud. "The Book of Ruth: A 'Feminist' Commentary to the Torah?" In Athalya Brenner, ed., *Ruth and Esther*, 24–49. FCB 2/3. Sheffield, UK: Sheffield Academic Press, 1999.

Fontaine, Carole R. "Facing the Other: Ruth-the-Cat in Medieval Jewish Illuminations." In Athalya Brenner, ed., *Ruth and Esther*, 75–92. FCB 2/3. Sheffield, UK: Sheffield Academic Press, 1999.

Fuchs, Esther. "The History of Women in Ancient Israel: Theory, Method, and the Book of Ruth." In Caroline Vander Stichele and Todd Penner, *Her Master's Tools? Feminist and Postcolonial Engagements of Historical-Critical Discourse*, 211–32. Global Perspectives on Biblical Scholarship 9. Atlanta: SBL Press, 2005.

———. "The Literary Characterization of Mothers and Sexual Politics in the Hebrew Bible." In Adela Yarbro Collins, ed., *Feminist Perspectives on Biblical Scholarship*, 117–36. SBLBSNA 10. Chico, CA: Scholars Press, 1985.

———. "Who Is Hiding the Truth? Deceptive Women and Biblical Androcentrism." In Adela Yarbro Collins, ed., *Feminist Perspectives on Biblical Scholarship*, 137–44. SBLBSNA 10. Chico, CA: Scholars Press, 1985.

Gitay, Zefira. "Esther and the Queen's Throne." In Athalya Brenner, ed., *A Feminist Companion to Esther, Judith, and Susanna*, 136–48. FCB 1/7. Sheffield, UK: Sheffield Academic Press, 1995; London and New York: T. & T. Clark, 2004.

———. "Ruth and the Women of Bethlehem." In Athalya Brenner, ed., *A Feminist Companion to the Book of Ruth*, 178–90. FCB 1/3. Sheffield, UK: Sheffield Academic Press, 1993.

Glancy, Jennifer A. "The Accused: Susanna and Her Readers." *JSOT* 58 (1993): 103–16. And in Athalya Brenner, ed., *A Feminist Companion to Esther, Judith, and Susanna*, 288–302. FCB 1/7. Sheffield, UK: Sheffield Academic Press, 1995; London and New York: T. & T. Clark, 2004.

———. "Susanna 1." In *WIS*, 157–58.

Green, Barbara. "The Plot of the Biblical Story of Ruth." *JSOT* 23 (1982): 55–68.

Greenstein, Edward L. "Reading Strategies and the Story of Ruth." In Alice Bach, ed., *Women in the Hebrew Bible: A Reader,* 211–32. New York and London: Routledge, 1999.

Grose, Thomas K. "Mixed Messages." In Susan Headen and Jeffery L. Sheler, eds., *Women of the Bible: Provocative New Insights,* 38–41. *U.S. News and World Report.* Special Collector's Edition, 2005.

Haag, Herbert, Dorothee Sölle, Katharina Elliger, and Marianne Grohmann. Trans. Brian McNeil. *Great Couples of the Bible.* Minneapolis: Fortress Press, 2006.

Honig, Bonnie. "Ruth, the Model Emigrée: Mourning and the Symbolic Politics of Immigration." In Athalya Brenner, ed., *Ruth and Esther,* 50–74. FCB 2/3. Sheffield, UK: Sheffield Academic Press, 1999.

Hopkins, Denise Dombkowski. "Judith." In *WBC,* 279–85.

Hyman, Naomi Mara. "Ruth and Naomi" and "Vashti and Esther." In *Biblical Women in the Midrash: A Sourcebook,* 135–148, 149–172. Northvale, NJ, and London: Jason Aronson, 1997.

Jacobus, Mary. "Judith, Holofernes, and the Phallic Woman." In *Reading Women: Essays in Feminist Criticism,* 110–36. New York: Columbia University Press, 1986.

Jensen, Jane Richardson. "Ruth according to Ephrem the Syrian." In Athalya Brenner, ed., *A Feminist Companion to the Book of Ruth,* 170–76. FCB 1/3. Sheffield, UK: Sheffield Academic Press, 1993.

Kates, Judith A., and Gail Twersky Reimer, eds. *Reading Ruth: Contemporary Women Reclaim a Sacred Story.* New York: Ballantine, 1994.

Kirk-Duggan, Cheryl A. "Black Mother Women and Daughters: Signifying Female-Divine Relationships in the Hebrew Bible and African-American Mother-Daughter Short Stories." In Athalya Brenner, ed., *Ruth and Esther,* 192–210. FCB 2/3. Sheffield, UK: Sheffield Academic Press, 1999.

Klein, Lillian R. "Honor and Shame in the Book of Esther." In Athalya Brenner, ed., *A Feminist Companion to Esther, Judith, and Susanna,* 149–75. FCB 1/7. Sheffield, UK: Sheffield Academic Press, 1995; London and New York: T. & T. Clark, 2004. And in *From Deborah to Esther: Sexual Politics in the Hebrew Bible,* 95–118. Minneapolis: Fortress Press, 2003.

LaCocque, André. *The Feminine Unconventional: Four Subversive Figures in Israel's Tradition.* Minneapolis: Fortress Press, 1990.

———. "La Shulamite." In *Subversives ou un pentateuch de femmes,* 133–63. Lectio Divina 148. Paris: Les Éditions du Cerf, 1992.

Lapsley, Jacqueline E. "The Word Whispered: Bringing It All Together in Ruth." In *Whispering the Word: Hearing Women's Stories in the Old Testament,* 89–108. Louisville, KY: Westminster John Knox Press, 2005.

Larkin, Katrina J. A. *Ruth and Esther.* Old Testament Guides. Sheffield, UK: Sheffield Academic Press, 1996.

Leneman, Helen. *The Performed Bible: The Story of Ruth in Opera and Oratorio.* Sheffield, UK: Sheffield Phoenix Press, forthcoming.

———. "Ruth and Boaz Love Duets as Examples of Musical Midrash." Lectio Difficilor, 1/2006. http://www.lectio.unibe.ch/06_1/leneman_love_duets.htm.

Levine, Amy-Jill. "'Hemmed In on Every Side': Jews and Women in the Book of Susanna." In Fernando F. Segovia and Mary Ann Tolbert, eds., *Reading from This Place,* vol. l, *Social Location and Biblical Interpretation in the United States,* 175–90. Minneapolis: Fortress Press, 1995. And in Athalya Brenner, ed., *A Feminist Companion to Esther, Judith, and Susanna,* 303–23. FCB 1/7. Sheffield, UK: Sheffield Academic Press, 1995; London and New York: T. & T. Clark, 2004.

———. "Ruth." In *WBC,* 84–90.

———. "Sacrifice and Salvation: Otherness and Domestication in the Book of Judith." In James C. VanderKam, ed., *"No One Spoke Ill of Her": Essays on Judith,* 17–30. SBL Early Judaism and Its Literature 2. Atlanta: Scholars Press, 1992. And in Athalya Brenner, ed., *A Feminist Companion to Esther, Judith, and Susanna,* 208–23. FCB 1/7. Sheffield, UK: Sheffield Academic Press, 1995; London and New York: T. & T. Clark, 2004. And in Alice Bach, ed., *Women in the Hebrew Bible: A Reader,* 367–76. New York and London: Routledge, 1999.

Masenya, Madipoane (ngwana 'Mphahlele). "Esther and Northern Sotho Stories: An African-South African Woman's Commentary." In Musa W. Dube, ed., *Other Ways of Reading: African Women and the Bible.* Atlanta: SBL; Geneva: WCC Publications, 2001.

———. "Their Hermeneutics Was Strange! Ours Is a Necessity! Rereading Vashti as African–South African Women." In Caroline Vander Stichele and Todd Penner, eds., *Her Master's Tools? Feminist and*

Postcolonial Engagements of Historical-Critical Discourse, 170–94. Global Perspectives on Biblical Scholarship 9. Atlanta: SBL Press, 2005.

———. "A Small Herb Increases Itself (Impact) by a Strong Odor: Reimagining Vashti in an African–South African Context," 27–49. *Old Testament Essays* 16 (2003): 332–42.

McKinlay, Judith E. "Reading Rahab and Ruth." In *Reframing Her: Biblical Women in Postcolonial Focus*, 37–56. The Bible in the Modern World 1. Sheffield, UK: Sheffield Phoenix Press, 2004.

———. "A Son is Born to Naomi: A Harvest for Israel." In Athalya Brenner, ed., *Ruth and Esther*, 151–57. FCB 2/3. Sheffield, UK: Sheffield Academic Press, 1999.

Meyers, Carol. "Returning Home: Ruth 1.8 and the Gendering of the Book of Ruth." In Athalya Brenner, ed., *A Feminist Companion to the Book of Ruth*, 85–114. FCB 1/3. Sheffield, UK: Sheffield Academic Press, 1993.

———. "'Women of the Neighborhood' (Ruth 4.17): Informal Female Networks in Ancient Israel." In Athalya Brenner, ed., *Ruth and Esther*, 110–27. FCB 2/3. Sheffield, UK: Sheffield Academic Press, 1999.

Milett, Craig Ballard. "The Father's Daughter" and "The Sister." In *Archetypes of Women in Scripture: In God's Image*, 23–38, 39–56. San Diego: LuraMedia, 1989.

Milne, Pamela J. "What Shall We Do with Judith? A Feminist Reassessment of a Biblical 'Heroine.'" *Semeia* 62 (1993): 37–58.

Mosala, Itumeling J. "The Implications of the Text of Esther for African Women's Struggle for Liberation in South Africa." In David Jobling and Tina Pippin, eds., *Ideological Criticism of Biblical Texts*. *Semeia* 59 (1992): 129–38.

Nadar, Sarojini. "A South African Indian Womanist Reading of the Character of Ruth." In Musa W. Dube, ed., *Other Ways of Reading: African Women and the Bible*, 159–75. Atlanta: SBL Press; Geneva: WCC Publications, 2001.

Niditch, Susan. "Esther: Folklore, Wisdom, Feminism and Authority." In Athalya Brenner, ed., *A Feminist Companion to Esther, Judith, and Susanna*, 26–46. FCB 1/7. Sheffield, UK: Sheffield Academic Press, 1995; London and New York: T. & T. Clark, 2004.

Nielsen, Kirsten. *Ruth*. Old Testament Library. Louisville, KY: Westminster John Knox Press, 1997.

Nowell, Irene. "Women of Courage and Strength: Judith, Susanna" and "Queen Esther." In *Women in the Old Testament*, 153–206. Collegeville, MN: Liturgical Press, 1997.

Ostriker, Alicia. "The Book of Ruth and the Love of the Land." *BibInt* 10 (2002): 343–59.

Ozick, Cynthia. "Ruth." In David Rosenberg, ed., *Congregation: Contemporary Writers Read the Jewish Bible*, 361–82. New York: Harcourt Brace Jovanovich, 1987.

———. "Ruth." In Athalya Brenner, ed., *A Feminist Companion to the Book of Ruth*, 191–214. FCB 1/3. Sheffield, UK: Sheffield Academic Press, 1993. And in Judith A. Kates and Gail Twersky Reimer, eds., *Reading Ruth: Contemporary Women Reclaim a Sacred Story*, 211–32. New York: Ballantine, 1994.

Pardes, Ilana. "The Book of Ruth: Idyllic Revisionism." In *Countertraditions in the Bible: A Feminist Approach*, 98–117. Cambridge: Harvard University Press, 1992.

Raheb, Viola. "Women in Contemporary Palestinian Society: A Contextual Reading of the Book of Ruth." In Silvia Schroer and Sophia Bietenhard, eds., *Feminist Interpretation of the Bible and the Hermeneutics of Liberation*, 88–93. JSOTSup 374. Sheffield, UK: Sheffield Academic Press, 2003.

Rashkow, Ilona. "Ruth: The Discourse of Power and the Power of Discourse." In Athalya Brenner, ed., *A Feminist Companion to the Book of Ruth*, 26–41. FCB 1/3. Sheffield, UK: Sheffield Academic Press, 1993.

Reinhartz, Adele. "The Greek Book of Esther." In *WBC*, 286–92.

Sakenfeld, Katharine Doob. "Naomi's Cry: Reflections on Ruth 1:20–21." In Brent A. Strawn and Nancy R. Bowen, eds., *God So Near: Essays on Old Testament Theology in Honor of Patrick D. Miller*, 129–43. Winona Lake, IN: Eisenbrauns, 2003.

———. *Ruth*. Interpretation. Louisville, KY: Westminster John Knox Press, 1999.

———. "Ruth and Naomi: Economic Survival and Family Values" and "Vashti and Esther: Models of Resistance." In *Just Wives? Stories of Power and Survival in the Old Testament and Today*, 27–49, 49–68. Louisville, KY: Westminster John Knox Press, 2003.

———. "Ruth 4, an Image of Eschatological Hope: Journeying with a Text." In Margaret A. Farley and Serene Jones, eds., *Liberating Eschatology: Essays in Honor of Letty M. Russell*, 55–67. Louisville, KY: Westminster John Knox Press, 1999.

Schuller, Eileen M. "Introduction to the Apocrypha." In *WBC*, 263–64.

Silver, Ursula. "Ruth and Naomi: Two Biblical Figures Revived among Rural Women in Germany." In Athalya Brenner, ed., *Ruth and Esther*, 93–109. FCB 2/3. Sheffield, UK: Sheffield Academic Press, 1999.

Sölle, Dorothée, et al. "Ruth, the Moabite," "Judith," "Esther," and "Susanna." In *Great Women of the Bible in Art and Literature*, 148–57, 206–19, 220–33, 234–43. Trans. Joe H. Kirchberger. Macon, GA: Mercer University Press, 1994.

Stanton, Elizabeth Cady. "The Book of Ruth." In Athalya Brenner, ed., *A Feminist Companion to the Book of Ruth*, 20–25. FCB 1/3. Sheffield, UK: Sheffield Academic Press, 1993.

Stocker, Margarita. *Judith: Sexual Warrior Women and Power in Western Culture*. New Haven, CT: Yale University Press, 1998.

Stoddard, Eve Walsh. "The Geneology of Ruth: From Harvester to Fallen Woman in Nineteenth Century U.K." In Raymond-Jean Frontain and Jan Wojcik, eds., *Old Testament Women in Western Literature*, 205–36. Conway, AR: UCA Press.

Trible, Phyllis. "A Human Comedy." In *God and the Rhetoric of Sexuality*, 166–99. Overtures to Biblical Theology. Philadelphia: Fortress Press, 1978.

———. "Naomi," "Orpah," and "Ruth." In *WIS*, 130–31, 133–34, 146–47.

———. "Two Women in a Man's World: A Reading of the Book of Ruth." *Soundings* 59 (1976): 251–79.

Turner, Mary Donovan. "Daughter Zion: Giving Birth to Redemption." In Cheryl A. Kirk-Duggan, ed., *Pregnant Passion: Gender, Sex, and Violence in the Bible*, 193–204. Semeia Studies 44. Atlanta: SBL, 2003.

van Dijk-Hemmes, Fokkelien. "Ruth: A Product of Women's Culture?" In Athalya Brenner, ed., *A Feminist Companion to the Book of Ruth*, 134–39. FCB 1/3. Sheffield, UK: Sheffield Academic Press, 1993.

van Henten, Jan Willem. "Judith as Alternative Leader: A Rereading of Judith 7–13." In Athalya Brenner, ed., *A Feminist Companion to Esther, Judith, and Susanna*, 224–52. FCB 1/7. Sheffield, UK: Sheffield Academic Press, 1995; London and New York: T. & T. Clark, 2004.

van Wijk Bos, Johanna W. H. *Ezra, Nehemiah, and Esther*. Louisville, KY: Westminster John Knox Press, 1998.

van Wolde, Ellen. "Texts in Dialogue with Texts: Intertextuality in the Ruth and Tamar Narratives." *BibInt* 5 (1997): 1–28.

Weems, Renita J. "Blessed Be the Tie That Binds (Naomi and Ruth)" and "A Crown of Thorns (Vashti and Esther)." In *Just a Sister Away: A Womanist Vision of Women's Relationships in the Bible*, 23–38, 99–110. San Diego: LuraMedia, 1989.

Weisberg, Dvora E. "The Widow of Our Discontent: Levirate Marriage in the Bible and Ancient Israel." *JSOT* 28:4 (2004): 403–29.

White, Sidnie Ann. "Esther." In *WBC*, 131–37.

———. "Esther: A Feminine Model for Jewish Diaspora." In Peggy L. Day, ed., *Gender and Difference in Ancient Israel*, 161–77. Minneapolis: Fortress Press, 1989.

Williams, Delores. "Breaking and Bonding." *Daughters of Sarah* 15, no. 3 (May/June 1989): 20–21.

Wolkstein, Diane. "Esther's Story." In Athalya Brenner, ed., *A Feminist Companion to Esther, Judith, and Susanna*, 198–206. FCB 1/7. Sheffield, UK: Sheffield Academic Press, 1995; London and New York: T. & T. Clark, 2004.

———. *Esther's Story*. New York: Morrow Junior, 1996.

Wyler, Bea. "Esther: The Incomplete Emancipation of a Queen." In Athalya Brenner, ed., *A Feminist Companion to Esther, Judith, and Susanna*, 111–35. FCB 1/7. Sheffield, UK: Sheffield Academic Press, 1995; London and New York: T. & T. Clark, 2004.

Yaron, Schlomith. "Sperm Stealing: A Moral Crime by Three of David's Ancestresses." Illustrated by Marc Chagall. *Bible Review* 17:1 (2001): 34–38.

Zlotnick, Helena. "From Jezebel to Esther: Fashioning Images of Queenship in the Hebrew Bible." *Bib* 82 (2001): 477–95.

Suggestions for Use in Religious Education Classes

This book has been designed for use both in academic courses and in religious education classes in churches and synagogues. The discussion questions at the end of each chapter are especially intended for the latter. I have found them to generate lively discussion. Ideally, participants should each have a copy of the book and read the portion that will be discussed in the upcoming session. When this is not possible, participants should at least be encouraged to prepare for class by reading the biblical text or texts that tell the biblical woman's story. When even this level of advance preparation is unrealistic, the biblical stories may be read aloud at the beginning of the class. This has the advantage of making the story fresh in everyone's mind. Biblical stories were originally told rather than read. Reading them out loud or retelling them in a group setting often is much more powerful than reading them silently alone.

The material in this book can be used over an entire academic year, or it can be condensed to fill a quarter of twelve or thirteen weeks. Individual stories can be lifted out and made the focus of a class as well. The story of Eve especially lends itself to such treatment. A class could easily spend four one-hour sessions on Genesis 2–3. The stories of Ruth, Esther, Susanna, and Judith also would make a good series.

For groups that wish to use this material over an entire academic year (September–May), the following outline is recommended:

FIRST QUARTER
    Weeks 1 and 2: Introduction
    Weeks 3 to 5: Story of Eve
    Week 6: Sarah
    Week 7: Hagar
    Week 8: The Daughters of Lot
    Week 9: Rebekah
    Week 10: Rachel and Leah
    Week 11: Dinah
    Week 12: Tamar
    Week 13: Potiphar's Wife

SECOND QUARTER
> Week 1: The Women of Exodus 1:8–2:10
> Week 2: The Women in Moses' Adult Life
> Week 3: The Daughters of Zelophehad
> Week 4: Rahab
> Week 5: Deborah
> Week 6: Jael
> Week 7: The Wife of Manoah
> Week 8: Delilah
> Week 9: Jephthah's Daughter
> Week 10: The Levite's Woman
> Week 11: Hannah, the Woman of Endor, and Rizpah
> Week 12: David's Most Important Wives
> Week 13: The Rape of Tamar, the Women of Tekoa and Abel

THIRD QUARTER
> Week 1: Abishag and Bathsheba, the Queen Mother, the Two Harlots,
>   and the Queen of Sheba
> Week 2: Jezebel, Athaliah, and the Two Cannibal Mothers
> Week 3: The Widow of Zerephath, an Unnamed Widow, and the
>   Shunammite Woman
> Week 4: The Women of the Prophets
> Week 5: The Women of the Wisdom Literature and the Song of Songs
> Week 6 and 7: Ruth
> Week 8 and 9: Esther
> Week 10: Susanna
> Week 11 and 12: Judith
> Week 13: Conclusions and Wrap-up

Those who wish to dig deeper into these stories may consult the notes at the end of the book and the bibliography for each chapter.